Who Lives, Who Dies, Who Decides?
Second Edition

This second edition of *Who Lives, Who Dies, Who Decides?* has been updated to consider the rising stakes for issues of life and death. Abortion, assisted dying, and capital punishment are among the most contentious issues in many societies and demand debate. Whose rights are protected? How do these rights and protections change over time and who makes those decisions? Based on the author's award-winning and hugely popular undergraduate course at the University of Texas, and highly recommended by *Choice* magazine, this book explores the fundamentally sociological processes which underlie the quest for morality and justice in human societies. The author's goal is not to advocate any particular moral "high ground" but to shed light on the social movements and social processes which are at the root of these seemingly personal moral questions and to ask readers to develop their own opinions.

Sheldon Ekland-Olson joined the University of Texas at Austin after completing his graduate work at the University of Washington in Seattle and Yale Law School. He is currently the Bernard and Audre Rapoport Centennial Professor of Liberal Arts and serving as the Director of the School of Human Ecology. For five years he served as Dean of the College of Liberal Arts and then for eight years as Executive Vice President and Provost of the university. He has authored or co-authored several books and numerous articles on criminal justice, prison reform, and capital punishment. Widely recognized for his commitment to teaching undergraduates, he is the recipient of numerous teaching awards. His current interests are reflected in the book, *Who Lives, Who Dies, Who Decides?*, an exploration of how communities have gone about justifying the violation of universally held moral imperatives.

He is married to his best friend, Carolyn. They have two children, well grown. These children have produced seven grandchildren, all, as it turns out, perfectly perfect.

Contemporary Sociological Perspectives

Edited by **Doug Hartmann**, University of Minnesota
and **Jodi O'Brien**, Seattle University

This innovative series is for all readers interested in books that provide frameworks for making sense of the complexities of contemporary social life. Each of the books in this series uses a sociological lens to provide current critical and analytical perspectives on significant social issues, patterns and trends. The series consists of books that integrate the best ideas in sociological thought with an aim toward public education and engagement. These books are designed for use in the classroom as well as for scholars and socially curious general readers.

Published:

Who Lives, Who Dies, Who Decides?

Abortion, Neonatal Care, Assisted Dying, and Capital Punishment

Second Edition

Sheldon Ekland-Olson

Routledge
Taylor & Francis Group

NEW YORK AND LONDON

This edition published 2015
by Routledge
711 Third Avenue, New York, NY 10017

and by Routledge
2 Park Square, Milton Park, Abingdon, Oxon, OX14 4RN

Routledge is an imprint of the Taylor & Francis Group, an informa business

First edition published 2012 by Routledge

Library of Congress Cataloging-in-Publication Data
Ekland-Olson, Sheldon, 1944–
    Who lives, who dies, who decides?: abortion, neonatal care, assisted dying, and capital punishment/Sheldon Ekland-Olson. — Second edition.
        pages cm — (Contemporary sociological perspectives)
    Includes bibliographical references and index.
    1. Life—Moral and ethical aspects. 2. Death—Moral and ethical aspects. 3. Suffering—Moral and ethical aspects. I. Title.
    BD435.E46 2014
    179.7—dc23
    2014026113

ISBN: 978-1-138-80879-9 (hbk)
ISBN: 978-1-138-80880-5 (pbk)
ISBN: 978-1-315-75045-3 (ebk)

Typeset in Adobe Caslon, Trade Gothic and Copperplate Gothic
by Florence Production Ltd, Stoodleigh, Devon, UK

MIX
Paper from
responsible sources
FSC   FSC® C014174
www.fsc.org

Printed and bound in the United States of America by Sheridan Books, Inc. (a Sheridan Group Company).

To:
My wife Carolyn
To:
My son Scott and his wife Jennette
My daughter Brooke and her husband Miki
To:
My wonderfully perfect grandchildren
Grant, Reid, Mia, Blake, Ana, Jessica, and Téa

BRIEF CONTENTS

DETAILED CONTENTS

The material covered travels over a varied landscape—eugenics, abortion, neonatal care, assisted suicide, lynching, and capital punishment. The single common theme is assessed social worth. In each case, the focus is upon two deeply important moral imperatives: life is sacred and should be protected. Suffering, once detected, should be alleviated. Comparing these otherwise distinct topics, we ask a single question: How do we go about justifying the violation of these deeply important, perhaps universal, moral imperatives, while holding tightly to their importance? The short answer is this: with empathy and logic, we draw boundaries and we resolve dilemmas. From time to time, science, technology, and crystallizing events disturb, clarify, and inform existing understandings of the implied sense of social worth. New resolutions of dilemmas and definitions of life's protective boundaries are called for. In this manner, moral systems evolve. They do so along a jagged and often contentious path.

The foundation of the Eugenics Movement in the United States is reviewed. This movement was grounded in the work of Charles Darwin. It was shaped and advanced by a small, interconnected network of well-regarded intellectuals, philanthropists, and political leaders. It soon reached coast to coast and took on national implications.

A major objective of the Eugenics Movement was to develop a model law that would be adopted nationwide. After several attempts, a basic template was agreed upon in the early 1920s. The State of Virginia was a leader. In 1927, the Supreme Court, in *Buck v. Bell*, legitimized Virginia's statute following a contrived trial and appeal. Numerous states soon adopted similar statutes. In 1933, the newly formed government of Adolf Hitler took note and adopted a close approximation of the laws passed in the United States. Some three years later, the model law's author, Harry Laughlin, was given an honorary degree from Heidelberg University in recognition of his work on racial cleansing.

Following World War II, the soul-searing consequences of policies defining some lives as less worthy of protection and support than others became glaringly evident. At the same time, revolutionary advances were being made in the biological sciences. Together, these scientific, technological, and cultural developments set the stage for a reconsideration of human and civil rights and the protective boundaries life.

As the rethinking of the boundaries of protected life progressed, legislation was proposed to formalize broad ethical principles and strengthen regulations of the medical profession. Early attempts failed. Four crystallizing events, involving medical experiments that reminded many of practices in Nazi Germany, precipitated legislative action and the launching of what came to be known as the bioethics movement.

PART II
THE EARLY MOMENTS AND MONTHS OF LIFE   125

An early focus of the bioethics movement was abortion. A rubella pandemic and the widely publicized story of a mother who had taken Thalidomide early in her pregnancy captured the nation's attention. Existing restrictive abortion laws came under increased criticism. Two Supreme Court cases involving the use of contraception set the stage for *Roe v. Wade* and a companion case, *Doe v. Bolton*. In Roe, the court confirmed what the contraception cases had established: there was a right to privacy. The court also established that a fetus was not a fully protected person under the Constitution. For many, this decision came like a "bolt from the blue."

Following *Roe v. Wade*, other cases addressed additional issues in seemingly contradictory decisions. Together, they infused a heated political debate that would last decades and reshape the political landscape. Basic questions regarding the legal and moral legitimacy of governmental actions were raised. Protests intensified. They eventually included clinic bombings and the murder of abortion providers.

Of particular concern were abortions performed late in pregnancy. Partial-birth abortions became a phrase of political art. Statutes were crafted. Early attempts foundered for failing to consider the health of the mother. After several failed attempts, a strange and strained federal statute was adopted, protecting life during the latter stages of pregnancy, not in principle but by anatomical markers as the infant emerged from the birth canal. Medical practices took account of, and adjusted to, these markers as late-term abortions continued.

The issues did not go away with birth. Medical advances made it possible to prolong the lives of young infants in ways previously not possible. Questions were raised about the wisdom of prolonging young lives in the face of birth defects and painful, debilitating conditions. New regulations were proposed and eventually refined. Questions remained. What were the boundaries of privacy for parental choice, and what were the boundaries of a life worth living? Who should decide? What should we do when parents wanted medical care continued, but physicians saw further treatment as futile? Given the uncertainty of prognoses, decisions are most frequently made in a sea of ambiguity.

PART III
THE BOUNDARIES OF TOLERABLE SUFFERING   225

Like the boundaries of life worth protecting, the boundaries of tolerable suffering are hazy. To make matters more uncertain, tolerance for suffering appears to shift over time. We adjust, even to life's most difficult moments. Advances in life-prolonging medical technologies in the mid twentieth century accentuated these long-standing issues as never before. Life could be prolonged, even when life had lost all meaning and when suffering was the result.

As life-prolonging technologies were perfected, life could be maintained even in the face of severe suffering and even when life approximated that of a vegetable. The protection of life and the alleviation of suffering were seen as frequently competitive. How was the resulting dilemma resolved? Patient autonomy had been affirmed many times over many years. Still, if a patient chose to end their life, no longer seen as worth living, there were competing, collective interests to prevent them.

Religious beliefs are central to how one approaches the end of life. Belief in an efficacious, caring god, a god who can be reached through prayer, is particularly important. For those who pray often, god should be trusted. Active intervention to hasten the end of life was far more likely to be opposed. Beyond religious beliefs, the practicalities of allocating health care entered the picture. What are the appropriate criteria for rationing health care. Age? Ability to pay? Are there lives less worthy of prolonging than others? When life reaches a certain point, are we simply prolonging death rather than protecting life? How do we best maintain the dignity of life that remains?

The right to die and death with dignity became phrases of political art. As so often happens, dramatic events crystallized thinking and clarified issues. A physician wrote an article about how he helped a patient die. Vigorous debate followed. How-to books were written, death machines were devised, and carefully crafted questions were posed. When life becomes unbearable, should we provide assistance to those who want to leave life? What form should such assistance take? If persons are unable to end their life, do they have a right to assistance? Voters went to the polls. Cases were taken to court. Conflicting opinions were issued. Much ambivalence remains as the debate continues.

Justifying the intentional infliction of suffering and the taking of life involves not only the removal of the otherwise protective boundaries of life, but also the demonization of a perceived threat. Lynchings following the Civil War in the United States provide one tragic example. Those already on the margins of life were most vulnerable. As blatant injustices became evident, new protections were devised. They were slow in coming. Additional egregious examples further energized reform efforts. In one instance, it took 40 years to exonerate nine young men who had been riding a train during the Depression, charged with rape, and sentenced to die. In another instance, two men were acquitted of the brutal torture and murder of a young teenager, a crime they admitted committing.

Reform efforts were grounded in a deep sense of injustice and a consequent withdrawal of legitimacy for practices then in place. The close linkage between contemporary patterns of capital punishment and lynching as a legacy of slavery was hard to miss and even harder to deny. It was most evident in cases involving a black offender, charged with raping or attempting to rape a white woman. A campaign to reform and then abolish existing capital- punishment practices was launched. Success was achieved when capital punishment, as then practiced, was declared unconstitutional. It was only a partial victory. Executions could continue if existing procedures were modified.

Newly crafted, now quite lengthy legal procedures yielded increased executions. Concerns remained. Once again, science and technology provided an important impetus for rethinking moral issues. Strong evidence became available that many persons were being wrongly convicted of capital offenses. In addition, the new procedures, in one sense clarifying, had become messy and meaningless for even some who had devised them. As this book goes to press, the standards and procedures are shifting, and the debate continues.

17   LESSONS LEARNED   414

The protective boundaries of life and the associated sense of social worth are structured and rearranged through exclusionary logic and the power of empathy. Moral evolution rarely progresses along a straight path. Instead, it winds along a jagged and often contentious route. Existing moral principles, judicial decisions, and legislated statutes are frequently not well fashioned to address new scientific findings and technologies. What has been called cultural lag ensues. To address this cultural lag, metaphors are built, analogies are drawn, empathy-generating images are fashioned, and stories are told. In the process, the legitimacy of existing understandings and practices is reassessed. Given the fundamental nature of the moral dilemmas in question, tension remains. From this tension, social movements are spawned. A general proposition emerges: dilemmas, especially ones involving competing and deeply important moral principles, produce cyclical social change. When the need to identify the protective boundaries of life is coupled with the need to establish the boundaries of tolerable suffering, unavoidable dilemmas emerge. Such dilemmas are, by definition, not resolvable. In an important sense, both sides are right. If so, tension will always remain. Perhaps this is the final lesson learned.

PREFACE TO THE SECOND EDITION

It has been three years since this volume was first published. Why the update? The basic argument remains the same. Through laws, religions, and customs we routinely justify the violation of deeply important moral imperatives aimed at protecting life and alleviating suffering, all the while holding tightly to the importance of our moral principles. We do so by drawing boundaries of social worth and setting priorities to resolve dilemmas.

Three events, worthy of note, have taken place since the initial volume appeared. The first is a dramatic increase in legislation aimed at curbing the availability and use of abortion. Between 2011 and 2013 more restrictions on abortion were enacted (205) across the U.S. than in the entire previous decade (189). These restrictions are being appealed and protested, providing excellent illustration yet again of what we have labeled Lesson Six in the final chapter: In many circumstances, unavoidable dilemmas, infused with uncertainty, emerge. The resolution of such dilemmas always leaves, by definition, residual tension. In such circumstances, when one argument prevails, the contrary position is likely to respond. Tension will always remain and cyclical change ensues.

The second set of recent events worthy of note underscores the importance of both logic and empathy when drawing the uncertain boundaries of life worthy of protection. In December 2013 a 13-year-old girl, Jahi McMath, was declared dead following a seemingly simple operation gone tragically wrong. The criteria used to determine her death were widely accepted, grounded in thorough development and discussion between the late 1960s and the early 1980s. The result being:

> An individual who has sustained either (1) irreversible cessation of circulatory and respiratory functions, or (2) irreversible cessation of all functions of the entire brain, including the brain stem, is dead. A determination of death must be made in accordance with accepted medical standards.

Everyone agreed. Jahi McMath's brain revealed absolutely no activity. In this sense death had occurred. The problem was that a ventilator and drugs were maintaining her breathing lungs and beating heart. Seeing these indicators of life, Jahi's parents, dealing with their grief over the tragic and unexpected loss of their young daughter, found it hard to let go. Jahi's mother noted simply, "I would probably need for my child's heart to stop to show me that she was dead. Her heart is still beating, so there's still life there." For their part, the attending physicians were uncomfortable maintaining a beating heart and breathing lungs in a dead person's body. When establishing the boundaries of protected life and the meaning of futility, the power of empathy and promise of hope sometime collide with logic and science.

The final set of recent events calling for note in this updated volume center on the uncertainties of removing the protective boundaries of life when we decide to execute someone. Even in states and regions of the U.S. where capital punishment is most frequently carried out, there is reluctance to kill persons who might not be accountable for their actions. We treat young persons different than adults, even when they perform very similar acts. Likewise, if a person has substantial intellectual disabilities, having the body of an adult but the mind of a child, adjustments in punishments are made. The question is: Where do we draw the line? In 2014, these issues came before the Supreme Court in a case, *Hall v. Florida*.

Freddie Lee Hall had been on death row just short of 36 years, awaiting execution for killing a young woman who was pregnant at the time. During his three-and-a-half decade stay on death row, the Supreme Court had held that it was unconstitutional to execute a person judged to be mentally retarded. The Court had left it to the States to determine what level should be used to determine retardation, or what came to be labeled substantial intellectual disability. In Florida the line was drawn at the score of 70 on the Wechsler IQ test. Freddie Lee Hall's test scores indicated he was at or just above this point. He could be executed. Problem was, the Wechsler IQ test, like all tests, was subject to variation from one administration to the next, yielding what is referred to as standard error of measurement (SEM). No allowance was made for the SEM in Florida.

In May 2014, the Supreme Court held that this lack of attention to SEM made the Florida law unconstitutional. Freddie Lee Hall's 36-year stay on death row would be extended further while this flaw was fixed. At this same time, nationwide concern over the use of capital punishment continued to gain momentum over the now widely acknowledged finding that we were deciding to kill innocent persons. Additional, largely unrelated questions also arose over the use and supply of drugs for lethal injections and the occurrence of botched executions.

While support for capital punishment continued at around 60 percent, in 2014 this was the lowest point it had been in decades, and there was a noticeable trend among States to repeal capital punishment statutes. As this volume goes to press, the debate continues, as some advocates assert the justification of taking life for deeds done while others press for abolishment of what is by many standards a messy and meaningless system.

PREFACE TO THE FIRST EDITION

This book has been a long time in the making. It flows from interests in the power of assessed social worth. Retrospective autobiographies are always chancy, but in my mind these interests began in the years I spent in law school, where as a student in the late 1960s I was more interested in the dynamics of life than the precedents of law. Although I was attending law school, I had no desire, and even less intention, to become a lawyer. This presented some problems, but more importantly it provided substantial freedom to let my mind wander over terrain others might not travel. In particular, I became interested in reform efforts then being directed at mental and penal institutions, and can still remember a light bulb flashing when the wording of the Thirteenth Amendment was brought to my attention. Slavery had been abolished, my professor noted, except as a punishment for crime. Duly convicted felons remained slaves of the state. From this much followed. By the late 1960s, a century after the passage of the Thirteenth and Fourteenth Amendments, this legacy of slavery was providing the motivating energy behind a broad-based prison reform movement, embedded in even broader based efforts to seek a more inclusive society.

At the time, I was working with Stanton Wheeler, a marvelous colleague with a sharp and creative mind. One thing led to another, and after leaving law school I found myself as a young professor of sociology at the University of Texas at Austin, who soon became involved with persons running the prisons in and around Huntsville. Over the ensuing decades, the Texas prison system has become a behemoth spread across a large state, but in the early 1970s it was a small, cloistered community in East Texas. Reforms of existing practices were slowly but surely finding their way behind the walls of institutions run much like plantations.

As prison reforms progressed, administrative control was restructured, long-established practices were declared unconstitutional, and unantici-pated consequences began to appear. Most prominent was a rise in prison violence. Prison gangs began to flex their muscle more overtly, inflicting violence up to and including death. The fissured structure of social worth, the sense of Us and Them, was present among the kept as well as the keepers. Contact with cellblock life and prison violence eventually led to death row and the study of capital punishment, where the protective boundaries of life are officially removed.

It is from these experiences that the power of social worth began to occupy my thinking. Serious interest in how the protective boundaries of life are defined, restructured, and removed began to take root. At the same time, given what I was seeing in the prison and capital punishment reform efforts, I developed a more general interest in social movements and the close linkage between a sense of injustice and the withdrawal of legitimacy from governmental practices. As luck would have it, about this time David Snow took a job offered by the University of Texas and was given an office just down the hall. Dave is an energetic soul with a mind that sparkles with ideas. Over the next several years, at lunch and in our offices, we would talk about football and swimming, but also, more relevant here, social movements and the importance of a sense of injustice and assessed legitimacy, the critical role moral entrepreneurs play, the organizing potential of social networks and interlocking organiza-tions, and the power of rhetoric to frame issues. I take this opportunity to express my appreciation to Dave for these still-valued conversations.

As sometimes happens, young professors are asked to develop new courses that will draw students. My mother had recently died from an illness that required my father to make a deeply disturbing decision to terminate treatment. The decision was forced by a lack of health insurance coverage for my mother's condition. This was not long after Elisabeth

Kübler Ross had released *On Death and Dying*, which covered the five stages of grief. Related research was just getting off the ground, and, as morbid as it sounded, I decided to develop a course, "On Death and Dying." I taught this course for several years, and it eventually evolved into an offering titled, somewhat less morbidly, "Life and Death Decisions." Most recently, I am happy to report, this course was listed by The Daily Beast as one of the 10 hottest courses in the nation. Now, I do not give much credence to such listings, but it brought a "Way to go Dad!" from my daughter, so that was reason enough to celebrate.

It is from this course and the background of experiences with prison life and capital punishment that *Who Lives, Who Dies, Who Decides?* emerged. While writing the book, I noticed the manuscript taking on a life of its own. What follows is not the book I had originally planned. As topics were covered and compared, insights were modified and reaffirmed, and a single question emerged. How do we, as a community, go about justifying the violation of deeply important moral imperatives? The emerging answer was twofold. We draw boundaries and resolve dilemmas. It also became quite evident while writing about eugenics, abortion, neo-natal care, assisted suicide, and capital punishment that moral assessments and their associated social movements evolve, not in a straight trajectory, but along a frequently jagged and contentious path. Sporadic advances in science, technology, and equally sporadic occurrences of crystallizing events are of central guiding influence.

I had spent some time with Ogburn's idea of cultural lag and the link between science and technology and the evolution of moral thinking. What I had not much thought about was the power of crystallizing events to clarify issues and galvanize effort. In each of the following chapters this influence is evident. Among those who study social movements, there is much conceptual common ground in the influence of *Buck v. Bell*, the Scottsboro Boys, Emmett Till, the invention of the kidney machine, the revelation of questionable medical experiments in the early 1970s, and the development of DNA fingerprinting in the 1990s. In each case, these widely divergent events provided clarity for the issues at hand and galvanized action leading to change.

Having written this book, I have come to appreciate the importance of one basic proposition. Just as supply and demand are linked in economic affairs, the evolution of moral systems is guided by a sense of injustice, assessed legitimacy, and pressure for change. The greater the sense of injustice, the greater the withdrawal of legitimacy, and the more intense the efforts for change. Rarely does social science reveal such a regular pattern embedded in the conceptual landscapes traveled. Supporting evidence is abundant throughout the following chapters.

ACKNOWLEDGMENTS

As this volume goes to press, I find myself indebted to many. For several years I have taught courses both large (Life and Death Decisions) and small (Boundaries and Dilemmas). Many of the ideas that follow were developed in these classes. I take this opportunity to thank all those who attended. We have had a good time, and I trust your lives have benefited. I know mine has. My friend and colleague Michael Adams was unbelievably generous with his time, insight, and sharp editorial eye. Thank you, Michael, and, yes, I know we have a debate to come. The early days of writing, when a finished manuscript remains a distant hope, are not always easy. Mary Ann Rankin, my colleague in the trenches of bureaucrademia, was supportive in many ways as the manuscript began taking shape, even when demands on her own time were beyond substantial. Thank you, Mary Ann. Your support and friendship meant and continues to mean a great deal.

Numerous persons were helpful with specific issues. Bill Winslade provided important clarifications on end-of-life decisions. Thank you, Bill. Professor Margaret Little, the current director of the Kennedy Institute of Ethics, provided important insights early on. Thank you, Maggie. My long-time friend, Jack Gibbs, knows how much our sessions at the Clay Pit have meant, but I will tell him anyway. Jack, your always-engaged mind continues to make me marvel. Our friendship and conversations have eased the sometimes-difficult experiences that come with writing a book such as this one. When writing about capital punishment reform efforts, I contacted Tony Amsterdam. We did not know one another, and many colleagues would have politely demurred. Tony did not. He responded with an open spirit and helpful material that is rarely seen. Thank you, Tony. You have become a role model for many. Add me to the list. I take this opportunity also to thank Danielle Dirks, Elyshia Aseltine, Julie Beicken, Jennifer Storch, and Meredith Rountree, graduate students with whom I have had the privilege of working. You have assisted me in many ways throughout the writing process, and I thank you. To Brooke Vuckovic, who also happens to be my daughter, I send love and thanks for her masterful editorial assistance and her many helpful suggestions that have made this a better book. I would also like to extend thanks to Gary Jensen of Vanderbilt University and Raymond De Vries of the University of Michigan for peer-reviewing the text at its draft stage. A thanks also to the reviewers who provided comments for this second edition:

Sandra Joy	Rowan University
William Winslade	University of Houston
Richard C. Gianni	Westwood College
Marlann Patterson	University of Wisconsin-Stout
Sue Lillyman	University of Worcester

Finally, for her tolerance of early morning writing sessions and the support she provides in ever so many ways, I thank my life-mate, Carolyn.

CHAPTER 1

A SINGLE QUESTION

The material covered in the following chapters travels over a varied landscape—eugenics, abortion, neonatal care, assisted suicide, lynching, and capital punishment. Why have these topics been brought together in a single volume? The common theme is assessed social worth. In each case, the focus is upon two deeply important moral imperatives: life is sacred and should be protected. Suffering, once detected, should be alleviated. Comparing these otherwise distinct topics, we ask a single question: How do we go about justifying the violation of these deeply important, perhaps universal, moral imperatives, while holding tightly to their importance? The short answer is this: with empathy and logic we draw boundaries and we resolve dilemmas. From time to time science, technology, and crystallizing events disturb, clarify, and inform existing understandings of the implied sense of social worth. New resolutions of dilemmas and definitions of life's protective boundaries are called for. In this manner moral systems evolve. We will find they do so along a jagged and often contentious path.

A Moral System Evolves

In the first part, A Moral System Evolves, we explore events leading to the what came to be called the Final Solution and, from there, to a re-energized concern with human and civil rights. Our account begins with Charles Darwin's recently released findings and proposed explanations of

1

evolution being used to improve and protect life. Some lives, some contributions to life were more worthy of protection and support than others. Feeble-minded and other unfit persons were likened to parasites and useless eaters. They were said to detract from and perhaps endanger the communities in which they lived. *LIFE*, writ large, could and should be protected by minimizing their presence. Preventing the creation of life among those deemed less worthy would not only protect *LIFE*, it would also minimize suffering.

Well-educated, influential moral entrepreneurs advanced the eugenics cause through a loosely connected network of organizations. One was the Eugenics Record Office in Cold Spring Harbor, located some 40 miles outside New York City on Long Island. Leading the charge was a young former schoolteacher, Harry Laughlin. Laughlin spent the better part of his life carefully drafting a model statute designed to yield a uniform national policy. Using Laughlin's template, laws were crafted and a contrived trial and appeal to the U.S. Supreme Court were advanced where Oliver Wendell Holmes, himself a proponent of minimizing the lives of those deemed less worthy, wrote the Supreme Court opinion in *Buck v. Bell*, famously stating,

> It is better for all the world, if instead of waiting to execute degenerate offspring for crime, or to let them starve for their imbecility, society can prevent those who are manifestly unfit from continuing their kind. The principle that sustains compulsory vaccination is broad enough to cover cutting the Fallopian tubes. Three generations of imbeciles are enough.

From this case much followed. In the end, the Government of Adolf Hitler, borrowing heavily from Laughlin's now legitimized template, expanded Holmes' rationale to limit, manipulate, and end the lives of persons deemed less worthy. When the soul-searing consequences of this exclusionary framework came to light, a counter-movement to secure more inclusive human and civil rights was energized.

Actions taken by the Nazis were barbarian and extreme. They had progressed step by little step. Many saw similar steps being taken in the United States. Two-and-a-half decades after the Nuremberg Trials, four crystallizing events underscored these fears. It came to light that physicians and scientists were radiating cancer patients in Ohio and other places not so much to cure cancer as to learn what happened to the human body in the event of an atomic-bomb attack. Within months it was learned that other medical researchers were feeding feces to retarded children to learn more of the causes and cures of hepatitis. Still others, desiring to protect the scientific integrity of their research, were refusing treatment, known to be effective, to men suffering from syphilis. Finally, it was learned that physicians and scientists were experimenting with recently aborted, soon-to-die, but still-living fetuses to secure additional knowledge about fetal development. In each instance, lives deemed less worthy were used to benefit *LIFE* and alleviate future suffering.

These studies shocked the nation. Parallels to the Nuremberg Trial of 23 German doctors following World War II were too obvious to miss. The stage was set for legislation "to identify basic ethical principles." Principles were proposed and adopted. A Bioethics Movement was born. New boundaries of protected life and tolerable suffering were developed, and new priorities were set for resolving dilemmas. In the process, a moral system evolved.

The Early Moments and Months of Life

Central to the Nuremburg Code and ideas flowing from it was the principle of individual autonomy. Absent compelling state interests, individuals had a right to choose what was done to their body. In the second part, The Early Moments and Months of Life, we wind our way through the debates, sometimes labeled wars, infusing the boundaries and dilemmas of choice, abortion, and neonatal care. Where are the boundaries of protected life to be drawn—prior to conception, at conception, at viability, inches from life? In the early months following birth, the protection of life and the alleviation of suffering sometimes conflict. Some infant lives, some moments early in life are deemed more worthy of protection and support than others. Deep disagreements are found. Who should decide?

Widely divergent answers have been proposed. These answers have been shaped by religious and political beliefs, as well as practices among physicians, sometimes hidden from public view. Political campaigns and social movements have been launched, up to and including the bombing of abortion clinics and the killing of abortion providers. These lethal actions have paradoxically been justified by a commitment to protect and support life. The cycle is complete when those killing abortion providers are themselves executed, again justified through a commitment to protect and support life.

A theme, running throughout the entire book, is that from time to time crystallizing events have drawn attention, clarified thought, and galvanized action. In the early 1960s, an Arizona law prevented a young mother, who happened to be a local host of a children's television program, from obtaining an abortion, even though she wanted another child, but had taken a drug associated with severe life-limiting, resource-draining birth defects. More broadly, and almost simultaneously, a rubella pandemic raised similar issues among a much large number of expectant mothers. For many, then-existing laws prohibiting abortion represented a tragic injustice. They increased the chances of defective births as well as the deaths of mothers seeking illegal abortions in unsanitary conditions. They could not command the respect and obedience of those governed. Then-existing laws prohibiting abortions should be changed.

A decade later, a Supreme Court decision shaped in large measure by these events and assessments came like a "bolt from the blue." It declared that a fetus developing in the mother's womb was not a fully protected person under the Constitution and that there were important rights to privacy protecting the mother's choice to have an abortion. For many, this was unconscionable. A pro-life movement was energized. Among those seeking to overturn *Roe* was a former abortion provider, using newly available ultrasound images to show what was said to be the "silent scream" of a fetus being aborted. President Reagan distributed the film to Congress. It was shown in churches and discussed in the media. Other, more jarring, images were advanced. Protests expanded, at times becoming lethal. Pro-life advocates echoed the charges of their antagonists: existing law was a tragic injustice; it could not command the respect and obedience of those governed. It should be changed.

In 1991, what came to be known as the Summer of Mercy called attention to second- and third-term abortions performed by a physician in Wichita, Kansas, Dr. George Tiller. Emotional political campaigns continued, clinics were bombed, an attempt was made to take Dr. Tiller's life, and other abortion providers were shot. A little over a decade later,

federal legislation outlawed "partial-birth abortions," similar to those that
so concerned the Summer of Mercy protesters.

This law was a strange and strained piece of legislation. It reflected
competing desires to protect the choices, life, and health of the mother
and the life of the almost-born child. It exemplified in specific detail the
need to establish the boundaries of protected life. It limited the taking
of life in late-term pregnancy, not in principle but by the vaginal location
of the fetus. Procedures adapted to meet the anatomical requirements of
the new law. Late-term abortions continued. The physician targeted by
Summer of Mercy protesters, now labeled by activists as "Tiller the Baby
Killer," was shot to death while worshipping at his church on Sunday
May 31, 2009. Among the assailant's supporters were persons long
associated with the more aggressive wing of the pro-life movement. For
these pro-life advocates, Dr. Tiller's murder was justified with reference
to biblical scripture calling for the taking of life to protect life.

The debates over the boundaries and dilemmas of early life and death
decisions have not been limited to life in the womb. For many years, there
was no known way to prolong the lives of infants labeled "monstrosities
at birth." With advances in medical technology, this changed. Life could
be prolonged, even in very difficult circumstances. The rhetoric defining
the assessment of newly arrived infants changed. Monstrosities at birth
became imperiled infants. Again, crystallizing events loomed large in the
evolving rhetoric and moral understanding. In Indiana, a young infant,
diagnosed with Down Syndrome, was allowed to die when his parents
refused permission to perform a relatively simple operation. Many were
appalled. Such infants, it was argued, deserved protection. Hastily crafted
regulations were put in place, but failed to account for many more difficult
circumstances when the infant's life was infused with far greater suffering,
when the prognosis of a life worth living was dim, and when medical
treatment seemed futile. Additional tragic stories came to light. Further
clarification of the Baby Doe Regulations ensued.

Even with this clarification, however, uncertainty remained. Where
are the protective boundaries of meaningful life to be drawn? Where are
the boundaries of tolerable suffering? What should be done when the
protection of life and the alleviation of suffering compete? Who should
decide? The power of unavoidable moral dilemmas to infuse the

uncertainties of life with tension is nowhere more evident than in the early moments and months of life. These same issues are found later in life.

The Boundaries of Tolerable Suffering

In the third part, The Boundaries of Tolerable Suffering, we repeatedly see how attempts to alleviate suffering come into conflict with efforts to prolong and protect life. Life-prolonging medical technologies frequently not only fail to relieve suffering, but in a very real sense become a source of suffering itself.

In the case of a young man severely burned in an explosion in the early 1970s, we hear his plea, "Please let me die." Had his accident occurred only a few years earlier he would have most certainly died. With new life-saving regimes in place, his pleas went unheeded, and his life was prolonged. Ten years later, he remained adamant in his claim that his autonomy should have been respected and his pleas heeded.

A year and a half after this tragic accident, pleas of a different sort came from the parents of a young woman. Their daughter had entered what had recently been labeled a persistent vegetative state. Medical technology was keeping her alive, but she had lost her functioning mind and was incapable of receiving or projecting information. This was not a life worth living. Her parents wanted to let their daughter peacefully leave her meaningless existence. Their pleas met both opposition and support. Eventually, noting her parents' loving concern, the recently established constitutional right to privacy in *Roe* and related decisions, and a long-established religious doctrine, a New Jersey court found in their favor. Amid protests, Karen Ann Quinlan's respirator was removed. She lived for another nine years. The resolution of her ordeal would have an even longer-lasting impact, becoming a cornerstone for the right-to-die movement.

Early legislative efforts to define the point where life becomes less worthy of support and protection had floundered amid charges and fears that such laws would reawaken the thoroughly repulsive euthanasia practices of Nazi Germany. The *Quinlan* case struck a nerve. Energized by this case, efforts to secure a right to die with dignity gained momentum. Public opinion shifted decidedly in favor of allowing doctors to end a patient's life by some painless means if the patient and family requested it. "Living Wills" became widely used and discussed. In 1976, California enacted the first piece of legislation to recognize that modern medical technology was prolonging life beyond natural limits, and that adults should have a fundamental right to control their medical care, including the decision to withhold or withdraw life-sustaining procedures. Similar legislation in other states followed.

This shift in the moral and legal landscape was further strengthened when a second case of a young woman in a persistent vegetative state came to the public's attention. This case eventually found its way to the U.S. Supreme Court. Here, the Court underscored a long-established principle. There was a clear and distinct right to refuse medical treatment. Nancy Cruzan was in a persistent vegetative state, unable to express her wishes, but, if clear and convincing evidence could be found regarding what her wishes would be, the request to terminate medical treatment should be honored. Such evidence was found. Again amid protests, the tube providing nutrition to Nancy was removed. Eleven days later she died. In reply to the right-to-life protestors gathered outside the hospital, Nancy's father wrote in his tribute to his daughter:

> Today, as the protestor's sign says, we gave Nancy the gift of death. An unconditional gift of love that sets her free from this twisted body that no longer serves her. A gift I know she will treasure above all others, the gift of freedom. So run free Nan, we will catch up later.

A decade and a half had passed between the cases of Karen Ann Quinlan and Nancy Cruzan. During this defining period in the right-to-die movement, numerous cases were taken to court and widely discussed. As with the abortion debates, religious beliefs and practices separated protagonists on one side or another. Most important, as reflected in public opinion polls, was the frequency with which respondents prayed. If you believed in an active, concerned god, a god within reach, a god willing to work as a partner, to intervene in your life, you were more likely to pray frequently. A caring, accessible god could be trusted to do what was best in your life. God should control the moment of death. Opposition to, or support for, assisted dying was patterned accordingly.

Whatever your religious beliefs and practices, health care was limited and expensive. Who should receive priority? Discussions of how to set limits emerged and heated up when the then governor of Colorado spoke to some elderly constituents gathered in Denver in March of 1984. "We've got a duty to die," Governor Lamm stated, "and get out of the way with all of our machines and artificial hearts and everything else like that and let the other society, our kids, build a reasonable life." He would later explain the context in which these words were spoken, but, in stating what he did, he prodded a more intense debate. Lamm's speech was followed closely by a lengthy treatment of the topic in Daniel Callahan's *Setting Limits: Medical Goals in an Aging Society*.

"Is it possible," Callahan wrote, "that medicine's triumphant reconstruction of old age has also unwittingly created a demographic, economic and medical avalanche, one that could ultimately (and perhaps already) do great harm—a demographic avalanche by harmfully increasing the number and proportion of the elderly." This distorted the ratio of old to young, Callahan continued, precipitating "an economic avalanche by radically increasing the burden of social and familial dependency; and a medical avalanche by lengthening life beyond a capacity to preserve its quality." Like Governor Lamm, Daniel Callahan was raising the idea that at some point we might have a duty to die. This sense that some lives were more worthy of support and protection than others raised long-noted concerns.

These concerns were not just for the elderly; they were also for the disabled. Here, too, the boundaries of tolerable suffering and lives worth living and protecting often collided. Who should decide? If a decision was left to the individual most directly involved, should assistance be provided when needed? Was there a right to this assistance? Around these questions, the debate progressed. Poignant stories appeared, and how-to books were written. A Michigan physician devised a machine patients could use to end their lives, as legislation, at first unsuccessful, was proposed to ensure access to death with dignity. Finally, in November 1994 the voters in Oregon approved Measure 16, the Oregon Death With Dignity Law. This law was countermanded by officials in Washington, DC, court cases were filed, and sequential opinions contradicted one another.

In 1997, in a decision characterized by its unanimous ambivalence, the U.S. Supreme Court decided two cases, one from Washington State and one from New York. There was no right to assisted suicide, the Court found, but there was also no reason to prohibit assistance. The decision should be left to the voters. A decade later, in November 2008, the voters of Washington State went to the polls and decidedly supported the nation's second Death With Dignity law. As of this writing, the debate continues.

Taking Life and Inflicting Suffering

In the final part, Taking Life and Inflicting Suffering, we walk through difficult and often deeply disturbing events characterizing the intentional infliction of suffering and death—lynching and capital punishment. The evidence is clear—there is a close connection between the two. This connection is grounded in the shadows of the Thirteenth Amendment and Section 1 of the Fourteenth Amendment to the Constitution.

Slavery was abolished by the Thirteenth Amendment, except as a punishment for crime. With passage, a duly convicted felon became a slave of the state, *civiliter mortuus*, civilly dead. His estate, should he have one, was to be administered like that of a dead man. Following the Civil War and ratification of the Thirteenth Amendment, former slaves could be re-enslaved and put to work, if convicted of a crime. They frequently were. As events unfolded, "duly convicted" was, and to some extent remains, a term of art. Section 1 of the Fourteenth Amendment aimed to clarify. No person was to be stripped of life, liberty, or property, without due process of law. Nor was anyone to be denied the equal protection of the laws.

These phrases, too, remain open to wide interpretation. Whatever else it might be, a criminal trial is a mechanism for removing the otherwise protective boundaries of life. We can do things to convicted felons that are forbidden when done to free citizens. We can constrain life, limit freedom, and in the extreme inflict death. Lacking explicit guidelines for juries and judges, the status passage from a free citizen to a convicted felon came to reflect the emotions and prejudices of the moment. In post-Civil War life, the line between a perfunctory criminal trial and lynching was often razor thin.

In a society fissured by a strong sense of Us and Them, equal protection of the law was hard to find. Convictions and punishment were quite simply and clearly differentially distributed across racial lines. Equality and due process for Us did not mean the same thing as equality and due process for Them. Sham trials and brutal lynchings were widespread and disproportionately inflicted upon former slaves and their descendants. For those seeking a more inclusive communal life, such blatant inequality generated a deep sense of injustice and withdrawal of legitimacy from existing practices.

This sense of injustice and the closely linked denial of legitimacy to then-operating laws energized social movements for change. Events such as transpired in the rural Arkansas communities of Hoop Spur, Helena, and Elaine in September 1919 served to crystallize thinking and galvanize these reform efforts. In the frenzy following a presumed insurrection among black farmers and sharecroppers, persons were tortured to secure confessions. Trials lasting minutes sentenced formerly free citizens to death. In this instance, appeals were taken, and the Supreme Court refined, ever so slightly, the boundaries of acceptable due process. For reformers, a foothold had been found.

A little over a decade later, in March 1931, as the Great Depression loomed large, nine young black men, looking for work and riding a freight train, were accused of raping two white women. Without access to legal counsel, they were convicted and sentenced to death, with the exception of the youngest, 13 years old, who was sentenced to life in prison. Again, the trials were perfunctory. These cases, too, were taken to the Supreme Court. The failure of the trial court to provide reasonable opportunity to secure defense counsel was found to be a clear denial of due process, as the Court found, "certain immutable principles of justice which . . . no member of the Union may disregard." It took four decades and the pronouncement of one-time adamant segregationist, Governor George Wallace, before the record was set straight on the innocence of those accused, now widely known as the Scottsboro Boys.

Two decades after the initial trials of the Scottsboro Boys, the movement to secure a more inclusive society was gaining momentum, as evidenced in *Brown v. Board of Education*. The year following this landmark case, a young teenager, Emmett Till, traveled from Chicago with his cousins to visit relatives in Mississippi. He was relaxing one day after work outside a local store. He had gone inside to buy some bubble gum and candy and apparently overstepped the boundaries of a peculiar chivalry when he whistled at the 21-year-old storekeeper. His brutalized body was found three days later in the river. Two suspects were arrested. They confessed to abducting Emmett, but denied killing him. After an abbreviated trial, Roy Bryant and J.W. Milam were acquitted. A few months later they confessed to the murder in a widely publicized article in *Look* magazine. The presence of obvious and brutal injustice was undeniable.

With these and numerous similar cases in the background, in 1963 a group of lawyers launched a campaign to first reform and then totally abolish a system of capital punishment soiled by the lingering legacy of slavery. It took almost a decade, but in June 1972 capital punishment, as then practiced in the United States, was declared arbitrary and capricious, and therefore unconstitutional. If the noted problems could be fixed, however, executions could resume. New guidelines were soon crafted, and trials were restructured to ensure full consideration of the character of the defendant and the circumstances of the crime.

On January 17, 1977, executions resumed. The process was no longer perfunctory. It took years. Still, problems remained. One broad-scale study showed that something on the order of two-thirds of the cases contained reversible error, and prominent Supreme Court Justices, once voting to sustain capital punishment, changed their minds, noting that the system they had helped construct had become messy and meaningless. They would no longer tinker, as Justice Blackmun put it, with the machinery of death.

Their concerns were heightened when clear evidence began emerging from new techniques for DNA profiling. Many innocent persons had been sentenced to death. Reform efforts expanded, and moratoria were declared. Within the decade between 2000 and 2010, the number of executions decreased from almost 100 to just under 50. There was a parallel decline in the number of persons sentenced to death, signaling a further decline in executions in the years ahead. As this book goes to press, the questions of when the protective boundaries of life should be removed for offenses committed remain grist for a frequently caustic and accusatory debate.

The Single Question

How do we go about justifying the violation of deeply important moral imperatives? We draw boundaries to establish social worth and we set priorities to resolve dilemmas. We begin with a movement to limit the number of individuals judged to be unfit.

PART I

A MORAL SYSTEM EVOLVES

CHAPTER 2

AN EXCLUSIONARY MOVEMENT IS BORN

In the aftermath of World War II, the troubling implications of an exclusionary mindset, defining some lives less worthy than others, became glaringly apparent. The soul-searing discovery of Nazi atrocities precipitated a broad-scale effort to clarify universal human rights and refine long-neglected civil rights. The goal was to reshape the boundaries of protected life in a more inclusive fashion. Efforts emerged to clarify the dignity and autonomy of the individual and to untangle the knotty problem of whether all human life, all moments in life are equally worthy of living, protecting, and prolonging. The consequent debates were accompanied by significant controversy. They had been brewing for many years.

Some Lives Are More Worthy Than Others

The story of Nazi atrocities is often told. Only more recently has this story been linked to the broadly influential framework of "applied biology" shared with colleagues in the United States as well as other European and Scandinavian countries. Important statutes and court cases in the United States predated and eventually served as a template for the National Socialist Government's exclusionary laws, defining some lives more worthy of support and protection than others. This template was grounded in a framework that came to be known as eugenics.[1]

The Eugenics Movement was in many ways an embodiment of progressive thought, a purposeful attempt to improve the quality of life

15

based on the belief that science provided an objective basis for moving toward a better future.[2] A Edwin Black notes,

> Eugenics was a movement of the nation's elite thinkers and many of its most progressive reformers. As its ideology spread among the intelligentsia, eugenics cross-infected many completely separate social reform and health care movements, each worthwhile in its own right.[3]

The list of progressive movements cross-infected included child welfare, prison reform, mental and public health, immigration rights, birth control, educational reform, and the priorities of numerous charitable foundations. Eugenics was not the intellectual property of a single political persuasion.

> Conservatives employed eugenic arguments to justify restrictions on birth control, suffrage, divorce, and women's educational and professional opportunities, while social radicals employed other eugenic arguments to assail them . . . Most defended capitalism, whereas others argued that only in a classless society would it be possible to separate the genetic wheat from the chaff.[4]

Early seeds for eugenics came in the writings of an economist turned demographer, Thomas Malthus. As the eighteenth century drew to a close, Malthus had written a brief but influential pamphlet: *An Essay on the Principle of Population—as it Affects the Future Improvement of Society*. His argument was simple. Humans need food. Humans enjoy sex. Sex produces offspring. Left unchecked, the population will grow geometrically. The food supply will grow arithmetically. Shortages will ensue, as sure as night follows day. These shortages will be differentially felt. Families should have no more children than they can support, otherwise, they produce an unfair burden on society.

Thomas Malthus died in 1834 in Bath, England. A second edition of his essay was published in 1836. It was around this time that a young Charles Darwin, not yet 30 years old and just returned from his circumnavigation of the globe on the *Beagle*, began what he called his systematic inquiry. According to Darwin's own account, Malthus provided important theoretical grounding for his work.

I happened to read for amusement Malthus on Population, and being well prepared to appreciate the struggle for existence which everywhere goes on from long-continued observation of the habits of animals and plants, it at once struck me that under these circumstances favourable variations would tend to be preserved, and unfavourable ones to be destroyed. The results of this would be the formation of a new species. Here, then I had at last got a theory by which to work.[5]

It would be some 20 years before *Origin of the Species* was published, but Darwin's paradigm-shifting *magnum opus* had begun. It is on the parsimonious foundation of demography, natural selection, survival of the fittest, and policies directed at assisting Nature's selection process for the good of the whole that the international Eugenics Movement was built.

Eugenics Becomes a Duty

In the early formative years of eugenics, no one was more important than the coiner of the term, Fancis Galton. Relying on his knowledge of animal husbandry Galton was firm in his belief that statistical analysis of data, carefully gathered, yielded important insights. Galton was convinced that the means could be found to give "the more suitable races or strains of blood a better chance of prevailing speedily over the less suitable."[6] These means, while imperfect, were more humane than the brutal processes of natural selection. Duty and virtue thus intermixed with utilitarian calculations. In one of his frequently cited, self-reflective passages, Galton noted,

> Man is gifted with pity and other kindly feelings; he has also the power of preventing many kinds of suffering. I conceive it to fall well within his province to replace Natural Selection by other processes that are more merciful and not less effective.[7]

To alleviate or avoid suffering, life should be manipulated. Intrigued by his cousin Charles Darwin's writings, Galton began gathering reams of data on determinants of success for persons considered luminaries of their times. He meticulously analyzed these data with statistical techniques he was then developing, techniques he refined with Karl Pearson. At the time, Galton's and Pearson's statistical techniques, still very much in use today, were revolutionary innovations aimed at discovering patterns in otherwise uncertain matters. They captured the attention of the world's best minds. Not only was the emerging field of eugenics acceptable, but, thanks in large measure to the works of Darwin, Galton and Pearson, eugenics also became compelling and respected among the intelligentsia.

Galton released an early version of his statistical study of luminaries in *Macmillan's Magazine* in 1865, and then in more detail in *Hereditary Genius* in 1869. With the appropriately cautionary notes of a conscientious scientist, he was bold in his assertions.

> I propose to show in this book that a man's natural abilities are derived by inheritance, under exactly the same limitations as are the form and physical features of the whole organic world . . . I shall show that the social agencies of an ordinary character, whose influences are little suspected, are at this moment working towards the degradation of human nature, and that others are working towards its improvement. I conclude that each generation has enormous power over the natural gifts of those that follow, and maintain that it is a duty we owe to humanity to investigate the range of that power, and to exercise it in a way that, without being unwise towards ourselves, shall be most advantageous to future inhabitants of the earth.[8]

In this introductory paragraph, Galton the scientist became Galton the policy advocate.

It is one thing to assert, "man's natural abilities are derived by inheritance." It is quite another to assert that little suspected influences are working towards "the degradation of human nature, and that others are working towards its improvement," that we have "enormous power" to influence the make-up of society, and that it is a duty owed to humanity to ensure these influences "shall be most advantageous to future inhabitants of the earth."

Embedded in these latter statements is the idea that boundaries between more and less valuable life can and should be drawn. For Francis Galton and many scientists and politicians paying attention, some lives were more worthy of cultivation, protection, and support than others. With this rationale, eugenics the scientific investigation became eugenics the progressive social movement.

Galton continued his work and in 1883 elaborated further on what he had in mind, coining and explaining a term for the enterprise. He wanted a word "to express the science of improving stock," a word "equally applicable to men, brutes, and plants." The term eugenics worked. It came from the Greek *eugenes*, "good in stock, hereditarily endowed with noble qualities." For Galton, the idea of improving the stock was not limited to judicious mating, but included "all influences that tend in however remote a degree to give to the more suitable races or strains of blood a better chance of prevailing speedily over the less suitable than they otherwise would have had."[9] The practical implications of exclusionary differential worth were beginning to grow.

Although early formal membership in eugenic associations was estimated to be less than 2,000 in both Britain and the U.S., there were a large number of small chapters, and the message was spreading. Eventually, loosely defined networks of individuals and organizations provided a semblance of common ideological footing and coherence for the Eugenics Movement. Karl Pearson is said to have "exulted" to Francis Galton, in 1907, "You would be amused to hear how general is now the use of your word *Eugenics*! I hear most respectable middle-class matrons saying if children are weakly, 'Ah that was not a eugenic marriage!'"[10] By 1910, eugenics had become one of the most frequently cited topics in the *Readers Guide to Periodical Literature*.[11]

At the turn of the century Galton was asked by the Anthropological Institute in London to deliver a lecture on his ideas. He titled his discussion, "The Possible Improvement of the Human Breed, Under the Existing Conditions of Law and Sentiment." Clearer understanding through data collection and analysis had taken place since his earlier works.

> The faculties of future generations will necessarily be distributed according to the laws of heredity, whose statistical effects are no longer vague, for they are measured and expressed in formulae. We cannot doubt the existence of a great power ready to hand

and capable of being directed with vast benefit as soon as we shall have learnt to understand and to apply it. To no nation is a high human breed more necessary than to our own, for we plant our stock all over the world and lay the foundation of the dispositions and capacities of future millions of the human race.[12]

There were boundaries to be drawn between more and less valuable forms of life, and "our" stock was better than "theirs."

In this same talk, Galton noted that the methods for "augmentation of the favored stock" might vary. Choices would have to be made. For Galton the statistician, naturalist, and policy advocate, some measures were better than others.

The possibility of improving the race of a nation depends on the power of increasing the productivity of the best stock. This is far more important than that of repressing the productivity of the worst. They both raise the average, the latter by reducing the undesirables, the former by increasing those who will become the lights of the nation. It is therefore all important to prove that favour to selected individuals might so increase their productivity as to warrant the expenditure in money and care that would be necessitated.

These two options would find different homes. Repression of undesirables, or what came to be called negative eugenics, would take deepest root and become most fully developed in the United States, Canada, Scandinavia, and Germany. Positive eugenics, or what might be called in later parlance affirmative action for the advantaged, would become the policy of choice among eugenic advocates in Great Britain.

Throughout the closing decades of the nineteenth century, a Malthusian future was looming as resources were strained by a severe depression. Prosperous citizens were having children at or just below replacement levels. Among the less prosperous and newly arrived immigrants, those least able to support their children, offspring were arriving at much higher rates. To make matters worse, society was providing a safety net for these less-advantaged persons. This "indiscriminate benevolence" for the poor was criticized, as it produced artificially long lifespans for the unfit. Survival of a thriving, prosperous society was at stake.[13] If left unchecked, these higher birth rates and artificially reduced death rates among society's least capable could mean only one thing—the slow but sure degrading of the population.

To curb this degradation, emphasis turned to procreation and migration. When it came to procreation, as Galton had pointed out, there were two options. The prosperous and well educated could be encouraged to have more children. Alternatively, the poor and less capable could be encouraged, gently or otherwise, to have fewer. As for migration, undesirable elements from abroad could be discouraged from entering the country. Eventually, strategies to reduce the proportion of those judged to be in the bottom 10 percent of the population—the submerged tenth as they were sometimes called—would take three forms: segregation in asylums, forced sterilization, and restrictive immigration policies.

The negative eugenic argument was attractively simple. Would not it be better to have a society enriched by those who are productive, healthy, emotionally stable, and smart, than one stifled by degenerate, feeble-minded, disabled, and criminal citizens? To protect *LIFE* writ large, the lives of those less worthy should be reduced in number. Knowing now where this argument led, it is almost automatic to be repulsed by the proposed journey.

How did well-educated individuals, schooled in the healing arts and the rigors and self-correcting mechanisms of science, supported by prominent, well-endowed philanthropic foundations, whose mission it was to make society better, go so badly wrong? Step by little step seems to be the answer. Step by step, in a climate of fear that the quality of *LIFE* was being threatened and needed protection. A loosely connected network of individuals and organizations, dedicated to the eugenics cause, began to chart the course toward a more secure future.[14]

A Base of Operation

The framing message and assumption of eugenics was differential worth. Some lives were more worthy of support and protection than others. There was research to be done. The fruits of research could be used for the betterment of all. Pioneering efforts took root in the American

Breeders' Association, the American Eugenics Society, the Galton Society, the Race Betterment Foundation and the Human Betterment Foundation.[15] No organization, however, was more important as an early base of operation than the Station for the Experimental Study of Evolution (SESE) and the Eugenics Record Office (ERO) at Cold Spring Harbor, Long Island, New York.

The SESE and ERO were launched through the efforts of a young entrepreneurial professor, Charles Benedict Davenport. Davenport, a biologist with mathematical training, received his PhD in 1892 from Harvard. His interests led him to the works of Francis Galton, Karl Pearson, and Gregor Mendel. He was eventually appointed to the editorial board of Karl Pearson's journal, *Biometrika*. Reviewing articles for this newly founded journal put him in touch with other like-minded scholars reporting their research on a wide range of related topics.

The empirical methods taking hold in biology at the time, especially those exploring the links between the ideas of Gregor Mendel and Darwin's evolutionary theories, needed a home. Davenport was convinced of the importance of this enterprise, noting the parallels between improving the quality of thoroughbred horses, hogs, cattle, and sheep and the vitality and strength of the human population. It was a promising, exciting enterprise, well worth pursuing.

While teaching at Harvard and then at the University of Chicago, Davenport began seeking funds to establish an independent laboratory. He had taught at a small summer institute on the northwestern shore of Long Island. He knew it would be an ideal location for the operation he had in mind. He knew also that the philanthropic Carnegie Institution of Washington (CIW) had just been founded, and that their funding priorities coincided with his interests.

Through an influential banker friend in Chicago, Davenport submitted a funding proposal to the Carnegie Institution's secretary aimed at exploring "the analytic and experimental study of the cause of specific differentiation—of race change."[16] The proposal was turned down. Davenport had failed to spell out, and the CIW had failed to recognize, the broader implications of what he had in mind. The CIW was most interested in proposals that would have broad-based practical impact. They were also interested in funding researchers and organizations that would coordinate efforts toward a common goal.

As young researchers often do, Davenport learned of this assessment and CIW's predisposition to broad-based practical projects that worked across disciplines. He rewrote his proposal and resubmitted. In December of 1903, he was awarded a grant with commitments "to continue indefinitely, or for a long time." The SESE was born.

As work moved forward, an alliance was immediately formed with the American Breeders Association (ABA), created in St. Louis, Missouri, the same year funding for the SESE was secured. At their first meeting, Davenport was elected to the ABA oversight committee and was instrumental in establishing the Eugenics Committee. This committee was charged, in the hereditary parlance of the day, to "devise methods of recording the values of the blood of individuals, families, people and races," with the overarching purpose of emphasizing "the value of superior blood and the menace to society of inferior blood."[17]

It became increasingly clear that carefully kept records and a repository for data were essential to the research being pursued. Plans began almost immediately to add such capacity. Again, funding was needed. In testament to the strength of weak ties[18] and the importance of a tenacious entrepreneurial spirit for the success of any social movement, Davenport knew that railroad magnate, Edward Henry Harriman, had recently died and had left control of his fortune to his wife, Mary Harriman. He knew also that Mary Harriman's daughter had been a student of his some three years earlier in the summer program at Cold Spring Harbor.

He wrote Mary Harriman, who was distributing a portion of her fortune through a philanthropic foundation devoted to providing individuals an opportunity to become "more efficient members of society." Harriman placed special emphasis on the use of scientific principles to secure a rational, orderly society.[19] What better match could there be than with the Station for the Experimental Study of Evolution? Renewing their acquaintance and noting his admiration for her philanthropic endeavors, Davenport suggested that the newly launched endeavor at Cold Spring Harbor would be a good fit for the priorities of the Harriman Foundation.

Of all the letters Mary Harriman received, reportedly some 6,000, Davenport's was one that stood out. Davenport and Harriman gathered for subsequent conversations to discuss what he had in mind and how it matched the goals of the Foundation. In the end, financial commitments were made, and the Eugenics Record Office came into being. Harry Laughlin, a former teacher and school superintendent from Missouri who had become acquainted with Davenport through the ABA and their mutual interest in the breeding of ranch and farm stock, was appointed to head up the ERO.

Funding from the CIW and the Harriman Foundation provided much-needed resources. These well-regarded funding sources provided added credibility and a place at the table with society's elite for the fledgling enterprise. The operation at Cold Spring Harbor was an operation to be taken seriously. It soon became "a meeting place for eugenicists, a repository for eugenics records, a clearinghouse for eugenics information and propaganda, a platform from which popular eugenic campaigns could be launched, and a home for several eugenical publications." The ERO, in short, "became a nerve center for the Eugenics Movement as a whole."[20]

From Cold Spring Harbor and the eventual expansion of related operations across the country, the Eugenics Movement evolved. Conferences were held, studies conducted, papers and books written, speeches given, sermons delivered, laws crafted and passed. Contrived lawsuits were filed, expert testimony was provided, and Supreme Court decisions were produced. It would be a long-lasting, far-reaching, and in the end quite troubling legacy.

Framing the Agenda

The Cold Spring Harbor operation worked hand-in-hand with the American Breeders Association.[21] The ABA was grounded in American Agricultural Colleges and Experiment Stations; both had been established as part of the Land Grant College or Morrill Act in 1862 and were dedicated to the improvement of agricultural crops and animal stock. Davenport had been elected to the ABA oversight committee, and in 1906 he helped establish a eugenics committee. The committee's charge was to develop methods for mapping eugenically relevant traits of families, individuals, and races, with the underlying assumption that some "blood lines" were beneficial and some detrimental to the health of society. Early human eugenics in the United States grew largely from the efforts of this ABA committee. Its membership was luminary.

David Starr Jordan, the first president of Stanford University, agreed to serve as chair. His colleagues on the committee included Alexander

Graham Bell and Luther Burbank. As indicated in a membership pamphlet put out by the ABA, their purpose was to advance the "interests of the Association that relate to human improvement by a better selection of marriage mates and the control of the reproduction of defective classes."[22] Much of the ABA's human eugenics initiative transferred to Cold Spring Harbor. Shortly after Harry Laughlin took the superintendent's job at the ERO, the task of producing an early report for Jordan's Committee became his responsibility.

David Starr Jordan, an ichthyologist by training, was well trained for this effort. In his early 30s he had been appointed president of Indiana University in 1885, six years after joining the faculty, making him the youngest university president in the country. Shortly thereafter he would become Stanford University's first president. His position and academic credentials put him in touch with prominent citizens in the nation's heartland and west coast, as well as colleagues he had attended school with on the east coast.

Jordan had long-standing interests in these matters. As a young professor in Indiana, he had become acquainted with Oscar McCulloch, the minister of the Indianapolis Congregational Church. A captivating orator and central figure in the social gospel and charity reform movements of the time, Reverend McCulloch was dedicated to improving the condition of man. He had been responsible for establishing numerous charitable organizations in the Indianapolis area. He sensed a degradation of society, spoke frequently of this in his sermons, and was a vocal advocate for change.[23]

Among his many causes, McCulloch was a frequent and outspoken critic of the injustices of capital punishment, advocating as well for a more humane prison system modeled after a recently constructed reformatory in Elmira, New York. Thanks in no small measure to Reverend McCulloch's efforts and influence, Indiana was the first state to establish a reformatory for women and girls. A parallel institution for men would soon follow. These reformatories would become the site of pioneering mandatory sterilization efforts.

Reverend McCulloch was impressed by Galton's research. He was drawn also to Richard Dugdale's study of an extended family in New York, first published in 1877, *"The Jukes" A Study in Crime, Pauperism, Disease and Heredity*. Dugdale's study provided, McCulloch believed, important insights into both cause and remedy of degenerate persons who so troubled and damaged the society he aimed to improve. There were stories of a similarly situated family involved in crime and socially degrading behavior throughout Indiana, and McCulloch decided to investigate.

He would later recall his first contact with the Ishmaels in the fall of 1877:

> There were gathered in one room, without fire, an old blind woman, a man, his wife and one child, his sister and two children. A half-bed was all the furnishing. No chair, table, or cooking utensils. I provided for their immediate wants, and then looked into the records of the township trustee.

From this initial meeting, McCulloch expanded his investigation over the next decade, eventually including over 250 families connected through an extended familial network, 30 of which were investigated in greater depth. In 1888, McCulloch presented his findings, at a National Conference of Charities and Corrections, held in Buffalo, New York, introducing the world to *The Tribe of Ishmael: A Study of Social Degradation.*

He began with an analogy. There were parallels, McCulloch noted, between this tribe and a small, free-swimming, parasitic crustacean, then being studied by a University of Chicago professor, Ray Lankaster.[24] Soon after birth, "an irresistible hereditary tendency seizes upon it." It attaches to a crab, losing in the process "the characteristics of the higher class, and becomes degraded in form and function." This parasitic behavior is transmitted to its offspring, and it stands "in nature as a type of degradation through parasitism, or pauperism."

With the parasitic-crustacean imagery in place, McCulloch continued. "I propose to trace the history of similar degradation in man. It is no pleasant study, but it may be relied upon as fact. It is no isolated case. It is not peculiar to Indiana." Nearing the end of his presentation, Reverend McCulloch underscored his analogy between those he had studied and the parasitic crustacean.

> They are a decaying stock; they cannot longer live self-dependent. The children reappear with the old basket. The girl begins the

life of prostitution, and is soon seen with her own illegitimate child. The young of the Sacculina at first have the Nauplius form common to their order. Then the force of inherited parasitism compels them to fasten themselves to the hermit crab. The free-swimming legs and the disused organs disappear. So we have the same in the pauper. Self-help disappears. All the organs and powers that belong to the free life disappear, and there are left only the tendency to parasitism and the debasement of the reproductive tendency.

Like parasites, the Tribe of Ishmael, from one generation to the next, sucked nutrients from society and in the process became useless dependents.

This energy-sapping degradation, McCulloch concluded, was hereditary. It was also pushed along by misplaced charity. "The so-called charitable people who give to begging children and women with baskets have a vast sin to answer for ... So-called charity joins public relief in producing still-born children, raising prostitutes, and educating criminals." For the moment, this preacher of the social gospel, this organizer of charitable organizations, and innovative reformatories, had apparently become disenchanted with a New Testament account of the final judgment involving those who were charitable and those who were not.[25]

McCulloch closed his presentation with a final admonition. "What can we do? First, we must close up official out-door relief. Second, we must check private and indiscriminate benevolence, or charity, falsely so-called. Third, we must get hold of the children." Whatever his findings and policy lessons drawn from the Tribe of Ishmael, by 1891, three years after presenting his findings, Oscar McCulloch, the minister, researcher, and social reformer had become president of the National Conference of Charities and Corrections. Shortly thereafter, at the age of 48, he would die an untimely death from his inherited Hodgkin's Disease.[26]

McCulloch's dehumanizing parasitic characterization of the Tribe of Ishmael, and those of the same ilk, however, was longer lasting and widely shared. In 1902, a decade after McCulloch's death, a president of what is today known as the American Association on Intellectual and Developmental Disabilities, M.W. Barr, made another presentation to the National Conference of Charities and Corrections. His topic: "The Imbecile and Epileptic Versus the Tax-Payer and the Community." His conclusion: "Of all dependent classes there are none that drain so entirely the social and financial life of the body politic as the imbecile, unless it be its close associate, the epileptic."[27]

Branching Out

By the time Reverend McCulloch's parishioner, David Starr Jordan, accepted his appointment as chair of the ABA's committee, charged with mapping traits beneficial or detrimental to the health of society, he had become a well-known academic. He left Indiana University to become Leland Stanford Junior University's (now, simply Stanford University) first president the same year Oscar McCulloch died. Armed with McCulloch's sermons, research, and policy conclusions, as well as his own work and the writings of other prominent academicians, Jordan became a linchpin for the eugenic movement on the west coast.

His position and academic standing made him attractive on the lecture circuit, both nationally and internationally. In 1898, he collected many of his writings in *Foot-Notes to Evolution: A Series of Popular Addresses on the Evolution of Life,* and published them along with supplemental essays by three of his colleagues at Stanford and the University of Pennsylvania. The next year, he gave a widely debated speech at Stanford, *The Blood of a Nation: A Study of the Decay of Races Through the Survival of the Unfit,* which was eventually published in 1902 and then reprinted by the American Unitarian Association in 1907, along with a related speech he delivered in Philadelphia at ceremonies celebrating the two-hundredth anniversary of the birth of Benjamin Franklin.[28]

By this time, the eugenic position of this one-time parishioner in Oscar McCulloch's Plymouth Church and now well-known and influential president of Indiana and Stanford universities had solidified. In *Blood of a Nation* he wrote,

> For a race of men or a herd of cattle are governed by the same laws of selection . . . In selective breeding . . . it is possible, with a little attention to produce wonderful changes for the better . . . To select for posterity those individuals which best meet our

needs or please our fancy, and to destroy those with unfavorable qualities, is the function of artificial selection.

President Jordan's perspective had been further shaped by several visits he made to the village of Aosta, located in a sparsely populated, scenic, alpine valley not far from majestic Mont Blanc, where Italy, France, and Switzerland converge. There he had observed a community of "cretins." Later, in his autobiography, he would recall this community in rather unsympathetic terms as "feeble little people with uncanny voices, silly faces, and sickening smiles, incapable of taking care of themselves."[29] By 1910, this community of cretins had all but died out as a result of segregation in an asylum where the Church would neither condone marriage, nor permit child bearing. Jordan drew upon this lesson of selective breeding through enforced segregation in the years just ahead.

With this background, prominence, and perspective, Stanford's president accepted the request from the ABA and the ERO to develop policy recommendations for human eugenics. In 1911, Jordan began work with Harry Laughlin on a study, funded in part by the Carnegie Institution, to explore the "best practical means for cutting off the defective germ-plasm in the human population." The Eugenics Movement was gaining momentum in a now nationwide network of connections.

It was also redefining itself and broadening its mission. The ABA changed its name to become the American Genetics Association. Its official publication, *American Breeders Magazine*, became the *Journal of Heredity*. A former Stanford student of Jordan's, Paul Popenoe, was appointed as its editor.

The Criteria for Exclusion

Understanding of heredity was primitive at best. The structure of DNA and genetic markers were nowhere on the horizon. Instead, researchers continued to rely on the distribution of traits as revealed in pedigree studies of familial networks, such as studies of the Jukes and the Ishmaels produced by Richard Dugdale and Oscar McCulloch.

A common thread in these endeavors was how to separate those unfit from the worthy and contributing. To better define these boundaries, Charles Davenport published *The Trait Book*,[30] a detailed listing of individual characteristics, predispositions, and behavioral tendencies. Guidelines for field observations, pedigree charts, and surveys were developed and widely distributed to physicians, teachers, social workers, and parents. Classification schemes to organize the data were devised. The feeble-minded, degenerate, perverts, morons, imbeciles, epileptics, and paupers were defined as lives less worthy. They were to be identified, isolated, minimized, and if possible eliminated.

While definitions of exclusionary boundaries remained loose and subject to wide interpretation among fieldworkers, continuing attempts were made to refine definitions and data-gathering techniques. Training was provided before sending persons, mainly women, into the field to observe and identify manifestations of the defined traits. To further assist these efforts, quantitative intelligence testing, being developed in France at the time, was adapted for family pedigree purposes.

As the Cold Spring Harbor operation was getting off the ground, French psychologists Alfred Binet and Theodore Simon designed the *Simon–Binet Scale* between 1905 and 1908. A few years later, Lewis Terman, a Stanford professor and colleague of David Starr Jordan, offered a modified version of the test, known as the Stanford–Binet test. A close associate of Charles Davenport and the ERO, Henry Goddard, translated the work of Binet and Simon into English and introduced break-off points to identify "morons," persons with marginal intelligence, from "imbeciles" (one category lower) and "idiots" (two categories lower).

Goddard was the director of the research laboratory at the Vineland Training School for Feebleminded Girls and Boys in New Jersey. He believed at the time that such children would grow up to have higher fertility rates than others and thus advocated tight controls on their ability to have children. As part of the growing network of eugenic cooperation, Goddard routinely made his patients available for family pedigree tracing and assessment and was intimately involved in writing reports for the ERO.

In one of these reports Goddard reviewed his impressions of the quality of the data being collected:

> The field worker goes out as the superintendent's personal representative with a letter recommending her (females were seen as most effective interviewers) and urging the parents, for the sake

of the child, to tell all they possibly can, and to send her to other relatives or to any one who may be able to give information, which may be used to help their child, or some one's child. The response has been full, free, and hearty. Parents do all in their power to help us get the facts. There is very rarely anything like an attempt to conceal facts that they know. Of course, many of these parents are ignorant, often feeble-minded, and cannot tell all that we should like to know. Nevertheless, by adroit questioning and cross-reference, we have been able to get what we believe to be very accurate data in a very large percentage of our cases.[31]

One can only speculate how these families might have responded had they known more fully that an underlying purpose of Goddard's studies was to limit the existence of persons such as themselves and families such as their own.

Whatever the response, later assessments of family pedigree studies were not kind. One particularly critical reviewer would note,

The movement continued to amass volumes of data on families and individuals by combining equal portions of gossip, race prejudice, sloppy methods and leaps of logic, all caulked together by elements of actual genetic knowledge to create the glitter of a genuine science.[32]

Goddard himself would eventually question the validity of his conclusions, along with their eugenic implications.

The early family pedigree studies of the Jukes and the Ishmaels, along with less well-publicized related research, however, would soon be joined by other works, including Goddard's widely disseminated and highly influential investigation of the Kallikaks[33] and Arthur Estabrook's reexamination of data on the Jukes.[34] Armed with the experience gained from his reexamination of the Jukes, Estabrook would become an expert witness in a contrived trial involving forced sterilization of a young woman in Virginia, Carrie Buck. His testimony would be joined by that of Harry Laughlin. This trial and subsequent appeal to the Supreme Court became the high-water mark for justifying governmental intrusion into the lives of those labeled as defective, feeble-minded parasites.

The Passing of the Great Race, authored by Madison Grant, a friend and professional associate of Davenport and the ERO, would also join this growing body of academic literature. These individuals and their works would play major roles as the Eugenics Movement continued its journey. Grant's work, widely translated, was greeted with mixed reviews. Columbia University professor and well-known anthropologist Franz Boaz and his soon to become equally famous student Margaret Mead were among its most severe critics. In contrast, it was favorably reviewed in *Science*, the journal of the American Association for the Advancement of Science.[35] Most infamously, it would be praised and used as a template by a young Adolf Hitler as he wrote *Mein Kampf* from his jail cell.[36]

The negative Eugenics Movement clearly had broad reach and influence. A relatively small, loose-knit circle of colleagues, centered at the ERO in Cold Spring Harbor, shaped the agenda. Their aim was to establish a nationwide program of mandatory sterilization grounded in statutory law. It began with David Starr Jordan's committee and a 200-page report largely written by Harry Laughlin.

Notes

1 For eugenics as a global social movement see: Deborah Barrett and Charles Kurzman, "Globalizing Social Movement Theory: The Case of Eugenics," *Theory and Society* 33 (2004): 487–527. For detailed accounts, see: Daniel Kevles, *In the Name of Eugenics* (New York: Knopf, 1985); Stefan Kühl, *The Nazi Connection: Eugenics, American Racism, and German National Socialism* (New York: Oxford University Press, 1994); Edwin Black, *War Against the Weak: Eugenics and America's Campaign to Create a Master Race* (New York: Four Walls Eight Windows, 2003); Alexandra Minna Stern, *Eugenic Nation: Faults & Frontiers of Better Breeding in Modern America* (Berkeley, CA: University of California Press, 2005).

2 Daniel Rogers, "In Search of Progressivism," *Reviews in American History* 10 (1982): 113–32.

3 Black, *War Against the Weak*, 125.

4 Diane B. Paul, *Controlling Human Heredity—1865 to the Present* (Atlantic Highlands, NJ: Humanities Press, 1995), 21.

5 Charles Darwin, (ed. by Barlow, N.) *The Autobiography of Charles Darwin* (1876) (London: Collins), 47.

6 Francis Galton, "Eugenics: Its Definition, Scope, and Aims," *The American Journal of Sociology* 10 (1904): 1–27.

7 Francis Galton, *Memories of My Life* (London: Methuen, 1908), 323.

8 Francis Galton, *Hereditary Genius* (New York: Macmillan & Company, 1869), 11.

9 Francis Galton, *Inquiries Into Human Faculty and its Development* (New York: J.M. Dent & Co. and London: E.P. Dutton & Co., 1883), 17, fn 1.

10   Quoted in Kevles, *In the Name of Eugenics*, 57.

11   Kevles, *In the Name of Eugenics*, 57–69. Philip R. Reilly, *The Surgical Solution: A History of Involuntary Sterilization in the United States* (Baltimore, MD: Johns Hopkins University Press, 1991), 18.

12   "The Possible Improvement of the Human Breed Under the Existing Conditions of Law and Sentiment," The Second Huxley Lecture of the Anthropological Institute, delivered on October 29, 1901.

13   Paul Popenoe and Roswell Johnson, *Applied Eugenics* (New York: The Macmillan Company, 1918).

14   For a thorough summary of this movement see: Julie Beicken's *Eugenics: An Elite Social Movement* (2010), Masters Thesis, University of Texas, Austin.

15   Kevles, *In the Name of Eugenics*. Garland E. Allen, "The Eugenics Record Office at Cold Spring Harbor, NY, 1910–1940: An essay in institutional history," *Osiris* 2 (1986): 225–64.

16   Allen, "The Eugenics Record Office," 229.

17   Black, *War Against the Weak*, 39.

18   Mark Granovetter, "The Strength of Weak Ties: A Network Theory Revisited," *Sociological Theory* 1 (1983): 201–33. David A. Snow, Louis A. Zurcher, and Sheldon Ekland-Olson "Social Networks and Social Movements: A Micro-Structural Approach to Differential Recruitment," *American Sociological Review* 45 (1980): 789.

19   Allen, "The Eugenics Record Office," 234.

20   Allen, "The Eugenics Record Office," 226.

21   Barbara A. Kimmelman, "The American Breeders' Association: Genetics and Eugenics in an Agricultural Context, 1903–13," *Social Studies of Science* 13 (1983): 163–204.

22   See Archival material collected by Beicken, "Eugenics," 512–15.

23   Genevieve C. Weeks, *Oscar Carleton McCulloch, 1843–1891: Teacher and Practitioner of Applied Christianity* (Indianapolis, IN: Indianapolis Historical Society, 1976), 130–56.

24   Sir Edwin Ray Lankester, *Degeneration, a Chapter in Darwinism* (London: Macmillan, 1880).

25   Book of Matthew 25:34–45.

26   Weeks, *Oscar McCulloch, 1843–1891*.

27   M.W. Barr, *Proceedings National Conference of Charities & Corrections*, quoted in Wolf Wolfensberger, *The Origin and Nature of our Institutional Models* (Syracuse, NY: Human Policy Press, 1975), 34.

28   David Starr Jordan, *The Human Harvest: A Study of the Decay of Races Through the Survival of the Unfit* (Cambridge, MA: American Unitarian Association, 1907).

29   David Starr Jordan, *The Days of a Man: Volume 1, 1851–189* (Yonkers-on-Hudson, NY: World Book Co., 1922), 314.

30   Charles B. Davenport, *Eugenics Record Office Bulletin No. 6, The Trait Book* (Cold Spring Harbor, NY, 1912).

31   Eugenics Record Office, *Bulletin No. 1, Heredity of Feeble-Mindedness* (Cold Spring Harbor, NY, 1911), 1.

32   Black, *War Against the Weak*, 105.

33 Henry Herbert Goddard, *The Kallikak Family: A Study in the Heredity of Feeble-Mindedness* (New York: The Macmillan Company, 1912).
34 Arthur H. Estabrook, *The Jukes in 1915* (Washington, DC: Carnegie Institute of Washington, 1916).
35 Frederick Adams Woods, "The Passing of the Great Race," *Science*, October 25 (1918): 419–20.
36 See Black, *War Against the Weak*, 274–6.

CHAPTER 3
LEGAL REFORM TO ELIMINATE DEFECTIVES

The legal effort to justify mandatory sterilization was carefully orchestrated. It began with Harry Laughlin's 200-page report on the "best practical means of cutting off the defective germ plasm in the American population," released in February of 1914.[1] The model law Laughlin would eventually craft and release in 1922 grew directly from this earlier report. Laughlin's 1922 proposal served as a template for laws enacted in the United States and upheld by the Supreme Court in the landmark case *Buck v. Bell* in 1927.[2] It also provided the foundation for Germany's early sterilization law enacted in 1933, shortly after Adolf Hitler came to power. In gratitude for his pioneering work, so helpful in guiding Germany's early efforts, Laughlin was awarded an honorary degree from Heidelberg University in 1936 for his work on "racial cleansing."[3]

The journey from Laughlin's 1914 report to the horrors of Nazi Germany was taken step by little step over three decades. It was guided by a question posed by cereal magnate, philanthropist, and physician, John H. Kellogg at the First National Conference on race betterment, also held in 1914. "We have wonderful new races of horses, cows, and pigs," Kellogg noted. "Why should we not have a new and improved race of men . . . a Race of Human Thoroughbreds."

How to Limit Defectives

Laughlin's 1914 report considered numerous alternatives to limit the number of human defectives. He reviewed the effectiveness of marital restrictions, polygamy, and euthanasia, but gave special emphasis to what David Starr Jordan had seen in the village of Aosta—physical isolation and mandatory sterilization—as the best means to advance the cause.

The priorities of Laughlin and his committee were clearly articulated:

> In light of the studies thus far made it is clear that the most promising agency for reducing the supply of defectives in the whole population at a rate making for the ultimate extinction of the antisocial strains must consist in the segregation of the members of these strains before their reproductive periods, and in the sterilization of such of them as are returned to society at large while still potential parents. Moreover, such a program to be generally effective must be nation-wide and consistently followed in its application.[4]

The committee, in some measure at the urgings of Alexander Graham Bell,[5] also considered positive eugenic strategies by encouraging "fit and fertile matings among the better classes." In the opinion of the committee, however, facilitating better-class mating was a more difficult, less efficient road to travel. The urgency of the situation demanded more direct and efficacious action.

Other strategies were also considered and rejected. In 1896, Connecticut had prohibited marriages involving epileptics, idiots or imbeciles, and other feeble-minded individuals. After their own review, the committee found these restrictive marriage laws unlikely to work as the targeted persons were "not amenable to law and custom."[6] Other potential methods for furthering the cause were equally fraught. The committee concluded that polygamy, or the "pure sire method," would work, but any program that advocated polygamy would be "doomed to failure" because it struck at "one of our most priceless heritages so laboriously wrought through centuries of moral struggle. It would be buying a biological benefit at vastly too great a moral cost." The same was true for mandatory abortion, infanticide, and involuntary euthanasia. "Preventing the procreation of defectives rather than destroying them before birth, or in infancy, or in later periods of life, must be the aim of modern eugenics."[7] Therefore, polygamy among the better classes was not morally acceptable. Neither was abortion, infanticide, or euthanasia. Sterilization and segregation in asylums of those defined as parasitic degenerates was, on balance, the best choice.

With the problem defined and the major strategy chosen, the task became developing a law consistently applied nationwide. There was much work to do. It would not be easy. Creating such an agenda, with accompanying model statutes would be like building and maintaining a finely tuned, well-oiled, complex machine. There were a multitude of moving parts with ample opportunity for the legal machinery to grind to a halt. As the committee noted:

> Even though the motive be proper and the principle correct, an ill-designed statute, or an indifferent public, careless institution authorities, derelict state executive agencies, lack of adequate appropriation—and perhaps many other factors, acting either separately or *en masse*, may disable or may even destroy altogether the service expected of the entire mechanism.[8]

A model statute was an initial step. If a coordinated national program was going to succeed, careful attention would have to be given to these matters. Harry Laughlin and his colleagues were clear in their goal as well as constraints.[9] Protecting individuals, preserving justice, honoring public opinion, and abiding by constitutional dictates—these were the legal and moral challenges for any model law. These were not empty platitudes. They had been gleaned from the committee's practical review of recent statutes and judicial findings.

Finally, the committee wanted to be clear about motives. Again pointing to their review of laws already on the books or being considered, as well as extra-legal practices being employed, they noted:

> Three motives appear to have prompted the sterilization of individuals in America, first, the eugenical, second the punitive, and third the therapeutic. This model statute should be based upon purely eugenical ideals and must not under any consideration nor in any measure be punitive or vindictive.[10]

They knew well that recent court cases had prohibited the use of mandatory sterilization as a response to a crime committee. It was considered a cruel and unusual punishment. Using it to advance the public good was more acceptable.

A Moral Entrepreneur Reviews the Landscape

A champion for the cause was needed, and Harry Laughlin stood ready. Perhaps more than any other single individual, he became the moral and policy entrepreneur for mandatory eugenic sterilization. An early instructive eugenic reform effort had taken place in Pennsylvania. Mandatory-sterilization legislation had passed the legislature with solid support, but was vetoed a week later by the governor. In Indiana, the home state of Oscar McCulloch and the professional launching pad for David Starr Jordan, efforts had been more successful. Harry Laughlin and his committee meant to learn from these experiences, as well as those in other states such as California, Oregon, Washington, New Jersey, New York, and Connecticut.

One lesson learned from the Pennsylvania experience was that clarity of proposed procedures and precision in moral and legal justification were essential. On March 21, 1905, both houses of the legislature in Pennsylvania had passed an "Act for the Prevention of Idiocy." Detailing various procedures and responsibilities, the bill began,

> WHEREAS, Heredity plays a most important part in the transmission of idiocy and imbecility . . . If, in the judgment of this Committee of Experts and Board of Trustees, procreation is inadvisable, and there is no probability of improvement of the mental condition of the inmate, it shall be lawful for the surgeon to perform such operation for the prevention of procreation as shall be decided safest and most effective.

While the bill had solid support in the Pennsylvania legislature, it had none from the state's governor, Samuel Pennypacker.

Governor Pennypacker found the bill wanting on several fronts. He began his veto message with a chiding, tongue-in-cheek comment:

> This bill has what may be called in propriety an attractive title. If idiocy could be prevented by an act of assembly, we may be quite sure that such an act would have long been passed and approved.

He went on to spell out in more detail why he felt the bill did not pass practical, legal, or ethical muster.

For one thing, the proposed law was vague in specification of permissible procedures to prevent procreation. The newly developed vasectomy might be a minor procedure, but salpingectomies, used to sterilize women, were not. Again with chiding derision Governor Pennypacker noted, "It is plain that the safest and most effective method of preventing procreation would be to cut the heads off the inmates." Why not choose this method?

The governor was skeptical also of the ethical wisdom that flowed from narrowly trained scientists and doctors. "Men of high scientific attainment are prone, in their love for technique, to lose sight of broad principles outside of their own domain of thought." In the governor's mind, this bill, whatever its asserted merits, reflected this professional narrow-mindedness and violated profoundly important ethical principles.

In prescient anticipation of what many years later would be called the Georgetown Principles of Bioethics,[11] Governor Pennypacker noted that doctor–patient trust was breached, patient autonomy was violated, beneficence neglected, malevolence imposed, and justice ignored. Taken together, "A great objection is that the bill … would be the beginning of experimentation upon living human beings, leading logically to results which can readily be forecasted." History and the Nuremberg Doctors' Trials would prove Governor Pennypacker right.

In closing his veto message, he quoted disapprovingly from an article he had recently read, in the eugenics journal *Heredity*:

> Studies in heredity tend to emphasize the wisdom of those ancient peoples who taught that the healthful development of the individual and the elimination of the weakling was the truest patriotism—springing from an abiding sense of the fulfillment of a duty to the state.

The governor did not agree, believing instead the proposed law would result in grave injustice. "To permit such an operation would be to inflict cruelty upon a helpless class of the community which the state has undertaken to protect." Samuel Pennypacker disagreed with the wisdom, justice, practicality, and legality of such a law. He was governor. He had veto power. A little over a week after the bill was passed, he exercised this power.

While the governor's action was not altogether popular, the legis=
lature did not attempt to override his veto. A short time afterward,
Pennypacker responded to a rowdy crowd protesting his action, "Gentlemen, gentlemen! You forget you owe me a vote of thanks. Didn't I veto
the bill for the castration of idiots?"[12] Governor Pennypacker left office
the next year.

Two years later, the experience in Indiana was different. Here, the
lessons learned from Oscar McCulloch and David Starr Jordan were first
put into practice and then into law. Working with inmates in Indiana's
reformatory, Dr. Harry Sharp had begun imposing vasectomies shortly
after the procedure was proposed in an article in the *Journal of the American
Medical Association* in 1899.[13] Sharp published two articles of his own,
one in the 1902 *New York Medical Journal* and another in the 1907 *Journal
of the American Medical Association*, extolling the virtues of the new surgical
procedure.[14] He confirmed claims that the patients he had vasectomized,
numbering over 200 even before an enabling law was passed, did better
in school, masturbated less frequently, felt stronger, and slept more
soundly. In addition, if released, they would have no more children.

Based on his experience, Sharp, as the Indiana Reformatory's chief
surgeon, began to lobby for legal change. He had been able to perform
his sterilizations without a legal statute in part because reformatories and
their outcast inmates were far from the public eye. For the most part,
legislative bodies and the courts took a hands-off approach to institutional
life. Although reformatories such as the one Sharp worked in were isolated
worlds apart,[15] having enabling legislation would provide legal cover if
needed.

Sharp was joined in his campaign by Indiana's nationally prominent
public-health pioneer, John Hurty. Hurty was then Secretary of the
State Board of Health. He was well known for his groundbreaking work
in sanitation, improved food and drug safety, and quarantine measures.
Given his accomplishments in public health, Hurty's was a voice to be
heard. He "saw little difference between public health and eugenics. From
his perspective, both involved broad-based sanitary measures guided by
the latest scientific discoveries and advances . . . undertaken for humani-
tarian purposes." Together, Hurty asserted, these measures were designed
"to end the suffering of unfortunates and maximize the overall health of
the body politic."[16]

Sharp and Hurty were persuasive. In 1907, Indiana became the first state to have an involuntary sterilization law. In the House, the vote was 59 to 22, in the Senate 28 to 16. The Indiana law was very close in word, procedure, and purpose to the law Governor Pennypacker had vetoed. This time, however, Governor J. Frank Hanley, three days after passage in the Senate, signed the bill into law.

The law's purpose was clear: it was designed "to prevent procreation of confirmed criminals, idiots, imbeciles, and rapists." The law was not designed to impose punishment for any crime. Instead, its design was eugenic, and its purpose public health. Discretion was granted to a committee of experts:

> If, in the judgment of this committee of experts and the board of managers, procreation is inadvisable, and there is no probability of improvement of the mental and physical condition of the inmate, it shall be lawful for the surgeons to perform such operation for the prevention of procreation as shall be decided safest and most effective.

Dr. Harry Sharp had argued that surgical and administrative procedures were safe, painless, fair, and positive in impact. Secretary Hurty agreed and confirmed the public health would be improved. There was a compelling collective interest in passing this law. Predictably, persons sterilized did not always agree. Several inmates, among the reported 119 men sterilized in Indiana Reformatory during the first year of the law's existence, took particular exception and wrote letters[17] to Hanley's successor, Governor Thomas Marshall, who would soon become Woodrow Wilson's vice president. These letters noted the perfunctory nature of the conversations leading to sterilization decisions and asserted that, whatever the law's stated eugenic purpose, its consequences were punitive and lacking in procedural safeguards.

These letters found a sympathetic ear in recently elected Governor Marshall. Shortly after his election, Governor Marshall became concerned enough to declare a moratorium. Given the isolated nature of institutional life and the resulting lack of data, it is not clear whether or to what extent sterilizations continued, but the stage was set to challenge such laws on constitutional grounds of due process, equal protection, and cruel and unusual punishment. Harry Laughlin and his committee took note of the governor's moratorium and associated concerns. They also noted similar concerns in other states.

Between March 1907, when Indiana's law was signed by the governor, and the February 1914 release of the Laughlin committee's recommendations, eleven additional states passed statutes similar to Indiana's. Four states, including Pennsylvania with its 1905 statute, passed laws that were vetoed or revoked in referendum. In other states, laws had been, or were being, appealed with challenges to due process, equal protection, and cruel and unusual punishment provisions of the state and federal constitutions. Nine states launched failed legislative efforts. Laughlin's committee aimed to learn lessons as they continued to craft their national strategy.

Nowhere did the eugenic sterilization movement take deeper root than in California, the adopted home of David Starr Jordan. The legislature enacted the state's first nonconsensual sterilization law in 1909. There was only one dissenting vote out of 63.[18] The governor signed the legislation into law. Modified several times over the years, and falling into some disuse after the revealed Nazi horrors of World War II, it was not until 1979 that California's sterilization statute was finally repealed in a social climate of heightened concern over governmental intrusion into individual lives.[19]

The first two decades of California's sterilization experience were summarized in *Sterilization for Human Betterment*, commissioned by the Human Betterment Foundation and published in 1929.[20] The HBF was a linchpin on the west coast for the Eugenics Movement. It had roots in, and functioned like, the ERO on the east coast and the Race Betterment Foundation in Michigan. Like these sister organizations, its board included many prominent figures in the Eugenics Movement, including David Starr Jordan and his professorial colleagues from the University of Southern California, Berkeley, Stanford, and Harvard.

The summary of the California experience was co-authored by the Foundation's major benefactor, E.S. Gosney, and President Jordan's protégé, Paul Popenoe. Given the clear activist agenda of the authors, and spotty record keeping across the country, there is reason to be skeptical of the precise numbers, trends, and comparisons in this volume. What is clear, however, in this and all other accounts, thanks in large measure to the prominence and organizational abilities of David Starr Jordan and the resources of E.S. Gosney, is that California was by far the most active state when it came to eugenics organizations and enforcement practices.

Gosney and Popenoe proudly reported that 6,255 eugenic sterilizations had been performed over the two decades between California's 1909 law and their 1929 report. This represented "practically three times as many official sterilizations as had been performed in all the rest of the United States." The years following would see further increase. Over the decades until final repeal, the most consistent estimate is that California accounted for something on the order of 20,000 eugenic sterilizations, a third of the nation's estimated total of 60,000.[21]

Framing a Legitimized Logic of Exclusion

As the Eugenics Movement gained momentum, the work of Darwin, Galton, Mendel, and their disciples was widely accepted and drawn upon. Defective hereditary traits could be uncovered and documented using the tools developed in family-pedigree investigations. Current beliefs and best available evidence suggested that the place to start was with those already on the margins of life, those persons housed in reformatory and penal institutions, as well as state institutions "for the insane, the feeble-minded, the epileptic, the inebriate, and the pauper classes."[22]

Laughlin and his committee recognized that not all inmates in these institutions would qualify for mandatory sterilization. Therefore, the second step for a legitimate exclusionary scheme needed to be procedural. Systematic case-by-case reviews would have to be done. Issues of due process and concern for equal protection would have to be addressed. The purpose of nonconsensual sterilization had to be clear, and Harry Laughlin would return time and again to what almost became a mantra. The aim of mandatory sterilization was not punishment. It was a public-health measure:

> [In both] intent and phrasing the proposed sterilization law should follow the strictest eugenical motives, and should be based upon the theory that sterilization is of such consequences that it should be ordered only by due process of law and only after expert investigation.

Family-pedigree studies were increasingly developed. This meant that all inmates prior to their release should be asked about their personal and family histories to determine the potential they had for producing defective offspring. The responsibility for determining such potential was given to an institutional eugenics commission, composed of persons "possessing expert knowledge of biology, pathology, and psychology." The head of each institution would have the responsibility of providing the eugenics commission with the inmate's "mental and physical conditions, innate traits, personal record, family traits and history."

In a bow to equity, the eugenics examination was to be carried out on all inmates prior to their release. For those found likely to be parents of "defectives," the eugenics commission would report its findings to a state court, including a recommendation for the appropriate sterilizing operation. The court would then examine the evidence, "allowing ample opportunity for the individual in question, or his relatives, guardian or friends to be heard." If the court concluded the individual had the potential for producing children who would "probably, because of inherited defective or anti-social traits, become a social menace or a ward of the state," the court would order the head of the institution "to cause to be performed . . . in a safe and humane manner, a surgical operation of effective sterilization before his or her release or discharge."

Laughlin's committee specified these principles in what they saw as a "Model Sterilization Law." They also outlined legal, ethical, and practical commentary on its various provisions. In the end, if states vigorously and consistently financed and enforced the recommended statute, they would not only meet constitutional, moral, and public opinion concerns but "in two generations practically cut off the inheritance lines and consequently the further supply of that portion of the human stock now measured by the lowest and most degenerate one-tenth of the total population."

A very precise schedule, complete with "Rate of Efficiency" graphs, was provided to achieve total elimination of defectives by 1985. In rough approximation, the total number of yearly sterilizations nationwide would rise from 92,000 in 1920; to 121,000 by 1930; 158,000 by 1940; 203,000 by 1950; 260,000 by 1960; 330,000 by 1970; and 415,000 by 1980. The stakes were high. The degenerate one-tenth constituted a "growing menace" to the nation's social welfare. Legal reforms should start immediately.

Although the agenda was ambitious, the committee believed its goals could be achieved "beginning on a small scale and keeping pace with institutional growth and scientific study." The program of recommended action could be accomplished "in a lawful, just and humane manner without detriment to, but on the contrary, to the great advancement of, national welfare." The call to action became a patriotic battle cry.

> Only those nations of history which have arisen to great effort to achieve a worthy end have long enjoyed a high plane of culture or have left contributions of worth to subsequent peoples. The purging of the defective traits from the blood of the American people is worthy of our best efforts.

The issues were now framed. The Laughlin report was released in February of 1914. Six months later, Germany declared war on France and invaded Belgium. The bloody war years (1914–18) consumed the nation's attention. The Eugenics Movement would have to wait. It would lose steam, but it would not come to a halt as it was supported by a receptive exclusionary climate.

A Receptive Exclusionary Climate

The eugenics cause was embedded in a broader cultural climate infused with an us-and-them mindset. Some lives were more worthy of protection, support, and encouragement than others. As Laughlin's committee sought legitimate ways to minimize the procreation of less worthy lives, the country was working its way through a rabidly racist and xenophobic period.

Jim Crow Laws had been passed in the closing years of the nineteenth century. These same years saw a sharp increase in lynchings. By 1914, lynchings were tapering off but continued at historically high levels through the 1920s.[23] The Ku Klux Klan (KKK), disbanded after the Civil Rights Act of 1871, was being reinvented.[24]

In 1916, Madison Grant published his widely read and instantly reprinted book, *The Passing of the Great Race*. Grant was closely associated with colleagues at Cold Spring Harbor and the Eugenics Movement on both the east and west coasts. He was a graduate of Yale University and Columbia Law School and couched his review of how demographic and migration patterns had shaped history, using rhetoric that drew at once on the self-correcting methods of science and the unbending, sometimes bombastic, convictions of a political activist.

Grant forewarned readers, "data will inevitably expand and perhaps change our ideas, but such facts as are now in hand and the conclusions based thereupon are provisionally set forth . . . necessarily in a dogmatic form."[25] These introductory remarks were accurate. Data expanded, ideas changed, and his book was a dogmatic, racist account of history. For Grant, not only was history driven by the migrations and interactions among races, Aryan Nordics were more hearty, intelligent, and industrious than those born of African, Asian, or southern and eastern European stock.

Grant was less worried about reducing the proportion of feeble-minded parasites through sterilization than he was about an even greater threat to the nation's strength—immigration. He concluded his first chapter on "Race and Democracy" with a cautionary note. Reliance on immigrants was the prelude to extinction as "immigrant laborers are now breeding out their masters and killing by filth and by crowding as effectively as by the sword."[26] In echoes of Oscar McCulloch, and in anticipation of arguments in years to come, he concluded his treatise with opposition to Emma Lazarus's words at the base of the Statue of Liberty.

Instead of welcoming the homeless and tempest tost, the huddled masses yearning to breathe free, Grant's belief was that "altruistic ideals" and "maudlin sentimentalism" had made America an "asylum for the oppressed" who were in fact leading the country toward a "racial abyss." His book's closing lines reflected his major worry. "If the Melting Pot is allowed to boil without control and we continue to follow our national motto and deliberately blind ourselves to all 'distinctions of race, creed or color'" those of Colonial descent would go the way of the "Athenian of the age of Pericles, and the Viking of the days of Rollo."[27]

When it came to persons of African ancestry, it was a matter of making sure a solid sense of rightful "place" was maintained. "As long as the dominant imposes its will on the servient race and as long as they remain in the same relation to the white as in the past, the Negroes will be a valuable element in the community." If, however, dominance was not achieved, these same people would be "destructive to themselves and to the whites. If the purity of the two races is to be maintained they cannot continue to live side by side and this is a problem from which there can be no escape."[28]

Madison Grant was not writing in a vacuum. At the same time, concern for lynchings was being voiced with increased urgency. The great migration of black citizens from south to north was gaining momentum, as persons began to lay the groundwork for what would become the National Association for the Advancement of Colored People. The violent summer of 1919 loomed just ahead. The fissuring sense of Us and Them, selective immigration, limited social intermingling among black and whites, and most certainly prohibitions against miscegenation would join hands with mandatory sterilization of defectives in the years just ahead.

The year just prior to the publication of Grant's book, *The Birth of a Nation*, a widely viewed, heroic depiction of the KKK, based on Thomas Dixon's book, *The Clansman*, was released covering many of the same themes. It was shown to Dixon's classmate at Johns Hopkins, President Woodrow Wilson, who reportedly gave it a positive review.[29] The recently reborn KKK made use of the film as a recruitment tool. Showings were sometimes greeted by counterbalancing protests, movie cancellations, and riots in several large cities.

In the more strictly eugenic arena, underscoring the themes that some lives are more worthy than others, *The Black Stork* was released the same year as *The Passing of the Great Race*. Shown over the next decade, this film made a strong connection between eugenics and doing god's will. It was a dramatization of the widely publicized experiences and practices of a Chicago surgeon, Harry Haiseldon. Dr. Haiseldon had allowed defective infants to die. His actions drew substantial public attention and generated both support and opposition.

Reflecting the wide dissemination of family-pedigree studies at the time, when asked about his practices, Haiseldon told a reporter, "What do you prefer—six days of Baby Bollinger or seventy years of the Jukes?"[30] Helen Keller, well known for her strong advocacy for persons with disabilities, herself a person Dr. Haiseldon might have let die as an infant, joined in support of the doctor's action. In a letter to *The New Republic*, written shortly after the publicity surrounding Haiseldon broke, Keller likened his actions to "weeding of the human garden that shows a sincere love of true life."[31]

The Black Stork,[32] in which Haiseldon himself played the part of the controversial doctor based on his own practice, depicted the courtship and marriage of two couples. Interlaced were parallels drawn with the breeding of cattle and horses and pleas for laws that would allow marriages only for couples who were certified as eugenically healthy. One marriage in the film resulted in the birth of a defective child. Following the mother's vision of a child's life filled with pain, derision, sorrow, and crime, and at the doctor's urgings, the child is allowed to die and ascend into the arms of a heavenly figure. In the second marriage, after some initial misplaced concern over the genetic heritage of the mother, a healthy child was born. The film ended with the husband in this latter couple noting, "Yes, we're fit to marry."[33]

Importantly, the film introduced a eugenics theme rejected by Laughlin's committee—the termination of defective lives. Mandatory sterilization to avoid the birth of "defectives" was one thing. Killing, or allowing to die, after birth was quite another, even if, as the images of the film implied, the baby ascended into the waiting arms of Jesus. The *Black Stork*, with its message of restricting marriages for eugenic reasons and letting defective infants die, was shown over the next several years. It was re-released with several edits in 1927, the same year as the Supreme Court's decision legitimizing eugenic sterilization in *Buck v. Bell*.

The underlying themes of terminating life or knowingly letting an infant die under various circumstances would become a major item of bioethical debate in the latter half of the twentieth century. Regardless of the bioethical debates to come, those intimately involved in the early Eugenics Movement clearly thought some lives more worthy of support and protection than others. Just as clearly, they thought governmental intrusion was called for. The strength of communal life was at stake. They would, on occasion, even consider the merits of euthanasia for "nature's mistakes."[34]

Whatever the underlying rationale, momentum for eugenic legal reform and governmental action to protect public health was regenerated in the years following the "war to end all wars." In particular, two new and eventually highly influential organizations were launched, each rooted in an existing national network of personal relations.

Mobilizing Resources and Networks of Support

The American Eugenics Society (AES) was conceived and developed in the early 1920s. Its chief architect, Henry Fairfield Osborne, was the president of the American Museum of Natural History and a collaborator with Madison Grant on *The Passing of the Great Race*. Harry Laughlin, Madison Grant, and Harry Crampton, a well-respected evolutionary biologist, joined Osborne in his AES initiatives. AES's major focus was public education. The aim was to move beyond the dry analysis of academic publications and conferences, beyond the elite circles of the Ivy League, the University of Chicago, and Stanford, to the heartland. If the Eugenics Movement was to succeed, resources would have to be mobilized, and networks of support would have to be expanded.

County-fair exhibits became a staple of this public-education campaign. They came complete with flashing lights demonstrating how high birth rates among the unfit, those "born to be a burden on the rest," were degrading the nation. "Fitter family" and "better baby" contests were organized at these same state fairs. Much like prize cows, chickens, and hogs, families and babies were judged by physical appearance, health, behavior, and intelligence. The winners were awarded medals and ribbons for demonstrating high-quality breeding.

As the AES was getting off the ground, the HBF was launched in California. Its core members included David Starr Jordan and Paul Popenoe. Connections with the ERO in New York, programs in Indiana, and the Race Betterment Foundation in Michigan were evident. In California, the wealthy citrus grower and philanthropist, Ezra Gosney, provided resources making the HBF perhaps the best-funded eugenics organization in the country.[35] In this California-based operation, resources were primarily aimed at data gathering and analysis, with particular emphasis on the impact and success of compulsory sterilization. Reports from the HBF, illustrated by Gosney and Popenoe's *Sterilization for Human Betterment*, were widely disseminated and discussed. Among those paying attention was the German government, but first additional legal refinements were needed.

The Legal Framework Clarifies

Laughlin's initial report to the ERO was released in 1914. By 1921, eight state laws had been challenged in state and federal appellate courts. They did not fair well. All but one was, either in whole or in part, overturned. This had a dampening effect on the Eugenics Movement, but, working with a colleague in Chicago, Judge Harry Olson, Laughlin took lessons from these appellate decisions as he refined his model sterilization law.

Many of the legal issues raised had come up just prior to the 1914 report. One was in New Jersey, home of Goddard's Vineland Training School for Feebleminded Girls and Boys. The then governor and future president, Woodrow Wilson, had signed the new law in 1911. It authorized the sterilization of the "feeble-minded (including Morons, Imbeciles, and Idiots), epileptics, rapists, and certain criminals and other defectives" who were confined in the State's reformatories and charitable and penal institutions.

An appeal was made on behalf of a young epileptic woman, Alice Smith.[36] Alice had been confined in New Jersey's State Village for Epileptics since 1902. Although her epilepsy was not contested, at the time of her hearing she had not had a seizure for five years. In May of 1912, a committee was convened to determine whether it was advisable that she be sterilized by salpingectomy. It determined that it was and so ordered. The committee's action was appealed to New Jersey's Supreme Court, where Justice Garrison, on behalf of two other colleagues, wrote the court's opinion. Neither he nor his colleagues were at all convinced that the mandated sterilization of Alice Smith was either wise or legal.

They noted in specific detail the seriousness of a salpingectomy. It involved "the incision or excision of the Fallopian tube, i.e., either cutting it off or cutting it out." Unlike a vasectomy, this procedure was "deep-seated surgery under profound and prolonged anaesthesia, and hence (involved) all of the dangers of life incident thereto, whether arising from the anaesthetic, from surgical shock or from the inflammation or infection incident to surgical interference." The statute's vague wording also bothered the judges, as its sterilization authority was broad enough to authorize an operation to remove any of a woman's organs essential for procreation—ovaries, fallopian tubes, and uterus.

Given this assessment, the reasons for state intervention for coercive sterilization had to be compelling. The stated motivating reason: public health. For these three New Jersey judges, this was a "novel" rationale, one that asserted the "theoretical improvement of society by destroying the function of procreation in certain of its members who are not malefactors against its laws." Similar to concerns Governor Pennypacker had articulated for his veto of Pennsylvania's 1905 legislation, they noted that, if they found the state's intervention legitimate in cases like Alice Smith's, "the doctrine we shall have enunciated cannot stop there."

There were other conditions besides epilepsy and the other enumerated statutory "defects" that might render persons a perceived burden to the common good. "Racial differences, for instance, might afford a basis for such (a policy) in communities where that question is unfortunately a permanent and paramount issue." Further,

> Even beyond all such considerations it might be logically consistent to bring the philosophic theory of Malthus to bear upon the police power to the end that the tendency of population to outgrow its means of subsistence should be counteracted by surgical interference of the sort we are now considering.

Having noted the logical destination of state intervention based on public-health concerns and differential assessment of social worth, the New Jersey court decided not to decide this issue. Constitutional issues surrounding collective interests that might permit or even call for state intervention remained cloudy. The Supreme Court would clarify this issue in *Buck v. Bell* a decade and a half hence.

There was, however, a less clouded constitutional issue. Equals should be treated equally. For cases such as Alice Smith's, it was clear "the force of the statute falls wholly upon such epileptics as are inmates confined in the several charitable institutions in the counties and State." If the public's health was accepted as a legitimate rationale and was to be protected by the elimination of procreation among epileptics and other "defectives," it would require "the sterilization of the vastly greater class who are not protected from procreation by their confinement in state or county institutions." If incarcerated epileptics were sterilized in the interest of the public's health, so should be non-institutionalized epileptics. Failure to do so would undermine the entire policy.

For Alice Smith, the New Jersey Supreme Court found "the present statute is invalid in that it denies . . . the equal protection of the laws to which under the Constitution of the United States she is entitled." Judged to be inequitable, the law was no law at all. Alice Smith would not be sterilized. The state could intrude in these extremely personal matters. It simply had to do so equitably. In the years ahead, issues came up in cases appealed in Michigan and New York, both decided in 1918.[37] These cases only underscored the importance of the equal protection issue.

Harry Laughlin took note as he modified his model statute released in 1922:

> All persons in the State who, because of degenerate or defective hereditary qualities are potential parents of socially inadequate offspring, regardless of whether such persons be in the population at large or inmates of custodial institutions, regardless also of personality, sex, age, marital condition, race, or possessions of such person . . .

This suggested wording involved a far more complicated political agenda and much deeper commitment to the eugenics cause. It did not catch on broadly in the United States. It would, however, be included in Germany's initial sterilization program.

The New Jersey, Michigan, and New York cases had raised issues of equal protection. Other cases from other states involved were based on the legitimacy of sterilization as punishment. These statutes would be modified. They use language that mimicked Laughlin's suggestion that nonconsensual sterilization be, "purely eugenic, that is, to prevent certain degenerate human stock from reproducing its kind. Absolutely no punitive element." In other instances, judicial appeals had revealed that sterilization against a person's will lacked provisions for "due process." Laws providing ample written notice, a hearing before a competent and impartial panel, with a subsequent right to appeal, fared better than laws without such provisions. This lesson, too, was incorporated in Laughlin's 1922 model statute.

While preparing his 1922 report, Laughlin had been working with Harry Olson, supervising judge for the Chicago Municipal Court. Judge Olson was also an active participant in the Eugenics Movement, at one time president of the Eugenics Research Association. Together, Olson and Laughlin decided that Laughlin's analysis and model statute should be widely distributed to politicians, judges, and activists across the country in an attempt to stimulate renewed interest in the faltering eugenic sterilization efforts.[38]

Laughlin's revised model statute provided a template for legislative change that would be widely debated.[39] With disagreements heard and debates held, many states eventually adopted some version of Laughlin's 1922 statutory template. Within two years of its release, some 15 states passed laws patterned to greater and lesser degree after Laughlin's recommended language. Among these, Virginia's law, passed two years later in 1924, would soon move to the national forefront.

A Landmark Case is Contrived

Reflecting the racial climate of the times as well as more specific eugenic interests, Virginia's dual-pronged 1924 legislation included the "Racial Integrity Act" and what came to be known as "The Sterilization Act." Both eventually became landmarks in U.S. constitutional law.

The Racial Integrity Act, greatly influenced by the writings of Madison Grant, required a racial description of all persons born in the state and marriage between "white persons" and "non-white persons." Some 40 years later, the wording prohibiting marriage across racial lines would be challenged and overturned in *Loving v. Virginia*.[40] Shortly thereafter, *Loving* would be cited in two companion cases, best known for honoring individual autonomy and firmly establishing the right to privacy—*Roe v. Wade* and *Doe v. Bolton*.[41] Virginia's Sterilization Act would reach the Supreme Court much sooner. The court's finding would be quite the opposite when it came to justifying state intrusion into an individual's privacy and autonomy.

To say the 1924 Virginia Racial Integrity and Sterilization acts reflected the climate of the times, both racial and eugenic, is not to say each was easily passed into law as part of a tidal wave of public consensus. They were not. In the case of the Sterilization Act, there was serious opposition.

Very specific individual interests and beliefs among a small group of influential politicians, lawyers, physicians, and administrators accounted for eventual legislative success.

Thanks to the meticulous work of Paul Lombardo,[42] we know the details of how three long-time personal friends and close professional associates, Albert Priddy, Aubrey Strode, and Irving Whitehead, crafted a successful strategy, not only for the passage of Virginia's sterilization statute, but also for its eventual affirmation in 1927 by the Supreme Court. The familiar names of Harry Laughlin, Harry Olson, Arthur Estabrook, and Henry Goddard were also in the mix. Justice Oliver Wendell Holmes, another prominent supporter of the Eugenics Movement, provided the sought-after stamp of approval.

By virtually any standard, *Buck v. Bell* is a landmark case. It not only stands as a high-water mark for the Eugenics Movement, but also as a grounding reference point for when state intrusion overrides individual autonomy when no criminal wrong has been asserted or proven. The story took almost 15 years to unfold. It begins about the time the ERO was getting off the ground in Cold Spring Harbor.

In 1910, Virginia, at the urgings of then state senator Aubrey Strode, established the Virginia Colony for Epileptics and Feebleminded, eventually known simply as the Lynchburg Colony. It was located in Strode's home district. It would become one of, if not the, largest such institution in the United States, and Virginia would become second only to California in the number of nonconsensual sterilizations performed.[43] The colony's first three-member governing board included Irving P. Whitehead, Aubrey Strode, and Dr. Albert Priddy, the Colony's first superintendent.

In 1911, shortly after taking over, Priddy urged the legislature to give serious thought to permitting sterilization of those under his care. He also urged that "defectives" sent to his institution be expanded to include more of the feeble-minded. In its next session, the legislature responded and specifically directed the commitment of feeble-minded "women of child-bearing age, from twelve to forty-five years of age." This, of course, meant the colony grew. It was growing in a time of scarce resources. Capacity pressures and economic constraints were also stretching other state institutions. Resources throughout the state became seriously strained, and, as organizations often do, avenues were explored to increase capacity at minimal cost.

In response, the state's Board of Charities and Corrections set up a committee to develop alternatives. Albert Priddy was asked to participate. The committee recommended broad-scale institutional sterilization. This would, among other things, allow the more capable among the feeble-minded to work outside the state's institutions at reduced costs to the state and without the risk of reproducing their kind.

Given the rhetoric in the committee's recommendations, as well as that found in Priddy's separate reports to the governor, there can be no doubt that the recommended sterilization of institutionalized individuals was grounded in the family-pedigree studies and policy recommendations of Dugdale, McCulloch, Goddard, Estabrook, Laughlin, and others. Phrases such as "blight on mankind," "burden too heavy," "rising tide of degeneracy," "non-producing and shiftless persons, living on public and private charity" were sprinkled throughout. Sterilization of inmates was needed for the "protection of society." It would have the beneficial side effect of saving money and increasing institutional capacity.

In the 1916 session of the legislature, Senator Strode, working with Dr. Priddy, introduced five separate bills related to the treatment of the feeble-minded. In what may have been the language of political compromise, designed to garner increased support, the most important of these proposals allowed sterilization without explicitly mentioning the procedure. Instead, the superintendent of the colony and members of the colony's board were given authority to use "such moral, medical and surgical treatment as they deem proper" to promote "the objects for which the institution is provided." One of the institution's objectives was "the protection of society."

Priddy's interpretation of the bill's language was clear. Within five days of the law's effective date, on June 9, 1916, he petitioned the colony's board for permission to sterilize eight women, using salpingectomy procedures. The three-member board responded in short order. With one member absent and one not responding, Whitehead alone provided written approval the same day Dr. Priddy's request was received. This quick turnaround soon became the rule. Requests to authorize sterilization and subsequent board approval were for the most part routine and perfunctory, with Priddy recommending and Whitehead approving, at times involving more than two dozen women in a single hearing.

Less than a year later, in March of 1917, the sterilization of two women, a mother and daughter, Miss Jessie Mallory and Mrs. Willie Mallory, was approved. The sterilizations were performed soon after approval. Two months later, the father and husband filed three suits. Two were for the release of the younger Mallory children who had been taken into custody in the same raid on the family home, while the father was absent. Two of the suits were successful and resulted in the release of the children. The third suit was for $5,000 in damages related to Mrs. Mallory's confinement and her subsequent forced sterilization.

In Mrs. Mallory's case, a jury returned a verdict in favor of Dr. Priddy. It was based on Priddy's defense that the sterilization had been performed for therapeutic reasons. Still, the judge was cautious and warned Priddy to discontinue his sterilization practices until the law could be clarified and strengthened. The judge was aware that depositions taken during the proceedings revealed serious questions about the legitimacy of the practices that resulted in Mrs. Mallory's commitment and sterilization.

Combing through these documents, Paul Lombardo uncovered Mrs. Mallory's recollection of how her commitment decision was made:[44]

> *Mrs. Mallory*: A doctor examined my mind and asked if I could tell whether salt was in the bread or not, and did I know how to tie my shoes. There was a picture hanging on the wall of a dog. He asked me if it was a dog or a lady. He asked me all sorts of foolish questions which would take too long for me to tell you.
>
> *Question*: What happened?
>
> *Mrs. Mallory*: Then the doctor took his pencil and scratched his head and said "I can't get that woman in," and Mrs. Roller said to them, "put on there, 'unable to control her nerves,' and we can get her in for that." That is about all.

If Mrs. Mallory's recollections were substantiated, the practices of Priddy and his colleagues would easily be questioned, and those responsible could be held legally responsible.

Dr. Priddy heeded the judge's concerns, but only in part. Sterilizations continued, but his stated rationale shifted. Instead of references to women of the "moron type," justifications for sterilizations were given, following the Mallory trial, in terms of relief of physical suffering for "pelvic disease" of unspecified origin.

While Priddy continued to claim he could treat his patients as he saw fit, he also understood his personal risks. Clearly, a new law was needed to provide adequate cover. Priddy provided a draft, but this time he lacked his main supporter. Senator Strode was away on an Army commission in Washington, DC, secured in part through the influence of his friend and political supporter, Irving Whitehead.

Priddy's proposed legislation failed, garnering only a single vote, that of the bill's sponsor. In later correspondence, a sympathetic physician colleague who had helped with the effort would note, "We were rewarded for our trouble by one vote and were laughed at by the law-makers."[45] It was clear the drafting expertise and political savvy and influence of Strode were missed. When Strode returned in 1919, joint efforts resumed.

There was support for eugenic sterilization in Virginia's assembly, but there was also growing opposition from respected scientists who questioned the scientific validity of family-pedigree studies and the claim that defects such as feeble-mindedness were hereditary.[46] Such traits might run in the same family, but that could be accounted for by any number of social, cultural, and economic explanations besides hereditary influence. The Catholic Church began speaking in louder voice, questioning the moral standing of mandatory sterilization, eventually culminating in Pope Pius XI's condemnation in 1930 of the practice of depriving persons of "a natural faculty by medical action."[47] Despite this growing opposition, after some initial false starts, in 1923, with the support of the General Board of State Hospitals, Priddy approached Strode again for his assistance in the next legislature.

This time Strode and Priddy used Laughlin's 1922 revised model sterilization statute as a touchstone for their proposed sterilization law. The bill, guided through the legislative process by Strode, reflected many of the details from Laughlin's template. It did not, however, provide for the sterilization of all "defectives," whether in or out of institutions. Instead, it provided for "the sexual sterilization of inmates of state institutions in certain cases." The legislation passed both houses of Virginia's assembly, with only two dissenting votes. Still, there were worries whether the statute would withstand an appeal. Other laws had passed in other states only to be declared unconstitutional. Care should be taken.

Shortly after the bill's passage, Dr. Priddy presented 18 sterilization petitions to the colony's board. All 18 were approved in a single hearing. Noting, however, the importance of securing legitimacy through the appellate courts, the board directed Priddy to work with Strode to prepare a test case. They agreed. No sterilizations should take place before the new law was tested in the courts and placed on firm legal footing.

After review, Priddy, Whitehead, and Strode agreed that acceptable procedural safeguards were in place. The purpose of the law was eugenic, not punitive, so this base, too, was covered. Equal protection, on the other hand, remained an issue. As Virginia's law covered only those who where institutionalized, equal protection concerns, similar to those Judge Garrison articulated in Alice Smith's case in New Jersey, remained a potential problem.

The Lynchburg Colony needed a compelling, safe case to run through the courts. They also needed a strategy that would ensure success. An 18-year-old woman, Carrie Buck, whose case had been one of the initial 18 petitions Priddy filed, was chosen. In a clear conflict of interest, Irving Whitehead was asked to represent Carrie Buck. Aubrey Strode was asked to take the case on behalf of the state. Priddy was the named defendant. It was a close-knit group. It would be a carefully coordinated effort. In the end, it would be hard to argue that Carrie Buck's interests had been defended.

For the state, Strode wrote to Arthur Estabrook, who had been his wife's social-work professor, asking him to assist in the evaluation of the Buck family. In addition, two doctors, Albert Priddy and Joseph DeJarnette, were asked to testify. Priddy's self-interest in the case was evident. Dr. DeJarnette's was only a little less so. Among other things, he had assisted Priddy in his failed legislative drafting, and had been the one complaining of legislative derision when their failed legislative attempt had generated a single vote, accompanied by laughter in the legislature.

Harry Laughlin, whom Priddy may have met during a visit to Judge Harry Olson's court a few years earlier, and who was certainly known by his leading role in the Eugenics Movement, was asked to provide a deposition as an expert witness. Although he did not talk with Carrie

Buck or any member of her family directly, Laughlin did receive correspondence from Priddy summarizing the case. He was quick to put it to use.

On the basis of this correspondence, Laughlin supported the claim that Carrie Buck was a feeble-minded and otherwise unfit individual whose traits were hereditary. In Laughlin's expert opinion, shaped by the letter he had received from Priddy, Carrie was a strong candidate for eugenic sterilization. With sometimes verbatim parroting of Priddy's words, Laughlin concluded that the Buck family belonged "to the shiftless, ignorant, and worthless class of anti-social whites of the South."

In Carrie's defense, Attorney Whitehead called no witnesses. Nor did he cross-examine or question in any detail witnesses or evidence provided by Strode. Carrie Buck had been chosen because of the assertion that her mother, she, and her daughter were all feeble-minded, and that there was a family history of immoral, anti-social behavior. Whitehead could have challenged all of these assertions with substantial, easily available, supporting evidence.[48] He did not. It was by any standard a shoddy and irresponsible defense.

The county circuit court affirmed the sterilization decision in February of 1925. Just a month prior to this decision, Dr. Priddy died, and his assistant James H. Bell took over as the colony's superintendent. The case was now titled *Buck v. Bell*. Appeal was taken to the Virginia Supreme Court of Appeals, where the county court's judgment was affirmed. Shortly after this decision, Strode and Whitehead jointly appeared before the colony board to celebrate their victory. They remained concerned, however, that the case had still not received affirmation from the U.S. Supreme Court. They aimed to secure a remedy.

Remembering that Strode and Whitehead were on opposite sides of the case, the notes of a subsequent meeting read in part,

> Colonel Aubrey E. Strode and Mr. I.P. Whitehead appeared before the Board . . . their advice being that this particular case was in admirable shape to go to the court of last resort, and that we could not hope to have a more favorable situation than this one.[49]

The assessment of the chances for success, by these clearly colluding lawyers, would prove correct.

The final step to firmly secure Virginia's Sterilization Act's constitutional legitimacy was the U.S. Supreme Court. Arguments were heard on April 22, 1927. A week and a half later, on May 2, Justice Oliver Wendell Holmes, on behalf of an eight–one court majority, issued the opinion affirming Virginia's sterilization statute.[50] The court found that Carrie Buck was a feeble-minded woman committed through appropriate procedures to the Virginia Colony for Epileptics and Feebleminded. She was the daughter of a feeble-minded mother and the mother of an illegitimate, feeble-minded child. The decision to sterilize her had been reached through compliance with "very careful provisions" that protected patients from possible abuse. "So far as procedure is concerned," the court concluded, "the rights of the patient are most carefully considered . . . there is no doubt" Carrie Buck "has had due process of law."

Turning from procedure to the issue of whether sterilization was ever appropriate as a eugenic public-health measure, Jutice Holmes grounded the opinion in the common good:

> We have seen more than once that the public welfare may call upon the best citizens for their lives. It would be strange if it could not call upon those who already sap the strength of the State for these lesser sacrifices . . . in order to prevent our being swamped with incompetence . . . The principle that sustains compulsory vaccination is broad enough to cover cutting the Fallopian tubes.

Closing with what reads like a frustrated comment from a member of the privileged class, Holmes wrote *Buck v. Bell*'s most famous sentence: "Three generations of imbeciles are enough." Perhaps never has such a strong condemning statement been written by such a respected jurist on the basis of such shoddy evidence. One can only speculate about whether it came in some measure from Holmes's personal and ardent support of the Eugenics Movement.[51]

The final paragraph of the *Buck* decision addressed the issue of equal protection stemming from the fact that the statute did not apply to the feeble-minded "multitudes outside." Holmes brushed this off as the "usual last resort of constitutional arguments." The law is never perfect, he noted. It "does all that is needed when it does all that it can." Case closed. Carrie Buck was sterilized five-and-a-half months later, on October 19, 1927.

The Floodgates Open

If ever there was a case that opened the floodgates, it was *Buck v. Bell*. Holmes's decision laid to rest issues of due process, equal protection, and the legitimacy of mandated sterilization. In support of the decision, prominent theologians and legal scholars would continue to assert, well into the 1950s, that the collective good could not be achieved "if the community may not defend itself, and is forced to permit the continued procreation of feeble-minded or hereditarily diseased children. Sterilization in such cases is not solely a matter of (personal control), but also of (state control.)"[52]

State legislatures across the country would likewise take notice. According to data collected by the HBF, by January 1933, 28 states had mandatory sterilization statutes. Starting the count in 1919, a total of just over 16,000 persons were non-voluntarily sterilized—roughly 7,000 males and 9,000 females. In some states, e.g., California, the ratio of males to females was roughly 1:1. In states such as Kansas, males were at higher risk at a ratio of 1.5. In other states, the ratio was heavily weighted toward females. For example, in Minnesota, approximately 10 females were sterilized for every male. By 1933, there had been a shift in these ratios toward more female sterilization when a new, simpler, and somewhat safer procedure, eventually known as the Pomery method of tubal ligation, was introduced to a wider audience in 1929.[53]

The states with the highest numbers of mandatory sterilizations were spread from coast to coast, with California leading the way at 8,500, Virginia 1,300, Kansas and Michigan 1,000, Oregon 900, and Minnesota 700. There was a dramatic rise in mandated sterilizations in 1929, and another, even higher, peak, roughly 5,000 nationwide, in 1932, the year prior to the passage of the initial German sterilization law. Subsequent yearly totals leveled off at roughly 3,000. This only slightly bumpy plateau held well into the 1940s.[54]

The isolated nature of institutions, a culture of professional independence among physicians, coupled with spotty record keeping across states and jurisdictions, mean that precise totals and comparisons are suspect. All accounts, however, corroborate a dramatic increase in the number of nonconsensual sterilizations following *Buck v. Bell*. Indeed, the totals reported are likely lower limit estimates.

Public-Health Measures Go Terribly Wrong

Justice Holmes wrote in *Buck* it would be strange if the State "could not call upon those who already sap the strength of the State for these lesser sacrifices . . . in order to prevent our being swamped with incompetence." In his opinion, as well as that of seven of his Supreme Court colleagues, the principle of supporting public health through mandatory sterilization was secure. In related, personal correspondence this same esteemed Justice, son of the privileged, had also expressed his support for "putting to death the inadequate" and "infants that didn't pass the examination."[55] This was the kind of extended exclusionary logic that so troubled Governor Pennypacker and Judge Garrison. These principles of law were broad enough to justify far more extensive state intervention into the lives of individuals. Persons could be used, without their consent, for the good of the whole.

In the wake of *Buck*, mandated sterilizations in the U.S. increased. On this there is no doubt. In subsequent years, the evidence is now clear, there were also a series of medical experiments carried out using those on the margins of life to support the common good. Nothing, however, compared with what was about to happen in Germany. Beginning with a broad-based mandatory sterilization law in mid 1933, patterned directly after Harry Laughlin's 1922 Model Statute, the journey toward the Final Solution began. It would take an independent path, but it drew heavily from the American experience. In July, 1933, six months after Adolf Hitler became Chancellor, *Gesetz zur Verhütung Erbkranken Nachwuchses* (Law for the Prevention of Genetically Diseased Offspring) was enacted.

This statute, clearly an amalgam of Laughlin's 1922 template and more broadly drawn German objectives, became effective on January 1, 1934. Following passage of the law, the next edition of *Eugenics News*, where Harry Laughlin was a member of the editorial board, published a favorable review of the German statute, beginning with the sentence, "Germany is the first of the world's major nations to enact a modern eugenical sterilization law for the nation as a whole." The parallels were noted with pride, "To one versed in the history of eugenical sterilization in America, the text of the statute reads almost like the 'American model sterilization law'."[56] In addition to Laughlin's model statute, Germany's newly formed government would also take note of Gosney and Popenoe's book, *Sterilization for Human Betterment*, and related work of the HBF.

Traveling through Germany in 1934, an HBF board member reported to Gosney that their work was playing

> a powerful part in shaping the opinions of a group of intellectuals who are behind Hitler in this epoch-making program. Everywhere I sensed that their opinions have been tremendously stimulated by American thought, and particularly by the work of the Human Betterment Foundation.[57]

A third element of American law and policy the Germans noted when passing the 1933 sterilization statute were the numerous statutes then on the books in the United States, statutes precipitated and legitimized by the U.S. Supreme Court's vindication of mandatory sterilization in *Buck v. Bell*.

The American roots of Germany's aggressive moves to limit "useless eaters" were further deepened through the financial support of the Rockefeller Foundation to the Kaiser Wilhelm Institute for Anthropology, Human Heredity, and Eugenics (founded in 1927) and the Kaiser Wilhelm Institute for Psychiatry. Located near the center of political power in Berlin and Munich and run by such academic and medical luminaries as Eugen Fischer, Fritz Lenz, Ernst Rüdin, and Otmar von Verschuer, these facilities became the leading force for eugenics in Germany. They would also eventually become closely tied to the sterilization of the so-called Rhineland Bastards, the infamous Aktion T-4 program, and medical experiments conducted in Auschwitz.[58]

The link between science and politics was crystal clear. A prominent German scientist and professor of medicine, Eugen Fischer, reporting on the activities of the Kaiser Wilhelm Institute he was directing in Berlin, noted optimistically in 1941:

> The coming victorious end of the war and the monumental extension of the "Greater German Empire" also present our research agencies with new tasks . . . In times like these [we have] to serve the immediate interests of the people, the war, and politics; but second, [we] must orient [ourselves] to the future as well as the present, for one can never know what practical effects pure

scientific research might have in the future ... No one could imagine that Gregor Mendel's studies of peas would provide the basis for a hereditary health legislation ... or that my study of bastards of 1908 could support race legislation.[59]

There is now a well-documented story that state-imposed atrocities, grounded in the idea that society's defective outcasts, those seen as a burden to society, those referred to as "useless eaters," could be sterilized or experimented upon, even to the point of disfigurement and death, for the good of the whole, began with the passage of Germany's encompassing sterilization law, explicitly patterned after Harry Laughlin's template. The underlying logic progressed step by step down a long and terrible road. These steps encountered political opposition along the way. They required political campaigns to generate support. They would take almost a decade to reach their final, tragic climax.[60]

Ironically, each step included commitment to the idea that life should be protected. Each step depended on exclusionary logic defining some lives as more worthy of protection, encouragement, and support than others. In order to protect *LIFE*, some lives could be sacrificed. If respect for the dignity and autonomy of those less worthy had to be suspended, so be it.

This was the logic of the Eugenics Movement, eventually taken to the extreme, that so worried Governor Pennypacker, Judge Garrison, and those who agreed with them. The debate and concerns would continue in the decades ahead. The revised understanding of the protective boundaries of life would be further informed by what came to be known as the biological revolution. The biological revolution and an awakened concern for more inclusive civil and human rights, taken together, would reshape a moral and legal framework.

Notes

1   Eugenics Record Office, *Bulletin No. 10A, Report to the Committee to Study and to Report on the Best Practical Means of Cutting Off the Defective Germ Plasm in the American Population: The Scope of the Committee's Work* (n.p., 1914); Eugenics Record Office, *Bulletin No. 10B, Report to the Committee to Study and to Report on the Best Practical Means of Cutting Off the Defective Germ Plasm in the American Population: The Legal, Legislative and Administrative Aspects of Sterilization* (n.p., 1914).
2   *Buck v. Bell* 274 U.S. 200 (1927).

3 Many of the ideas in Laughlin's report had been presented and discussed at the First National Conference on Race Betterment, held the month prior to the release of the 1914 report in Battle Creek, Michigan.

4 Eugenics Record Office, *Bulletin No. 10B, Report to the Committee to Study and to Report on the Best Practical Means of Cutting Off the Defective Germ Plasm in the American Population: The Legal, Legislative and Administrative Aspects of Sterilization* (1914), 9.

5 Letter from Alexander Graham Bell to Charles B. Davenport. Quoted in Black, *War Against the Weak*, 90.

6 Eugenics Record Office, *Bulletin No. 9, State Laws Limiting Marriage Selection: Examined in the Light of Eugenics* (n.p., 1913).

7 Eugenics Record Office, *Bulletin No. 10A*, 55.

8 Eugenics Record Office, *Bulletin No. 10B*, 76.

9 Eugenics Record Office, *Bulletin No. 10B*, 12.

10 Eugenics Record Office, *Bulletin No. 10B*, 12.

11 Tom L. Beuchamp and James F. Childress, *Principles of Biomedical Ethics*, 5th ed. (New York: Oxford University Press, 2001).

12 Cited in Kevles, *In the Name of Eugenics*, 109.

13 Albert J. Ochsner, "Surgical Treatment of Habitual Criminals," *Journal of the American Medical Association* 53 (1899): 867–8.

14 Harry C. Sharp, "The Severing of the Vasa Differentia and its Relation to the Neuropsychiatric Constitution," *New York Medical Journal* 46 (1902): 411–14. Harry C. Sharp, "Vasectomy as a Means of Preventing Procreation of Defectives," *Journal of American Medical Association* 51 (1907): 1897–1902.

15 Erving Goffman, *Asylums: Essays on the Social Situation of Mental Patients and Other Inmates* (Garden City, NY: Anchor Books, 1961).

16 Alexandra Minna Stern, "'We Cannot Make a Silk Purse Out of a Sow's Ear': Eugenics in the Hoosier Heartland," *Indiana Magazine of History* 103 (1) (March, 2007). Available online at: www.historycooperative.org/cgi-bin/justtop.cgi?act=just top&url=.

17 Stern, "'We Cannot Make a Silk Purse Out of a Sow's Ear'", par. 12.

18 In the Senate, the vote was 21 to 1. In the House, it was 41 to 0.

19 Legislation repealing the law was precipitated by a class action suit, *Madrigal v. Quilligan*, involving coerced postpartum tubal ligations of predominantly working-class women of Mexican origin. See Stern, *Eugenic Nation*, 200.

20 E.S. Gosney and Paul Popenoe, *Sterilization for Human Betterment* (New York: The Macmillan Company, 1929).

21 Stern, *Eugenic Nation*.

22 The following quotes are all taken from the Laughlin Committee report.

23 See, for example, Stewart E. Tolnay and E.M. Beck, *A Festival of Violence: An Analysis of Southern Lynchings, 1882–1930* (Urbana, IL and Chicago: University of Illinois Press, 1995).

24 David Chalmers, *Hooded Americanism*, 3rd ed. (Durham, NC: Duke University Press, 1987).

25 Madison Grant, *The Passing of the Great Race* (New York: Charles Scribner's Sons, 1916), xxiv.

26   Grant, *The Passing of the Great Race*, 12.
27   Grant, *The Passing of the Great Race*, 263.
28   Grant, *The Passing of the Great Race*, 87–8.
29   Some suspected Dixon, a friend and former classmate of Wilson's, might have been the source of positive comments attributed to the president.
30   Martin S. Pernick, *The Black Stork: Eugenics and the Death of "Defective" Babies in American Medicine and Motion Pictures Since 1915* (New York: Oxford University Press, 1996), 41. See also, chap. 8.
31   Helen Keller, "Physicians' Juries for Defective Babies," *The New Republic* 18 December (1915): 173–4. For a discussion of apparent contradictions in Helen Keller's public pronouncements, see John Gerdtz, "Disability and Euthanasia: The Case of Helen Keller and the Bollinger Baby" (paper presented at the sixteenth University Faculty for Life Conference, 2006).
32   The film was also titled, *Are You Fit to Marry?*
33   The 1927 version of the film is housed at the Kennedy Institute of Ethics.
34   Foster Kennedy, "The Problem of Social Control of the Congenitally Defective: Education, Sterilization, Euthanasia," *American Journal of Psychiatry* 99 (1942): 13–16.
35   Philip R. Reilly, "Involuntary Sterilization in the United States: A Surgical Solution," *The Quarterly Review of Biology* 62 (1987): 153–70.
36   *Smith v. Board of Examiners of Feeble-Minded*. 88 A. 963, decided Nov. 18, 1913. Among other reasons, this case is interesting as, later in his life, Harry Laughlin would find that he, too, was epileptic. Many critical commentators would note the irony of Laughlin's diagnosis in later years.
37   *Haynes v. Lapeer* Cir. Judge, 201 Mich. 138, 144–5, 166 N.W.938, 940–1 (1918); *Osborne v. Thomson*, 103, Misc. 23, 33–6, 169 N.Y.S. 638, 643–5, aff'd; 185 App. Div. 902, 171 N.Y.S. 1094 (1918).
38   Harry Laughlin, *Eugenical Sterilization in the United States* (Chicago: Psychopathic Laboratory of the Municipal Court of Chicago, 1922).
39   Charles Davenport, Laughlin's boss, was much less adamant about sterilization and more in favor of simple, institutional segregation. He also felt that Laughlin's obsessive attention to sterilization was having negative political consequences.
40   *Loving v. Virginia*, 388 U.S. 1 (1967).
41   *Roe v. Wade*, 410 U.S. 113 (1973). *Doe v. Bolton*, 410 U.S. 179 (1973).
42   Paul A. Lombardo, "Three Generations, No Imbeciles: New Light on *Buck v. Bell*," *New York University Law Review* 60 (1985): 30–62. *Buck v. Bell* 274 U.S. 200 (1927). The following summary is based on Lombardo's account.
43   For a documentary detailing sterilization in the Lynchburg Colony see: *The Lynchburg Story: Eugenic Sterilization in America*, Stephen Trombley, Director; Bruce Eadie, Producer. Worldview Pictures Production (1994).
44   Lombardo, "Three Generations, No Imbeciles," 41, fn 59.
45   Lombardo, "Three Generations, No Imbeciles," 45, fn 79.
46   For example, in addition to the questions raised by anthropologists such as Franz Boaz and Margaret Mead, Nobel Laureate, Hermann Joseph Muller, known for his work establishing a link between radiation and genetic mutation, had spoken out strongly against the implications of the family-pedigree studies at the Third International Congress of Eugenics.

47   Pius XI, "On Christian Marriage," in *Five Great Encyclicals* (New York: Paulist Press, 1939), 96–7.

48   See Lombardo's review in "Three Generations, No Imbeciles," 50–5.

49   Cited by Lombardo, "Three Generations, No Imbeciles," 56.

50   *Buck v. Bell* 274 U.S. 200 (1927).

51   See Albert W. Alschuler, *Law Without Values: The Life, Work, and Legacy of Justice Holmes* (Chicago: University of Chicago Press, 2000), 27–30.

52   Joseph Fletcher, *Morals and Medicine* (Princeton, NJ: Princeton University Press, 1954), 168.

53   E. Bishop, and W.F. Nelms, "A Simple Method of Tubal Sterilization," *NY State Journal of Medicine* 30 (1930): 214–16.

54   Philip R. Reilly, "Involuntary Sterilization in the United States: A Surgical Solution," *The Quarterly Review of Biology* 62 (1987): 162.

55   Alschuler, *Law Without Values*, 27–30.

56   "Eugenical Sterilization in Germany," *Eugenical News* 18 (1933): 89–94.

57   The full paragraph from the letter reads:

> You will be interested to know that your work has played a powerful part in shaping the opinions of a group of intellectuals who are behind Hitler in this epoch-making program. Everywhere I sensed that their opinions have been tremendously stimulated by American thought, and particularly by the work of the Human Betterment Foundation. I want you, my dear friend, to carry this thought with you for the rest of your life, that you have really jolted into action a great government of 60,000,000 people.

Cited in Black, *War Against the Weak*, 277.

58   Peter Weingart, "German Eugenics Between Science and Politics," *Osiris* 2nd series, 5 (1989): 260–82.

59   Quoted in Weingart, "German Eugenics", 276.

60   Robert Jay Lifton, *The Nazi Doctors: Medical Killing and the Psychology of Genocide* (New York: Basic Books, 1986). See also, Leo Alexander's now widely cited article: "Medical Science Under Dictatorship," *The New England Journal of Medicine* 241 (2) (1949): 39–47.

CHAPTER 4

REDRAWING THE BOUNDARIES OF PROTECTED LIFE

In the mid twentieth century, theologians, philosophers, physicians, lawyers, politicians, social scientists, and activists joined debate in a world where civil and human rights were being rethought, and where judgments regarding the protective boundaries of life were lagging behind advances in science and technology. General Omar Bradley's Armistice Day speech three short years after two atomic bombs had been dropped on Japan is exemplary. Addressing his audience, Bradley warned:

> Our knowledge of science has clearly outstripped our capacity to control it ... Man is stumbling blindly through a spiritual darkness while toying with the precarious secrets of life and death. The world has achieved brilliance without wisdom, power without conscience. Ours is a world of nuclear giants and ethical infants.[1]

While General Bradley was most concerned with war in an atomic age, his point echoed across the social landscape. Moral and ethical frameworks were lagging dramatically behind scientific advances.

Similar concerns were voiced in a field soon to be known as bioethics. In pursuit of moral and ethical clarification, symposia were held, books written, academic and policy centers established, journals founded, governmental commissions convened, reports issued, regulations enacted, social movements launched, and Supreme Court decisions released.

On all fronts, the goal was a clearer understanding of the boundaries of tolerable suffering and protected life, the meaning and importance of social worth, the dignity and respect accorded to autonomous individuals, and the allocation of legitimate authority to those who would decide the fate of others.

Resolution remained elusive. Thirty years after General Bradley's remarks, a Catholic theologian, Richard McCormick, in an article appearing in a recently established periodical dedicated to exploring bioethics, noted, "Because times, circumstances, and perspectives change, sometimes dramatically, the viability of some of our most treasured value judgments depends on the accuracy of their formulation in our time."[2] Two-and-a-half decades later, in witness to the continuing uncertainties and contentious nature of the issues encountered, Leon Kass, a physician deeply concerned with the ethics of medical research would add, "The evils we face are intertwined with the goods we so keenly seek: cures for disease, relief of suffering, preservation of life. Distinguishing good and bad thus intermixed is often extremely difficult."[3]

Six full decades had passed since Nazi atrocities had been uncovered. Agreement remained elusive. What was clarity and accurate assessment for some was obfuscation and flawed, even dangerous, thinking to others.

An Awakening

There was one point, however, on which everyone agreed—Nazi doctors during World War II had engaged in barbaric behaviors. The stark nature of the suffering inflicted was jolting. As such events sometimes do, the revelations crystallized thinking and galvanized action. The proceedings of the Nuremberg Doctors' trial revealed what the pursuit of scientific knowledge, void of an inclusive understanding of, and respect for, the autonomy and dignity of the individual, can render. Something had to be done. The world's abrupt recognition that such reasoning had gone terribly wrong marked "a new beginning in the moral traditions of medicine, a beginning that would become bioethics."[4]

Doctors on trial in Nuremberg pointed to similar practices, laws, and policies in the United States and other countries. Nazi doctors believed that life was sacred and should be protected, but, like Justice Holmes, Harry Laughlin, and David Starr Jordan, they also believed some lives were more worthy of protection and support than others. Individual rights could be suspended and the dignity of individuals ignored, so that other, more worthy lives might be enhanced, prolonged, and protected, and the social fabric strengthened.

The initial public response to the revealed Nazi atrocities, as intense as it was, was muted by a distancing collective disbelief. The quite specific roots the Nazi medical experiments shared with the Eugenics Movement advanced by Stanford University's first president, spearheaded by the director of the ERO at Cold Spring Harbor, legitimized by the Supreme Court, implemented in numerous sterilization statutes, and underwritten by the Rockefeller Foundation's contributions to the Kaiser Wilhelm Institutes in Germany, and what eventually came to be known as the T-4 unit and the Nazi euthanasia program,[5] were rarely mentioned.

German doctors and the system they defined were barbaric, but they were an anomaly. The war was over. The Allies had won. It was time to punish the anomalous, barbaric offenders and move on. Less attention, one is tempted to say none, was paid to how others in the medical profession had not been, and were not now, "immune from seduction by social, political, or economic organizations that seek to corrupt medicine for their own agendas."[6] In the years immediately following World War II and for most of the following two decades, the American medical research community considered the Doctors' Trial and the Nuremberg Code largely irrelevant to its own work.[7]

The broader cause for concern, however, was not lost on everyone. Shortly after World War II, a Human Rights Commission was convened, chaired by Eleanor Roosevelt, with prominent members including a Pulitzer Prize winner and an eventual Nobel Peace Laureate. The commission's goal was to identify the common ground on which all humans walked and principles by which all should be guided. Evidence would be collected from countries and cultures around the world. The unleashing of the atomic bomb on two Japanese cities had brought an increased urgency to their efforts. As the former First Lady and now the Commission's chair noted,

> We came into a new world—a world in which we had to learn to live in friendship with our neighbors of every race and creed and color, or face the fact that we might be wiped off the face of the earth.[8]

Eleanor Roosevelt had been a long-time champion of human and civil rights. She and her Commission colleagues were motivated by the recognition that "disregard and contempt for human rights" had resulted in "barbarous acts which have outraged the conscience of mankind." Their tenacious willingness to cut through the Gordian knot of international relations in what Winston Churchill characterized as "anxious and baffling times,"[9] eventually produced the *Universal Declaration of Human Rights*. This Declaration did not emerge as whole cloth. It was woven, partially unraveled, and then rewoven through several drafts over a period of just under two years. The Commission's initial meeting was convened in Lake Success, New York, in January 1947, a half-hour drive from Cold Spring Harbor, where Harry Laughlin had headquartered his efforts to advance the exclusionary cause of eugenics.

The Declaration, drafted by eight delegates from countries on opposite sides of various political coalitions, drew unifying moral suasion from the "recognition of the inherent dignity and . . . equal and inalienable rights of all members of the human family." As specific manifestations of this grounding principle became evident, however, the Declaration's 30 articles became wide-ranging and in many ways ill-focused. Initial articles dealt with the right to life, liberty, security, and the prohibition of slavery, torture, and inhuman and degrading punishment (Articles 3, 4, and 5). Attention then turned to the more contentious freedoms of movement, thought, religion, and expression (Articles 13, 18, and 19), and finally to such society-specific matters as the right to join trade unions, the right to equal pay for equal work (Article 23), and the right to rest and leisure (Article 24).

The Declaration was an impressive document. It signaled the hopes of mankind and asserted the equal worth of all humans. The broadly cast net and attendant lack of focus, however, diluted its impact. More highly focused moral sustenance for an evolving moral framework would come from elsewhere. Some six months after the UN approved of the Universal Declaration of Human Rights, a Boston physician, also motivated by the dangers of an exclusionary mindset where some lives are deemed more worthy of living and protecting than others, but much more focused in his concerns with medical research, published a widely influential article in the *New England Journal of Medicine* (*NEJM*).[10]

Dr. Leo Alexander had been one of the architects of the Nuremberg Code. He was worried. He knew the Nazi horrors had not sprung up instantly, but had been reached in small, incremental steps. He saw early danger signs among his medical colleagues in the United States. He issued a warning:

> Whatever proportions these crimes finally assumed it became evident to all who investigated them that they had started from small beginnings. The beginnings at first were merely a subtle shift in emphasis in the basic attitude of the physicians. It started with the acceptance of the attitude, basic in the euthanasia movement, that there is such a thing as life not worthy to be lived.

In Dr. Alexander's mind, many of his colleagues had "been infected with Hegelian, cold-blooded, utilitarian philosophy . . . early traces of it can be detected in their medical thinking that may make them vulnerable to departures of the type that occurred in Germany." He wanted his readers to know that, all too frequently, if a patient could not be cured, physicians too often developed a sense of failure and the "nonrehabilitable sick" too easily became "unwanted ballast."

For Leo Alexander,

> The original concept of medicine and nursing was not based on any rational or feasible likelihood that they could actually cure and restore . . . The Good Samaritan had no thought of nor did he actually care whether he could restore working capacity. He was merely motivated by the compassion in alleviating suffering.

Curing disease and prolonging life were important, but, if success and the objectives of medicine were totally defined in these terms, there were dangers. For Dr. Alexander, high priority should also be paid to the deep-seated responsibility to attend to the quality of life and the alleviation of suffering.

As his article was read and his ideas discussed, it became clear Dr. Alexander was not alone. Particularly noteworthy were the efforts of Cicely Saunders, a London nurse turned physician. In 1948, a short time before Alexander published his *NEJM* article, Saunders had been working as an "almoner," a distributor of alms, in a large London hospital. Among those she cared for was a dying Jewish émigré from Poland. Motivated by this and similar experiences, Nurse Saunders enrolled in medical school and, as a physician, became the driving force behind what eventually became the international Hospice Movement, known for its embrace of the dying process and its dedication to honoring the alleviation of suffering.[11]

Both Saunders and Alexander were wedded to the idea that the alleviation of suffering had equal standing with prolonging life. As Saunders would frequently note, "We do not have to cure to heal." The meaning and core importance of the alleviation of suffering, sometimes at odds with curing diseases and prolonging life, would become a central point of contention as the field of bioethics matured in the decades ahead. The impetus for heightened attention were advances in science, medical technologies, and what had been labeled cultural lag.[12]

Science, Technology, and Cultural Lag

The idea of cultural lag is straightforward. Science produces new knowledge. New knowledge is fashioned into innovative technologies. New technologies, especially those associated with the protection of life and the alleviation of suffering, call for moral and ethical refinements. The disjuncture between science, technology, and existing assessments of suffering and the protective boundaries of life is an important impetus for reshaping moral, legal, and ethical frameworks.

So it was in mid-twentieth-century United States. Restrictive abortion and contraception statutes had been largely drafted in the late 1800s when pregnancy, in the absence of antibiotics and refined medical procedures, routinely produced a serious threat to the health and life of the mother, and when equally threatening abortion procedures provided an important fallback remedy for controlling parenthood and family size. Restrictive abortion laws were crafted with these health risks in mind, but they put physicians who provided abortion services, as well as mothers seeking to limit their family size, at risk of becoming felons. By mid twentieth century, things had changed. Thanks to antibiotics and improved medical procedures, abortion and carrying a child to term were far safer. The state had less compelling reasons to regulate a physician's judgment and a woman's choice, especially in the early stages of pregnancy.

Confronted with these advances and deeply important yet competing values, and relying on vaguely specified legal standards, legislative bodies across the country in the 1960s produced the first widespread shift in abortion laws since the late 1800s. These legislative reforms were shaped by a legal template emerging from a long moribund project, brought to life following World War II and guided by another prominent figure in the Nuremberg Trials, a person deeply concerned with the dignity and autonomy of the individual and appropriate limitations on state power.

Herbert Wechsler, a widely respected professor at Columbia Law School, was an assistant attorney general when he helped craft the strategy for the trials at Nuremberg. Shortly thereafter, in 1951, he assumed the reins of the American Law Institute's (ALI) project to produce a Model Penal Code (MPC). This effort was designed to bring coherence and fairness to the rules and regulations governing the coercive power of the state. There was a sense that the criminal law was vague in construction, not well adapted to current knowledge, and sometimes too sweeping in its intervention.

The ALI's reform initiative had begun decades before, but had languished. The experiences of the war just finished and the subsequent Nuremberg trials provided the crystallizing event needed for renewed effort. Writing in the *Harvard Law Review* shortly after taking the reins of the Model Penal Code project, Wechsler outlined the initiative's importance.

> Whatever views one holds about the penal law, no one will question its importance in society. This is the law on which men place their ultimate reliance for protection against all the deepest injuries that human conduct can inflict . . . By the same token, penal law governs the strongest force that we permit official agencies to bring to bear on individuals. Its promise as an instrument of safety is matched only by its power to destroy . . . Nowhere in the entire legal field is more at stake for the community or for the individual.[13]

Of most immediate relevance for the soon-to-be-born bioethics movement was section 230.3 of the Model Penal Code, "Abortion." An initial draft was released for comment in 1959. The final version was presented in 1962.

The model abortion statute proposed by Wechsler's ALI project addressed the gap between medical advances and existing legal practices. Broader exceptions to strict abortion prohibition, based on recent assessments of the health risk to the mother, were recommended. These recommendations would be incorporated into many state statutes several years before the Supreme Court reached its landmark decisions outlining a trimester framework for the shifting boundaries protecting life, privacy, and individual autonomy.

Abortion was not the only issue. Wechsler's ALI project and suggested revisions to abortion statutes were embedded in a much broader sense of a scientific revolution. The existing moral and legal frameworks were simply not up to the task. It was a well-recognized and increasingly discussed problem. Aldous Huxley, in a reflective forward to his *Brave New World*, first published in 1932, reminded his readers, "The theme of the *Brave New World* is not the advancement of science as such; it is the advancement of science as it affects human individuals."[14] *In vitro* fertilization and techniques to prolong the lives of young infants exemplified such scientific advancements. Many felt artificially conceived infants might be grossly abnormal and should be prohibited. Newborn infants suffering from formerly lethal conditions could now be kept alive. But was this the best thing to do? As with abortion, the questions became: Who should decide and on what basis?

James Watson, co-discoverer in 1953 of the double-helix structure of DNA, commented just months after the landmark *Roe v. Wade* decision, "We have to reevaluate our basic assumptions about the meaning of life." The severity of most birth defects was not discovered until after birth. Watson, citing his colleague Francis Crick, provocatively suggested,

> If a child were not declared alive until three days after birth, then all parents could be allowed the choice that only a few are given under the present system. The doctor could allow the child to die if the parents so chose and save a lot of misery and suffering.[15]

Intentionally provocative or not, and as outlandish as Watson's suggestion seemed to many, the delayed declaration of protected life had been

proposed prior to Watson's statement and would receive serious consideration in the years ahead.[16]

Similarly, a pioneering practitioner in the use of artificial organs to
sustain life, Dr. Belding Scribner, noted in his 1964 presidential address
to the American Society for Artificial Internal Organs,[17] "It is becoming
increasingly clear that the moral and ethical guidelines handed down to
us through the centuries are becoming more and more inadequate to
govern our lives." Scribner urged his medical colleagues to join lawyers,
theologians, and philosophers to "explore the possibility of some sort of
joint effort in finding solutions to these vexing and urgent problems."

William Ogburn, Aldous Huxley, James Watson, and Belding Scribner
were joined by many others in their concern for the technology-driven
need to reexamine the protective boundaries of life and related moral and
ethical guidelines. Currently used moral touchstones needed rethinking.
Legal scholars of all political persuasions agree, the U.S. Constitution
does not mention contraception, abortion, or privacy. Likewise, no sacred
text, be it the Qur'an, the Torah, the Bible, Buddhist Precepts, or Vedic
Texts, has anything to say about cloning, *in vitro* fertilization, or genetic
defects. Similarly, little direct guidance can be found from Socrates,
Hippocrates, or Emmanuel Kant when it comes to brain-activity definitions of death, the harvesting and allocation of organs for transplantation,
the use of kidney dialysis machines, or the moral implications of a
persistent vegetative state.

And yet, there was a plethora of moral questions to resolve. Do genetic
defects, debilitating accidents, or disease-driven suffering yield lives
less worthy of living and protecting? Is fetal research similar to experimentation on human beings without their consent? When does human
life become more like a vegetable? Scarce resources must be rationed.
Should "social worth" play a role when deciding who should receive organ
transplants and other life-prolonging resources? Can we, should we, define
death so as to maximize the chances that harvested organs will be successfully transplanted? Through analogies, metaphors, logic, and empathy-
generating stories and events, our sense of the protective boundaries of
life evolves. Given the uncertainty of outcomes and shadowed legal and
moral principles, disagreements emerge. Given the profound importance
of the moral imperatives involved, these disagreements frequently become
intense and, on occasion, even deadly.

A Crystallizing Event and Rationing Health Care

As is often the case, large questions frequently emerge from small beginnings. This became evident when a doctor, Belding Scribner, working with engineering colleagues at the University of Washington in Seattle, developed a u-shaped arteriovenous cannula shunt, lined with the recently developed material Teflon. This small device, first used in 1960, provided dramatically improved chances of surviving end-stage kidney disease. Patients confronting a 100 percent chance of near-term death might now have access to multi-year survival.

In the beginning, the machines and procedures were limited, cumbersome, and expensive. Who should have access? Were some lives more worthy of saving than others? Who should decide? Answers to the ethical dilemmas and boundaries of relative worth provided new impetus for rethinking how we rationed health care and thereby played an important role in the transformation of the health care system.[18] After three patients had been successfully treated using the improved dialysis machine, the University of Washington Hospital administration informed Dr. Scribner that no new patients were to be accepted. The procedure was too expensive, and the facilities too limited. What to do?

In short order, the Seattle Artificial Kidney Center, connected with nearby Swedish Hospital, was established. The Center would open for business in January 1962. It would have three beds, associated dialysis equipment, and supporting medical personnel. Given the dramatic success of the new technology, demand for these new facilities immediately far exceeded supply.[19] Using the three beds, each patient would have to be hooked up for at least 10 hours, twice weekly. In the beginning, it was decided that five patients could be served. Plans were put in place to expand this to 10. Decisions would have to be made. Who should have access? Who should decide?

Two committees were set up. One, the Medical Advisory Committee, made up of physicians and a psychiatrist, would determine the initial pool of eligible patients. Screening would be based on emotional stability and medical prognosis. A second committee, the Admissions Advisory Committee, was to determine who from this initial pool would be chosen. This seven-member committee included a lawyer, housewife, official of state government, banker, minister, labor leader, and surgeon. The membership was specifically designed to provide a non-medical assessment of the potential patients.

Random selection and first-come-first-served strategies were considered and rejected. Decisions would be made on the basis of relative social worth. The role of the admissions committee,

> was to assess the relative worth of a candidate to their family and the community in terms of the degree of dependence of others upon the candidate's continuing existence, and the rehabilitative potential and moral value or worth of the candidate.[20]

As impressive as the technological advances in dialysis were, it would be the necessity to ration health care guided by these vaguely specified criteria of relative worth that would capture the public's attention.

Shortly after the new dialysis center opened and the advisory committees convened, *Life* magazine, widely read for its pictorial spreads and accompanying journalistic accounts, sent a young west-coast staff writer, Shana Alexander, to Seattle to develop a story. The story turned out to be the longest piece ever published by *Life*.[21] Its author would later characterize it as the most "awesome and disturbing story" she had ever worked on.[22] Thirty years later, a conference would be held in Seattle, bringing together 42 of the 60 individuals identified as bioethics pioneers, to commemorate Alexander's article as a crystallizing event in the launching of the bioethics movement.[23]

Social Worth and Rationed Health Care

Alexander's story presented an early glimpse of how the uncertain assessment of social worth would dominate bioethics and the rationing of health care in the years ahead. In one sense it was déjà vu. It was the same question raised by the Eugenics Movement. Instead of regulating the ability to have children and thereby protect the health of the broader community, social worth would be used to allocate life-prolonging resources. Increasingly effective immunosuppressant drugs and successful organ transplants were being developed, as were methods to maintain the lives of infants and adults who would have certainly died in the recent past. The questions were not likely to go away any time soon.

When allocating access to the dialysis machine, the uncertain potential for medical complications led to a decision to eliminate persons over 45 years of age. The uncertain potential that children might be traumatized by dialysis procedures and dietary restrictions limiting normal growth meant pre-teenagers were also eliminated. Finally, candidates were limited to residents of the state of Washington, as they had to start somewhere, and most of the money for the dialysis program had come from state taxpayers. To choose from among this pool of Washington residents, not too young and not too old, a list of possible considerations was drawn up. It included age, sex, marital status, number of dependents, income, net worth, educational background, nature of occupation, past performance and future potential, emotional stability, and such things as whether special considerations should be given to the social worth of parents with children at home.

Beyond these rough and ready rationing guidelines, there was little clarity. After briefing the admissions committee, a doctor recalled, "We told them frankly that there were *no* guidelines, they were on their own. We really dumped it on them." Committee members wanted to maximize their objectivity and therefore blocked knowledge of the attending physician and the name of the patient from their deliberations. If personal knowledge entered in, they would excuse themselves from the decision. Piece by piece, a template for assessing differential social worth began to take shape. It was a work in progress.

Ambiguities in judgments of relative worth, as well as refinements in the committee's thinking, became evident as their deliberations proceeded. Details were reconstructed in Alexander's article:

> *Minister*: How can we compare a family situation of two children, such as this woman in Walla Walla, with a family of six children, such as patient Number Four—the aircraft worker?
>
> *State official*: But are we sure the aircraft worker can be rehabilitated? I note he is already too ill to work, whereas Number Two and Number Five, the chemist and the accountant, are both still able to keep going.
>
> *Labor leader*: I know from experience that the aircraft company where this man works will do everything possible to rehabilitate a handicapped employee . . .

Housewife: If we are still looking for the men with the highest potential for service to society, then I think we must consider that the chemist and the accountant have the finest educational backgrounds of all five candidates.

Surgeon: How do the rest of you feel about Number Three—the small businessman with three children? I am impressed that his doctor took special pains to mention that this man is active in church work. This is an indication to me of character and moral strength.

Housewife: Which certainly would help him conform to the demands of the treatment . . .

Lawyer: It would also help him to endure a lingering death . . .

Uncertainty was unavoidable. Social worth was a matter of personal preference. As the lawyer on the committee noted in an interview with Alexander,

I believe that a man's contribution to society should determine our ultimate decision. But I'm not so doggone sure that a great painting or a symphony would loom larger in my own mind than the needs of a woman with six children.

Committee members were also aware that implications of their criteria would soon expand. Successful organ transplants were just around the corner. As the surgeon on the admissions committee noted,

Medically speaking, I am not a disciple of this particular approach to kidney disease. But in the larger view, this project will not just benefit one disease—it will benefit all aspects of medicine. We are hoping someday to learn how to transplant live organs. So far, the body will not accept foreign tissue from another person, but eventually we will find a way to break this tissue barrier.[24]

The surgeon had reason to be optimistic. In the mid to late 1950s and early 1960s, work on kidney transplants was proceeding. In 1963, one year after the surgeon's interview, a spate of articles appeared in medical journals signaling promising success in the use of immunosuppressant drugs and related kidney transplant therapies.[25] Other successful organ transplants, including pancreas, liver, and heart, would take place over the next four years. As these rapid-fire revolutionary developments were taking place, and as additional dialysis centers were opened, the need for a refined moral and ethical framework with accompanying decision-making structures became ever more evident.[26]

In a subsequent study of patient access to early organ transplants and kidney dialysis, Renée Fox and Judith Swazey uncovered some early general patterns.[27] Specific cases illustrated these general findings. A young, ne'er-do-well man, repentant of his ways once he found out about his renal failure, stood less of a chance than a 30-year-old father with seven dependants who would become wards of the state were he to die. A "responsible" wife and mother was chosen over a young woman known to be a prostitute. As reasonable as these decisions might seem, and as preferable as they might be to a strictly random, first-come-first-served rationing process, there were objections to the underlying, ambiguous assumptions of what constituted social worth.

By 1965, an estimated 800 persons were on hemodialysis in some 121 centers spread across the country. Even with this impressive expansion, the demand continued to far outdistance available resources. Estimates put the number of persons in need of hemodialysis between 60,000 and 90,000, with an increased number of between 5,000 and 10,000 each year.[28] Patient selection and the rationing of access could not be avoided. For many, deciding whose life to protect and whom to let die on the basis of the social-worth criteria was disturbing and offensive.

A sharp articulation of these objections came from a physician, Director of Community Services at Cedars–Sinai Medical Center, and his colleague, a professor of law at UCLA.[29] Their critique appeared following the rapid increase in the number of dialysis centers. At about the same time, two successful heart transplants had taken place, first in Cape Town, South Africa, and then in Houston, Texas. Given the rapidly expanding utility of hemodialysis, the promising, though still limited, organ-transplant procedures, and the daunting costs and very clear restrictions on patient access, this early critique of the newly developed selection procedures reflected a sense of urgency. In their introduction, the physician and law professor wrote,

> The spectacular recent advances of medical science have created
> unprecedented legal and ethical problems . . . Medical science is

creating and allocating resources of the greatest value; use of the
resource means life, denial means death ... If society, with its
chief instrument, law, does not tame technology, technology may
destroy our sense of ethics—and man himself.

Pandora's box had been opened. With the expansion of hemodialysis
and organ-transplant programs, the debate widened. If not social worth,
then what? How should the boundaries protecting one life above another
be drawn? If all lives are of equal value, why not set up a random selection
procedure? Why not operate on a first-come-first-served basis? As
procedures are expensive, why burden the rest of society with the high
cost of treatment, when this money could be used for other and perhaps
better purposes? Why not let market forces determine access and simply
save those who can pay? While each of these options presented problems,
the authors of the *UCLA Law Review* piece concluded, "Any of these
methods is preferable to selection by ad hoc comparative judgments of
social worth." Many others disagreed with this conclusion. These
disagreements would endure.

Stories Are Told, Doctrines Explored

As physicians, philosophers, lawyers, and theologians struggled to clarify
rationing standards for dialysis and organ transplants, they took notice
of a *Harvard Law Review* article, written some 15 years earlier by
Lon Fuller,[30] an influential legal philosopher known for exploring the
connection between law and morality, between aspirations and duties.
He had recently presented and published a series of related lectures at
Yale Law School.[31] Although his influence on the field of bioethics was
felt early, his more lasting influence would eventually flow through the
works of one of his students, Ronald Dworkin.[32]

In his 1949 article, Fuller told a story to make his point. It involved
trapped spelunkers, who, after rolling dice, chose a companion to kill and
eat in order to survive. The surviving spelunkers were tried, convicted of
murder, and sentenced to hang. They appealed their case. Through the
opinions of the appellate judges, Fuller explored various moral and legal
issues related to the protection and termination of life under such dire
circumstances. In the end, the conviction was affirmed, and the defendants
were hanged.

This contrived account, while dramatic and based in general outline on actual and well-known cases, was of limited use as metaphor for choosing hemodialysis and organ-transplant patients. In Fuller's story, persons directly in need were making the decision to kill one of their companions so they might live. The spelunkers' plight was further removed from immediate dialysis and organ-transplant concerns in that the major issues were the legitimacy of the conviction and sentence of death, not the legitimacy of the criteria for the spelunkers' decision-making.

The writings of another lawyer–philosopher, Edmond Cahn, also drew attention. The same year as Fuller's spelunker article appeared, Cahn had published *The Sense of Injustice*, in which he explored equity and just deserts as they impacted perceptions of injustice and the legitimacy of actions taken. While clearly relevant to the choice of patients for dialysis and organ transplants, Cahn's ideas were developed in a time when such choices were rarely contemplated, let alone immediately present as unavoidable necessities. How did they apply to rationing health care? Not clear, was the answer. Some additional clarity was found in Cahn's second book, published seven years before the Seattle hemodialysis clinic was established. In one section, "The value of being alive," the actual cases underpinning Fuller's contrived spelunkers were explored. One case involved an overloaded longboat cast adrift in freezing seas when the mother ship struck an iceberg. Decisions of who should be cast overboard to save the rest were made by the first mate.

Cahn recounted the tragic events,

> The sailors rowed and the passengers bailed, but the over-weighted long-boat, drifting between blocks of floating ice, sank lower and lower as a steady rain fell on the sea. The wind began to freshen, the sea grew heavy, and waves splashed over the bow. Then, after the first mate had twice given the order, Holmes (a seaman) and the rest of the crew began to throw the male passengers overboard. Two married men and a little boy were spared, but the fourteen remaining male passengers were cast over, and two women— devoted sisters of one of the victims—voluntarily leaped to join their brother in his death. The long-boat stayed afloat. The next morning Holmes spied a sail in the distance, exerted himself heroically to attract notice of the passing vessel, and eventually brought the rescue of everyone left in the boat.[33]

When the survivors returned to Philadelphia, there was talk of prosecution. All but Holmes disappeared. Holmes was put on trial, convicted, and sentenced to six months of hard labor, in addition to the nine months he had spent in jail awaiting trial.

What lessons could be learned from these experiences? For Cahn, "Every human life has some value." But, under some circumstances, some may be more worthy than others. How to decide? "The courts give us very little additional information by which to ascertain the elements of that value," Cahn concluded. In some cases "life prospects" might be considered, but how are these to be assessed? Here, the legal system provided some additional guidance, but revealed more about what should not be considered than what should. "Lawyers and judges may here join hands with moralists and philosophers and declare that the degree of happiness to be attained by a human being does not depend on wealth or status."

Given the continuing elusiveness of the criteria for determining differential social worth, and viewing all life as valuable, Cahn turned to the virtue of volunteers. Let the virtue of those most immediately involved determine the outcome. In the longboat, virtue was rare, and volunteers were few. Selfish interests dominated. Most male passengers did not volunteer to lighten the boat. Instead, "before being thrust into the sea, they had tried by offers of bribes and by main force to stay aboard." Lacking virtuous volunteers and acceptable criteria for assessing social worth, relying on the invisible hand of destiny became ever more attractive.

Killing some so that others might live was not acceptable to Cahn. This was far less defendable than proceeding so that all would live or die according to destiny. "While life remains there may be ground for hope and no one can be quite certain that a rescuing sail will not come into sight."[34] In the end, absent volunteers and clear criteria for choosing, Cahn was personally drawn to this option, "If none sacrifice themselves of free will to spare the others—they must all wait and die together."

Life is sacred and should be protected. The problem is, in the lifeboat circumstances, protecting some meant killing others. For Cahn, intentionally killing, even in these extreme circumstances, was not acceptable. This might be a reasonable conclusion for lifeboat ethics or, as Cahn put it, for "morals of the last days," but those looking for guidelines when allocating hemodialysis and organ transplants among patients found little guidance.

With transplants and dialysis, the choice, no matter if by casting lots or social worth, was not who should be killed first, but who should first be rescued. Doing good, knowing harm would result, was a pervasive, long-contemplated problem. For many, intention, not outcome, was the prime consideration. Choosing to save a life, knowing but not intending that others would die, did not have the same moral standing as intentionally taking a life so that others might live. Likewise, the moral equivalence of removing a respirator or administering a pain-relieving drug to alleviate suffering, knowing it would bring about the end of life, was viewed with mixed reactions.[35]

Theologians had struggled with these issues for centuries. Intending and pursuing good, knowing that bad might also result, had even acquired the status of a doctrine—the Doctrine of Double Effect. Thanks to the revival of *virtue ethics*[36] and in particular the works of two Oxford University colleagues, G.E.M. (Elizabeth) Anscombe, "more rigorously Catholic than the Pope," and Philippa Foot, a "card-carrying atheist,"[37] the importance of intention and the Doctrine of Double Effect began to receive increased interest.

Anscombe and Foot were both schooled in analytic philosophy and heavily influenced by Austrian-born philosopher, Ludwig Wittgenstein. Their writings, along with those of their analytic-philosopher colleagues, were aimed more to engage fellow academics than the general public. Their prose could be both obscure and terse. Once, in a two-sentence reply to a 20-page, densely written article exploring the double-effect doctrine as applied to the permissibility of abortion when the mother's health was at stake, Anscombe wrote with conciseness befitting her Austrian mentor:

> The nerve of Mr. Bennett's argument is that if A results from your not doing B, then A results from whatever you do instead of doing B. While there may be much to be said of this view, still it does not seem right on the face of it.[38]

On other occasions, exchanges were more broadly developed, enlightening, and accessible. In an article published just after Anscombe's abbreviated reply, Philippa Foot introduced, again in the context of abortion, what came to be known as the Trolley Problem.[39] The Trolley

Problem eventually took numerous forms. Whatever the specifics, it always presented a forced choice. Bad could always result from a choice for the good. Was there a difference between acting and not acting, between commission and omission? The Trolley Problem and related metaphors, illustrating the double effect of intended and unintended consequences, would arise repeatedly in the years ahead.[40] While the field of bioethics had yet to be launched, by the late 1960s broad guidelines, some obscure, some more evident, were beginning to take shape.

The Decade of Conferences

The beauty and utility of general concepts such as "social worth," "intention," and "double effect" are that they shed common light on otherwise diverse situations such as eugenics, abortion, neonatal care, patient choice, and both active and passive euthanasia. When applied to particular situations, however, fog always remains.

So it was throughout the 1960s, the "decade of conferences,"[41] as doctors, philosophers, theologians, social scientists, lawyers, and political activists wrote papers, published books, convened symposia, identified criteria, crafted principles, and drafted laws to frame the meaning of what came to be known as bioethics: a framework that would provide useful guideposts for finding our way through "the rapid and awesome advances of contemporary science in controlling the physical and mental processes of human life."[42]

Some of these conferences, such as the Dartmouth Convocation on Great Issues of Conscience in Modern Medicine held in 1960,[43] and the *Sanctity of Life* symposium, held at Reed College in March of 1966, were broad in scope. Sweeping questions were asked:

> Could one identify the forces in society that determine how valuable one man holds the life of another? Do adequate guide-lines exist in law, theology, or in the liberal arts? Are the biomedical sciences, dedicated to preserving health and prolonging life, taking undue liberties in the guise of improving man's condition?[44]

Within these broad questions, conference participants tackled topics ranging from eugenics and the creation of sperm banks to global issues of environmental degradation, nuclear war, and how the elimination of certain diseases might impact population growth among the world's most impoverished people.

Other symposia were more narrowly organized around particular issues. Proceedings from one such conference, drawing participants from eight countries, were published in 1966 as *Ethics in Medical Progress: With Special Reference to Transplantation*. One reviewer of the conference would note, "This book might well have been sub-titled 'What Price My Kidney?'"[45]

Broadly drawn or narrowly focused, these gatherings brought together a stellar array of the academic and professional elite.[46] With the exception of abortion and recently awakened concerns for the environment, broad-based political action groups had yet to assert themselves. Instead, the public was "seen as an audience, waiting for scientists to bring solutions to the problems they have created."[47] Conferences were informed by the now widely hailed double-helix structure of DNA. Several other promising advances, limiting the spread of disease and providing life-saving technologies, such as hemodialysis, organ transplantation, and respirators, were also drawing substantial attention. Conference participants grappled repeatedly with forced-choice dilemmas of who should live and who should die, reflecting an awakened awareness that scientific knowledge and all good intentions might go terribly wrong. Innovations benefiting some could and did have negative, even devastating, implications for others.

This issue was brought forcefully to the fore, not in conference deliberations, but through the writings of a single marine biologist, Rachel Carson, working largely in isolation. Carson, who had worked for the Fish and Wildlife Service and written eloquently for over a decade about the interconnectedness of life,[48] received a letter in 1958 from a friend in Massachusetts noting the disturbing deaths of a large number of birds on Cape Cod. The deaths had apparently resulted from spraying dichloro-diphenyl-trichlorethane (DDT), a chemical developed and used to control typhus and malaria during World War II. The use of DDT had undoubtedly saved hundreds of thousands, perhaps millions, of lives and dramatically expanded agricultural production. Indeed, its discovery resulted in Paul Hermann Müller receiving the 1948 Nobel Prize. Rachel Carson, however, had been convinced for a number of years that the benefits of DDT and other insecticides were accompanied by substantial dangers to the environment. Such insecticides, she suggested, would better be called biocides.

Prompted by her friend's letter, Carson pressed forward and wrote *Silent Spring*, first serialized in the *New Yorker* in 1962, and later that same year published in book form. Bowing to the importance of intended and unintended outcomes, she dedicated the book to Albert Schweitzer, quoting him in the front piece as warning, "Man has lost the capacity to foresee and to forestall. He will end by destroying the earth."

Writing in a style compelling to the general public and strongly opposed or ignored by prominent individuals, corporations, and organizations, Carson's work would eventually be credited with setting in place the cornerstone for the American environmental protection movement.[49] Carson was not unalterably opposed to the search for effective control of insects spreading disease or destroying crops. She was, however, keenly aware that the positive effects of insecticides were penetrating the food chain and accumulating in the tissues of plants and animals, leading to the possibility of altering "the very material of heredity upon which the shape of the future depends."

All she was arguing, she stated in her introductory chapter, "The obligation to endure," was "that control must be geared to realities, not to mythical situations, and that the methods employed must be such that they do not destroy us along with the insects."[50] Carson's message was clear: the broad-scale use of currently available insecticides, no matter how well intentioned, was a threat to the circle of life. Life in its broadest sense needed protecting.

The double-edged sword of positive advances yielding negative side effects was also evident among those concerned with what came to be labeled the demographic transition. Thanks to medical science, poor countries were experiencing dramatically lowered death rates. Until there were comparable adjustments in the birth rate, these areas of the world would experience an exploding population confronted with an inadequate food supply. Echoes of Thomas Malthus, who had so captured the attention of Charles Darwin and Francis Galton, were once again heard in projections of impending famines.[51] Until adjustments were made, widespread starvation, the demographers predicted, was the most likely side effect of improved control over infectious disease.

Flawed Judgment and Sloppy Science

Not all negative consequences of otherwise positive advancements resulted from vague definitions, forced-choice dilemmas, and unforeseen inter-connections between life-enhancing innovations and life-damaging outcomes. Some came directly from flawed judgment and sloppy science. Addressing these issues during the 1966 Reed College *Sanctity of Life* conference, Dr. Henry K. Beecher noted, "One often hears it said these days that moral choices are always among shades of gray, never between black and white. This, of course, is not true."[52]

What most concerned Beecher were experiments using humans without their consent. This was a black and white issue. It should not be done. Beecher had set the stage for his damning critique in an article in the *Journal of the American Medical Association* in 1959.[53] His conference talk was largely an update of this article, as well as a reprise and elaboration of his more recently published piece in the *NEJM*, which would help precipitate medical research reforms in the years just ahead.[54]

Dr. Beecher had personal experience to draw upon. He was an endowed faculty member at Harvard Medical School, and, while controversial, he was generally considered among the world's foremost anesthesiologists. He was well versed in the Nazi human experiments, which had led to the trial of 23 doctors, of whom seven had been executed and nine others sent to prison. He knew well that the Nuremberg Code began with the sentence: "The voluntary consent of the human subject is absolutely essential."

Henry Beecher also knew that violations of this principle, as well as the more recently adopted Declaration of Helsinki,[55] were not restricted to the horrors of Nazi medical experiments. They were present in research being done in reputable hospitals and universities across the country. They were prevalent in the clandestine experiments conducted by the CIA on mind-altering drugs and mind-control techniques. The military was doing research involving human subjects to better understand radiation effects associated with the fallout from atomic-bomb use and testing.[56] How was this different than what the Nuremburg doctors had been convicted of doing? Beecher knew and acknowledged that even some of his own practices were not above reproach. Leo Alexander's earlier warning that Americans should be aware that Nuremberg Code violations were present in their own midst was clear.

With this background and the knowledge that his colleagues attending the Reed College conference in Oregon would be uncomfortable with his message, Dr. Beecher set out to document his concerns. Early in his talk, he related a story recently reported in a New York City newspaper.

> Thirty-four infants, whose mothers are in the state reformatory for women here, have been fed live polio virus in their milk in a scientific experiment.
> They were given a weakened virus to determine their antibody response while they still had temporary immunity acquired from their mothers. The work was in connection with a search for a live polio virus capable of being taken by mouth and producing long immunization with a single dose for each type of polio virus.

The problem was, Beecher told his audience, the focus of clinical research was not on healing the patient. It was investigating the disease. Persons were being used to achieve a "greater good." There were clear dangers in such investigations. As serious as they already were, Beecher continued, they were likely to increase in the coming years owing to increased federal funding, the promise of new knowledge, and academic pressure on investigators to produce results.

In his more specifically written *NEJM* elaboration of his Reed College discussion, Beecher presented 22 studies, culled from some 50 he had been looking into. In his introductory paragraph he noted,

> Evidence is at hand that many of the patients in the examples to follow never had the risk satisfactorily explained to them, and it seems obvious that further hundreds have not known that they were the subjects of an experiment although grave consequences have been suffered.

Some might argue, he continued, that the benefits of these experiments outweighed the concerns. He was not among them. There were other, more important, quite well-established values at stake. Quoting Pope Pius XII, Dr. Beecher emphasized his basic point: "science is not the highest value to which all other orders and values . . . should be subordinated."

The problem for Beecher was not intentional harm. Instead,

> During ten years of study of these matters it has become apparent that thoughtlessness and carelessness, not willful disregard of the patient's rights, account for most of the cases encountered. Nonetheless, it is evident that in many of the examples presented, the investigators have risked the health or the life of their subjects.

In later years, additional confirming evidence became plentiful. A prominent physician later interviewed on this topic reported:

> So I felt that we've got to find a better way to justify research, because there's no question there are problems with children . . . we studied the effects of heat stress on babies, and the justification was that the death rate from summer diarrhea was very high in the world. And so we showed what happened under the circumstances. But it was really, looking back, totally unethical. We used Black babies from an orphanage, and there was no consent. There were no parents. The whole thing was—we justified it by finding nice adoptive homes for these babies instead of being in an orphanage.[57]

Beecher's argument was compelling. Further evidence only confirmed his assertions. Tighter controls to minimize carelessness were needed. The need would become glaringly clear in the early 1970s, when three highly questionable studies, including one Beecher had noted, came to the public's attention. All three involved underprivileged patients at the social and economic margins of life, patients whose lives were deemed less worthy of careful protective safeguards than others.

When Dr. Henry Beecher was speaking in Oregon and publishing in the *NEJM*, publicity surrounding these troubling events was yet to come, but reforms were in the works.[58] First, however, there was another matter in need of immediate attention. Once again, dramatic scientific and technological breakthroughs called for a rethinking of the protective boundaries of life.

Harvesting for Life

Concerns with the ethics of using human subjects in clinical studies had led Harvard to establish a Standing Committee on Human Studies, with Dr. Beecher as its chair. Dr. Joseph Murray, who would eventually be awarded the Nobel Prize in Medicine for his work on kidney transplants, was one of Beecher's colleagues. Both were well aware of unresolved ethical issues raised by rapidly improving organ transplant procedures and the increasing effectiveness of immunosuppressant drugs. They were also convinced these issues, like the ethics of medical research involving humans, would become increasingly pressing. There was an immediate need of clarification.

Two months prior to the first successfully transplanted human heart, taken from a young car accident victim where the moment of death was somewhat hazy, Beecher wrote to the dean of the Harvard Medical School suggesting that the Human Studies Committee's charge be expanded. His rationale was clear. "Both Dr. Murray and I think the time has come for a further consideration of the definition of death. Every major hospital has patients stacked up waiting for suitable donors."[59] To maximize the chances of a successful transplant, organs should be removed as close to the moment of death of the donor as possible. When was removal ("harvesting" entered the vocabulary) appropriate? Surely not before the donating patient was dead, but when did death occur?

Well-established common-law definitions of death were no longer as useful as they once were. They relied on the absence of cardiorespiratory activity. Readily available technology now meant respiration and blood circulation could be artificially maintained for years in some cases. Waiting too long to harvest organs meant they would deteriorate. Harvesting too soon presented obvious ethical and legal issues. Defining death in terms too closely tied to probabilities of successful transplantation presented vexing problems too obvious to ignore. The outdated definition of death made so evident by new technologies demanded attention.

These issues came to a head when, late in the evening of December 3, 1967, in Cape Town, South Africa, Dr. Christiaan Barnard transplanted a heart taken from a young woman in her early 20s, Denise Ann Darvall. Denise had been critically injured in a car accident earlier that morning, suffering a skull fracture and serious brain injuries. She could not be kept alive without "artificial" means. Around 9:00 that evening, her heart and kidneys were removed, with the permission of her father.

Her kidneys were given to a young boy.[60] The recipient of her heart was a 55-year-old grocer, Louis Washkansky. Dr. Barnard's operation drew worldwide attention, and, although Mr. Washkansky survived less than three weeks, he was seen as the recipient of the first successful human heart transplant. Given the circumstances surrounding Denise Darvall's organ removal and transplantations, the pressing nature of broader ethical questions loomed large. More such operations were sure to come. A clearer example of cultural lag could not be imagined.

Shortly after Washkansky's death on December 21, 1967, the dean of Harvard Medical School, on January 4, 1968, heeded Beecher and Murray's request and established what came to be known as the Harvard Brain Death Committee. Henry Beecher would be its chair. Physicians dominated the committee, but additional members were chosen for their expertise in theology, history, law, and ethics. These same issues were drawing attention in Washington, DC.

Deference to Doctors

Concern for the ethics of medical research, along with the drama of the first human heart transplants[61] and other rapidly advancing medical technologies and procedures, had captured the attention of some in the U.S. Senate. Prominent among them was future presidential candidate and then senator Walter Mondale. In 1968, a month after the Harvard committee began its work, Senator Mondale introduced legislation to establish a Presidential Study Commission on Health Science and Society. Hearings were held in March and April as Mondale called upon a parade of prominent physicians and scientists, both for and against such a commission. These included Henry Beecher, speaking in favor of establishing the Study Commission, and Christiaan Barnard, who drew a packed hearing room when he testified in strong opposition.

Beecher reaffirmed his belief that there were limits beyond which medical science, even in search of life-enhancing remedies, should not pass. These needed to be better defined, and a Study Commission would be useful. Theologian Kenneth Vaux agreed, and, with biblical allusion to the consequences of passing these limits, noted, "what will it profit us if we gain the whole world and forfeit our soul?"[62]

The repetitive argument from those in opposition to establishing a governmental commission was that so-called new ethical questions were not new at all. Doctors had addressed them for centuries. If new questions did arise, answers could and should be found in the common sense of those best informed about medical matters, those most directly connected to the patients—physicians. Government commissions were cumbersome and would produce needless, counterproductive regulations. As the now celebrated heart surgeon, Dr. Barnard, put it, "I do not think the public is qualified to make the decision . . . You must leave it in the people's hands who are capable of doing it."[63]

Christiaan Barnard's argument carried the day. Mondale's 1968 hearings closed without producing legislation. Trust in those "capable of doing it," for the time being, remained secure. This would soon change.

A Harvard Committee Redefines Death

While Senator Mondale's hearings were proceeding, Beecher's Harvard committee continued its work to define the boundaries of death. Members were united in what they saw in need of clarification. They finished in short order, publishing their recommendations as a special communication to the *Journal of the American Medical Association*, seven months, almost to the day, after the committee was formed.[64]

Technology had reduced the utility of the common-law conception of death. Resuscitative and other life-sustaining measures had "led to increased efforts to save those desperately injured." Sometimes, these efforts were only partially successful. The result was "an individual whose heart continues to beat but whose brain is irreversibly damaged." The burden on patients, their families, and hospital personnel was great. The rationing of health care again seemed unavoidable. Comatose patients occupied hospital beds better utilized for others in need. Finally, and here the problem became most sensitive, the committee noted it was increasingly clear that "obsolete criteria for the definition of death can lead to controversy in obtaining organs for transplantation."[65]

Beecher's committee aimed to develop criteria more closely attuned to then available medical procedures and technologies to determine a "*permanently* nonfunctioning brain." They agreed on three tests, to be confirmed, when possible, by a fourth. All four tests were to be repeated at least 24 hours later, with no change evident. Finally, the Harvard committee noted that the validity of these repeated tests depended on the absence of potentially masking conditions of hypothermia and central nervous system depressants, such as barbiturates. Final decisions were to be made by the physician-in-charge.

The Brain Death Committee wanted to be as clear as possible. Defining the cessation of life had deep moral significance. Existing common-law standards involving irreversible cessation of circulatory and respiratory functions had become outdated by new technologies.[66] In cases such as Denise Darvall's, long-used indicators of life could be kept in the viable range with artificial means potentially for years, even when the portion of the brain that made us human had permanently stopped functioning. The medical community, the committee concluded, was "ready to adopt new criteria for pronouncing death . . . in an individual sustaining irreversible coma as a result of permanent brain damage."

While there was some controversy, and an alternative brain-stem standard was eventually adopted in the United Kingdom, the Harvard committee's recommendations were widely accepted and formally adopted. Kansas was the first state to enact related legislation in 1970. Many states would follow. Troubling cases, such as that of Karen Ann Quinlan, would emerge in the years just ahead.

By 1980, there was a growing consensus that legal language defining death should be uniform. A Presidential Commission was convened, resulting in the Uniform Determination of Death Act (UDDA). Both traditional and brain-death criteria were included. The wording read:

> An individual who has sustained either (1) irreversible cessation of circulatory and respiratory functions, or (2) irreversible cessation of all functions of the entire brain, including the brain stem, is dead. A determination of death must be made in accordance with accepted medical standards.

The UDDA was patterned after the Harvard Brain Death Committee's recommendations, informed by common-law practices, refined by intervening events and discussions, and approved by the American Medical Association (AMA) and the American Bar Association in 1980 and 1981, respectively. The aim was to provide comprehensive bases for determining death in all situations.

The brain-death criteria were hailed as one of the great achievements in refined medical ethics. The nagging sense, however, that the criteria were connected to organ transplantation, with other attendant ethical issues, remained troubling. A decade and a half after the UDDA was proposed, Peter Singer, known for his practical approach to ethics, direct writing style, and the assertion that some lives or moments in life were more worthy of protection than others, saw the criteria for defining the boundary between life and death as confirmation of his position:

> This change in the definition of death has meant that warm, breathing, pulsating human beings are not given further medical support. If their relatives consent . . . their hearts and other organs can be cut out of their bodies and given to strangers. The change in our conception of death that excluded these human beings from the moral community was among the first in a series of dramatic changes in our view of life and death.[67]

A Paradigm for Protected Life

As important as these refinements were, for many the cultural lag remained. The stage for what came to be known as the bioethics movement was firmly set in 1969, when theologian James Gustafson organized a final gathering of the decade of conferences. The Yale Divinity School, where Gustafson taught, and the Yale School of Medicine were the cosponsors. The conference would prove to be highly influential.

"One hopes we can move beyond the conference procedure," Gustafson wrote, "to a more disciplined, careful, long range way of working in which areas of disagreement can not only be defined but in part at least overcome." What was needed, Gustafson concluded, was the mobilization and organization of resources, "interdisciplinary work within universities or centers that have personnel and resources for the arduous tasks of intensive and long-term work."[68]

Gustafson organized the 1969 gathering with these objectives in mind. Its featured speaker, around whom the proceedings were organized, was Paul Ramsey. It would later be written that this "massive" conference was enlivened by vigorous panel responses to Ramsey's presentations and "marked the beginnings of a new and astoundingly influential scholarly practical discipline."[69]

Ramsey was a widely recognized, outspoken Christian ethicist from Princeton, known as an acute analytic scholar and a sometimes acerbic, argumentative, and strong-willed talker. At previous conferences throughout the decade he had repeatedly challenged, to not always receptive colleagues, the "shallowness of scientists' moral thinking about abortion and genetics." He would do so again, though this time his criticisms would be broader based and more fully developed.

Having received the first grant given by the Joseph P. Kennedy, Jr. Foundation for studying medical ethics, Ramsey took the unusual step of preparing for his presentations by spending the better part of the spring semesters in 1968 and 1969 talking with and observing doctors and scientists at Georgetown University School of Medicine. Drawing on this experience and his background as a theologian and ethicist, he organized his presentations into four lectures: "Updating Death," "Caring for the Dying," "Giving and Taking Organs for Transplantation," and "Consent in Medical Experimentation."

Thanking various participants attending the Yale conference, with wry, self-deprecating humor, Ramsey recalled, when delivering the first of his lectures, the words of a wise colleague:

> I should say that these lectures will ask more questions than they will answer, will pose questions that may be unanswerable, will answer questions seldom asked and particularly questions physicians never thought of asking, and won't answer the questions doctors did ask.
>
> I stipulate that to do any one of these things shall be deemed success and that I enroll in any of these undertakings only on a "Pass–Fail" basis. Stiffer competition or any more severe judgment would be too much for me.

Those in attendance, mostly northeastern physicians and Ivy League academics, may have smiled at these disarming introductory comments from a colleague they knew to be strong-willed and self-assured. Their smiles would soon fade. They recognized a scholarly tour de force when they saw one. As an extension and elaboration of his lectures, a year after the conference, Yale University Press published Ramsey's *The Patient as Person*.

Ramsey wove his lectures and book together with the Biblical concept of *fidelity to covenant*.

> We are born within covenants of life with life. By nature, choice, or need we live with our fellowmen in roles and relations. Therefore we must ask, "What is the meaning of the *faithfulness* of one human being to another in every one of these relations?" This is the ethical question.

He aimed to clarify "the meaning of *care*, to find the actions and abstentions that come from adherence to *covenant*, to ask the meaning of the *sanctity of life*, to articulate the requirements of steadfast *faithfulness* to a fellow man." He would explore the human significance of medical relations "in which some decision must be made about how to show respect for, protect, preserve, and honor the life of fellow man." For most, including a prominent chronicler of the history of bioethics, Ramsey's integrated presentations, both written and spoken, marked nothing less than a paradigm shift for "doing ethics."[70]

Together, Ramsey's lectures and book extended and enriched the human rights principles embedded in the hastily crafted Nuremberg Code. They provided further grounding for the worried musings of Leo Alexander and Henry Beecher. They specified and humanized the philosophic generalizations of G.E.M. Anscombe and Philippa Foot regarding the importance of intentions and the Doctrine of Double Effect. They would soon inform revitalized congressional hearings and reports.

With his lectures completed and *The Patient as Person* published, Ramsey's work became, without question, a cornerstone for the agenda of a field for which a term was about to be coined. They might "rightly be called the founding preaching and scriptures of the field of bioethics."[71]

Notes

1 "An Armistice Day Address," Boston, MA, November 10, 1948, *The Collected Writings of Omar N. Bradley*, vol. 1: 584–9.
2 Richard McCormick, "The Quality of Life, the Sanctity of Life," *Hastings Center Report* 8m (1978): 30–6.
3 Leon R. Kass, *Life, Liberty and the Defense of Dignity: The Challenge of Bioethics* (San Francisco, CA: Encounter Books, 2002), 3.
4 Albert R. Jonsen, *The Birth of Bioethics* (New York: Oxford University Press, 1998), 134.

5 "The Rockefeller Foundation and the Kaiser Wilhelm Institute," *Science* 84 (1936): 526–7.
6 Micahel A. Grodin and George J. Annas, "Legacies of Nuremberg: Medical Ethics and Human Rights," *Journal of the American Medical Association* 276 (1996): 1682–3. David J. Rothman, *Strangers at the Bedside* (New York: Basic Books, 1991): 15–50.
7 Rothman, *Strangers at the Bedside*, 31. Indeed, the Nuremberg Doctors' Trial seems to have been an important prod for the formal articulation of the AMA statement of ethics.
8 For a detailed account of this committee's work and eventual declaration, see Mary Ann Glendon, *The World Made New: Eleanor Roosevelt and the Universal Declaration of Human Rights* (New York: Random House, 2001), Chap. 2. See also, Eleanor Roosevelt, "The Promise of Human Rights," *Foreign Affairs* 26 (1948): 470–7.
9 Taken from Winston Churchill's "Sinews of Peace" speech (eventually known as the "Iron Curtain" speech for the sentence: "From Stetting in the Baltic to Trieste in the Adriatic an iron curtain has descended across the Continent.") Speech given at Westminster College in Fulton, Missouri, March 5, 1946.
10 Leo Alexander, "Medical Science Under Dictatorship," *New England Journal of Medicine* 241, 2 (1949): 39–47.
11 David Clark, *Cicely Saunders—Founder of the Hospice Movement: Selected Letters 1959–1999* (New York: Oxford University Press, 2005). Shirley De Boulay, *Cicely Saunders: Founder of the Modern Hospice Movement* (Cambridge: Hodder & Stoughton, 1984).
12 William Ogburn, *On Culture and Social Change*, Ed. Otis Dudley Duncan (Chicago: The University of Chicago Press, 1964): 86–95.
13 Herbert Wechsler, "The Challenge of a Model Penal Code," *Harvard Law Review* 65 (1952): 1098.
14 Aldous Huxley, foreword to *Brave New World*, by Aldous Huxley (New York: Harper Collins, 1993), xi.
15 "Children From the Laboratory," *AMA Prism*, (1973): 13.
16 Michael Tooley, "Abortion and Infanticide," *Philosophy and Public Affairs* 2 (1972): 37–65. Helga Kuhse and Peter Singer, *Should the Baby Live?: The Problem of Handicapped Infants* (New York: Oxford University Press, 1985).
17 Belding H. Scribner, "Ethical Problems of Using Artificial Organs to Sustain Human Life," *Transactions of the American Society for Artificial Internal Organs* 10 (1964): 209–12.
18 Albert Jonsen, *The New Medicine & the Old Ethics* (Cambridge, MA: Harvard University Press, 1990). David J. Rothman, *Strangers at the Bedside: A History of How Law and Bioethics Transformed Medical Decision Making* (New York: Basic Books, 1991).
19 Scribner, in his 1964 presidential address, noted that some 10,000 "ideal candidates" who could have been treated had died. Belding H. Scribner, "Ethical Problems of Using Artificial Organs to Sustain Human Life," *Transactions of the American Society for Artificial Internal Organs* 10 (1964): 209–12.
20 C.R. Blagg, (1998) "Development of Ethical Concepts in Dialysis: Seattle in the 1960s," *Nephrology* 4 (1998): 236.
21 Shana Alexander, "They Decide Who Lives, Who Dies: Medical Miracle and a Moral Burden of a Small Committee," *Life*, November 9 (1962): 103–28.

22 Speech given at the Birth of Bioethics Conference, Seattle, September 1992.

23 Albert R. Jonsen, "The Birth of Bioethics," *Special Supplement, Hastings Center Report* 23, 6 (1993): S1.

24 This account of Seattle's first dialysis center is gleaned largely from Alexander, "They Decide Who Lives, Who Dies" *Life*, November 9 (1962): 106–23.

25 J.E. Murray et al., "Kidney Transplantation in Modified Recipients," *Annals of Surgery* 156 (1962): 337–55; T.E. Starzl, T.L. Marchioro, and W.R. Waddell, "The Reversal of Rejection in Human Renal Homografts with Subsequent Development of Homograft Tolerance," *Surgery, Gynecology, and Obstetrics* 117 (1963): 385–95; D.M. Hume et al., "Renal Homotransplantation in Man in Modified Recipients," *Annals of Surgery* 158 (1963): 608–44; M.F. Woodruff et al., "Homotransplantation of Kidney in Patients Treated by Preoperative Local Radiation and Postoperative Administration of an Antimetabolite," *Lancet* 2 (1963): 675–82; J.E. Murray et al., "Prolonged Survival of Human Kidney Homografts by Immunosuppressive Drug Therapy," *New England Journal of Medicine* 268 (1963): 1315–23.

26 A.H. Katz and D.M. Proctor, "Social–Psychological Characteristics of Patients Receiving Hemodialysis Treatment for Chronic Renal Failure," *Public Health Service* (1969) Kidney Disease Control Program, July.

27 Renée Fox and Judith Swazey, *The Courage to Fail: A Social View of Organ Transplants and Dialysis* (Chicago: University of Chicago Press, 1978): 232.

28 Figures cited by David Sanders and Jesse Dukeminier, Jr., "Medical Advance and Legal Lag: Hemodialysis and Kidney Transplantation," *UCLA Law Review*, 15 (1968): 366.

29 Sanders and Dukeminier, Jr., 357–413.

30 Lon Fuller, "The Case of the Speluncean Explorers," *Harvard Law Review*, 62 (1949): 616–45.

31 Lon Fuller, *The Morality of Law* (New Haven, CT: Yale University Press, 1964).

32 See, for example, Ronald Dworkin, *Life's Dominion: An Argument About Abortion, Euthanasia, and Individual Freedom* (New York: Alfred A. Knopf, 1993). See also, Ronald Dworkin, Thomas Nagel, Robert Nozick, John Rawls, Thomas Scanlon, and Judith Jarvis Thomson as amici curiae in support of respondents, *State Of Washington v. Harold Glucksberg Dennis C. Vacco, Attorney General Of New York v. Timothy E. Quill* 521 U.S. 793 (1997).

33 Edmond Cahn, *The Moral Decision: Right and Wrong in the Light of American Law* (Bloomington, IN and London: Indiana University Press, 1955): 61–2.

34 Here, Cahn referred to another jurist colleague who had written along similar lines: Benjamin Cardozo, "What Medicine Can Do for Law," in *Selected Writings of Benjamin Nathan Cardozo*, Ed. M.E. Hall (1947).

35 James Rachels is generally given credit for launching this debate in the context of bioethics. See his "Active and Passive Euthanasia," *New England Journal of Medicine* 292 (1975): 78–80. For important early critique see: Paul T. Menzel, "Are Killing and Letting Die Morally Different in Medical Contexts?" *Journal of Medicine and Philosophy* 4 (1979): 269–93. For later assessment, when bioethics had matured as a field and cases were appearing in courts all across the nation, see: Howard Brody, "Causing, Intending, and Assisting Death," *Journal of Clinical Ethics* 4 (1993): 112–17.

36 G.E.M. Anscombe, "Modern Moral Philosophy," *Philosophy* 33 (1958). G.E.M. Anscombe, *Intention* (Cambridge, MA: Harvard University Press, 1957).

37 Z. Vendler, "The Grammar of Goodness: An Interview With Philippa Foot," *Harvard Review of Philosophy* 6 (2003): 32–44.

38 Johnathan Bennett, "Whatever the Consequences," *Analysis* 26 (3) (January, 1966): 83–102. G.E.M. Anscombe, "Note on Mr. Bennett," *Analysis* 26 (6) (June, 1966): 208.

39 Philippa Foot, "The Problem of Abortion and the Doctrine of the Double Effect," *Oxford Review* 5 (1967).

40 See, for example, Judith Jarvis Thomson, "A Defense of Abortion," *Philosophy & Public Affairs* 1 (1971), and "Killing, Letting Die, and the Trolley Problem," *The Monist* 59 (1976): 204–17. P.S. Woodard, Ed., *The Doctrine of Double Effect: Philosophers Debate a Controversial Moral Principle* (Notre Dame, IN: University of Notre Dame Press, 2001).

41 So labeled by Albert R. Jonsen, in *The Birth of Bioethics* (New York/Oxford: Oxford University Press, 1998): 13. Jonsen's book remains the most comprehensive account of the emergent bioethics movement.

42 From the dust jacket of *Life or Death: Ethics and Options* (Seattle, WA: University of Washington Press, 1966), a publication of edited papers presented at a symposium on *The Sanctity of Life*, held at Reed College, March 11–12, 1966.

43 *Dartmouth Alumni Magazine* 53, 2 (1960).

44 *Life or Death: Ethics and Options* (1966), a publication of edited papers presented at a symposium on *The Sanctity of Life* (Seattle, WA: University of Washington Press): ix.

45 C.P. Harvey, "Ethics in Medical Progress: A Ciba Foundation Symposium," *The Modern Law Review* 30 (1967): 591–3.

46 For one listing of many of the prominent players focusing on medical aspects of these issues see: Albert R. Jonsen, Ed., "The Birth of Bioethics," *Special Supplement, Hastings Center Report* 23, 6 (1993): S 16.

47 Jonsen, *The Birth of Bioethics*, 15.

48 Rachel Carson, *Under the Sea Wind* (New York: Oxford University Press, 1941); Rachel Carson, *The Sea Around Us* (New York: Oxford University Press, 1950); Rachel Carson, *The Edge of the Sea* (Boston, MA: Houghton. Mifflin & Co., 1955).

49 Thanks in large measure to Carson's work, the National Environmental Policy Act was passed in 1969. See, Jack Lewis, *EPA Journal*, November 1985: "*Silent Spring* played in the history of environmentalism roughly the same role that *Uncle Tom's Cabin* played in the abolitionist movement. In fact, EPA today may be said without exaggeration to be the extended shadow of Rachel Carson."

50 Carson, *Silent Spring*, 8–9.

51 William Paddock and Paul Paddock, *Famine—1975* (Boston, MA: Little, Brown & Co., 1967). Paul Ehrlich, *The Population Bomb* (New York: Ballantine Books, 1968).

52 H.K. Beecher, Ed., "Medical Research and the Individual," in *Life or Death: Ethics and Options* (Seattle, WA: University of Washington Press, 1968), 116.

53 "Experimentation in Man," *Journal of the American Medical Association* 169 (1959): 461–78.

54 Beecher, "Ethics and Clinical Research."

55   Adopted by the 18th World Medical Assembly, Helsinki, Finland, June 1964.

56   See Alfred W. McCoy, *A Question of Torture: CIA Interrogation, From the Cold War to the War on Terror* (New York: Henry Holt & Company, LLC, 2006): 21–59. Eileen Welsome, *The Plutonium Files: America's Secret Medical Experiments in the Cold War* (New York: The Dial Press, Random House, 1999).

57   See Interview with Robert E. Cooke, *Oral History of the Belmont Report and the National Commission for the Protection of Human Subjects of Biomedical and Behavioral Research*, 5. See also M.H. Pappworth, "Human Guinea Pigs: A Warning," *The Twentieth Century* (1962): 66–75.

58   See Memorandum issued by the Research Grants Division of USPHS on February 8, 1966. Statement of policy.

59   Cited in David J. Rothman, *Strangers at the Bedside* (New York: Basic Books, 1991): 160–1.

60   There was some short-lived controversy in apartheid South Africa as Denise was white and the recipient of her kidneys, 10-year-old Jonathan van Wyk, was "coloured."

61   Denton Cooley, operating in Houston, Texas, performed a second human-heart transplant in June this same year.

62   Cited in Jonsen, *The Birth of Bioethics*, 92.

63   Quoted in Rothman, *Strangers at the Bedside*, 172–3.

64   Special Communication, "A Definition of Irreversible Coma, Report of the Ad Hoc Committee of the Harvard Medical School to Examine the Definition of Brain Death," *Journal of American Medical Association* 205 (1968): 337–40.

65   The motivating importance of improved organ-transplant procedures for a new definition of death was clear. While Beecher and his committee were doing their work, another AMA committee was convened to establish ethical guidelines for organ transplantation. This report was approved in June of 1968, just prior to the release of the brain-death recommendations, and formally published in 1969. See, American Medical Association, *Guidelines for Organ Transplantation*. Judicial Council Opinions and Reports (Chicago: American Medical Association, 1969): 11–12.

66   The committee pointed to a widely cited reference, *Black's Law Dictionary*, where physicians were to determine the "total stoppage of the circulation of the blood, and a cessation of the animal and vital functions consequent thereupon, such as respiration, pulsation, etc."

67   Peter Singer, "Is the Sanctity of Life Ethic Terminally Ill," *Bioethics* 9 (1995): 308.

68   James Gustafson, "Review of *Life or Death: Ethics and Options*," *Commonweal* 89 (1968): 27–30.

69   Margaret Farley, foreword to *The Patient as Person: Explorations in Medical Ethics*, 2nd ed., Ed. Paul Ramsey (New Haven, CT: Yale University Press, 2002).

70   See Albert R. Jonsen, "The Structure of an Ethical Revolution: Paul Ramsey, the Beecher Lectures, and the Birth of Bioethics," in *The Patient as Person: Explorations in Medical Ethics*, 2nd ed., Ed. Paul Ramsey (New Haven, CT: Yale University Press, 2002): xvi–xxvii.

71   Jonsen, "The Structure of an Ethical Revolution," xvi–xxvii.

CHAPTER 5

CRYSTALLIZING EVENTS AND ETHICAL PRINCIPLES

The 1960s was the decade of conferences, capstoned by the publication of *The Patient as Person*. These conferences set the stage for the founding of a field—bioethics—and the creation of two centers embodying James Gustafson's call for "interdisciplinary . . . intensive and long-term work." With the intellectual stage set, the 1970s ushered in what might be called the decade of crystallizing events. These events focused attention, clarified issues, galvanized effort, and precipitated a call for legislatively defined moral principles. The human tragedies embedded in these events energized legal reform efforts more effectively than conference presentations ever could.

A Term is Coined

Conference discussions throughout the 1960s encouraged a growing number of publications that covered the protective boundaries of life and tolerable suffering in the broadest sense.[1] It became clear that perspectives from the humanities, social, behavioral, and natural sciences, engineering, and medicine should be joined. An early proposal for addressing the broad set of issues identified came from an oncologist working at the medical school at the University of Wisconsin in Madison.

Professor Van Rensselaer Potter was interested in the links between health and environmental carcinogens. Margaret Mead, the anthropologist, had inspired him with her calls for interdisciplinary study in an "age when the very survival of the human race and possibly of all living creatures depends upon our having a vision of the future for others which will command our deepest commitment."[2] Potter had written various articles on related topics throughout the 1960s, and in 1971 he brought some of his ideas together in a small volume, *Bioethics: Bridge to the Future*.[3] By most accounts, this marked the coining of the term, bioethics.[4] In his own words, Potter aimed "to contribute to the future of the human species by promoting the formation of a new discipline, the discipline of *Bioethics*."

For this Wisconsin oncologist, what was needed was recognition of

> the fact that human ethics cannot be separated from a realistic understanding of ecology in the broadest sense. *Ethical values* cannot be separated from *biological facts*. We are in great need of a Land Ethic, a Wildlife Ethic, a Population Ethic, a Consumption Ethic, an Urban Ethic, an International Ethic, a Geriatric Ethic, and so on.

Thus framed, in Potter's call for a field of bioethics one could hear echoes of General Omar Bradley, Rachel Carson, and a host of ecologists, community planners, and demographers worried more about the survival of the planet than the ethics of medical experimentation, physician–patient relations, and the protected boundaries of individual lives.

Potter mentioned medical research, boundaries defining the beginning and ending of life, and criteria for the allocation of scarce, life-prolonging medical resources, but these issues appeared almost as afterthoughts in his discussions. For many others, "bioethics" would focus most heavily not on Potter's ecological issues but on the protective boundaries marking the beginning and ending of life and the meaning and boundaries of tolerable suffering.

Two Centers Frame the Debate

While Potter was gathering his papers for publication and coining a term, two research and teaching centers were being organized, and the loosely knit Society of Health and Human Values[5] was being founded largely by those who had organized and participated in the conferences of the 1960s. The Hastings Center, located on the Hudson River a little over an hour's drive from New York City, and the Kennedy Institute of Ethics,[6] at Georgetown University in Washington, DC, would become the dominant framers of what came to be known as the bioethics movement.

The Hastings Center, by design, aimed to carve out a new field of scholarly discourse. Articles appearing in *The Hastings Center Report* (*HCR*) would shape much of the scholarly discussion in the years ahead. It became in many ways a "Leader of leaders."[7] The Kennedy Institute's strategic location in the nation's capital, along with its ability to mobilize resources and organize effort, would be called upon repeatedly in support of numerous governmental commissions and landmark legal cases.

The initial task for both the Kennedy Institute and the Hastings Center was to clarify what bioethics, as an interdisciplinary enterprise, should look like. Little emphasis was placed upon the abstract formulations of logicians and analytic philosophers; more was placed upon, as Daniel Callahan, the first director of the Hastings Center, put it, developing a discipline "so designed, and its practitioners so trained, that it will directly—at whatever cost to disciplinary elegance—serve those physicians and biologists whose position demands that they make the practical decisions."[8] Fledgling bioethicists were drawn to the practical issues embedded in several high-profile events coming to light in the early 1970s. These events reinvigorated Senator Mondale's failed 1968 congressional hearings. Drawn to these matters and encouraged by the stated purposes of their primary benefactor, members of the newly established Kennedy Institute launched an "applied" endeavor, aimed in large measure at ethical questions of medical research and practice. Trust and singular reliance on the common sense of physicians who, as Christiaan Barnard had put it in testimony before Senator Mondale's 1968 Committee, were "capable of doing it" began to break down as troubling events shifted political priorities and calls for action. As one observer noted, "The formal birth of bioethics really began by Congressional mandate!"[9]

Four Crystallizing Events

In 1971, Senator Mondale, along with 17 congressional cosponsors, reintroduced his 1968 proposal for a commission for the "study and evaluation of the ethical, social, and legal implications of advances in biomedical research and technology." Senator Mondale was one of the founding members of the Hastings Center, and his proposal to Congress was published in the first edition of the *HCR*, "The Issues Before Us."

This reprint was accompanied by a short inset, written by Paul Ramsey, who urged the medical profession, scientists, and legislators, to give these issues the serious attention they deserved. It was too easy, Ramsey warned, "to raise ethical questions with a frivolous conscience and to no serious purpose." For Ramsey, serious purpose meant that lawmakers, physicians, and scientists needed to be prepared to "stop the trial or procedure in question in the event that the 'ethical finding' should turn out to be murder or deception or other serious wrong to actual or (now) hypothetical human beings." Initially, Senator Mondale's renewed call for legislative action gained little real traction, passing the Senate, but failing to gather much attention in the House. Revelations of disturbing, issue-clarifying events, calling for serious focused action changed this.

Just months after the senator from Minnesota presented his proposal, the *Washington Post*, on October 8, 1971, carried a front-page story with the headline, "Pentagon Has Contract to Test Radiation Effect on Humans." The lead paragraph stated,

> For the past 11 years, the Pentagon has had a contract with the University of Cincinnati to study the effects of atomic radiation on human beings. The prime purpose of the study, according to the contract, has been to "understand better the influence of radiation on combat effectiveness."

The head of the Cincinnati research team, Dr. Eugene Saenger, was quoted in the final paragraph of the article, reaffirming his belief in the legitimacy and value of the project:

> There is a need to investigate the effects of radiation on human beings to give support to the military . . . These are tough problems that should not be swept under the rug, and I personally think the work we are doing is damned important.

Patients receiving radiation all had cancer. They were poor, with little education, and unable to pay for private physicians. Just over 60 percent were of African–American heritage. All were drawn to the hospital seeking help. There was little or no hope that the full-body radiation treatment many received would help them personally, but there was the belief that, by monitoring such radiation effects, something valuable could be learned to assist military personnel on the battlefield or citizens in the event of an atomic attack. In the minds of many, in a time of mutually assured destruction (MAD), the potential knowledge gained was "damned important." The full extent to which similar radiation experiments were being conducted across the country during the Cold War would not come to light until years later.[10]

One thing, however, was immediately clear. There were strong parallels between the Cincinnati research and the practices and rationale German doctors had for conducting medical experiments during World War II. Such similarities were what had worried Leo Alexander and Henry Beecher. In Cincinnati, as in Germany, experiments were designed to shed light on how to protect the military under life-threatening conditions. In both instances, medical research, known to create painful and even lethal effects, was designed to advance knowledge, not improve the health of patients being treated. In both instances, experiments were carried out without fully informed consent of the persons being studied. In both instances, the privileged and well-situated members of society were nowhere to be found. In Cincinnati, as in Germany, one could easily detect the implied dehumanizing question: If patients of less social worth are going to die anyway, why not use them for the greater good? Had not just such a rationale been used by Justice Holmes in *Buck v. Bell*?

The *Washington Post* revelation of the Cincinnati radiation experiments did not create instant and widespread moral outrage. It did, however, capture the attention of a few legislators and a young assistant professor of English, Martha Stephens, along with some of her colleagues at the University of Cincinnati. Actually, according to Professor Stephens' own account, it was not the story in the *Washington Post* that had captured her attention. A colleague had shown her a similar story in the *Village Voice*, a widely circulated weekly publication of the "underground press" in New York City. In subsequent discussions, members of the University of Cincinnati's Junior Faculty Association (JFA), a group of untenured professors, decided that, as university citizens, they were responsible for what took place on campus and that they should not "rely on reporters outside to tell us what was happening; we ourselves should find out and let the people know."[11]

As a young faculty member, Stephens took it upon herself to approach the director of the university's medical center to get further details. It took some convincing. The director was reluctant to release and noted in paternalistic comments that English professors might not understand the technical details. After several persistent visits, however, one afternoon Stephens walked into the director's office and saw a large stack of documents on the director's desk. "Here they are, if you really want them," he told her. She walked out of the office with "about six hundred pages of double-spaced transcript in several dark brown folders." Over the holidays she read the material and began to write a report to her colleagues on the JFA.

It was a sobering experience. "I had long been used to reading plays and novels of tragic deaths, full of pity and sorrow," she later recalled. But she had not been "used to *this* pity, *this* sorrow . . . of people sick and confused coming for help and then being brutally abused." She read profiles doctors had appended to their annual reports: "I could readily see . . . that one patient had died six days after radiation, and others on day seven, day nine, day ten, fifteen, twenty, twenty-two, and so on." "It was clear," she concluded, "that these tests would have to be brought to an end and that any of us on campus who could help must do so." With her reading and research completed, on January 25, 1972, just under four months after the initial *Washington Post* story broke, Stephens' seven-page report, addressed to "the campus community," was released in a press conference held by the JFA.

One person attending the press conference was a reporter from the *Washington Post*. He took the report and wrote a story that appeared the next day.[12] At this same time, Senator Edward Kennedy was working with Senator Mondale and others to revive congressional interest in more effective regulation of medical experiments involving humans. Kennedy saw the *Post* story and read the JFA's conclusions into the Congressional Record the same day they were reported. Following the press conference, Kennedy asked one of his aides to begin working with Professor Stephens and her colleagues. The medical community was challenging the JFA report, and Kennedy wanted to find out more. The aide later told Stephens and her colleagues, "We have sent the JFA report out to our medical sources and they have told us it makes a very damaging case against these doctors." Within two months, Senator Kennedy and Ohio Governor John Gilligan met with the University of Cincinnati's president, Warren Bennis, and reached agreement on stopping the research in question.

Momentum for reform involving tighter controls of medical research was building. It was further energized when revelations regarding experiments using young children on Staten Island came to light the same month Martha Stephens and her colleagues released their JFA report. Again, there were charges of serious wrong being done to persons on the margins of protected life.

In his 1966 *NEJM* article, Henry Beecher had pointed to a research project that had taken place in an institution for mentally retarded children. He had not identified the institution by name or location, but the study was described as being directed "toward determining the period of infectivity of infectious hepatitis." It involved the "artificial induction of hepatitis . . . in an institution of mentally defective children in which a mild form of hepatitis was endemic."

In a later account, the experiments were described in greater detail. "The experiments typically involved injecting some of the unit residents with gamma globulin and feeding them the live hepatitis virus (obtained from the feces of . . . hepatitis patients)." At the same time, a "control" group was "fed the live virus without the benefit of gamma globulin, to ascertain that the virus was actually 'live,' capable of transmitting the disease, and to measure the different responses."[13]

Consent forms describing the study in general terms were provided, but there is evidence that the parents' request to have their child admitted to the over-crowded institution would be denied if they did not consent. What was very clear to Beecher, writing in 1966, was the study's violation of a resolution, extending the Nuremberg Code and adopted by the World Medical Association, that "Under no circumstances is a doctor permitted to do anything which would weaken the physical or mental resistance of a human being except from strictly therapeutic or prophylactic indications imposed in the interest of the patient." In no case was it "right to risk an injury to 1 person for the benefit of others."

Beecher's anonymous account of this intentional induction of hepatitis into institutionalized "mentally defective" children was included among

21 other projects of concern. As more information became available, it became clear that the institution was Willowbrook, the same over-crowded, squalid, poorly tended institution Senator Robert F. Kennedy had described in 1965 as bordering on a "snake pit."

In many ways, Willowbrook was a legacy of institutions for the "feeble-minded" established in the heyday of the Eugenics Movement. The mandatory sterilization policies may have subsided, but residents were still seen as less worthy members of society and kept in conditions likened to dogs in a kennel. Beecher's account and Senator Robert Kennedy's characterization had only scratched the tip of a very much larger iceberg. The badly deteriorated, severely under-funded conditions and practices within the walls of Willowbrook remained out of the public's view.

In November of 1971, this lack of attention changed. A Willowbrook doctor had been organizing parents and staff to protest the abysmal conditions and mistreatment of children, an effort that got him fired. This same doctor approached a friend and local television reporter, Geraldo Rivera, asking that Rivera document the "horror" at Willowbrook. He wanted Rivera to see one section in particular where "there are sixty retarded kids, with only one attendant to take care of them. Most are naked and they lie in their own shit."[14] He had a key. He could get Rivera in. Twenty-five years later, Rivera, by then a well-known muckraking reporter, would recall that when he unlocked the door and stepped inside it was "*the* defining moment" of his life.[15]

Rivera's filming of conditions in Willowbrook was aired in early January 1972. It captured national attention. By mid March, a suit was filed by the New York Civil Liberties Union (NYCLU) on behalf of approximately 5,400 Willowbrook residents. After three years in the courts and pro-tracted legal negotiations, a consent decree was signed in May of 1975 establishing new standards of care for mentally retarded persons and a dramatic reduction in the size of the institution. Eventually, the full story would be chronicled in *The Willowbrook Wars*, published in 1984. As bad as the conditions at Willowbrook were, there was more to come.

On July 25, 1972, some five months after the NYCLU filed its class action suit on behalf of the residents at Willowbrook, yet another troubling story broke, this time in the *Washington Evening Star*. The headline read, "Syphilis Patients Died Untreated." The story was picked up nationwide, and the next day the *New York Times* ran a parallel article: "Syphilis Victims in the U.S. Study Went Untreated for 40 Years." The lead sentence left little doubt:

> For 40 years the United States Public Health Service has conducted a study in which human beings with syphilis, who were induced to serve as guinea pigs, have gone without medical treatment for the disease and a few have died of its late effects, even though an effective therapy was eventually discovered.

The study had begun in 1932, involving "about 600 black men, mostly poor and uneducated, from Tuskegee, Ala., an area that had the highest syphilis rate in the nation at the time."

If appalling institutional conditions and hepatitis research done on young retarded children on Staten Island and the radiation studies performed on cancer patients unable to secure alternative medical care in Cincinnati had awakened the conscience of some in Congress, it can rightly be said the account of the Tuskegee syphilis experiment scarred the congressional soul. It is hard to imagine a more dramatic, inescapable example of the country's racist legacy than what took place in Macon County, Alabama, over a 40-year period between 1932 and 1972.

Taken together, these three revelations of highly questionable medical research and practice left little doubt: some lives were deemed less worthy than others by the very physicians charged with their healing.[16] Some persons were less likely to be protected. Their suffering was more likely to be tolerated. Their use for the benefit of others—even if it meant the infliction of harm, suffering, and death—was more likely to be justified.

Physicians and medical personnel involved in the Macon County syphilis study offered a few weak justifications, but these were hard, perhaps impossible, to sustain. Members of Congress reacted with shock. Senator William Proxmire, Democrat from Wisconsin, and a member of the Senate subcommittee that oversaw public-health budgets, called the Tuskegee study "a moral and ethical nightmare."[17] The assistant secretary of health and scientific affairs of the Department of Health, Education, and Welfare, when interviewed, reacted similarly. An official in the Venereal Disease Branch of the Center for Disease Control, where responsibility for the study resided in its final years, suggested, "a literal death sentence was passed on some of those people." "It is simply incredulous," he continued, "that such a thing could have ever happened. I honest to God don't understand it."[18]

It could no longer be easily argued, as Christiaan Barnard and others had done in Senator Mondale's 1968 hearings, that the common sense and professional judgment of physicians involved in research should be fully trusted. By November of 1972, a Science Policy Committee reported, "Never before have the issues [of medical research] been given such wide publicity or discussed so frankly as has been the case in recent months."[19] In a later thorough account, it was written, "More than any other experiment in American history, the Tuskegee Study convinced legislators and bureaucrats alike that tough new regulations had to be adopted if human subjects were to be protected."[20] Senator Mondale's repeated calls for action were about to be heard.

These calls would come to fruition in 1973 hearings held by Senator Edward Kennedy, supported by his Senate colleague, Jacob Javits. They would be further energized by one more account of ethically questionable science—the use of newly aborted fetuses in federally funded research. These came into sharp focus just months after the Supreme Court's landmark abortion decisions, this time in the *Washington Post* on April 10, 1973. The story prompted a phone call from Eunice Shriver, who was executive vice president of the Joseph P. Kennedy, Jr. Foundation, the prime benefactor of the Kennedy Institute. She was calling the Institute's director and friend, obstetrician, Dr. André Hellegers.

A visiting colleague at the Kennedy Institute, self-described as a recently appointed professor "in the fledging field of bioethics," was having lunch with Dr. Hellegers at the time.

> As we were eating lunch, a waiter called him to the phone. After ten minutes, Dr. Hellegers returned, saying in his British-tinged Dutch accent, "That was Eunice Shriver. She wanted to discuss what should be done to stop the fetal research that was reported in this morning's *Post*."[21]

The article, "Live-Fetus Research Debated," led with the sentence, "The possibility of using newly-delivered human fetuses—products of abortions—for medical research before they die is being strenuously debated by federal health officials." "Most scientists feel," the *Post* article continued, "that it is both moral and important to health progress to use some intact, living fetuses—fetuses too young and too small to live for any amount of time—for medical study . . . Such tiny infants, if delivered intact, may often live for an hour or so with beating heart after abortion. They cannot live longer without aid, primarily because their lungs are still unexpanded. But artificial aid—fresh blood and fresh oxygen—might keep them alive for three to four hours." A well-known genetics researcher was quoted in support of the research:

> I do not think it's unethical. It is not possible to make this fetus into a child, therefore we can consider it as nothing more than a piece of tissue. It is the same principle as taking a beating heart from someone and making use of it in another person.

Others quoted in the article were not readily drawn to this analogy and instead turned to alternative comparisons, expressing deep empathy for the humanity of the fetus and drawing the boundaries of life quite differently. Using a not-yet-dead but soon-to-die fetus for medical research was more like experimenting on a person without their consent.

Prompted by the revelation of the Alabama syphilis study, the National Institutes of Health (NIH) had reopened the fetal-research discussion. The parallels were readily apparent. Dr. Hellegers was quoted in opposition. "It appears that we want to make the chance for survival the reason for the experiment." When a colleague probed, "Isn't that the British approach?" Hellegers responded, "It was the German approach, 'If it is going to die, you might as well use it.'" Hellegers was concerned. The boundaries of protected life were important. They were being breached. "I include the live fetus inside the human race whether it is inside or outside the uterus." "Who are you to ask [for informed consent]," Hellegers asked, "the fetus that cannot give consent, or a mother who has already consented to the fetus' destruction?"

Where should the boundaries of protected life be drawn? How should the potential benefits of scientific research be balanced against competing values? Who should decide? These were gripping, profoundly important matters. They should not be left solely to the discretion of physicians and scientists doing the research. They were not to be dealt with behind closed doors, pressed this way or that by the politics of the moment. They should be fully aired in the light of day. Abiding principles, commanding public respect, were at stake.

Three days later, a second article appeared in the *Washington Post* in which the NIH gave assurances that it "does not now support" nor would it in the future support research on "live aborted human fetuses anyplace in the world." These assurances were made before an audience of some 200 Roman Catholic high-school students. One of the young organizers of this gathering was 17-year-old Maria Shriver, daughter of Eunice Shriver, and later the First Lady of California.

The students were not altogether convinced. Referring to a federal advisory group who supported the continuation of "planned scientific studies" of the fetus under "carefully safeguarded" conditions, one student probed, "Why are they drawing up guidelines if they don't intend to use live fetuses?" It was a good question. It turned out the student's skepticism was justified. A third *Post* article appeared two days later, reporting that the NIH was in fact funding fetal research and that some funded researchers were doing their investigations by traveling to Finland and other countries where live fetuses and fetal tissue were more accessible. The story would continue to unfold.

One of the first faculty members to join Hellegers at the Kennedy Institute had been LeRoy Walters. He had received a divinity degree from the Associated Mennonite Seminaries and his PhD in Christian ethics in 1971 from Gustafson's program at Yale. He was later asked about the concern over the NIH research:

> After the *Roe v. Wade* decision by the U.S. Supreme Court early in '73, I think people were considering the abortion question in new ways. Rumors started to float that NIH was funding some research involving living fetuses, and, though NIH denied it, I think over the course of that year it became quite clear that NIH was indeed funding such research. There were also reports found in the medical literature of quite grisly experiments involving the decapitation of live fetuses after they had been delivered through hysterotomy. So I would say it became both an ethical issue and a political issue.[22]

Still, the NIH appeared to be tightening down, leading one advocate of continued fetal research to worry, "What I fear is that the new NIH action may make the situation so rigid that all research in this area may now be foreclosed." This would be a mistake:

> Rather than it being immoral to do what we are trying to do, it is immoral—it is a terrible perversion of ethics—to throw these fetuses in the incinerator as is usually done, rather than to get some useful information.

These same arguments would be heard some three decades later, as molecular biology and associated technologies made it possible to engage in pluripotential stem cell research.[23]

In 1973, however, attention was focused on mid-term fetuses. Should this still living but not yet viable tissue be used in research to advance life-enhancing knowledge? Or, were the fetuses fully protected members of the human family, infants not to be manipulated by researchers, even to advance the common good?

The civil-rights implications of the Cincinnati, Willowbrook, and Tuskegee experiences, coupled with the abortion and right-to-life implications of the fetal research, created a powerful bipartisan coalition. Something needed to be done. Years later, the "fledging" bioethicist having lunch with Dr. Hellegers when he took the call from Eunice Shriver had become the leading historian of the bioethics movement. He wrote,

> It might be said that the bipartisan support for the legislation was motivated by the two prominent cases of the moment. The Tuskegee scandal cried out to liberals as a blatant violation of civil rights and an example of racism. The fetal research question, with its abortion implications, aroused conservatives in the pro-life camp.[24]

The stage was set for what would be the first-ever legislation calling for a government body "to identify basic ethical principles."

The Search for Common Principles

This historic legislation (Public Law 93–348) emerged in 1974 from Senator Kennedy's committee and a parallel effort by Representative

Paul Rogers in the House. President Nixon signed the bill into law in mid July. Congress had established the National Commission for the Protection of Human Subjects of Biomedical and Behavioral Research. Eleven commission members were sworn in on December 3, 1974. The first order of business was to develop recommendations on fetal research. This had become Congress's first priority, and the legislation had placed a four-month deadline on this report. There was a sense of urgent concern "that unconscionable acts involving the fetus may have been performed in the name of scientific inquiry, with only proxy consent on behalf of the fetus."[25] Until the commission's recommendations were received, there would be a moratorium on federally funded research involving "a living human fetus, before or after the induced abortion." The only exception would be research to assure the survival of the fetus.

Albert Jonsen, a member of the commission and chronicler of these events, would later note they decided to meet two days each month over the life of the project. The pressure of the congressional deadline for the fetal-research recommendations, however, "required an even more intense schedule for the first four months, during which we met seven times." The question confronting members of the commission was "on the face of it, distressing: should a living fetus be used for research? It was also perplexing because the research done on fetuses was aimed at the health of future fetuses."[26] Protective boundaries of life would have to be drawn. Values embedded in profound dilemmas would have to be weighed. The debates were "long, tortuous, and often contentious."

Jonsen also recalled that these four months would prove to be "seminal ones for bioethics." They represented a new way of doing ethics. It was in the public arena. It was outside the closed doors of academic conferences and beyond the private ruminations of scholars. As Patricia King, another member of the commission, would recall on the occasion of the twenty-fifth anniversary commemoration of the *Belmont Report*,

> It was the first national commission to operate totally in public ... the most daunting thing was to discuss issues like fetal research and abortion in public ... not behind closed doors and emerging with a consensus. The consensus had to be hashed out in front of an audience. That is quite un-nerving ... It was quite astonishing.[27]

In the end, the commission issued its report, after closer to five months than four, with one well-respected member submitting a reluctant dissent. The dissenter was not willing to consider the fetus less than human.

Once described as an "amiable, rumpled old bear," who "warmed the ground where he stood,"[28] David Louisell was a professor of law at the University of California, Berkeley. He was known for his kind demeanor and sharp wit, but also for his interest in the legal and moral implications of the biological revolution and strong opposition to the *Roe v. Wade* and *Doe v. Bolton* decisions released some two-and-a-half years earlier.[29]

The commission had issued 16 recommendations, which dealt with therapeutic as well as nontherapeutic research directed toward the fetus and pregnant mother, along with several provisions for the conduct of such research. Professor Louisell found two of these recommendations —the fifth and sixth—of particular concern. These two allowed for "nontherapeutic research directed toward the fetus in anticipation of abortion" and "nontherapeutic research directed toward the fetus during the abortion procedure and the nontherapeutic research directed toward the nonviable fetus *ex utero*."

With echoes of concerns voiced by Dr. André Hellegers, concerns that had helped precipitate the commission's creation, Professor Louisell asserted the commission's fifth and sixth recommendations were misguided, "insofar as they succumb to the error of sacrificing the interests of innocent human life to a postulated social need." He continued,

> For me the lessons of history are too poignant, and those of this century too fresh, to ignore another violation of human integrity and autonomy by subjecting unconsenting human beings, whether or not viable, to harmful research even for laudable scientific purposes.

Louisell's disagreement was not over the general ethical principles being applied by his colleagues. These he found to reflect "unquestioned morality." Rather, his objections were to where the boundaries of protected life were drawn and how the embedded dilemmas were balanced when the agreed-upon general principles were applied to particular situations.

Recommendation 5 dealt with research on the fetus in anticipation of abortion. Given the Supreme Court's abortion decisions, this law professor knew he was on thin ice legally when it came to asserting the personal autonomy and integrity of the nonviable fetus still in the womb. It did not matter. In his mind, the Court's erroneous construction of the "legal fiction of 'potential' human life," the acceptance of the idea that "human life must be 'meaningful' in order to be deserving of legal protection," and the concept of "partial human personhood," had handed the commission "an all but impossible task."

It was a task, nevertheless, they needed to perform. Abraham Lincoln's response to the *Dredd Scott* decision, a ruling where persons of black African descent were declared non-citizens, came to mind. Louisell argued that, like *Dredd Scott*, decisions such as *Roe* and *Doe* need not be extended to other situations. Even if the Court had excluded the unborn from the full protective boundaries of personhood, we should resist extension of this idea to other contexts. Research on an unborn fetus, in anticipation of abortion, was an anathema. Professor Louisell could see "no legal principle which would justify, let alone require, passive submission to such a breach of our moral commitment."

Recommendation 6 was, if anything, more troubling. It spoke of the "nonviable fetus *ex utero*." Up until that time, Louisell noted, both in law and society, a nonviable fetus *ex utero* would have been seen simply "as an infant." In his judgment, "all infants, however premature or inevitable their death, are within the norms governing human experimentation generally. We do not subject the aged dying to unconsented experimentation, nor should we the youthful dying."

Rejecting extension of the life-defining boundaries and rationale of the *Roe* and *Doe* decisions, Louisell anchored his argument in concerns similar to those expressed by Leo Alexander and Henry Beecher. He was also mindful of implications of Eleanor Roosevelt and the United Nation's efforts to identify universal human rights.

> I would, therefore, turn aside any approval, even in science's name, that would by euphemism or other verbal device, subject any unconsenting human being, born or unborn, to harmful research, even that intended to be good for society. Scientific purposes might be served by nontherapeutic research on retarded children, or brain dissection of the old who have ceased to lead "meaningful" lives, but such research is not proposed—at least not yet . . . Is it

the mere youth of the fetus that is thought to foreclose the full protection of established human experimentation norms? Such reasoning would imply that a child is less deserving of protection than an adult. But reason, our tradition, and the U.N. Declaration of Human Rights all speak to the contrary, emphasizing the need of special protection for the young.

In addition to the specific research guidelines, the commission was charged with identifying "the ethical principles which should underlie the conduct of biomedical and behavioral research with human subjects." Commission members convened to address this task in mid February, 1976, some two years after being sworn in. They gathered at the Belmont House, in Elkridge Maryland, about a 45-minute drive outside the nation's capitol. The eventual report would take its name from this bucolic setting.

The Belmont Report and the Georgetown Principles

In 1977, after the twenty-seventh meeting of the commission, a group of commissioners, consultants, and staff convened in the San Francisco study of Albert Jonsen. There had been several interim discussions and listings of possible principles with accompanying drafts of the report. The aim was to produce text that would be "succinct, easily comprehensible, and relevant to research practice."[30]

Three principles for medical research were settled upon—respect for persons (autonomy), beneficence, and justice. By design, these principles and associated guidelines were general in nature and broad in scope. They had been gleaned from the specific problems addressed. On June 10, 1978, the commission, at its forty-second gathering, finally approved a report—the Belmont Report. It, along with an extended companion book written by two young professors at about the same time, would become widely referenced touchstones in the years just ahead.

A philosophy professor associated with the Kennedy Institute at Georgetown University, Tom Beauchamp, had been asked to join the staff and take responsibility for writing what was initially referred to simply as the "Belmont Paper." By his own account, Professor Beauchamp had no sense of the widespread and lasting impact this work would have. Instead he felt he "was the new-kid-on-the-block on the staff" and that he "was getting the dregs of the assignment. Because it was what nobody else wanted to do."[31] To complete this endeavor, Beauchamp began working with his colleague Jim Childress on what would become their highly influential book, *Principles of Biomedical Ethics*.

There was some disagreement on specifics as these two works progressed, but, in the end, the Belmont Report and *Principles of Biomedical Ethics* were written simultaneously, the one influencing the other. By design, both aimed to encapsule important elements of a "common morality," principles "shared by all morally decent persons," which were "woven into the fabric of morality in morally sensitive cultures."[32] Taken together, these overlapping works would become highly influential benchmarks for bioethics. As attention increased, the framing importance of the principles enunciated, especially as developed by Beauchamp and Childress, would be referenced, and not always favorably, as the Georgetown Mantra.

When it came to the first principle: respect for persons or the idea of *autonomy*, most persons, even physicians directly involved in the recently revealed examples of disturbing medical research, would agree that individuals deserved respect as autonomous agents, and that persons with diminished capacities, such as children and the mentally handicapped, were entitled to protection.

The same held true for *beneficence*. Beneficence did not simply mean engaging in discretionary kindness or charity. Charity was a sought-after virtue, but there was more. There was a strong obligation to secure the well-being of persons, to "do no harm," and to "maximize possible benefits and minimize possible harms."

Finally, little disagreement would be found with the principle that *justice* should be advanced and protected. This seemed obvious. Given the injustices so evident in Cincinnati, Willowbrook, and Tuskegee, however, there was a need to state and clarify the obvious. Equitable treatment should be provided. There should be "fairness in distribution" of the benefits of medical research, and selected categories of persons should not be asked to shoulder an unfair amount of the burden.

Although developed in the context of medical research, these principles were applicable to a wide range of related issues. They provided a "common coin of moral discourse." As a later observer, writing in the

HCR, would put it, "The Babel of information formerly thought to be relevant to an ethical decision has been whittled down to a much more manageable level through the use of principles."[33]

Still, questions and criticisms emerged.[34] The enunciated principles failed as a straightforward guide to action. What did the "principlism" framework contained in the Belmont Report and the work of Beauchamp and Childress mean in particular situations?[35] How did these principles help resolve the sometimes competing demands to alleviate intolerable suffering and to protect life?

Bioethics in Action

As the field of bioethics matured, the newly minted principles were applied, and decisions were made, as cases emerged in specific contexts and particular circumstances. Lacking an explicit ethical road map, specific decisions became works in progress. Checklists were developed to assist physicians and ethics committees.[36] Still there were ambiguities.

Life is inherently valuable and should be protected. The alleviation of suffering and aversion to its creation are deeply seeded in our makeup. There is virtually no disagreement on these statements. Most would also agree, respect for the dignity and autonomy of the individual should be honored. Justice, accomplished through a sense of equality, opportunity, and just desserts should command respect.

When these broad principles are applied within specific circumstances, however, individuals grapple with competing conceptions of a meaningful life, tolerable suffering, and social worth. Disagreements emerge. Who should decide? Given the core importance of the imperatives involved, competing social movements are spawned, issues are framed, power is exercised, and laws are crafted and protested. Within this emotion-laden, dilemma-balancing, boundary-drawing, situational ethical matrix, justifications for violating otherwise binding moral imperatives emerge. These are the issues before us. We begin with abortion.

Notes

1   See, for example, Jacquelyn H. Hall and David D. Swenson, *Psychological and Social Aspects of Human Tissue Transplantation: Annotated Bibliography* (U.S. Department of Health, Education, and Welfare, 1968). James Carmody, *Ethical Issues in Health Services: A Report and Annotated Bibliography* (National Center for Health Services Research and Development, 1970).

2 Margaret Mead, "Toward More Vivid Utopias," *Science* 126 (1957): 957–61.
3 Van Rensselaer Potter, *Bioethics Bridge to the Future* (New York: Prentice Hall, 1971).
4 There is some academic debate over just who coined the term "bioethics." See Warren Thomas Reich's companion articles: "The Word 'Bioethics': Its Birth and the Legacies of Those who Shaped its Meaning," *Kennedy Institute of Ethics Journal* 4 (1994): 319–35; and "The Word 'Bioethics': The Struggle Over its Earliest Meanings," *Kennedy Institute of Ethics Journal* 5 (1995): 19–34.
5 See Thomas K. McElhinney and Edmund D. Pellegrino, "The Institute of Human Values in Medicine: Its Role and Influence in the Conception and Evolution of Bioethics," *Theoretical Medicine* 22 (2001): 291–317.
6 Originally called the Joseph and Rose Kennedy Institute for the Study of Human Reproduction and Bioethics.
7 M.L. Tina Stevens, *Bioethics in America: Origins and Cultural Politics* (Baltimore, MD: Johns Hopkins University Press, 2000), Chap. 2.
8 Daniel Callahan, "Bioethics as a Discipline," *The Hastings Center Studies* 1 (1973): 66–73.
9 Dianne N. Irving, "What is Bioethics?" (presented at the American Bioethics Advisory Commission, Washington, DC, 2000): 1–66.
10 See, Eileen Welsome, *The Plutonium Files: America's Secret Medical Experiments in the Cold War* (New York: The Dial Press, 1999). For an account of the Cincinnati radiation research, see Martha Stephens, *The Treatment: The Story of Those Who Died in the Cincinnati Radiation Tests* (Durham, NC: Duke University Press, 2002). For more contemporary accounts, see: Jerome Stephens, "Political, Social, and Scientific Aspects of Medical Research on Humans," *Politics and Society* 3 (1973): 409–27. Richard N. Little, Jr., "Experimentation with Human Subjects: Legal and Moral Considerations Regarding Radiation Treatment of Cancer at the University of Cincinnati College of Medicine," *Atomic Energy Law Journal* 13 (1972): 305–30.
11 This account of what transpired on the University of Cincinnati campus is taken from Stephens' reflections in *The Treatment: The Story of Those Who Died in the Cincinnati Radiation Tests* (Durham, NC: Duke University Press, 2002): 3–14.
12 Stuart Auerbach, "Faculty Study Hits Whole-Body Radiation Plan," A3.
13 David J. Rothman and Sheila M. Rothman, *The Willowbrook Wars* (New York: Harper & Row Publishers, 1984), 16.
14 Rothman and Rothman, *The Willowbrook Wars*, 16.
15 Stuart Warmflasher, *Unforgotten: Twenty-five Years After Willowbrook*, Jack Fisher, Director (City Lights Pictures).
16 As dramatic as these revelations were, there was still more. In July, 1973, *Relf v. Weinberger*, was filed in the district court in the District of Columbia on behalf of two young, mentally retarded black girls, ages 12 and 14, who had been involuntarily sterilized. During the hearings, it was learned that an estimated 100,000–150,000 similarly situated cases had been sterilized annually under federally funded programs. The effects of *Buck v. Bell* were alive and well. The district court found such procedures to be "arbitrary and unreasonable" and ordered an end to the practice. As the case wound its way through the courts, federal regulations were changed to meet the new, stricter standards for "informed consent" that were emerging. In 1977, *Relf* was remanded back to the district court for dismissal, as the issue became moot.

Parallel concerns were raised about the use of prisoners in medical research and the use of psychosurgery for behavior control. Psychosurgery for behavioral control had also become an issue depicted in the movie, *A Clockwork Orange*, and Michael Chrichton's novel *The Terminal Man*, as well as a Februrary, 1973 article in *Ebony* magazine by B.J. Mason. See also, Robert M. Veatch and Sharmon Sollitto, "Human Experimentation: The Ethical Questions Persist," *The Hastings Center Report* 3 (1973): 1–3.

17 Quoted by Jean Heller, "Syphilis Victims in the U.S. Study Went Untreated for 40 Years," *The New York Times* (July 26, 1972).

18 James H. Jones, *Bad Blood: The Tuskegee Syphilis Experiment* (New York: The Free Press, 1981): 206–7. *Atlanta Constitution*, July 26, 1972, 1A.

19 Science Policy Division, Congressional Research Service, Library of Congress, "Genetic Engineering, Evolution of a Technological Issue," report to the Subcommittee on Science, Research and Development, House Committee on Science and Astronautics, November 8, 1972, 40.

20 Jones, *Bad Blood*, 214.

21 Jonsen, *The Birth of Bioethics*, 94

22 Interview with LeRoy B. Walters, PhD (2004) Oral History of the Belmont Report and the National Commission for the Protection of Human Subjects of Biomedical and Behavioral Research, 1–2.

23 See *Guidelines for Human Embryonic Stem Cell Research* (Washington, DC: National Academies Press, 2005).

24 Jonsen, *The Birth of Bioethics*, 98.

25 *Report and Recommendations: Research on the Fetus*, The National Commission for the Protection of Human Subjects of Biomedical and Behavioral Research, 1.

26 Jonsen, *The Birth of Bioethics*, 100–1.

27 Patricia King, *The Belmont Commemoration*, Video.

28 John E. Coons, "David W. Louisell, In Memoriam," *California Law Review* 66 (1978): 934.

29 David Louisell and John T. Noonan (1970) "Constitutional Balance," in *The Morality of Abortion*, Ed. J. Noonan; David Louisell, "Biology, Law and Reason: Man as Self-Creator," *American Journal of Jurisprudence* 16 (1971): 1; David Louisell, "Euthanasia and Banthasia: On Dying and Killing," *Catholic University Law Review* 22 (1973): 723, 737.

30 Albert R. Jonsen, "On the Origins and Future of the Belmont Report," in *Belmont Revisited: Ethical Principles for Research With Human Subjects*, Eds. James F. Childress, Eric M. Meslin, and Harold T. Shapiro (Washington, DC: Georgetown University Press, 2005), 3–11.

31 Oral History of the Belmont Report and the National Commission for the Protection of Human Subjects of Biomedical and Behavioral Research, Interview with Tom Lamar Beauchamp, 6.

32 See Tom L. Beauchamp, "The Origins and Evolution of the *Belmont Report*," in *Belmont Revisited: Ethical Principles for Research With Human Subjects*, Eds. James F. Childress, Eric M. Meslin, and Harold T. Shapiro (Washington, DC: Georgetown University Press, 2005), 12–25; Tom L. Beauchamp, "The Origins, Goals, and Core Commitments of *The Belmont Report* and *Principles of Biomedical Ethics*," in *The Story*

of Bioethics: From Seminal Works to Contemporary Explorations, Eds. Jennifer K. Walter and Eran P. Klein (Washington, DC: Georgetown University Press, 2003).

33   John H. Evans "A Sociological Account of the Growth of Principlism," *Hastings Center Report* 3 (2000): 31–8.

34   K. Danner Clouser and Bernard Gert, "A Critique of Principlism," *The Journal of Medicine and Philosophy* 15 (1990): 219–36.

35   See: Edwin R. Dubose, Ronald P. Hamel, and Laurence J. O'Connell, Eds., *A Matter of Principles? Ferment in U.S. Bioethics* (Valley Forge, PA: The Trinity Press International, 1994).

36   See Albert R. Jonsen, Mark Siegler, and William Winslade, *Clinical Ethics*, 4th ed. (New York: McGraw Hill Companies, 1998).

PART II

THE EARLY MOMENTS AND MONTHS OF LIFE

CHAPTER 6

A BOLT FROM THE BLUE: ABORTION IS LEGALIZED

When does abortion become infanticide? Drawn less starkly, when does life possess properties that bring it under the "life is sacred and should be protected" umbrella? Given the high probability of disagreement, who should decide?

Many answers have been given to these now familiar questions. Religions have evolved beliefs, legislatures have passed laws, courts have articulated findings, and individuals have made choices. Politicians have taken positions, waged campaigns, won and lost elections. Scholars have worried over the fine points of philosophical and legal arguments. Activists have produced statistics, argued for the rights of the disabled, underscored the importance of privacy and choice, organized right-to-life demonstrations, bombed clinics, and murdered abortion providers. Throughout, an erratic pendulum-like swing of law, policy, and opinion, energized by the tensions of moral dilemmas and disagreements over whether all stages of human life are equally worthy of protection and support, has been generated.

This was clearly evident in the United States in the decades spanning the late nineteenth and mid twentieth centuries, when abortion was widely defined as a crime and when "periods of tolerance were punctuated by moments of severe repression."[1] The tension is no less evident in the decades following two companion, agenda-setting Supreme Court decisions in 1973,[2] legalizing abortion and seen by some as a "bolt from the blue."

Almost immediately, advocates for a woman's right to control her own body confronted those calling for protections of the unborn from the earliest moment of potential life. Interlaced were competing perceptions of injustice and legitimacy. Although manifested in any number of communities across time and around the globe,[3] these forces collided in the United States with renewed fury in what came to be called the abortion wars.

It may be that life is sacred—something that defines the core of our being, something of intrinsic value[4]—and should be protected is a moral principle always operable. The question is, when is this principle applicable. The most encompassing of all boundaries are those flowing from the idea that all life, at least all human life, is intrinsically, equally, and deeply important. There are no human lives, no moments of life more worthy of protection than others. Here, the boundaries of life do not necessarily attach to individual human beings. Instead, they encircle *LIFE* writ large. Such a view produces a very broad umbrella of protection. It anchors the Catholic Church's rationale for the regulation of contraception.

> Each and every marital act must of necessity retain its intrinsic relationship to the procreation of human life . . . We are obliged once more to declare that the direct interruption of the generative process already begun . . . [is] to be absolutely excluded as lawful means of regulating the number of children. Equally to be condemned, as the magisterium of the Church has affirmed on many occasions, is direct sterilization, whether of the man or of the woman, whether permanent or temporary . . . Similarly excluded is any action which either before, at the moment of, or after sexual intercourse, is specifically intended to prevent procreation— whether as an end or as a means.[5]

If laws were grounded in this theocratic proscription, there could be little doubt. *LIFE*, even *before* conception, would be protected. Not only would eugenics and mandatory sterilization be opposed, voluntary contraceptive measures of all kinds would be illegal. Not so long ago, throughout much of the United States, they were.

From Comstockery to the Right to Privacy

In the early 1870s, Anthony Comstock began a crusade as a quintessential moral entrepreneur.[6] Comstock was a Connecticut native who had recently returned from the Civil War and moved to New York City. He launched his efforts in the years just prior to the publication of Dugdale's study of the Jukes in New York's Hudson Valley. Comstock was appalled by the prostitution he saw on the city's streets. He was offended by readily available material he considered obscene, material including explicit advertisements for various birth-control measures. These threatened the public good. Something had to be done. As Harry Laughlin shaped the Eugenics Movement with his model sterilization law, so did Anthony Comstock shape the campaign to prohibit the production, availability, and distribution of obscene materials and articles of immoral use, including contraceptive devices.

In 1872, Comstock completed his model legislation and traveled to Washington, DC. By March of 1873, using Comstock's template, Congress passed a federal law, an "Act for the Suppression of Trade in, and Circulation of, Obscene Literature and Articles for Immoral Use." It would eventually become known simply as the Comstock Law. As related to contraception, it read:

> whoever, within the District of Columbia or any of the Territories of the United States ... shall sell ... or shall offer to sell, or to lend, or to give away, or in any manner to exhibit, or shall other-wise publish or offer to publish in any manner, or shall have in his possession ... any drug or medicine, or any article whatever, for the prevention of conception, or for causing unlawful abortion, or shall advertise the same for sale, or shall write or print, or cause to be written or printed, any card, circular, book, pamphlet, advertisement, or notice of any kind, stating when, where, how, or of whom, or by what means, any of the articles in this section ... can be purchased or obtained, or shall manufacture, draw, or print, or in any wise make any of such articles ... shall be imprisoned at hard labor in the penitentiary for not less than six months nor more than five years for each offense, or fined not less than one hundred dollars nor more than two thousand dollars, with costs of court.

Within a few years, a majority of states had passed similar laws. One of the stricter versions came in 1879 in Comstock's home state. In Connecticut, even married couples were vulnerable to a jail term for the use of birth control. Although difficult to enforce, especially when it came to the use of birth-control methods, these efforts almost immediately gave rise to a counter-crusade, the birth-control movement, and another moral entrepreneur, the enigmatic Margaret Sanger.[7] Sanger is credited with founding the American Birth Control Movement, which eventually evolved into the Planned Parenthood Federation of America. Driven by a sense of injustice and the repression of women, Sanger and those committed to the increased availability of birth-control methods challenged, even to the point of going to jail, the legitimacy of the Comstock laws.

For Sanger and her colleagues, these statutes allowed inappropriate governmental intrusion into the private lives of citizens. They manifested long-standing inequality for women and the repression of their ability to control their bodies and enjoy their lives. They meant that the poor would have more children. Disproportionately, these children would cause trouble and turn to crime, increasing the need, perhaps for eugenic measures, but most certainly for public-welfare and protective police measures. For Sanger and those who agreed, the case was clear. Persons should be able to plan their families effectively. There were means to do so. For both personal and collective-good reasons, contraceptive measures should be widely available.

In the 1930s, when the severe economic consequences of the Great Depression were felt, these arguments became ever more persuasive. Controlling the number of children became increasingly important, not only for the collective public health, as the eugenicists were arguing, but also for the well-being of individual families and prospective parents facing severe economic threats.

United States v. One Package of Japanese Pessaries marked an important turning point. Working with a physician friend in New York City in a conscious strategy of confrontational politics, Sanger had a box of sperm-blocking vaginal diaphragms (pessaries) sent from Japan. When customs officials confiscated the package, an appeal was filed, and, in 1936, the Circuit Court of New York[8] held that the package could, indeed must, be delivered, with no legal consequences for either the sender or receiver. Although the jurisdiction of this court was limited, the impact of the decision was broad. The winds of change, signaling increased availability and distribution of birth-control materials, began to blow in a consistent direction.

As demand for contraception grew, the market responded. Pharmaceutical companies expanded research and development operations, eventually producing what came to be known simply as The Pill. An early version, Enovid, was approved for the U.S. market for the regulation of menses in the late 1950s. In 1960, it was submitted to the Food and Drug Administration and approved as a birth-control pill. By today's standards, this approval was quite expeditious, proceeding as it did prior to the more thorough review protocols that emerged from the health concerns raised shortly thereafter by drugs such as Thalidomide. The approval of Enovid, along with numerous other birth-control drugs that followed, marked a dramatic improvement in both the effectiveness and convenience of birth-control options. Given this increased effectiveness and convenience, as well as the profits that could be made, challenges to state intervention began in earnest.

A version of the 1879 Connecticut Comstock statute remained on the books. Executive director of the Planned Parenthood League of Connecticut, Estelle Griswold, along with her medical director, Lee Buxton, a member of the Department of Obstetrics and Gynecology at Yale Medical School, gave a married couple information and medical advice on how to prevent conception. Following an examination, they prescribed a contraceptive measure for the wife's use. This was against the law. They were convicted. They appealed their conviction, and eventually their case was argued before the Supreme Court in March of 1965 in *Griswold v. Connecticut*.[9] A little over two months later, the birth-control prohibitions of the Connecticut statute, grounded in almost century-old legislation, were declared unconstitutional.

For most, this was an easy case. All nine of the Supreme Court justices, even those dissenting with the decision, saw the cultural lag in existing laws and agreed this anti-contraception statute was not wise, and, in the words of Justice Stewart, writing in dissent, perhaps even "silly" and "asinine":

> I think this is an uncommonly silly law. As a practical matter, the law is obviously unenforceable, except in the oblique context

of the present case. As a philosophical matter, I believe the use of contraceptives in the relationship of marriage should be left to personal and private choice, based upon each individual's moral, ethical, and religious beliefs. As a matter of social policy, I think professional counsel about methods of birth control should be available to all, so that each individual's choice can be meaning-fully made. But we are not asked in this case to say whether we think this law is unwise, or even asinine.

Justice Stewart's point was clear. Laws were not unconstitutional simply because judges felt they were unwise or otherwise out of line with their personal beliefs about the economic or social health of the community. Nor was the job of a judge to issue court decisions from personal convictions that the Constitution was more generally out of step with the times and in need of modification. Ironically, the same judge who had so forcibly noted, "three generations of imbeciles are enough," had made these points many years earlier.[10] The disagreement among the nine justices deciding *Griswold* was not over the substance of the Connecticut statue, but over who should resolve the perceived flaws.

Nowhere in the Constitution is birth control mentioned. Nowhere in the Bill of Rights are there references to family planning. Why, then, were laws prohibiting the use of birth-control methods unconstitutional? Assuming that any decision by the Supreme Court would need to be anchored in the Constitution, not personal beliefs, where should the justices look? Specific reasons were found in the penumbras of general principles. "The Bill of Rights," Justice Douglas argued for the majority in *Griswold*, "have penumbras, formed by emanations from those guarantees that help give them life and substance."

In particular, the court found protections of individual autonomy embedded in the not precisely articulated implications of the First, Fourth, Fifth, Ninth, and Fourteenth Amendments. The common penumbral collection point, Justice Douglas argued, was the right to privacy.

The present case, then, concerns a relationship lying within the zone of privacy created by several fundamental constitutional guarantees. And it concerns a law which, in forbidding the use of contraceptives, rather than regulating their manufacture or sale, seeks to achieve its goals by means having a maximum destructive impact upon that relationship. Such a law cannot stand in light of the familiar principle, so often applied by this Court, that a governmental purpose to control or prevent activities constitutionally subject to state regulation may not be achieved by means which sweep unnecessarily broadly and thereby invade the area of protected freedoms.

Whether Justice Douglas had in mind the unnecessarily broad sweep of legal provisions Justice Holmes had supported in *Buck v. Bell* is difficult to tell. Whether he also thought of the tragic consequences of medical experimentations without a patient's consent was unclear. Whatever the roots of his reasoning, the majority of the court found the sweep of the Connecticut statute unnecessarily broad. Married couples should have the right to choose to use contraceptive measures.

In a case decided some seven years later,[11] this right was extended, for reasons of equity, to unmarried persons as well. In this case, William Baird had been convicted of two offenses committed while lecturing on contraception to an audience at Boston University. He had exhibited contraceptive articles and, at the end of the lecture, had given a package of Emko vaginal foam to a young woman in the audience. By so doing, he was in violation of Massachusetts' law. Baird's convictions were appealed. The Supreme Court's rationale for overturning the conviction was straightforward.

If under *Griswold* the distribution of contraceptives to married persons cannot be prohibited, a ban on distribution to unmarried persons would be equally impermissible. It is true that in *Griswold* the right of privacy in question inhered in the marital relationship. Yet the marital couple is not an independent entity with a mind and heart of its own, but an association of two individuals each with a separate intellectual and emotional makeup. If the right of privacy means anything, it is the right of the individual, married or single, to be *free from unwarranted governmental intrusion into matters so fundamentally affecting a person as the decision whether to bear or beget a child* [emphasis added].

The arrest and conviction of William Baird had occurred in Connecticut's New England neighbor, Massachusetts. It was not an unwelcome event for Baird. As a participant with a group of birth-control activists engaged in confrontation politics, Baird had been prodding law-enforcement officials for some time to arrest him for breaking birth-control laws he considered unjust. His Boston University lecture had been part of these activities.

With these two Supreme Court decisions, victory could be declared. New England had been the region of the country with the most stringent Comstock laws. These laws were now dead. The boundaries of *LIFE* protected by the community's legal system did not extend prior to conception to choices regarding contraception. In addition, and importantly, to those paying attention, the last sentence in the above excerpt was important. The court had done more than establish the right of unmarried persons to use contraceptive measures, free from governmental interference. The stage was set to restrict governmental intrusion even further. Privacy included decisions to "bear or beget a child."

The right to privacy, found in the penumbras of the Bill of Rights and the Fourteenth Amendment, was thereby established. In the time between *Griswold and Baird*, the Supreme Court had also overturned the 1924 Virginia law prohibiting interracial marriages in 1967.[12] Although the constitutional grounding for this latter decision was racial discrimination, the right to choose your marriage partner had clear implications for individual autonomy and the general right to make very personal choices without governmental intrusion.

Legal scholars would continue to argue over whether privacy could be found in the shadowed language of the Constitution, but for most citizens the articulated restrictions on governmental intrusion when it came to contraception and choosing a marriage partner seemed quite reasonable. There were realms of individual autonomy and dignity into which the government should not intrude. Now the question became, was the decision to terminate pregnancy in the same category? Here, there was far less consensus.

Although privacy and the right to choose are important, very few argue they are absolute. How far does the right to privacy extend, and where does the autonomy and sanctity of the newly forming life, with associated protections, begin? At what point does state intrusion become compelling?

Potential for Life, Potential for Suffering

The court's conclusions regarding privacy, however vague or clear, anchored in penumbras of constitutional language or not, were not reached in a vacuum. Importantly, a broad-based civil rights movement designed to establish a more inclusive structuring of society and a more equitable standing for women in particular was gaining momentum. In addition, stunning advances in understanding the process of reproduction were being secured. Techniques to observe, determine, and understand intra-uterine developments were improved. Life-prolonging medical protocols and organ-transplantation procedures were introduced and perfected. Immediately prior to the *Roe* decision, a series of lectures had been given at Yale University that resulted in the publication of *The Patient as Person*. As detailed previously, these lectures and publication marked an important moment for a soon-to-be-thriving field of study — bioethics.

Justices in the Supreme Court were clearly aware of these events. They were also aware of heightened concerns about the potential quality of life for the yet-to-be-born. These concerns were intensified first by the side effects of the drug Thalidomide and then by a pandemic associated with what came to be known as congenital rubella syndrome. Alleviation of the potential suffering of the yet-to-be-born would collide with the imperative to protect potential life.

In 1962, Sherri Finkbine was the host of a Phoenix-based edition of the popular children's show, *Romper Room*. She was also the mother of four children under the age of seven and pregnant with what would be her fifth child. Early in her pregnancy, she had been taking a drug her husband, a local high-school teacher, had purchased on a trip to London to help her sleep and deal with morning sickness. This drug turned out to be the strongest available dosage of Thalidomide. When she became aware, through recently released clinical reports, that Thalidomide might be associated with very serious, crippling birth defects, she went to her doctor for advice. He "firmly" suggested that she have a therapeutic abortion. As she later recalled, "In talking it over with my [obstetrician], he said, 'Sherri, if you were my own wife and we two had four small children, and you really wanted a fifth child, I'd say start again next month under better odds.'"[13]

At that time in Arizona, early-term abortions were available through a walking-on-the-edge-of-the-law interpretation of the Arizona statute wherein the woman's physician agreed that abortion was appropriate, and a three-member therapeutic abortion board at the hospital concurred. Although her doctor recommended against going to a local Catholic hospital where her last baby had been born, he was confident that approval would be a mere formality at a local public hospital. It was. The procedure was scheduled for the next Monday morning.

Knowing that a local Air National Guard unit had been recently assigned to duty related to the Berlin Wall crisis, and fearing that some of these families might also purchase the drug as her husband had done, Finkbine decided to call a friend who worked for the local newspaper to relate her story and alert others. Monday morning the bold headline read, "Baby-deforming drug may cost woman her child here." Reading the headline and recognizing that their approval of this, as well as many other therapeutic abortions, might cross a line in any strict reading of the Arizona statute, hospital doctors and administrators immediately cancelled the scheduled procedure.

What initially promised to be an almost automatic approval soon became something quite different. The national wire services picked up the story. Prominent papers across the country, as well as the international press, ran features. Sherri and her husband received thousands of letters. Death threats were made, and FBI protection for the Finkbines was secured. Eventually, after being turned down for her application to have an abortion in Japan, Sherri Finkbine was granted permission to go to Sweden, where she had an abortion in the fourth month of her pregnancy. There, the doctor reported the fetus was so seriously deformed it would not have survived. In the aftermath, both Sherri and her husband lost their jobs, Sherri being told by the vice president of the NBC affiliate that she was no longer fit to handle children.[14]

By all accounts, this heart-wrenching, widely publicized case marked an important crystallizing event, clarifying issues and motivating reform. As one author, echoed by many others, noted, the refusal to grant a legal abortion in these dramatic conditions marked a point "when a diffuse dissatisfaction with the law began to crystallize into an organized movement to change the law."[15]

Further impetus for change came from an unexpected source. Rubella or "German measles" had been recognized for more than 200 years.[16] In the early 1940s, it had been linked to a wide range of abnormalities, including congenital heart defects, deafness, cataracts and glaucoma, and severe to moderate psychomotor retardation, along with a mortality rate approaching 10–15 percent. Epidemics of rubella seemed to occur on an irregular cycle of six to nine years. A large-scale pandemic swept across Europe and the United States between 1964 and 1966. Estimates of the impact found their way to 1969 Senate hearings[17] and indicated in the United States there had been some 50,000 abnormal pregnancies, including 20,000 newborns with birth defects and something on the order of 30,000 fetal deaths. Physicians, women, and families all over the country struggled with how to balance conflicting beliefs, demands, and feelings. Abortion laws were restrictive, but, as illustrated in Arizona, open to interpretation and physician discretion. Public opinion polls indicated a fairly even split in support for abortion when birth defects were anticipated.

The issue came to a head in 1966 when a member of the California Board of Medical Examiners, who had taken a strong stance against abortion, initiated proceedings to revoke the licenses of nine prominent, well-respected San Francisco physicians who had been performing abortions for mothers exposed to rubella. Their actions were contrary to an almost century-old California statute rooted in Comstock-era legislation.[18] Faced with the loss of their licenses, a spokesman for the physicians, who came to be known as the "San Francisco Nine," questioned the law's legitimacy based on their professional responsibilities. "We do not believe that violation of an archaic statue is unprofessional conduct."[19] For these physicians, the law was archaic and unjust, preventing a humane, professional response to families confronting potentially tragic situations. They were not alone.

A Social Movement Splinters

In the 1950s, concerned physicians, along with the organizational legacy of Margaret Sanger, Planned Parenthood, had joined hands with a group of legal scholars to draft a model abortion statute as part of the American Law Institute's MPC initiative.[20] The Comstock laws were only one example of penal codes throughout the country in need of rethinking and reform. The section of the MPC dealing with abortion was completed in 1959. It provided for abortions when there was substantial risk to the physical or mental health of the pregnant woman, when congenital defects were indicated, and when the pregnancy was the result of rape, incest, or "felonious intercourse." This template would serve much the same purpose as Harry Laughlin's work on a model statute for eugenic sterilization had done in 1922, as well as Comstock's original template prohibiting contraception. It guided and made uniform the statutes passed by states in the coming years.

With this model statute in hand, a few states passed new legislation in the early to mid 1960s to allow abortions in the case of rape and when the woman's physical or mental health was at stake. It was, however, the widespread publicity of Sherri Finkbine's experience with Thalidomide, along with the threat of birth defects resulting from the rubella outbreak and the resulting move to prosecute nine highly respected physicians, that galvanized reform efforts.

In response to these crystallizing events, the public conscience awakened. Personal and professional networks were activated, resources secured, and plans of action developed. Some 200 physicians from all across the country, along with deans of 128 medical schools, filed a brief on behalf of the San Francisco Nine.[21] Their concerns would be broadened immediately by other activists encouraged by the right to privacy secured the previous year in *Griswold*. These crosscutting efforts would soon divide the abortion-reform movement. The splintering was evident prior to the threat to revoke licenses of the San Francisco Nine and would deepen as reformers asked, "Who should decide?"—physicians, advisory boards, or women?[22]

Efforts to reform California's Comstock-era abortion statute were initiated in 1961, a year before Sherri Finkbine's struggle with the effects of Thalidomide. A bill was filed, based on the ALI's proposal. Hearings were held, but the bill died in committee. Two years later, in the aftermath of the now widespread concern with Thalidomide, the Society for Humane Abortion (SHA) was founded in San Francisco. SHA soon became a well-organized effort to collectively argue for a woman's unbridled right to choose.

This effort was spearheaded by Patricia Maginnis, quoted by one of her colleagues as stating, "Law enforcement from [the Attorney General of California] to the policeman on the street, realizes that once the law stands trial in court, it will collapse."[23] She aimed to make this happen. An active supporter of the 1961 reform legislation, Maginnis, once described as a frail, yet tough woman with a high-pitched voice, a flamboyant style, and words that stung, had become convinced that the proposed changes in the law were too timid. Leaving the final decision in the hands of individual physicians and hospital therapeutic abortion committees, such as had been done in Arizona, was a mistake. Instead, the SHA argued, "The termination of pregnancy is a decision which the person or family involved should be free to make as their own religious beliefs, values, emotions, and circumstances may dictate."[24]

Thus, there were competing interests among advocates for reform of the abortion laws—women's rights advocates bumped against physicians and others who would leave the decision in the hands of the doctors and therapeutic committees. Members of the SHA were unequivocal in arguing for the primacy of a woman's right to choose. As a result, there was a growing concern among physicians about their loss of professional discretion, along with criminal liabilities they might confront. With these competing versions of reform framed, a second round of hearings was held in the California legislature in 1964.

By then, the rubella pandemic was at full force. The heart-wrenching impact of the Thalidomide tragedies was evident. Each of these events shifted and intensified the debate. On the one hand, laws needed to be reformed to remove the criminal liability of physicians and to directly address the need for professional discretion. On the other hand, having a child with severe physical or mental problems would not only affect the existing family, but also future decisions to have additional children. Mothers should have a controlling say in the pattern and consequences of their child-bearing.

In counterbalance, the Catholic Church's leadership continued a strong lobbying effort in opposition to abortion in any form. Ironically, they also found strength in the Thalidomide and rubella events. Did not concerns for the quality of life of the yet-to-be-born child recognize there was a life worthy of protection? In what sense did the potential for birth defects make this life less valuable? Tests and existing evidence might suggest the high probability of birth defects, but very little about how severe these defects might be. How much would the quality of life be reduced and suffering encountered? What difference did it make?

These are not easy questions. No easy answers were forthcoming. Given competing interest groups—professional, personal, and religious—the 1964 hearings in the California legislature again ended in no formal action, this time following a much more contentious debate. The now heated and divisive political climate surrounding abortion reform in California was mirrored in New York, Colorado, Illinois, and other states.

Previously, physicians had surmised that easing the restrictive physician discretion laws would be relatively straightforward, as it would simply formalize existing practices into law. Following the 1964 hearings, however, it was clear that those calling for abortion on demand, as well as those adamantly opposed to abortion under any circumstances, were generating strong, effective opposition to leaving the decision in the hands of doctors and hospital committees. Organized efforts to advance the interests of physicians and therapeutic abortion committees would be required.

Like-minded colleagues supporting a bill patterned after the ALI physician discretion recommendations decided to convene a meeting. This gathering included professors, lawyers, social workers, and public-health professionals. Out of these meetings and discussions, the California Committee on Therapeutic Abortions (CCTA) was formed. Drafting statements aimed at convincing the public that the current law was inequitable and a barrier to good health care was the first order of business.[25] With carefully crafted statements in hand and a plan of action developed, the CCTA launched an initiative to educate the public and solicit support for the Beilenson Bill, named after the sponsoring Beverly Hills state senator, Anthony Beilenson.

This time, they were successful. In 1967, the Beilenson Bill passed. The campaign of the CCTA had received unexpected support from a backlash against the effort to professionally "defrock" the San Francisco Nine. Money, a letter-writing campaign, and a nationwide support group among physicians coalesced to pressure the California legislature for reform of the state's 1872 statute.

The Beilenson Bill included provisions for physician discretion and the establishment of therapeutic abortion boards. These individuals and boards could consider both the physical and mental health of the woman and circumstances when the pregnancy was the result of rape or incest, including cases of statutory rape when the woman was below the age of 15. Addressing the issue of potential birth defects, all initial versions of the bill also included provisions for the consideration of "fetal indications."

Given that much of the impetus for reform had emerged from the rubella outbreak and the Thalidomide scare, these latter provisions were to be expected. Last-minute negotiations with the governor and his advisers, however, led to the deletion of this portion of the bill. In the end, Governor Ronald Reagan, later known for his adamant anti-abortion stand,[26] signed the Beilenson Bill, without the provisions for "fetal indications." With the governor's signature, this bill became one of the most important pieces of abortion legislation to date. As important as this legislation was, counter-pressures inherent in the deeply embedded moral dilemmas would not go away. These opposing pressures would be highlighted with the conviction of a doctor who was an active member of the CCTA.

A Bolt from the Blue

Even as the Beilenson Bill was being crafted, debated, and passed, an abortion case was winding its way to the California Supreme Court. A young, then unmarried, woman had become pregnant. She and the father had seen Dr. Leon Belous on television advocating change in California abortion laws. Dr. Belous was a long-practicing physician specializing in obstetrics and gynecology. He was also a member of the Board of Directors of the California Committee on Therapeutic Abortion. The couple had written down his telephone number from the television show and later called him, asking for assistance in securing an abortion.

After an examination confirmed her pregnancy, the woman and the father pleaded in an emotional office visit with Dr. Belous for assistance. There was no immediate threat to the woman's health. There were no indications of fetal defects. Nevertheless, the couple told the doctor they would secure an abortion, one way or another, even if they had to go to Tijuana, Mexico. Dr. Belous insisted he did not perform abortions, but, in response to their continued pleadings and his concern for the mother's health and safety if she went to Tijuana for an abortion, he gave them a telephone number of an acquaintance who performed abortions in a neighboring city. He also gave the woman a prescription for antibiotics and instructed her to return for an examination if she decided to go through with the abortion.

The abortion was performed. As the mother was resting, the police, having been informed that an unlicensed doctor from Mexico was performing abortions, came into the office-apartment to arrest him. In the process, they discovered notebooks containing the names of other patients and numerous physicians, including Dr. Belous. On the basis of this information, they arrested Dr. Belous under the same 1872 statute used against the San Francisco Nine.

Dr. Belous was convicted after a jury trial in 1967, the same year the Beilenson Bill was passed. He received a $5,000 fine and two years' probation. He appealed this decision to the Supreme Court of California. In many ways foreshadowing the U.S. Supreme Court's *Roe* and *Doe* decisions, and cited in both, the California court overturned the conviction, finding the wording "necessary to preserve her life" too vague and uncertain to pass California constitutional muster. They also noted the recent finding in *Griswold*, as well as several of their own decisions that protected "right of privacy" or "liberty" in matters related to marriage, family, and sex.

As a final consideration of the state's duty to balance protections of the mother with those of the unborn, the court held "there are major and decisive areas where the embryo and fetus are not treated as equivalent to the born child," and that "the law has always recognized that the pregnant woman's right to life takes precedence over any interest the State may have in the unborn." With these conclusions, the Supreme Court of California became the first in the nation to strike down an abortion statute.[27] It did so in a classic case of abortion on demand.

Throughout the 1960s, the collective climate of perceived injustice and illegitimacy was strong. The Civil Rights Movement was in full swing. In 1963, Martin Luther King, Jr. had been arrested in Birmingham, Alabama, where he wrote and disseminated his widely read, "Letter from Birmingham Jail." That same year, he, along with some 200,000 supporters, had gathered in Washington, DC, for what became his "I have a dream" speech. A year later, the landmark 1964 Civil Rights Act was passed and signed into law by President Johnson. Urban riots spread across the country, including one in Watts, California, in 1965. That same year, Malcolm X was shot to death while delivering a speech in the Audubon Ballroom in the Washington Heights district of New York City. By 1966, "Black Power" had become part of the political discourse. In 1968, Martin Luther King, Jr. and Robert Kennedy were shot, and protests against the Vietnam War were gaining momentum.

In 1970, National Guardsmen shot and killed four students and wounded nine others during a war protest on the Kent State campus in Ohio.

It was in this climate, when every public opinion poll indicated a substantial decline in the trust, respect, and perceived legitimacy of governmental actions and policies, that the National Organization for Women was launched. NOW, eventually claiming half a million members, soon became a rallying point for a wide range of the Women's Movement. Although the right of a woman to choose to terminate her pregnancy was originally not a central concern NOW addressed, for many it was a cornerstone. As one activist associated with the Society for Human Abortion reported in a subsequent interview:

> Without that right, we'd have about as many rights as the cow in the pasture that's taken to the bull once a year. You could give her all those rights, too, but they wouldn't mean anything; if you can't control your own body you can't control your future.[28]

One of NOW's founders, Betty Friedan, soon became convinced and joined forces with author Lawrence Lader and prominent physician Dr. Benard Nathanson. These three, high-profile advocates for abortion rights helped convene a group of like-minded colleagues, and, in 1969, the National Association for the Repeal of Abortion Laws (NARAL), eventually known as NARAL Pro-Choice America, was founded.

Before the founding of NARAL, Lader had published an influential book titled simply, *Abortion*, as well as an earlier, well-received biography of Margaret Sanger. Using Sanger as a model, Lader had been one of the architects of the abortion movement's "confrontation politics." This strategy had resulted in a number of arrests, including the 1968 arrest of a Washington, DC, abortion provider, Dr. Milan Vuitch, whose case eventually came to the Supreme Court. In 1971, one day before the justices agreed to hear *Roe v. Wade* and *Doe v. Bolton*, the Court issued an intentionally crafted compromise in the Vuitch case,[29] finding that the concept of the woman's health included psychological as well as physical well-being and establishing the importance of a physician's professional judgment and discretion in abortion decisions. *United States v. Vuitch*, along with Lader's book, *Abortion*, would be repeatedly cited in the *Roe* and *Doe* decisions.

The third cofounder of NARAL, Bernard Nathanson, was a New York physician and at one time director of the largest abortion clinic in New York City. Perhaps reflecting, at a personal level, the moral dilemma playing out on the public stage, he soon became alienated from the practice of abortion and, after the *Roe* and *Doe* decisions, joined forces with the right-to-life movement. He would go on to produce and narrate the widely circulated, and some would claim incendiary, film, *The Silent Scream*.

These personal, professional, and association networks, embedded in, and bridging across, such organizations as ALI, SHA, CCTA, NOW, and NARAL, mobilized resources in a nationwide social movement to secure more liberalized abortion laws. By 1972, the year prior to the *Roe* and *Doe* decisions, some 16 states had enacted liberalized abortion statutes based largely on the Model Penal Code of the ALI.[30] Four states, including California after the *Belous* case and a subsequent decision in 1972 declaring portions of the 1967 abortion legislation unconstitutional, had statutes allowing for abortion on demand, as long as it was performed by a licensed physician.

Two days after *Roe* and *Doe* were announced, the *New York Times* editorialized that the decisions offered "a sound foundation for final and reasonable resolution" of the abortion debate. Many abortion activists were ready to declare, "Mission accomplished." Except for the political clout of the Catholic Church, the right-to-life advocates had yet to gather counterbalancing effectiveness.

This would change with the Supreme Court's action in *Roe* and *Doe*. What advocates for freedom-of-choice and physicians' discretion hailed as a victory had an opposite and galvanizing effect on those who opposed abortion. *Roe* and *Doe* went against everything they believed in. How could the Supreme Court say the Constitution of the United States— THE CONSTITUTION OF THE UNITED STATES!—excluded the unborn from fully protected persons?

As Kristin Luker notes from her interviews with activists, the mobilizing impact of Justice Blackmun's majority opinion was immediate—a bolt from the blue. More people joined the pro-life movement in 1973 than in any other year, reporting they were moved to do so the very day the decision was handed down.[31]

These now awakened activists would soon become a force to be reckoned with. They would advance a very different conception of the protected boundaries of life than the Supreme Court had outlined and would draw upon personal and faith-based networks to mobilize resources and build an empathetic identification with the unborn child from the moment of conception. If the law of the land did not protect life, the law of the land was unjust and illegitimate. It needed to be changed, ignored, or intentionally disobeyed. Some went even further, advocating violent action—up to and including the taking of life to protect life. The vehemence of the reaction was not altogether anticipated by the Supreme Court justices, crafting an opinion to more clearly draw the boundaries around protected life.

Notes

1   Leslie J. Reagan, *When Abortion Was a Crime: Women, Medicine, and Law in the United States, 1867–1973* (Berkeley, CA: University of California Press, 1997), 14.

2   *Roe v. Wade*, 410 U.S. 113 (1973). *Doe v. Bolton*, 410 U.S. 179 (1973).

3   See Rebecca Cook, "Developments in Abortion Laws: Comparative and International Perspectives," *Annals of the New York Academy of Sciences, Medical Ethics at the Dawn of the 21st Century* 913 (2000): 74–87. See also, www.newsbatch.com/abort.htm.

4   Something is intrinsically valuable "if its value is *independent* of what people happen to enjoy or want or need or what is good for them . . . Something is sacred or inviolable when its deliberate destruction would dishonor what ought to be honored." Ronald Dworkin, *Life's Dominion: An Argument About Abortion, Euthanasia, and Individual Freedom* (New York: Alfred A. Knopf, 1993): 71–4.

5   Pope Paul VI, "On the Regulation of Birth," *Humanae Vitae Encyclical*, July 25, 1968.

6   See Howard Becker, *Outsiders: Studies in the Sociology of Deviance* (New York: The Free Press of Glencoe, 1963), 147–63.

7   Esther Katz, Cathy Moran Hajo, and Peter C. Engelman, Eds., *The Selected Papers of Margaret Sanger* (Urbana, IL and Chicago: University of Illinois Press, 2003).

8   *United States v. One Package of Japanese Pessaries*, 86 F.2d 737 (2nd Cir. 1936).

9   *Griswold v. Connecticut*, 381 U.S. 479 (1965).

10 Oliver Wendell Holmes, dissent in *Lochner v. New York*, 198 U.S. 45 (1905).

11 *Eisenstadt v. Baird*, 405 U.S. 438 (1972) 405 U.S. 438.

12 *Loving v. Virginia*, 388 U.S. 1 (1967).

13 See Kristin Luker's interviews as reported in *Abortion and the Politics of Motherhood* (Berkeley, CA: University of California Press, 1984): 62–5.

14 James Risen and Judy L. Thomas, *Wrath of Angels: The American Abortion War* (New York: Basic Books, 1998), 14.

15 R. Sauer, "Attitudes to Abortion in America, 1800–1973," *Population Studies* 28 (1974): 53–67.

16 Jude Nicholas, "Congenital Rubella Syndrome, Neuropsychological Functioning and Implications Illustrated by a Case Study," 9330 Dronninglund, Denmark: Nordic Staff Traning Centre for Deafblind Services (NUD) 2000.

17   Statement by Virginia Apgar, M.D., vice president for medical affairs, The National Foundation—March of Dimes, to Subcommittee on Health, Senate Committee on Labor and Public Welfare, June 30, 1969.

18   C.E. Joffe, T.A. Weitz, and C.L. Stacey, "Uneasy Allies: Pro-Choice Physicians, Feminist Health Activists and the Struggle for Abortion Rights," *Sociology of Health and Illness* 26 (2004): 775–96.

19   *Honoring San Francisco's Abortion Pioneers—A Celebration of Past and Present Medical Public Health Leadership* (San Francisco: Center for Reproductive Health Research & Policy, 1953).

20   Sanford Kadish, "Fifty Years of Criminal Law: An Opinionated Review," *California Law Review* 87 (1999). Drew Halfmann, "Historical Priorities and the Response of Doctors' Associations to Abortion Reform Proposals in Britain and the United States, 1960–1973," *Social Problems* 50 (2003): 567–91.

21   *Honoring San Francisco's Abortion Pioneers—A Celebration of Past and Present Medical Public Health Leadership* (San Francisco, CA: Center for Reproductive Health Research & Policy, 1953).

22   Luker (1984) has provided a detailed, well researched, and wonderfully balanced book on these and associated events.

23   Lawrence Lader, *Abortion II: Making the Revolution* (Boston, MA: Beacon Press, 1973), 32.

24   Reagan, L. (1997): 223–224.

25   Luker (1984): 84.

26   Ronald Reagan, "Abortion and the Conscience of the Nation," *The Human Life Review* (1983).

27   *People v. Belous*, 71 Cal.2d 954, 458 P.2d 194, 80 Cal.Rptr. 354 (1969)

28   Luker (1984): 97.

29   Greenhouse (2005): 76–8.

30   Edward Duffy, *The Effects of Changes in the State Abortion Laws* (Washington, DC: U.S. Department of Health, Education, and Welfare, Public Health Service, 1971).

31   Luker (1984): 137.

CHAPTER 7

MAN'S LAW OR GOD'S WILL

When *Roe v. Wade*, from Texas, and *Doe v. Bolton*, from Georgia, were originally scheduled for argument before the Supreme Court in 1971, there were only seven justices on the court. For reasons of failing health, two justices had retired in September of that year. As a result, Chief Justice Burger set up a committee to screen cases and recommend which were controversial enough to be postponed until a full nine-member court could be convened, and which could move forward easily with only seven justices participating. Having heard mainly from broad-based, well-organized constituencies favoring liberalized abortion laws, and having been influenced by the searing impact of the Thalidomide tragedies and widespread birth defects resulting from the rubella pandemic, the initial thinking was that the abortion cases could be quietly decided on narrow grounds.

In a note written several years later to then Chief Justice Rehnquist, Justice Blackmun recalled his participation on this committee:

> I remember that the Old Chief appointed a screening committee, chaired by Potter, to select cases that could (it was assumed) be adequately heard by a Court of seven. I was on that little committee. We did not do a good job. Potter pressed for *Roe v. Wade* and *Doe v. Bolton* to be heard and did so in the misapprehension

that they involved nothing more than an application of *Younger v. Harris*. How wrong we were.[1]

Landmark Cases Take Shape

Blackmun's original draft of a possible decision in the *Roe* case, written in 1971, ran to some 17 pages and concentrated on the relatively narrow question of whether the wording of the Texas statute was too vague. There was no need, Blackmun felt, to even consider privacy and the rights of the fetus. This narrowly drawn approach, however, met with opposition from other members of the still seven-justice court.

A related case from Georgia, *Doe v. Bolton*, was heard at the same time. Whereas the *Roe* case from Texas reflected a law firmly rooted in late-nineteenth-century legislation, the case from Georgia was of more recent vintage. It directly reflected recommendations made in 1959 by the ALI. Both cases raised issues of privacy, which had been addressed in several recent Court cases. *Eisenstadt*, in particular and perhaps purposefully, had incorporated wording, "If the right to privacy means anything, it is the right . . . to bear or beget a child."[2]

Clearly, this wording had implications for abortion cases such as *Roe* and *Doe*. Given the ensuing discussion among the justices, the court decided to reargue both cases when the court was at full strength. Eventually, the *Roe* decision, now three times as long as Blackmun's original draft, would be the lead case. It addressed privacy as applied to a woman's right to decide to terminate her pregnancy, the state's dual interest in protecting the life and health of the mother and the boundaries of protected life for the fetus.

The court released its *Roe* and *Doe* decisions on January 22, 1973. This date was not accidental. Chief Justice Burger, President Nixon's first appointment to the court, feared the decision might be politically embarrassing to the president. He delayed submitting his short, concurring opinion until two days before President Nixon was sworn into office for his second term. This delayed the release of the *Roe* and *Doe* decisions until after Inauguration Day.[3] Immediate political embarrassment was avoided, but the controversy remained very much alive. The *Roe* and *Doe* decisions intensified the debate, set the stage for questioning the legitimacy of the law on moral as well as procedural grounds, and thereby lit the fuse for violence.

Legitimacy Questioned

A few months after the *Roe* decision, a well-respected Yale law professor, John Hart Ely, sowed the early seeds of questioned legitimacy in an article that became one of the most widely cited pieces in the history of the *Yale Law Journal*.[4] For Ely, it was not so much what was decided, but who made the decision. The influence of Ely's piece stemmed in part from his thoughtful articulation of his argument. It was further strengthened because he was himself a supporter of abortion rights. "Were I a legislator," Ely wrote, "I would vote for a statute very much like the one the Court ends up drafting."[5]

The Supreme Court, however, should not be in the business of drafting legislation. To secure legitimacy for their decisions, the court needed to make a connection with constitutional issues and not ground their findings in personal values or policy preferences. This, Ely argued, had not been done.

> Even though a human life, or a potential human life, hangs in the balance, the moral dilemma abortion poses is so difficult as to be heartbreaking. What they [the Supreme Court justices] fail to do is even begin to resolve that dilemma so far as our governmental system is concerned by associating either side of the balance with a value inferable from the Constitution. *Roe* was a bad decision because it was a groundless intrusion by one branch of government into matters best left to the jurisdiction of another.

The majority of justices on the court, of course, disagreed. Indeed, the court had anticipated much of Ely's argument:

> We forthwith acknowledge our awareness of the sensitive and emotional nature of the abortion controversy, of the vigorous opposing views, even among physicians, and of the deep and seemingly absolute convictions that the subject inspires. One's philosophy, one's experiences, one's exposure to the raw edges of human existence, one's religious training, one's attitudes toward life and family and their values, and the moral standards one establishes and seeks to observe, are all likely to influence and to color one's thinking and conclusions about abortion.

Our task, of course, is to resolve the issue by constitutional measurement, free of emotion and of predilection. We seek earnestly to do this.

A little over two decades later, the abortion debate had gained intensity. It dominated political campaigns. Additional court decisions had been released, and disagreements over abortion had become part of what some saw as a cultural war.[6] A symposium on the topic was published in 1996, by a group of influential scholars, in *First Things*.[7] Editors of *First Things*, commenting on what they saw as the Supreme Court's abuse of power, were worried.

They wondered whether, "We are witnessing the end of democracy." These same editors asserted in even more dramatic terms, "Law, as it is presently made by the judiciary, has declared its independence from morality. Among the most elementary principles of Western Civilization is the truth that laws which violate the moral law are null and void and must in conscience be disobeyed." "What is happening now," the editors continued, "is the displacement of a constitutional order by a regime that does not have, will not obtain, and cannot command the consent of the people." This left the editors wondering "whether we have reached or are reaching the point where conscientious citizens can no longer give moral assent to the existing regime."

These are very serious assertions. For contributors to the symposium, the questioned legitimacy of judicial usurpation of legislative decisions went beyond considerations of abortion, but abortion was the linchpin. As one claimed, "The Supreme Court made abortion the benchmark of its own legitimacy, and indeed the token of the American political covenant."[8] As might be expected, such claims generated a good deal of controversy, even among contributors to the symposium and those serving on the editorial advisory board.[9] For some citizens, more removed from the academic fine points being drawn, the case was clear. Driven by an allegiance to a higher law they found in biblical scripture, withdrawal of legitimacy was complete. An unjust law was no law at all. Violence followed.

A Clash of Absolutes?

As the battleground of *Roe* and *Doe* took shape, abortion laws then in effect dated mainly from the latter half of the nineteenth century.

Over these years, medical advances had been made. Law lagged behind. When the majority of laws criminalizing abortion were enacted, antiseptic techniques and antibiotics were not widely used or available. It could be argued, indeed it was argued, that the real focus of these early criminal abortion laws was not to protect the unborn. Rather they were designed to protect the life of the pregnant woman.

As the *Roe* Court put it:

> The State has a legitimate interest in seeing to it that abortion, like any other medical procedure, is performed under circumstances that insure maximum safety for the patient. This interest obviously extends at least to the performing physician and his staff, to the facilities involved, to the availability of after-care, and to adequate provision for any complication or emergency that might arise. The prevalence of high mortality rates at illegal "abortion mills" strengthens, rather than weakens, the State's interest in regulating the conditions under which abortions are performed.

Medical procedures had been vastly improved since the late 1800s. Abortion during the early months of pregnancy was now safer than childbirth, suggesting a minimal need for state intervention. On the other hand, abortion during the last stages of pregnancy continued to involve serious risks, and therefore regulation of procedures, facilities, and physician qualifications was more compelling.

With this understanding, the court constructed a sliding scale for justifying state intervention. For maternal health and safety, the state had compelling reasons to regulate abortion in the later stages of pregnancy. There were fewer compelling reasons in the early months. The question became how to segment what was in truth a continuum. A similar sliding scale confronted the court as it turned to the life-defining boundaries surrounding the embryo, fetus, or unborn child.

Two polar positions for protecting life's boundaries were proposed by the lawyers arguing *Roe*: (1) No protections, with abortion on demand; (2) full protection from the moment of conception. The court rejected both. Abortion is indeed a medical procedure, but so are appendectomies and root-canal treatments. More is at stake. The biological properties of the embryo, whatever your view of abortion, raise different questions about the protective boundaries of life than pulling a tooth or removing an appendix. The right to privacy was broad enough to include a mother's decision to terminate her pregnancy, but there were limits.[10]

In many ways, echoing those who had argued against restrictions on contraception, those arguing for abortion on demand noted that governmental intrusion would yield numerous and substantial burdens on the woman. Becoming a mother or adding additional children to the family might lead to a distressful life and future. Unwanted children might bring economic hardships, abuse, and neglect, or an otherwise poor upbringing for the child. Stigma might be attached to unwed motherhood.

After their review of such arguments, the court concluded:

> On the basis of elements such as these, appellant and some *amici* argue that the woman's right is absolute and that she is entitled to terminate her pregnancy at whatever time, in whatever way, and for whatever reason she alone chooses. With this we do not agree ... We, therefore, conclude that the right of personal privacy includes the abortion decision, but that this right is not unqualified and must be considered against important state interests in regulation.

For the majority of the court, the interrupted potential for life inherent in contraception and not-yet-joined gametes was one thing. Terminating a pregnancy after gametes combined was another. There were protections that needed to surround post-conception, prenatal life.

With abortion on demand set aside, the court turned to the protective boundaries of life and whether they were fully present at the moment, more accurately during the process, of conception and thus compelling of a decision prohibiting abortion. Noting that anti-abortion laws stemmed in large measure from legislation coincident with the Comstock Laws, the court probed deeper into history for insight. Wide variation was found.

The Persian, Greek, Roman, Jewish, and Christian traditions, the court noted, had all taken stands, varying from one time and place to another. Similarly, common and statutory law reflected shifting definitions of where and when the protective boundaries of life should be drawn—quickening, ensoulment, and live-birth. After this brief review of history, the court concluded that, in a comparison with the early nineteenth century, "a woman enjoyed a substantially broader right to terminate a pregnancy than she does in most States today."

What to do with this review of history? There was no crystal-clear answer. The boundaries of protected life were hazy. The court decided not to decide. "We need not resolve the difficult question of when life begins." The majority's decision noted:

> When those trained in the respective disciplines of medicine, philosophy, and theology are unable to arrive at any consensus, the judiciary, at this point in the development of man's knowledge, is not in a position to speculate as to the answer.

Instead, the court turned to the potential for life:

> A legitimate state interest in this area need not stand or fall on acceptance of the belief that life begins at conception or at some other point prior to live birth. In assessing the State's interest, recognition may be given to the less rigid claim that as long as at least potential life is involved, the State may assert interests beyond the protection of the pregnant woman alone.

The court, in its contraception decisions, had concluded that the potential for life inherent in the act of intercourse did not open the doorway for governmental intrusion. Conception, however, concretized the potential for life. Still there were ambiguities. For one thing, there was evidence, as the court stated, "to indicate that conception is a 'process' over time, rather than an event." The argument anchoring life's protected boundaries on "potential" would be long lasting. Continuing advances in the understanding of conception, both inside and out of the womb, at the cellular and molecular levels, as a process rather than a moment, along with prenatal assessments of the potential quality of life, would provide grist for the mill among bioethicists, politicians, and legal scholars in the years ahead.[11]

More settled was the idea that two sets of "fundamental rights" were involved—the health of the mother and the potential life she carried. There was a compelling state interest in limiting and protecting both.

Where to draw the boundaries? The nine-month gestation period was divided into three trimesters.

During the first trimester, when the health risks of an abortion were low, even lower than those of carrying the pregnancy to term, there was no compelling reason for state intervention. On this basis, the attending physician, in consultation with the mother, should be free to determine, without interference from the state, whether the mother's pregnancy should be terminated. When it came to the potential life the mother was carrying, the point of compelling state interest came with "viability," the point at which the fetus was capable of "meaningful life outside the mother's womb." Given then available and rapidly improving medical technology, this probabilistic point was said to be somewhere between six and seven months after conception. After this point, state regulations designed to protect the interests of the unborn child could go so far as to prohibit abortion, except when necessary to preserve the "life or health" of the mother.

With this reasoning in place, the *Roe* court found the Texas abortion statute unconstitutional and summarized its findings as follows:

(a) For the stage prior to approximately the end of the first trimester, the abortion decision and its effectuation must be left to the medical judgment of the pregnant woman's attending physician.
(b) For the stage subsequent to approximately the end of the first trimester, the State, in promoting its interest in the health of the mother, may, if it chooses, regulate the abortion procedure in ways that are reasonably related to maternal health.
(c) For the stage subsequent to viability, the State in promoting its interest in the potentiality of human life may, if it chooses, regulate, and even proscribe, abortion except where it is necessary, in appropriate medical judgment, for the preservation of the life or health of the mother.

Still, the boundaries for the legitimate protection of life of both the mother and fetus remained hazy. The mother's health and life were included. Did this include mental as well as physical health? How threatening or debilitating did the threat to health have to be? These issues were more directly addressed in the companion case from Georgia,

Doe v. Bolton. The protective boundaries were broadly drawn. Threats to the mother's health included, "all factors—physical, emotional, psychological, familial, and the woman's age—relevant to the well-being of the patient."

The boundaries for considering the health of the mother were wide. They even extended to the family. Any remaining ambiguities were to be resolved by physicians. As Justice Blackmun wrote for the majority in *Doe* (when physicians were, by and large, still assumed to be men), "This allows the attending physician the room he needs to make his best medical judgment. And it is room that operates for the benefit, not the disadvantage, of the pregnant woman."

As for the newly forming life, protections were attached to potential. After conception, there was some point or span of time where viability was achieved. Viability was defined in terms of probabilities of survival and meaningful life outside the womb. Although it was unclear when this occurred, or what was meaningful, the point or process was clearly linked to scientific advances and available medical technologies and protocols. The timing of viability might be adjusted in the future.

And so the stage was set. Protecting the sanctity of life was an uncertain, contentious matter. The shifting boundaries of protected life were divided into three-month increments determined by potential. For the fetus, it was the increasing potential for a viable, meaningful life, vaguely specified. For the mother, it was the increasing potential threat to her health and life, broadly defined. These roughly hewn trimester boundaries generated wide-ranging debate, eventually infused with a fury not altogether anticipated.

The Supreme Court had been careful to "resolve the issue by constitutional measurement, free of emotion." They found in the penumbras of the Bill of Rights and the Fourteenth Amendment the right to privacy. They did not find full protections for prenatal life. Instead, they were persuaded that "the word 'person,' as used in the Fourteenth Amendment, does not include the unborn."

The Power of Empathy

This exclusionary conclusion, reached through the constraining influence of legal reasoning, would not be viewed with such steely-eyed detachment by a significant portion of the population. For many, it became a clarion call for action. These now aroused advocates campaigned with increased energy and pointed to ultrasound images of the unborn child to build empathy for its humanity. Poster-sized pictures of late-term abortions were carried to the streets to generate disgust at what the Supreme Court had wrought. They searched the penumbras of scriptures, just as Supreme Court justices had done with the Constitution. Convinced that innocent lives were being taken, demonizing analogies were drawn with Nazi Germany. A small minority would hear direct messages from God and launch a violent and sometimes murderous campaign to protect life.

The power of empathy is nowhere more apparent than in the conversion of Dr. Bernard Nathanson. In his self-reflective book, *The Hand of God*, he wrote, "When ultrasound in the early 1970s confronted me with the sight of the embryo in a womb, I simply lost my faith in abortion on demand."[12] Dr. Nathanson's conversion had not been immediate. It evolved over a period of years, with early signs manifest in his November 1974 *New England Journal of Medicine* article. In this article, which turned out to be one of the most provocative in *NEJM*'s publication history, Nathanson continued his support for abortion unregulated by law, but wrote with divided spirit and a "deeply troubled mind."

"Our sense of values," Nathanson wrote, "has always placed the greatest importance upon the value of life itself." With a completely permissive legal climate for abortion, which he still believed "we must have," there was "a danger that society will lose a certain moral tension that has been a vital part of its fabric. In pursuing a course of unlimited and uncontrolled abortion over future years," he continued, "we must not permit ourselves to sink to a debased level of utilitarian semi consciousness . . . We must work together to create a moral climate rich enough to provide for abortion, but sensitive enough to life to accommodate a profound sense of loss."

By the early 1980s, Nathanson had changed his mind and decided to work with a colleague and, with the aid of ultrasound technology, videotape what happened during an abortion of an 11–12-week-old fetus. He later recounted that, in the editing studio, the emotional impact of the visual images was so great that his colleague decided to abandon his abortion practice. Nathanson himself had stopped doing abortions five years earlier, but recalled that he was "shaken to the very roots of my soul" by what he saw. The empathetic human bonding generated by the visual images of the unborn was inescapable. His conversion was complete.

Dr. Nathanson had been a prominent activist in the pro-choice movement, being one of the founders of NARAL. Early signs of his shifting
opinion did not go unnoticed by the growing number of right-to-life
supporters. Nathanson's still grainy videotape was shown during his subsequent lectures. Eventually, the videotape was edited further and made
into a film, *The Silent Scream*. The explicit purpose was to generate empathy for the pain inflicted on the fetus during abortion and to underscore
the human qualities of the developing fetus in the womb. It began with
a voice-overlay, "Now we can discern the chilling silent scream on the
face of this child who is now facing imminent extinction."

Overly dramatic, as many claimed, or not, this short introduction
reflected the film's message.[13] The impact was as immediate as it was
dramatic. It was shown in the White House to President Reagan, who
had recently published "Abortion and the Conscience of the Nation." The
president provided members of Congress with a copy of the film. News
accounts and editorials appeared, and screenings were held in churches
across the country.

For many, *The Silent Scream* was mind opening and conscience
prodding. It was praised for raising public awareness of the evils of
abortion, much like Harriet Beecher Stowe's *Uncle Tom's Cabin* had done
for slavery. It was also vilified as visually misleading and scientifically
inaccurate.[14] Accepted or not, the intended spoken and visual message of
the film was clear. We were not dealing with a nonperson outside communal boundaries of protection, as the Supreme Court had held. We were
dealing instead with a human being, fully deserving of all the protections
a moral community can offer.

This conclusion raised very troubling issues. Why would we even
remotely tolerate what *The Silent Scream* claimed to be the tearing apart
of a baby? Moderates advocating a pro-life position were willing to consider exceptions in cases of rape, incest, under-age pregnancies, and birth
defects. Why? In what sense were the lives of these unborn children less
worthy of protection?

Protests and Rescue Missions

Protests and disruptive actions escalated. Eventually, a small, loosely
connected, isolated, and tragically violent network declared war against

the "baby killers" in abortion clinics across the country. Between 1977 and 1978, there were 12 reported cases of clinic bombings or arson.[15] By 1979, a group of individuals had become disenchanted with what they saw as the timid, compromising position of the National Right to Life Committee. These individuals, headed by Paul and Judie Brown, broke off and founded the American Life League (ALL). A short time later, in 1980, Joseph Scheidler, a former Benedictine monk widely considered the godfather of the early activist anti-abortion movement, organized the founding of the Pro-Life Action League (PLAL). Both ALL and PLAL were as uncompromising in their mission as Patricia Maginnis and SHA had been in their earlier advocacy of abortion on demand.

Maginnis and SHA had lobbied and activated supporters for placing abortion decisions solely in the hands of the mother. For members of ALL and PLAL, there were no acceptable abortions. For these activists, "abortion is the unjust, premeditated taking of an innocent human life." Abortion equaled murder. Thus framed, the call for confrontational politics among these now highly energized activists intensified.

The stated mission of the PLAL was to save unborn children through "non-violent direct action." In pursuit of this mission, they published a manual, *Closed: 99 Ways to Stop Abortion*, at around the same time as the release of *The Silent Scream*. This how-to guide, which began with the sentence, "This book is based on the equation that abortion equals murder," outlined a collection of methods for protesting and preventing abortion. The tactics were based on the premise that:

> No social movement in the history of this country has succeeded without activist(s) taking to the streets. Activism, including demonstrations, pickets, protests, and sit-ins, is necessary not only to save lives, but to garner public attention, bring the media into the struggle, and shake politicians into recognizing the determination of anti-abortion supporters.

Early emphasis was given to "sidewalk counseling." The objective was simple. Sidewalk counselors were encouraged to "come between the baby who is scheduled to be killed and the doctor who will do the killing." Volunteers, armed in most cases with their Catholic beliefs and prayers, would gather in front of clinics and approach women or their friends and family, as they were walking across the parking lot or up the sidewalk to the clinic. All they wanted was to talk for a moment. Statements such as the following were part of videotaped conversations taking place in front of an abortion clinic and eventually embedded in a training and motivational tape for sidewalk counseling, *No Greater Joy*:

> Could I talk to you a minute? I have some information on the lawsuits that have been brought against this clinic.
>
> Could I talk to you a minute? We are trying to warn persons about this clinic. Do you see, these are pictures of ambulances in the parking lot. This is not a safe medical facility. Women have died here.
>
> Are you pregnant? Do you need help?
>
> I am a priest. Many girls come to confession with me. They have pain in them and they want to commit suicide . . . There is incredible guilt and pain for years, and they (nodding toward the clinic entrance) do not tell them because they are making money.

This 40-minute film, created by Joseph Scheidler and PLAL, depicted volunteers at work, carrying bibles, rosaries, and models of fetuses, similar to those used in *The Silent Scream*.

The objective of *No Greater Joy* was to mobilize resources by encouraging viewers to get involved. Viewers were told their counseling would be responsible for a baby being born and that this was a beautiful thing. They were encouraged to believe they were cooperating with God in the most important fight on the face of the earth. The sidewalk counseling tactics shown were calm, supportive, and conversational. They did not always turn out that way. Eventually, the tape was updated with free access on the Internet and accompanying advice on what to do "If somebody tells me to 'shut up' or to go away."[16]

All tactics outlined in *Closed* were not as calmly persuasive as those presented in *No Greater Joy*. Some were designed to obstruct, shock, and disgust. A subset of these were depicted in a second videotape, *Face the Truth*, also produced by PLAL.[17] Joseph Scheidler introduced this film with reference to the importance of grotesque images of late-term aborted fetuses.

The film began with a voice-over: "*Face the Truth* is a bold new public education initiative that brings the reality of abortion to the highways and downtown intersections of cities and towns across America, confronting those who have turned away from the tragedy of our age." With protesting citizens, mothers, and their children shown carrying greatly enlarged, dramatic and grotesque poster-sized photos of dismembered, aborted fetuses in the background, Scheidler's introductory statement was followed by another voice-over: "America is in a death epic. We have killed 47 million children. That's unconscionable and something has to be done, and we are doing what has to be done. We are showing America the face of abortion."

The framing objective was clear. The protective boundaries of life should be drawn at the earliest possible moment of conception. Like the visual images of holocaust victims in World War II and starving children in underdeveloped countries, the purpose was to generate empathy, a sense of injustice and illegitimacy, and a demand for change. The strong message was straightforward: life is sacred and should be protected. Life begins at conception. Existing laws are illegitimate, unjust, and immoral. They are no law at all. As one icon of the anti-abortion movement put it, "The bottom line is that at a certain point there is not only the right, but the duty, to disobey the State."[18]

These efforts and messages were securing a broader public. They permeated and were reflective of a national network of aroused organizations and individuals.[19] Once aroused by a sense of injustice and illegitimacy, backed by motivating disgust, empathy, and how-to recipes for action, these organizations and individuals expanded their now morally demanded actions.

Violence Increases

Following the rise in clinic arson and bombings in the late 1970s, there was a drop-off in violence directed at abortion clinics and staff. In 1984–5, the years *The Silent Scream* and *Closed: 99 Ways to Stop Abortion* were released, things changed. On Christmas Day, 1984, three clinics were bombed by a small group of young activists associated with a local Assembly of God church in Pensacola, Florida. They had come to identify their activities with the Old Testament story of Gideon, the slayer of those who offered infant sacrifices to Baal, referring to their protest efforts as the Gideon Project.[20] One of the suspects, soon arrested, claimed his actions had been "a birthday gift for Jesus." It turned out that one motivating factor had been the showing of graphic images and films at his church. They had left a "strong impression."

These young activists were only loosely connected with PLAL and Joseph Scheidler, but Scheidler, along with other national anti-abortion figures, would attend the trial and speak favorably of their activities in the media. Additional connections between this emerging, loosely connected and increasingly violent network of "pro-lifers" would soon become even more evident.

The Gideon Project was not an isolated incident. Between 1984 and 1985, the number of bombings and arson incidents at abortion clinics, as reported by the National Abortion Federation, rose dramatically to 52, more than quadrupling what had happened in the previous high-water mark between 1977 and 1978. An additional 107 bomb threats were recorded. Death threats also peaked at 45 during these same two years. Among these incidents was the bombing of the National Abortion Federation's headquarters, a national organization of professional abortion-service providers.

In addition, in 1984, Supreme Court Justice Harry Blackmun, who had written the *Roe* decision, received a death threat from a militant anti-abortion organization, which was implicated in the kidnapping of an abortion doctor and his wife in Illinois. The threat against Justice Blackmun was received in October at about the time an anti-abortion activist had disrupted the highly regimented atmosphere of Supreme Court hearings. A few months later, in February 1985, a bullet passed through the window of Justice Blackmun's home. No one was injured, but this incident marked the first time a Supreme Court justice had been the subject of a shooting investigation.

The increasingly aggressive militancy, now violent, did not go unnoticed. Criminal charges were lodged, arrests made, lawsuits filed, counter-demonstrations planned. Among moderates, disillusionment and a sense of betrayal set in. As one angry advocate of nonviolent, pro-life strategies put it, "The work we're doing, it totally shoots it down. There are a lot of minds and hearts to win over. Blowing up clinics only hardens hearts."[21] Less moderate anti-abortion religious groups joined forces, organized additional clinic blockades, and gave birth to new organizations.

Operation Rescue

In the early years of anti-abortion efforts, the Catholic Church had been the dominant force. When Protestant fundamentalists joined the cause, motivated by Francis Schaeffer's *A Christian Manifesto*, they moved center stage. One adherent, a young, charismatic Pentecostal minister, Randall Terry, still in his 20s, had become closely aligned with the efforts of PLAL and Joseph Scheidler. In 1986, with their relationship strained over how aggressive the anti-abortion forces should be, Terry joined others in the formation of Operation Rescue.

At the time, Scheidler was facing a series of lawsuits, and there is some indication that Operation Rescue emerged at least in part to avoid legal battles being launched against Scheidler and PLAL. Whatever its genesis, Operation Rescue was far more confrontational. It took seriously and applied to abortion the admonitions of Proverbs 24:11: "Deliver those who are being taken away to death, and those who are staggering to slaughter." Within Operation Rescue, sidewalk counseling and other comparatively modest protests gave way to massive demonstrations and blockades.

In response, in 1986, noting the destructive nature of protests across the country and in particular the recent destruction of property and injuries to staff in a Florida clinic, the National Organization of Women (NOW), joined by two reproductive-health clinics, filed a class-action lawsuit against Joseph Scheidler and eventually a second suit against Randall Terry and their respective organizations. NOW charged that Scheidler and Terry, along with their associates and organizations, had turned to violence, threats of violence, and extortion to close clinics down. It would be some 20 years before the Supreme Court settled the issues NOW raised.[22]

Organized and led by Randall Terry, the first major Operation Rescue clinic blockade took place in 1987, in Cherry Hill, New Jersey. A sympathetic reporter covered the event:

> Over 200 people were arrested . . . in the nation's largest "rescue mission" for unborn children, conducted at the Cherry Hill Women's Center in Cherry Hill, New Jersey. The protestors, who flew in from 19 different states at their own expense, came to the

clinic to be trained in the civil disobedience tactic of barring pregnant women from abortion facilities in order to save the lives of unborn babies.[23]

A subsequent assessment suggested the activities in Cherry Hill were transformative, "Clinic sit-ins and blockades were no longer small, isolated local events; they had suddenly become the most important form of political expression in the entire national debate over abortion."[24]

It was not until the next year, however, at the 1988 Democratic Convention in Atlanta, Georgia, that Operation Rescue came to prominent national attention. A large protest was organized, and again several hundred arrests ensued. Terry was interviewed shortly after the demonstrations.[25] Just as Supreme Court justices had found justification in the penumbras of the U.S. Constitution for its judicial interpretations, Terry found justification for his activities in his interpretation of scriptures:

> *Interviewer*: What is the philosophy behind Operation Rescue?
>
> *Terry*: The foundation of Operation Rescue is a call to people and the Church to repent. The Church has sinned before God by allowing children to be ripped apart and mothers to be exploited. We have sat idly by and have done virtually nothing.
>
> *Interviewer*: Why are those being arrested in Atlanta withholding their names? Why are they identifying themselves as "Baby John Doe" or "Baby Jane Doe"?
>
> *Terry*: We are withholding our names because the unborn children we represent have no names and no voice. We are identifying with them. We are making a statement to the system by identifying with their suffering. We want their plight to be known to the American people.
>
> . . .
>
> *Interviewer*: How do you justify violating the law in your fight against abortion?
>
> *Terry*: Easily. When God's law and man's law conflict, Scripture clearly teaches that man is not to obey that law. Some examples are when the three Hebrew children were thrown into the fire, when the apostles were jailed for preaching the Gospel, and when the stone was rolled away from the Lord's tomb. That was in

defiance of a man-made law. God never gave the government a blank check to do what it wants to do. It is a heresy to teach Christians to obey a law which runs counter to His law.

Between 1988 and 1989, some 24,000 arrests related to abortion-clinic protests were made.[26] These two years marked a dramatic peak in mass-action clinic blockade and protest activities. In the years just prior, anti-abortion supporters had tried and failed to enact a constitutional amendment to ban abortions. An initiative to pass a life-begins-at-conception federal statue had likewise floundered. There was more success at the state level, especially in Missouri, where the state legislature stepped in where the *Roe* court had demurred. Life, the law stated, began at conception.

Roe Reexamined

The Reagan years were coming to a close. Sandra Day O'Connor was now on the Supreme Court. William Rhenquist had become Chief Justice, and Antonin Scalia assumed his duties in 1986. Robert Bork had been nominated for a seat on the court, but was rejected by the Senate largely for his conservative and anti-*Roe* views. A colleague of Judge Bork had been put forward, but withdrawn. Anthony Kennedy was finally selected to fill the vacancy in 1988. As the 1980s drew to a close, by most accounts, the seven–two majority in the *Roe* and *Doe* cases had become something closer to five–four. In 1989, this shifting mixture of proclivities among Supreme Court justices became evident in a case emerging from the recently passed Missouri statute, *Webster v. Reproductive Health Services*.

Several aspects of the law were at issue, including its definition of when life started, but the major magnet for controversy was the determination of "viability" and the utility of the trimester structure. Although the court did not overturn *Roe*, it was close. There was no clear majority, only pluralities for differing versions of the court's findings. Chief Justice Rhenquist, joined by two of his colleagues, Justices White and Kennedy, concluded:

> *Roe*'s rigid trimester analysis has proved to be unsound in principle and unworkable in practice ... The *Roe* framework is hardly consistent with the notion of a Constitution like ours that is

cast in general terms and usually speaks in general principles. The framework's key elements—trimesters and viability—are not found in the Constitution's text, and, since the bounds of the inquiry are essentially indeterminate, the result has been a web of legal rules that have become increasingly intricate, resembling a code of regulations rather than a body of constitutional doctrine. There is also no reason why the State's compelling interest in protecting potential human life should not extend throughout pregnancy rather than coming into existence only at the point of viability. Thus, the *Roe* trimester framework should be abandoned.

An even harsher assessment was provided by Justice Scalia: "It thus appears that the mansion of constitutionalized abortion law, constructed overnight in *Roe v. Wade*, must be disassembled doorjamb by doorjamb, and never entirely brought down, no matter how wrong it may be."

As much dissention as there was in the court in *Webster*, for *Roe*, the center held, and it was not overturned. Nevertheless, the door was opened ever so slightly, and legislators in Pennsylvania entered. They passed a statute that was immediately challenged. In addition, following *Webster*, there was a flurry in the media and law journals predicting a sea change. A year after *Webster*, however, the initial *Roe*-will-be-overturned prognostications were dying down.[27]

For anti-abortion advocates, however, knowing that Presidents Reagan and Bush had now appointed the majority of the court, the Pennsylvania statute offered a ray of hope. The law was challenged. Critics of *Roe* were disappointed, as Justice O'Connor, in *Planned Parenthood v. Casey*,[28] writing for the majority stated, "We are led to conclude this: the essential holding of *Roe v. Wade* should be retained and once again reaffirmed."

This affirmation of *Roe* came on the heels of heightened clinic blockades. Questions began to surface in the rank-and-file of the anti-abortion movement. How much impact on the number of abortions were they having? Not much seemed to be the answer. The Centers for Disease Control and other organizations were reporting that the number of recorded abortions was holding steady at somewhere between 1.3 million and 1.6 million a year.[29] Although the precise figures could be questioned, the consensus was that the number of abortions during these years was at a plateau. Faced with this apparent lack of effectiveness, some activists withdrew from protest activities. Others, however, increased even further the intensity of their actions. A major milestone came in the year just prior to *Casey*, in Wichita, Kansas. It would eventually play out almost twenty years later in the shooting death of a local abortion provider.

The Summer of Mercy

By the early 1990s, facing challenges to his leadership, increased financial pressure, and emotional strain from a stay in jail, Randall Terry had relinquished his position as formal leader of Operation Rescue. The organization's confrontational orientation and organizing influence, however, remained. Energy and resources were gathered to launch one last major undertaking.

They focused on three abortion clinics in Wichita, Kansas, in what came to be known as the Summer of Mercy. They gave special attention to a clinic run by Dr. George Tiller. Tiller was advertising nationally his services to provide elective abortions in the second and third trimesters. Entrances to Tiller's and two other Wichita clinics were blocked. Police were called out. Somewhere between 2,500 and 3,000 arrests were made, mainly for minor offenses such as trespassing. A federal judge issued decrees, based on post-Civil War legislation designed to limit intimidation and deprivation of civil rights.[30]

When local police were not cooperative, the judge asked federal marshals to enforce his decrees. President Bush countermanded the judge's orders. After almost seven weeks of protest, orders, counter-orders, and substantial national publicity, some 25,000–35,000 persons (estimates varied) gathered in Wichita State University's stadium in late August. The state's governor, the city's mayor, and several high-profile anti-abortion activists, including leaders of organizations such as the recently disbanded Moral Majority and the recently established Christian Coalition, joined them. The aim was to underscore their common cause and celebrate their commitment to the "Hope for the Heartland." These citizens and organizations were a political force to be reckoned with.[31]

A political landscape of mutual demonization had taken shape. Dr. George Tiller became "Tiller the Baby Killer." Persons who favored the right to choose were characterized as murderers. Persons adamantly opposed to abortion under any circumstances were painted as narrow-minded religious fanatics. Following the success of the Summer of Mercy, similar events were organized elsewhere, though they did not attract nearly as much attention. Counteracting lawsuits continued. In 1992, prompted by events in Wichita and similar protests in other cities, the bipartisan Freedom of Access to Clinic Entrances (FACE) Act was filed in the U.S. Congress. This first attempt failed. This would change.

While this bill was being debated, a case examining the applicability of the Ku Klux Act of 1871 for regulating clinic blockades, used by the federal judge in Wichita, had reached the Supreme Court for a second hearing. Justice Department attorney, John Roberts, Jr., who in 2005 would become the seventeenth Chief Justice of the Supreme Court, argued the case for the Bush Administration, suggesting that the federal judge in Wichita had been wrong.

As actions of protestors were even-handed, Roberts argued, attempts to prevent abortion were not discriminatory. Resolution of the issue should be left to state-legislative bodies and courts. Lawyers for NOW and women's health clinics disagreed. They saw a nationwide and systematic conspiracy to intimidate abortion providers and to prevent women from exercising their civil rights. Limiting such discriminatory actions was precisely what the drafters of the 1871 Act had in mind.

The Supreme Court, in another split vote, sided with attorney Roberts and the Justice Department.[32] Abortion clinics and their clients would have to look elsewhere for protections. Given the emergence of fringe elements in the anti-abortion camp and the warlike rhetoric being used, the need for protections would soon become clear.

Taking Lives to Save Lives

Two months later, on March 10, 1993, shortly after the twentieth anniversary of *Roe*, Dr. David Gunn, who provided services in clinics in Alabama, Georgia, and Florida, became the first abortion provider to be murdered by anti-abortion extremists. Gunn had been targeted after his picture, phone number, and address appeared on a "Wanted" poster created by Operation Rescue and distributed at an Alabama rally held in support of Randall Terry.[33] The poster read,

WANTED: FOR MURDER
AND CRIMES AGAINST HUMANITY
TO DEFENSELESS UNBORN BABIES.
GUNN IS HEAVILY ARMED
AND DANGEROUS.

Confronted outside his Pensacola office by protesters carrying posters reading "David Gunn Kills Babies," Dr. Gunn was shot three times as he got out of his car on a Wednesday morning by a man dressed in a gray suit shouting, "Don't kill any more babies." The previous Sunday, this same man, it turned out, had asked his congregation to pray for Dr. Gunn's soul and conversion.

The assailant was Michael Griffin. He had grown up in Pensacola. Similar to participants in the Gideon Project, he was an active member of a local Assembly of God church. He had been influenced by what his attorneys characterized as the relentless rhetoric and graphic images shown to him by his preacher, a local anti-abortion extremist and former KKK member.[34]

The minister was the regional director of Rescue America, an organization evolved from Operation Rescue. He had been instrumental in leading the protest outside the clinic where Dr. Gunn was shot. Shortly after Dr. Gunn's murder, the minister was quoted as saying, in apparent reference to the FACE legislation, "There's talk of making protesting abortion clinics a felony. If you start talking about that, people are just going to find other ways of dealing with it."[35] This conservative zealot had also been one of the organizers of the 1986 incident in Pensacola, which precipitated NOW's suits against Scheidler and Terry. It would not be the last time persons involved in this loosely connected network would be implicated in lethal violence.

A few months after the shooting dead of Dr. Gunn, Dr. George Tiller, the major focus of the Summer of Mercy demonstrations, was wounded in a botched attempt on his life as he was leaving work one evening. Shelley Shannon, the admitted assailant and a participant in the Summer of Mercy, was a sympathizer with Michael Griffin. She, too, had become convinced that more drastic action was called for. Shannon's intensified convictions, along with her destructive and violent actions directed at other clinics, largely on the west coast, are documented in court records as well

as her diary and letters sent to family and friends. Like others, she turned
to her God's word and prayer for support.

Of Michael Griffin, she wrote:

> He didn't shoot Mother Teresa, he shot a mass murderer such
> as Saddam Hussien [sic] or Hitler. I don't even think it is accu-
> rately termed "murder." God is the only one who knows whether
> Gunn would ever have repented or if he would have killed another
> 5,000 babies and probably 3 or 4 more women, who probably
> weren't Christians either, and then died with even more to con-
> demn him . . . I am not convinced that God didn't require it of
> Michael to do this. It is possible. I am praying God will push
> more of us "off the deep end."

In this same diary entry, she continued,

> I am glad for those who are publicly refusing to condemn Michael
> Griffin. I'm sure there will be more of these works. Mine is clear.
> This morning in bed it seemed God asked, "Is there any doubt?"
> . . . Again He asked, "Is there any doubt?" I could recognize some
> fear and other things. The third time He asked, "Is there any
> doubt?" No, Lord. Please help me do it right.

A short time later, referencing a verse from Isaiah 6:8 ("Then I heard
the voice of the Lord saying, 'Whom shall I send? And who will go for
us?' And I said, 'Here am I. Send me!'"), Shelley Shannon took a bus
from Grants Pass, Oregon, to Oklahoma City, rented a car at the airport,
drove some 160 miles north to Wichita, Kansas, and "went off the deep
end" to become one of those messengers of God she was praying for.
She later wrote from jail to her daughter about first going into the clinic
and then back outside to wait until Dr. Tiller and a woman employee
left work that evening:

> I dressed up and fixed my hair different and went inside (had a
> gun in a purse) and got a look around, but couldn't find Tiller.
> [She left the clinic and waited outside until persons, including
> Dr. Tiller emerged.] I ran up [to Tiller's car] and shot through

the window, I think 6 times. I turned around and aimed at the lady, but I didn't shoot. It seemed like God (or an angel?) said, "Run for your life Shelley!" So I ran. Ran through a little creek spot & up to where the car was . . . Tried not to look suspicious . . . Got in, and drove off.

Shelley Shannon had only slightly wounded Dr. Tiller, and he began driving after her, but soon stopped. She eluded her pursuers and headed back south to Oklahoma City, where she was apprehended as she turned in her rental car at the airport. Later, at trial, it would be revealed that Rachelle Ranae "Shelley" Shannon had been leading a double life for some time. For many of her friends, as reported shortly thereafter, hearing that she was involved in this shooting and, as it was soon revealed, arson, bombings, and vandalism at several other clinics, was like hearing that "Minnie Mouse had bombed the White House."

The shootings of Drs. Gunn and Tiller drew substantial public attention and concern. The FACE legislation had failed to pass Congress in 1992. Following the murder of Dr. Gunn and the shooting of Dr. Tiller in 1993, the bill was reintroduced and supported by a bipartisan coalition of senators and representatives, including presidential candidate and Kansas Senator Bob Dole.

This time, it passed.[36] The House approved the bill on May 5, 1994. One week later, the Senate agreed. A good deal of testimony and relevant data had been gathered. Between 1977 and 1993, more than 1,000 acts of violence against providers of reproductive-health services had been reported. In addition to the murder of Dr. David Gunn, there had been at least 36 bombings, 81 arsons, 131 death threats, 84 assaults, 2 kidnappings, 327 clinic invasions, 71 chemical attacks, and more than 6,000 blockades and related disruptions of reproductive-health clinics.

On May 26, 1994, President Clinton signed the FACE legislation into law. While the Supreme Court had found the Ku Klux Act of 1871 inapplicable, FACE provided the sought-after protections for those seeking abortions and those providing services by making it a federal crime to use force, the threat of force, or physical obstruction to injure, intimidate, or interfere with persons obtaining or providing reproductive-health services.

Reported incidents of clinic protest activities, as recorded by the National Abortion Federation, tapered off. The number of blockades had been 83 and 66 in 1992 and 1993, respectively. In 1994, there were 25, and, in 1995, the total was 5. The number of attendant arrests and reported instances of vandalism likewise dropped. There would be an increase in picketing and peaks of more threatening activity in later years, such as the increase in anthrax threats in 2001, but there was a sense among supporters and opponents alike that the FACE Act was having an impact.

Still, there were problems. Four additional murders and eight attempted murders occurred in 1994. These murders, justified by extremists, were condemned, in varying degrees, by high-profile religious organizations, such as the Southern Baptist Convention, and activists such as Bernard Nathanson, John Cardinal O'Connor, Ann Scheidler, and Gary North.[37] For these individuals and organizations, taking life to protect life did not make sense. Others disagreed. Their efforts would continue.

The Army of God

The first murder of an abortion provider linked to the anti-abortion protest movement had been in 1993. For many anti-abortion activists, the dramatic escalation of lethal violence in 1994 was disconcerting and soundly condemned. The majority of moderates began withdrawing from the aggressive, and now illegal, forms of protest. Leadership among the anti-abortion activists was in disarray. There were efforts to open more constructive dialogues among pro- and anti-abortion rights groups.[38]

For a small but highly motivated minority, however, commitment to lethal action continued. For these individuals, the time had come for a violent response to the killing of children. They had waited long enough, perhaps too long. The injustice and illegitimacy of existing laws were clear. They were witnessing a holocaust, and they were no longer going to stand idly by. Parallels with the Nazis and the abolition of slavery and the violent anti-slavery actions of John Brown were repeatedly invoked.[39] Biblical scriptures were used to justify and frame their actions, and to demonize abortion providers. One such group called themselves the Army of God.

Shelley Shannon's letters and diary, along with her testimony and evidence presented at her trial, shed important light on how violence was spreading in contagion-like fashion among a small, isolated, and loosely connected group of extreme adherents to the anti-abortion cause. In particular, the Army of God's manual, dug up in Shannon's back yard following her arrest, brought increased and unintended attention to this shadowy organization.

The Army of God manual, which was revised on an irregular yearly cycle, was intended to provide how-to instructions on increasingly destructive and violent methods of protest and clinic obstruction, including the killing of abortion providers. The Army's loose-knit structure was evident in the manual, where it was claimed the Army of God was real, but members rarely

> communicate with one another. Very few have ever met each other. And when they do, each is usually unaware of the other's soldier status. That is why the Feds will never stop this Army. Never. And we have not yet even begun to fight.

The history of this organization remains clouded, but folklore indicates the original version of the Manual was drafted by some of the jailed Operation Rescue protesters at the 1988 Democratic Convention. In a later edition of the manual, the religious footing for their violent response to increased federal regulations was starkly stated in an explicit warning:

> We, the remnant of God-fearing men and women of the United States of Amerika, do officially declare war on the entire child killing industry. After praying, fasting, and making continual supplication to God for your pagan, heathen, infidel souls, we then peacefully, passively presented our bodies in front of your death camps, begging you to stop the mass murder of infants. Yet you hardened your already blackened, jaded hearts. We quietly accepted the resulting imprisonment and suffering of our passive resistance. Yet you mocked God and continued the Holocaust. No longer! All the options have expired. Our Most Dread Sovereign Lord God requires that whosoever sheds man's blood, by man shall his blood be shed. Not out of hatred of you, but out of love for the persons you exterminate, we are forced to take arms against you. Our life for yours—simple equation. Dreadful.

Sad. Reality, nonetheless. You shall not be tortured at our hands. Vengeance belongs to God only. However, execution is rarely gentile [*sic*].

Reflecting these same sentiments, Neal Horsley, a central figure in the Army of God,[40] wrote a piece, "Understanding the Army of God," shortly after a clinic bombing in Birmingham, Alabama, for which Eric Rudolph was eventually convicted, and where an off-duty policeman was killed, and a woman seriously injured.

> As I point out . . . these presently United States of America are actually at war. Like the bombs planted by the IRA in Ireland, the bombs might be terrorist but they are not cowardly when war has been declared and responsibility for the military actions are accurately assigned . . . If all the previous evidence did not make it clear, the bomb in the Birmingham clinic should prove to all that the Army of God has entered this warfare . . .
>
> Do not expect this war to end until legalized abortion is repealed. The Army of God is an evanescent, amorphous, autonomous and spontaneous eruption of individuals . . . People enraged by the war being waged in this nation against God's children will continue to engage in terrorist actions. Because the government of the USA has become a godless and apostate body, the people who rise up in arms against such idolatry deserve the name "The Army of God."[41]

The sense of injustice was deep. Legitimacy for the government was withdrawn. Those involved in the baby-killing industry had hardened their blackened, jaded hearts. A demonizing sense of Us and Them was complete. Violence followed. This destructive and lethal violence would be systematically advocated by fellow travelers in the Army of God, including its chaplain, Michael Bray, who wrote *A Time to Kill*, wherein he argued it was justifiable to kill abortion doctors. Similarly, Eric Rudolph wrote,

> I am not an anarchist. I have nothing against government or law enforcement in general. It is solely for the reason that this

government has legalized the murder of children that I have no allegiance to nor do I recognize the legitimacy of this particular government in Washington . . . Because I believe that abortion is murder, I also believe that force is justified in an attempt to stop it.[42]

It was a former Presbyterian minister, Paul Hill, however, who provided the most extensive exposition of the position taken by this loosely connected group of self-acknowledged terrorists. Following several days of protesting, in late July, 1994, Hill shot and killed Dr. John Britton, along with his armed escort, seriously wounding the escort's wife in the process. Dr. Britton had been recruited to Pensacola, in part to replace the services of Dr. Gunn. Hill, who admitted the killings, was convicted and sentenced to death. While awaiting execution, he brought together and expanded his writings in a manuscript, *Mix My Blood With the Blood of the Unborn*.

Hill was executed before he was able to finish his book. In the week just prior to his execution, Hill and his supporters decided that the manuscript would be published in its unedited condition. Subsequently, one of Hill's friends and confidants, Rev. Donald Spitz, then director of Pro-life Virginia, put the unedited manuscript online.[43] The grounding principle was succinctly stated: "It is certain that the innocent should be defended with the means necessary, and since the unborn are innocent, it is equally certain that they should be defended with the means necessary."

Two weeks after Paul Hill had killed Dr. Britton and his escort in Pensacola, Florida, a *Time* article appeared, asking the question, "Why not kill the baby killers?" This short piece began and ended with a nod to Hill's logic.

> The logic of Paul Hill—that abortion equals baby killing, that there is a "holocaust" going on and that therefore killing an abortionist is "justifiable homicide"—may be insane, but it is more consistent than the logic of those who share all of Hill's premises but reject his conclusion . . .
>
> Even someone who believes that abortion is murder might reasonably conclude that killing abortionists is not justified

because America is not Nazi Germany: we are a democracy under the rule of law. But once a group accepts the premise that the laws enacted by a democratic society are no legitimate deterrent in efforts to prevent "baby killing," it becomes harder to see what is wrong with stopping the murders by killing the murderers. The Operation Rescue people are not pacifists. They do not believe in the principle that violence is always wrong, even in response to violence. So why not kill the doctors? Paul Hill understands their logic better than they do.[44]

On September 3, 2003, Paul Hill became the first person executed for killings associated with abortion clinics. His last recorded words were an appeal to the Golden Rule:

> Two of the last things I'd like to say, if you believe abortion is a lethal force, you should oppose the force and do what you have to do to stop it. May God help you to protect the unborn as you would want to be protected.[45]

Other clinics were bombed, and doctors performing abortions were killed and assaulted,[46] but with Paul Hill's execution we came full circle. This former Presbyterian minister, calling on a higher law, justified killing those he charged with killing babies. He in turn was executed. Both life-ending actions were justified by invoking the imperative, "Life is sacred and should be protected." They differed only in how they defined the protective boundaries of life, their sense of injustice, and the legitimacy given to the actions taken.

Some six years later, on May 31, 2009, the story continued. Dr. George Tiller, who had escaped Shelley Shannon's attempted murder, was shot to death while attending church. His assailant's defense was justified homicide. Following Dr. Tiller's murder, Randall Terry released a statement:

> George Tiller was a mass-murderer. We grieve for him that he did not have time to properly prepare his soul to face God. I am more concerned that the Obama Administration will use Tiller's killing to intimidate pro-lifers into surrendering our most effective

rhetoric and actions. Abortion is still murder. And we still must call abortion by its proper name: murder.

Those men and women who slaughter the unborn are murderers according to the Law of God. We must continue to expose them in our communities and peacefully protest them at their offices and homes, and yes, even their churches.[47]

More direct justifications for Tiller's murder instantly appeared on outlets for the Army of God, one titled "A Just End to a Violent, Wicked Man."[48] Following Dr. Tiller's murder, violent actions aimed at abortion providers seemed to taper off. Political efforts to make it more difficult to secure an abortion gained energy.

In early 2014, the Guttmacher Institute reported[49] an unprecedented wave of state-level abortion restrictions, which had begun in 2010. Indeed, between 2011 and 2013 more laws were enacted (205) than in the entire previous decade (189). There was a pattern of consistency and imitation across the country, led by those who identified themselves with what had become known as the Tea Party. Frequently seen were laws mandating that women seeking an abortion be shown an ultrasound of the fetus as well as be made to listen as the physician read a scripted description of the fetus. Other laws strengthened requirements that abortion providers upgrade their facilities and have admitting privileges at a nearby hospital (e.g., within 30 miles.) Still other laws limited public funding otherwise provided to underwrite the services of such organizations as Planned Parenthood.

For supporters aiming to reduce abortions, these laws were hailed as increasing necessary information to fully inform women contemplating an abortion as well as to ensure safe procedures. For those in opposition, those who saw these laws as part of a War on Women, the underlying purpose was clear. Each and every law was aimed at making securing an abortion more difficult, either through heightened emotion or increased costs for both doctors and abortion-seeking women.

Whatever the rationale for or opposition to the tidal wave of new laws between 2011 and 2013, the data were clear. For some 40 years, public opinion had remained relatively stable, with support for the legality of abortion in the mid- to high 70 percentage-point range[50], with a relatively even split in those identifying as pro-life and those identifying as pro-

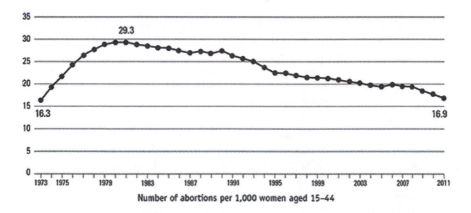

Figure 7.1 In 2011, the U.S. abortion rate reached the lowest level since 1973. Guttmacher Institute, Facts on induced abortion in the United States, Fact Sheet, 2014, http://www.guttmacher.org/pubs/fb_induced_abortion.html, accessed June 11, 2014.

choice. In comparison, over these same 40 years, there had been a consistent gradual decline in the rate of abortions among women aged 15–44.

Stable public opinion and downward trends in abortion rates were one thing, calls for further change were another. Dr. George Tiller had been best known, revered, and reviled for his willingness to provide late-term therapeutic abortions, when the fetus was, as some would note, mere inches from life. In the 1990s, what came to be referred to as partial-birth abortions moved center stage.

Notes

1 Linda Greenhouse, *Becoming Justice Blackmun: Harry Blackmun's Supreme Court Journey* (New York: Times Books Henry Holt & Company, 2005), 80.
2 *Griswold v. Connecticut*, 381 U.S. 479 (1965); *Eisenstadt v. Baird*, 405 U.S. 438 (1972) 405 U.S. 438.
3 Greenhouse, *Becoming Justice Blackmun*, 100.
4 John Hart Ely, "The Wages of Crying Wolf: A Comment on *Roe v. Wade*," *Yale Law Journal* 82 (1973): 920–49.
5 Ely, "The Wages of Crying Wolf," 926.
6 James Davison Hunter, *Cultural Wars: The Struggle to Define America* (New York: Basic Books, HarperCollins, 1991). See also, however, Morris P. Fiorina, with Samuel J. Abrams and Jeremy C. Pope, *Culture War? The Myth of a Polarized America* (Pearson Longman, 2006).
7 *Symposium: The End of Democracy? Judicial Usurpation of Politics* November, 1996.
8 Hittinger, "A Crisis of Legitimacy," 25.

9   One prominent contributor, Robert H. Bork, while standing by his critical analysis, wished the editors had not made their suggestions and noted in a follow-on letter to the editors, "The necessity for reform, even drastic reform, does not call the legitimacy of the entire American 'regime' into question." In another letter to the editors, a member of the *First Things* Editorial Board resigned, suggesting that the editors had "raised so grave and, in my opinion, irresponsible an issue, and given it such prominence, that I cannot, in good conscience, continue to serve."

10 In a bow to the eugenic past, the court would justify limits on a woman's privacy by citing *Buck v. Bell*. The principle of *stare decisis* was alive and well.

11 See for example, Teresa Iglesias, "*In Vitro* Fertilisation: The Major Issues," *Journal of Medical Ethics* 10 (1984): 36. Peter Singer, *Practical Ethics* (Cambridge: Cambridge University Press, 1993). Massimo Reichlin, "The Argument From Potential: A Reappraisal," *Bioethics* 11 (1997): 1–23

12 Bernard Nathanson, *The Hand of God: A Journey From Death to Life by the Abortion Doctor Who Changed His Mind* (Washington, DC: Regnery Publishing, 1996), 140.

13 See www.silentscream.org/silent_e.htm.

14 See "The Facts Speak Louder Than *The Silent Scream*," Planned Parenthood, www.plannedparenthood.org/news-articles-press/politics-policy-issues/abortion-access/anti-abortion-video-6136.htm.

15 The National Abortion Federation began compiling these and related statistics in 1977.

16 http://prolifeaction.org/sidewalk/packet.htm.

17 http://prolifeaction.org/truth/howto.htm.

18 Francis Schaeffer, *A Christian Manifesto* (Westchester, IL: Crossway Books, 1981), 120.

19 Dallas A. Blanchard, *The Anti-Abortion Movement and the Rise of the Religious Right* (New York: Twayne Publishers, 1994).

20 Dallas A. Blanchard and T.J. Prewitt, *Religious Violence and Abortion: The Gideon Project* (Gainesville, FL: University Press of Florida, 1993).

21 Risen and Thomas, *Wrath of Angels*, 94.

22 See *Scheidler, et al., v. National Organization for Women (NOW), et al.* and *Operation Rescue v. NOW, et al.* Argued November 30, 2005; decided February 28, 2006.

23 http://forerunner.com/forerunner/X0425_Cherry_Hill_Rescue.html.

24 Risen and Thomas, *Wrath of Angels* (1998): 263.

25 http://forerunner.com/forerunner/X0471_Randall_Terry_Interv.html.

26 The National Abortion Federation.

27 David Shaw, "'Abortion Hype' Pervaded Media After Webster Case," *Los Angeles Times*, July 4, 1990.

28 505 U.S. 833 (1992).

29 As reported by Alan Guttmacher Institute and Centers for Disease Control.

30 The Ku Klux Act of 1871.

31 See www.dr-tiller.com/mercy.htm.

32 *Jayne Bray, et al., Petitioners v. Alexandria Women's Health Clinic et al.*

33 *Washington Post*, March 11, 1993.

34 *New York Times*, March 5, 1994.

35 *Washington Post*, March 11, 1993.

36   Freedom of Access to Clinics Entrances (FACE) Act—Statute 18 U.S.C. § 248.

37   The Nashville statement of conscience: Why the killing of abortion doctor is wrong, September, 1994. "Killing Abortionists: A Symposium," *First Things*, December (1994): 24–31. Gary North, *Lone Gunners for Jesus: Letters to Paul J. Hill* (Tyler, TX: Institute for Christian Economics, 1994).

38   See, for example: www.npr.org/news/specials/roevwade/.

39   See Evan Carton, *Patriotic Treason: John Brown and the Soul of America* (New York: Free Press, 2006).

40   HBO's 2000 America Under Cover documentary, *Soldiers in the Army of God*, featured Horsley, along with Paul Hill, Bob Lokey, and Michael Bray.

41   This piece was later revised and posted on his website, christiangallery.com. In his introduction to the revised article, Horsley writes:

> I originally wrote this article in the immediate aftermath of a Birmingham abortion clinic bombing in 1997 when someone—Eric Rudolph?—sent a note saying the Army of God had planted the bomb. Post 9/11/2001, the only thing I add to what I wrote before is to point out that Muslim terrorists call themselves the Army of God just as this abortion clinic bomber did. It is most remarkable that President George W. Bush has finally acknowledged and admitted and declared the war that had gone undeclared in this nation ever since 1973 when the government of the USA in *Roe. v. Wade* effectively declared war against the children of God. If you want to understand the Army of God in the USA, read the article entitled "Exploding the Myth of the Army of God."

42   Rudolph had become widely known after hiding in the woods of North Carolina for some five years before being captured and facing four trials in four separate jurisdictions for his violent activities. See, www.armyofgod.com/EricRudolphHome page.html.

43   www.armyofgod.com/PHillbookIntro.html. Among other topics, Hill's manuscript sets out a point-by-point rebuttal of the Southern Baptist Convention's denunciation of the use of violence by anti-abortionists.

44   Michael Kinsley, "Why Not Kill the Baby Killers?" *Time*, August 15, 1994.

45   www.clarkprosecutor.org/html/death/US/hill873.htm.

46   In addition to Drs. John Britton and David Gunn, in 1994, two receptionists were killed in Massachusetts and Virginia. In 1998, a security guard at a clinic was killed in Alabama. In this same year, Dr. Barnett Slepian was shot to death in his home in New York. In addition, as reported by the National Abortion Federation, there were numerous attempted murders and assaults during this same time period.

47   Cited: www.christiannewswire.com/news/8967610531.html.

48   See www.armyofgod.com/GeorgeTillerBabyKillerIndex.html.

49   www.guttmacher.org/pubs/gpr/17/1/gpr170109.html.

50   See for example www.gallup.com/poll/1576/abortion.aspx.

CHAPTER 8

INCHES FROM LIFE

Dr. George Tiller had been labeled "Tiller the Baby Killer" by those opposed to his late-term abortion practice. Those who condemned his practices advocated violence, even lethal violence, to stop him. They were convinced they were doing God's will, taking life to protect life. Although extreme, such activists were embedded in a national social movement. The high-water mark came with the 1991 Summer of Mercy, where the immediate objective was to close down three local clinics, with special attention given to the one run by Dr. Tiller, who advertised nationally the late-term-abortion services he provided. Standing in opposition were those committed to respect the dignity and autonomy of a woman and the protection of her health.

A local federal judge issued an injunction to end the clinic blockades in Wichita. His orders were backed by the use of federal marshals. The president of the United States, George H.W. Bush, sympathetic to the demonstrators, countermanded the judge's action. Lawsuits were filed. One involved a young Justice Department attorney in his late thirties, John Roberts, who argued before the Supreme Court on behalf of Jayne Bray and her husband, Michael Bray, who had authored the anti-abortion book, *A Time to Kill: A Study Concerning the Use of Force and Abortion.*

In January, 1993, the Court agreed with Roberts and found the federal judge in Kansas had overstepped his authority. The use of federal force was not justified.[1] A little over a decade later, in 2005, Attorney Roberts would become Chief Justice of the Supreme Court. In 2007, he joined four of his colleagues in a decision that upheld the Partial-Birth Abortion Ban Act of 2003, signed into law by President George W. Bush.[2] This Act outlawed a subset of late-term-abortion procedures that had so troubled and outraged those opposed to Dr. Tiller's practice.[3] The boundary where abortion became infanticide was clarified. It was inches from birth.

This answer had been presaged during the oral argument in *Roe* in an exchange between Robert Flowers, assistant attorney general for the State of Texas, and justices Marshall and Stewart. Referring to a Texas statute, Justice Marshall probed its meaning:

> *Mr. Justice Marshall*: What does it [the statute] mean?
> *Mr. Flowers*: I would think that—
> *Mr. Justice Stewart*: That it is an offense to kill a child in the process of childbirth.
> *Mr. Flowers*: Yes, sir. It would be immediately before childbirth, or right in the proximity of the child being born.
> *Mr. Justice Marshall*: Which is not an abortion.
> *Mr. Flowers*: Which is not—would not be an abortion. Yes sir, you're correct, sir. It would be homicide.[4]

Words and Images

The applicability of moral principles and the perceived legitimacy of law depend on how issues are framed: on the analogies drawn, the meaning assigned to words, and the emotional impact of images. During the 1990s, phrases evolved, acronyms were employed, and illustrations produced, all to frame the moral meaning of ending a pregnancy at the very edge of where, all agreed, life is present.

One such phrase, "partial-birth abortion," was used to label the 2003 Act signed into law by President Bush. It was not a medical phrase. It was a phrase of political art, crafted by social activists and politicians. It evolved from a description of a newly developed medical procedure outlined by Dr. W. Martin Haskell at a national abortion risk management seminar, held in Dallas in September 1992.[5] Dr. Haskell was the physician–owner of a women's center in Cincinnati, Ohio. He had performed over 700 abortions using what he called dilation and extraction

(D&X) procedures. These procedures were easier and safer than the more commonly used dilation and evacuation (D&E) methods. He wanted to let his colleagues know how it was done.

Dr. Haskell was no activist and had not been threatened directly by persons such as Michael Griffin or Paul Hill, but he was aware they opposed what he did. His practice and perspective precisely illustrated what so troubled the organizers of the Summer of Mercy. In a subsequent interview, he related, "Pro-life activist Randall Terry recently said to me that he was going to do everything within his power to have me tried like a Nazi war criminal."[6] When talking with his colleagues at the abortion risk management seminar, however, this was not the risk Dr. Haskell had in mind. He was interested instead in reducing the medical risks in late second-trimester and early third-trimester abortions, offering details on a safe, quick outpatient procedure he had developed.

"Dilation and extraction is an alternative method for achieving late second trimester abortions to 26 weeks," Dr. Haskell reported. "It can [also] be used in the third trimester." In Dr. Haskell's experience, D&X was a preferable alternative to the classic D&E, as well as to various infusion and induction methods designed to soften fetal tissue for easier removal.

Haskell's detailed description was laced with technical descriptors: "sterile urea intra-amniotic infusion," "previous day's Dilapan," lysis, autolysis, transducer, Metzenbaum scissors, and Bierer or Hern forceps. These terms were understood by his professional colleagues, but, for those dedicated to protecting the almost-born child and convincing the broader public of the evils they saw, they were mere distractions from the tragedy taking place.

Other portions of Haskell's presentation did, however, catch their attention. Perhaps unwittingly, Dr. Haskell, when describing the technical details, also highlighted the humanity of the fetus and thereby generated empathy for the infant and repulsion for the actions being described. "The surgeon introduces a large grasping forceps," Haskell began. "He moves the tip of the instrument carefully towards the fetal lower extremities . . . [closes] its jaws to firmly and reliably grasp a lower extremity . . . and pulls the extremity into the vagina."

With a lower extremity in the vagina, Dr. Haskell continued, the skull frequently lodged at the internal cervical opening. At this point the surgeon would "hook the shoulders of the fetus" to increase the tension. Maintaining the tension,

> the surgeon takes a pair of blunt curved Metzenbaum scissors in the right hand. He carefully advances the tip, curved down, along the spine and under his middle finger until he feels it contact the base of the skull under the tip of his middle finger . . . the surgeon then forces the scissors into the base of the skull . . . Having safely entered the skull, he spreads the scissors to enlarge the opening.

With the scissors removed, a suction catheter is introduced into the hole and the surgeon, "evacuates the skull contents. With the catheter still in place, he applies traction to the fetus, removing it completely from the patient."

In an interview a year following his presentation, Haskell was asked, "Does it bother you that a second trimester fetus so closely resembles a baby?" "I really don't think about it," he responded. "Sure it becomes more physically developed but it lacks emotional development. It doesn't have the mental capacity for self-awareness. It's never been an ethical dilemma for me." Later in the same interview he was asked, "Does the fetus feel pain?" Admitting some ignorance, he again drew the humanizing line at self-awareness, likening the fetus to a pet:

> I'm not an expert, but my understanding is that fetal development is insufficient for consciousness. It's a lot like pets. We like to think they think like we do. We ascribe human-like feelings to them, but they are not capable of the same self-awareness we are. It's the same with fetuses.[7]

Why had he developed these procedures? To reduce risks to the mother and to ease the task facing the physician. The widely used D&E procedures involved dismembering the fetus inside the uterus and evacuating the pieces. After twenty weeks of gestation, fetal tissue could become tough and difficult to pull apart, thus complicating the operation and increasing the risk to the mother. Alternative procedures for softening fetal tissue, such as the infusion of a saline solution or other chemicals to terminate the life of the fetus *in utero* involved risks of infection.

As a result, Cincinnati hospitals, where Dr. Haskell practiced, discouraged these procedures.

The D&X procedures were not terribly complicated and had been developed somewhat simultaneously by others. While performing D&Es, Dr. Haskell had shifted his techniques almost by accident. When asked "What led you to develop D&X?" he responded:

> I noticed that some of the later D&Es were very, very easy . . . the easy ones would have a foot length presentation, you'd reach up and grasp the foot of the fetus, pull the fetus down and the head would hang up and then you would collapse the head and take it out. It was easy.[8]

For physicians, the procedures described might have been clinically straightforward and helpful. For others, they were a jarring offense against life. The doctor *grasped the foot* of the fetus. The surgeon's *fingers hooked the shoulders*. Scissors were advanced *along the spine* until they contacted the *base of the skull*, where they were inserted and expanded to create an opening through which a *catheter was placed to suck out the contents*. This caused the *skull to collapse* and thus be more easily removed through the birth canal.

Anti-abortion activists did not miss the disturbing humanizing implications. Starting with Bernard Nathanson's film, *The Silent Scream*, anti-abortion advocates had attempted to frame the abortion debate through graphic images and rhetoric, picturing the fetus in the sanctuary of the womb as a small, delicate, vulnerable person deserving of, in every way, our full respect and protection. During the early stages of pregnancy depicted in Nathanson's film, these images and conclusions were ambiguous. The ultrasound images were grainy and hard to decipher. The fetal models used in the film were misleading. Claims of early-term fetal suffering could be and were questioned.

More dramatic were the words of Dr. Haskell. They matched graphic, bloody, and, for many, shocking photos carried along roadsides, on college campuses, and in front of abortion clinics by protesters in Joe Scheidler's *Face the Truth* initiative.[9] These photos were of late-term abortions. They were so graphic they caused many on-lookers, even committed anti-abortionists, to turn away. With Dr. Haskell's clinical depiction of late-term abortion procedures, a compelling case could be made in a clear, yet less alienating manner. Anti-abortion advocates had been handed a gift.

Unwittingly, a doctor, well experienced with abortions, was making their case for them. D&X abortions involved the intentional killing of a partially born human being, in many cases occurring beyond the point of *viability* of 24–28 weeks, alluded to in *Roe*. Unlike first-trimester abortions, the late-term fetus took on easily identified human qualities and was clearly capable of experiencing pain.

This became evident in testimony a later congressional hearing was offered by a self-described pro-choice nurse, attending the D&X abortion of a 26½-week fetus:

> The baby's little fingers were clasping and unclasping, and his feet were kicking. Then the doctor stuck the scissors through the back of his head, and the baby's arms jerked out in a flinch, a startle reaction, like a baby does when he thinks that he might fall. The doctor opened up the scissors, stuck a high-powered suction tube into the opening and sucked the baby's brains out. Now the baby was completely limp. I was really completely unprepared for what I was seeing. I almost threw up as I watched the doctor do these things.[10]

Actions taken during late-term abortions might be described as dilation and extraction, or D&X, for clinicians. For others, they were the destruction of a small, vulnerable human being. The procedures were a repulsive abomination.

The National Right to Life Committee (NRLC) was the first to take up the charge on a national scale. As flawed as its message was, they were aware that *The Silent Scream* had been an effective call to action. Its title drew attention; even its grainy ultrasound images and illustrative not-always-to-scale fetal models generated empathy, commitment, and action. Using Dr. Haskell's description of his procedures, they aimed to do the same thing.

Images, originally easily reproducible, cartoon-like sketches drawn by an Oregon activist, Jenny Westberg,[11] and later refined into color representations for the Internet, were produced and disseminated.[12]

They depicted Dr. Haskell's description of D&X procedures. Their message was clear. The life of a small, vulnerable baby was at risk, the last picture showing the instant when the suction catheter was placed in the infant's skull.

Westberg's early images drew the attention of Keri Harrison, who would draft the 1995 Partial-Birth Abortion Ban legislation, carried by a Florida congressman, Charles Canady: legislation eventually vetoed by President Clinton. For Harrison, it was simple:

> To think that a human being would actually hold a little baby in his or her hand, and then kill it—that's what got me. If you're holding that child in your hand, and knowingly killing the child, you can't argue any more that it's not really a human being. You just can't do it.[13]

A dramatic phrase was needed to capture the procedure, a phrase that would be accurate and compelling, but not a phrase that would connect their efforts with the alienating fringe elements of the anti-abortion movement. "Late-term abortion" was too ambiguous and encompassing. It also left the sense that the procedure was fully covered by the *Roe* and *Doe* decisions.

In D&X procedures, the fetus was moved into the birth canal. It was in many ways similar to a premature birth. If the cervix dilated a bit more, the child would emerge through the birth canal without assistance. All this was visually apparent from the Westberg drawings. Harrison would later recall that, while throwing around terms with Representative Canady and NRLC lobbyist, Douglas Johnson, "We called it the most descriptive thing we could call it."[14] The fetus was indeed just inches from birth. "Partial-birth abortion" was decided upon as the phrase to frame the message.

Protecting Health as Well as Life

A bill, the "Partial-Birth Abortion Ban Act of 1995," was drafted. It passed Congress in December. It would amend Title 18 of the United States Code by inserting language following Chapter 73. The first two paragraphs, laced with legal language, drew the most attention.

(a) Any physician who, in or affecting interstate or foreign com-
merce, knowingly performs a partial-birth abortion and thereby
kills a human fetus shall be fined under this title or imprisoned
not more than two years, or both. This paragraph shall not apply
to a partial-birth abortion that is necessary to save the life of a
mother whose life is endangered by a physical disorder, illness,
or injury: Provided, that no other medical procedure would suffice
for that purpose. This paragraph shall become effective one day
after enactment . . .

As used in this section, the term "partial-birth abortion" means
an abortion in which the person performing the abortion partially
vaginally delivers a living fetus before killing the fetus and
completing the delivery.

The legislation had solid support in Congress, but not enough to override
a presidential veto.[15]

When explaining his veto, President Clinton did not refer to "partial-
birth" abortions, but rather that he had "long opposed late-term abortions
except where necessary to protect the life or health of the mother." Threats
to the mother's life had been included. "Health" had been left out. Had
the bill included an exception for "serious health consequences," consequences including "serious physical harm, often including losing the ability
to have more children," President Clinton would have signed it. Indeed,
he noted, "I would sign it now."

Concluding his remarks, the president wanted everyone to know he
understood and agreed with "the desire to eliminate the use of a procedure
that appears inhumane. But to eliminate it without taking into consideration the rare and tragic circumstances in which its use may be necessary
would be even more inhumane." Both Congress and President Clinton
wanted to protect life and alleviate suffering. They disagreed on where
the boundaries should be drawn and how competing values should be
resolved.

Why had supporters of the bill not included a "health" exception? Why
were others so adamant that this be done? Those opposing the "health"
exception recalled the language of *Roe's* companion case, *Doe v. Bolton*,
wherein the court had defined health broadly to include, "all factors

—physical, emotional, psychological, familial, and the woman's age— relevant to the well-being of the patient." This was no boundary at all. Anyone could conceivably claim a "health" exception. Opening the door to the health exception would be opening the floodgates to the disregard for life. It would mean partial-birth abortions on demand.

Advocates for the health exception, by contrast, focused on circumstances where suffering and damage to life's chances were severe. Some fetuses, if born, would have debilitating deformities or severe brain damage, sometimes detected late in the pregnancy. A meaningful life for the yet-to-be-born infant was precluded. In many cases, letting the child be born and fighting for its ultimately unattainable survival meant a severe strain on the financial and emotional resources of the family. More immediately, in some, albeit rare cases, not allowing late-term abortions represented a threat to the health and physical well-being of the mother, including her ability to have children in the future. The uncertain boundaries of tolerable suffering, like the thresholds for life, were shrouded in mist. The mechanisms of the law, useful for general policy, but hamhanded in individual cases, should not intrude. These difficult, often tragic, decisions should be left to persons most directly involved.

President Clinton's veto was issued on April 10, 1996. Those committed to respecting the autonomy of mothers, families, and their physicians to make these intensely personal decisions were relieved. Those concerned with what they saw as the taking of life just inches from birth and an emerging culture deemphasizing the sanctity of life were incensed. They did not plan to let the issue drop.

In an impassioned speech, urging his colleagues to override President Clinton's veto, Representative Henry Hyde anchored his message in a passage taken from Dostoevsky, "Man can get used to anything, the beast!" Hyde foresaw profound, society-wide consequences:

> It is not just the babies that are dying for the lethal sin of being unwanted or being handicapped or malformed. We are dying, and not from the darkness, but from the cold, the coldness of self-brutalization that chills our sensibilities, deadens our conscience and allows us to think of this unspeakable act as an act of compassion.[16]

Henry Hyde was not alone. A week after his veto, President Clinton received a letter of protest from the National Conference of Catholic Bishops. With "deep sorrow and dismay," those signing the letter found the president's veto "beyond comprehension for those who hold human life sacred." These religious leaders were convinced the president's action would ensure "the continued use of the most heinous act to kill a tiny infant just seconds from taking his or her first breath outside the womb." They found the president's assessment of "health" too broad, noting:

> If a woman is "too young" or "too old," if she is emotionally upset by pregnancy, or if pregnancy interferes with schooling or career, the law considers those situations as "health" reasons for abortion. In other words, as you know and we know, an exception for "health" means abortion on demand.

The archbishops of Chicago, Philadelphia, Washington, Baltimore, Boston, Los Angeles, Detroit, and New York, along with the president of the National Conference of Catholic Bishops, signed the letter. They saw President Clinton's veto as taking

> our nation to a critical turning point in its treatment of helpless human beings inside and outside the womb. It moves our nation one step further toward acceptance of infanticide. Combined with the two recent federal appeals court decisions seeking to legitimize assisted suicide, it sounds the alarm that public officials are moving our society ever more rapidly to embrace a culture of death.

They resolved to be "unremitting and unambiguous in our defense of human life."

Partial-Birth Abortion Ban legislation, very close to its original form, was reintroduced in the next session of Congress. The lobbying, hearings, and outcome were the same. By October 8, 1997, the bill had passed both houses of Congress. The health exception was not included. President Clinton issued his veto on October 10, 1997. Again, among supporters of the ban, there was an outcry of dismay, sorrow, and disgust. Those seeking to strengthen respect for the health, autonomy, and integrity of mothers, fathers, their families, and physicians breathed yet another sigh of relief. While passage of the bill had garnered more support, it was still a few votes shy of what was needed to override the president's veto.[17]

The Political Landscape

By this time, the issue of abortion had long been a central pillar of political campaigns. President Clinton and Congress were seemingly not far apart. Disagreement remained on exemptions for health consequences, consequences President Clinton specified as "serious physical harm, often including losing the ability to have more children."

National public opinion polls painted a mixed picture. One 2002 review of all major public polling done to date found, "wide variation in support for partial-birth abortion bans, ranging from 77 percent in one poll . . . to 49 percent in another." The review continued,

> When not providing respondents with specific legislative details about the timing of the procedure or the life of the mother exception, and indicating a doctor is involved, the survey question yields net opposition to the ban; only 43 percent favor banning the procedure while 51 percent are opposed.[18]

Using more general wording, the highly respected National Opinion Research Center, affiliated with the University of Chicago, had been conducting annual national polls on related topics since 1972. A consistent 85–90 percent of the population responded "Yes" when asked, "Please tell me whether or not you think it should be possible for a pregnant woman to obtain a legal abortion if the woman's own health is seriously endangered by the pregnancy?" These General Social Surveys included additional questions about such things as the respondent's social class, education, political leanings, and religious commitments and practices. Wide variation across the social landscape was consistently noted. Religious commitments and practices were of particular importance.

Perhaps most telling was the question, "About how often do you pray?" Possible responses ranged from "several times a day" to "never." Those praying several times a day were four times more likely to oppose abortion, even when there were serious threats to the mother's health, than those reporting they never prayed. Similar patterns were evident for other

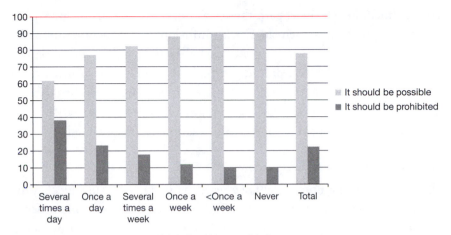

Please tell me whether or not you think it should be possible for a pregnant woman to obtain a legal abortion if there is a strong chance of serious defect in the baby?
About how often do you pray?

Figure 8.1 Support for Abortion, When There is an Indication of Birth Defects, by How Often Respondent Prays.

contingent circumstances, such as serious birth defects, where respondents were asked, "Please tell me whether or not you think it should be possible for a pregnant woman to obtain a legal abortion if there is a strong chance of serious defect in the baby." As one would expect, given these findings, the frequency with which one prayed was also closely linked to opposition to abortion on demand.

Clearly, those who spent time praying every day drew the early protective boundaries of life, and balanced the importance of the mother's life and health and the baby's life chances differently than those who prayed less often or never. Frequency of prayer was more predictive of an individual's opinion than various forms of affiliation, though the two were clearly related. The same polls found self-declared "fundamentalists" or "evangelicals" were more likely to pray daily than those aligning themselves with "mainline" or "liberal" denominations.[19] This religion-infused variation had not escaped political campaign strategists. Networks were activated and campaigns carried out.

Some 30 states passed legislation in one way or another banning partial-birth abortions. Wording used in these statutes reflected a coordinated, national agenda. The outlawed procedures focused on those Dr. Haskell had outlined. For the most part, these statutory bans did not include other late-term procedures such as D&E, infusion, or induction methods. Ironically, the politics of crafting the "partial-birth" wording and empathy-inducing images of D&X procedures had yielded legislation focused on procedure and location of the unborn, not on outcome. Partial-birth abortion laws focused on *how* the pregnancy was terminated, not on whether the life of a nearly born child was intentionally ended.

A Strange and Strained Argument

Dismembering the unborn fetus *in utero*, as was done using D&E procedures, or employing the various "softening" techniques of other procedures were by and large not covered by the state statutes or the proposed federal legislation. Instead, although specific wording differed here and there, the focus was on vaginal placement of a substantial portion of the unborn child for the purpose of performing procedures the physician knew would kill the child.

The state statutes were challenged in court. The first to reach the Supreme Court came from Nebraska in *Stenberg v. Carhart*.[20] It had been challenged just two days after its passage. On June 28, 2000, in the midst of a closely contested presidential campaign, the Supreme Court handed down an aggressively argued five–four decision declaring the Nebraska law unconstitutional. Two reasons were given. Most obviously, the Nebraska statute lacked an exception for protecting the "health" of the mother. President Clinton's later assessment was not simply his personal preference. It was grounded in this decision. Five of the Court's nine justices found that this omission violated precedents set out in *Roe*, *Doe*, and *Casey*. In addition, the definition and description of what Nebraska legislators had in mind by "partial-birth-abortion" procedures was deemed too ambiguous.

There had always been potential confusion between D&X and D&E procedures. Dr. Haskell had noted the link when describing how the fortuitous location of a foot meant the fetus could be easily pulled into the birth canal. The Nebraska statute focused on D&X procedures, but included

> deliberately and intentionally delivering into the vagina a living unborn child, *or a substantial portion thereof* [emphasis added], for

the purpose of performing a procedure that the person performing such procedure knows will kill the unborn child and does kill the unborn child.

What did "substantial portion" mean? A foot? Two legs? The torso? In his oral argument before the court, Nebraska's attorney general pointed to legislative debate for clarification. One senator had asked the bill's sponsor, "You said that as small a portion of the fetus as a foot would constitute a substantial portion in your opinion. Is that correct?" The sponsoring senator had agreed, "Yes, I believe that's correct."

This being the case, D&E and D&X procedures shaded into one another. Surely, protected life should not depend solely on the chance location of a foot. What happened if a D&E procedure turned into D&X while the abortion was taking place? The majority of the court concluded there was too much overlap. This left physicians at risk of prosecution, and the woman with too few acceptable options, creating a "substantial obstacle" and an "undue burden" on her choices in violation of the court's findings in *Casey*.

When it came to defining the protective boundaries of life, this was a strange and strained argument. Nebraska's law was unacceptable because it did not specify clearly where the fetus was when life was taken. Justice Scalia, writing in dissent, and referring to D&X procedures as "live-birth" abortions, berated the majority's rationale, noting that overturning Nebraska's ban on "this visibly brutal means of eliminating our half-born posterity is quite simply absurd." Justice O'Connor, disagreeing and concurring with the majority, noted that, if the statute had been limited to D&X procedures and included a health exception, "the question presented would be quite different." Given the question posed, however, their reasoning was sound.

Sound or absurd, the vote was five–four, and the ruling was released. Nebraska's statute banning partial-birth abortions was overturned. Given similar wording in statutes in more than two dozen other states,[21] the impact was national. Those working to ban partial-birth abortions were dealt a serious setback. The battle to determine when early life was fully protected, however, was not over.

Proponents for the ban took lessons from the Supreme Court's assessment of Nebraska's law. These lessons would influence their next steps.

In November 2000, George W. Bush was elected president, by the narrowest of margins. On December 12, 2000, the Supreme Court certified his election some six months after Nebraska's *Stenberg* decision. Although his administration would be consumed with other matters, President Bush was far more sympathetic, indeed, committed, to the banning of partial-birth abortions than his predecessor.

The Political Landscape Shifts

By October 2003, taking into account the court's assessment of the Nebraska statute, federal legislation was revised, hearings were held, amendments were considered, revisions were made, and votes were taken. The Partial-Birth Abortion Ban Act of 2003 did not contain a health exception for the mother, but it did clarify various other issues. It passed both houses of Congress by wide margins.[22] President Bush, on November 5, 2003, signed the Act into law.

At the signing ceremony, the president underscored his strong support, grounded in reverence for all young lives. "The best case against partial-birth abortion," he said, "is a simple description of what happens and to whom it happens. It involves the partial delivery of a live boy or girl, and a sudden, violent end of that life. Our nation owes its children a different and better welcome. [Applause] The bill I am about to sign protecting innocent new life from this practice reflects the compassion and humanity of America."

During the signing ceremony, President Bush may or may not have been aware of experiences such as those Gretchen Voss wrote about a few months later in the *Boston Globe*.[23] She and her husband, Dave, had gone to see ultrasound images of their developing baby. "As images of our baby filled the black screen, we oohed and aahed like the goofy expectant parents." From the technician's expression, however, it soon became evident something was wrong. A few minutes later, the expectant parents were meeting with their doctor. The ultrasound image had revealed the fetus had an open neural tube defect. The extent of the problem was not clear, and they were advised to go to another hospital in Boston for further diagnosis.

The news was not good:

> Instead of cinnamon and spice, our child came with technical
> terms like hydrocephalus and spina bifida. The spine, she [the

doctor] said, had not closed properly, and because of the location of the opening, it was as bad as it got. What they knew—that the baby would certainly be paralyzed and incontinent, that the baby's brain was being tugged against the opening in the base of the skull and the cranium was full of fluid—was awful. What they didn't know—whether the baby would live at all, and if so, with what sort of mental and developmental defects—was devastating. Countless surgeries would be required if the baby did live. None of them would repair the damage that was already done.

For Gretchen and Dave, the Partial-Birth Abortion Ban Act of 2003 did not reflect life-affirming compassion but a callous, misguided attempt to prohibit humane responses to deeply personal tragedies.

President Bush's attempt to ban partial-birth abortions threatens all late-term procedures. But in my case, everyone said it was the right thing to do—even my Catholic father and Republican father-in-law . . . Though the baby might live, it was not a life that we would choose for our child, a child that we already loved. We decided to terminate the pregnancy. It was our last parental decision.

Later, after Dave's brother had left a tearful message on their answering machine, Gretchen found her husband, "kneeling on the floor in our bathroom, doubled over and bawling, his body quaking."

Life and suffering, boundaries and dilemmas—there were no truly satisfying answers. Still, proponents on both sides pressed forward. The question now became whether the new federal statute, lacking as it did an exception for the mother's health, would clear the constitutional hurdle any better than the Nebraska law.

Legal Details

Drafters had gone to great lengths to ensure it would. The omission of a "health" exception, however, seemed to fly in the face of the Nebraska ruling. The omission was intentional. The congressional reasoning was blunt. The first paragraph of the Act read, "A moral, medical, and ethical consensus exists that the practice of performing a partial-birth abortion

... is a gruesome and inhumane procedure that is never medically necessary and should be prohibited." Congress based this blanket claim on hearings it had held.

From these hearings it was concluded:

> Congress finds that partial-birth abortion is never medically indicated to preserve the health of the mother; is in fact unrecognized as a valid abortion procedure by the mainstream medical community; poses additional health risks to the mother; blurs the line between abortion and infanticide in the killing of a partially-born child just inches from birth; and confuses the role of the physician in childbirth and should, therefore, be banned.

Congress had made a major effort to develop the factual basis for this conclusion through sworn testimony. Their well-developed findings deserved the court's deference. There was no need for a "health" exception. Others would disagree—the findings were not at all clear-cut and should be questioned.

The second problem the Supreme Court had found with the Nebraska statute was the meaning of the phrase "substantial portion" of the fetus outside the womb. How much was enough? Also of concern was the chance that what started as a common D&E procedure might unintentionally become a partial-birth D&X. To deal with these issues, Congress included quite specific wording.

> The term "partial-birth abortion" means an abortion in which ... the person performing the abortion deliberately and intentionally vaginally delivers a living fetus until, in the case of a head-first presentation, the entire fetal head is outside the body of the mother, or, in the case of breech presentation, any part of the fetal trunk past the navel is outside the body of the mother for the purpose of performing an overt act that the person knows will kill the partially delivered living fetus.

Clearly, there were now specific anatomical landmarks for the protected boundaries of life. In the case of head-first presentation, the full head must be outside the mother's body. In the case of a breech presentation, it was beyond the navel.

The rationale for these markers was not provided, nor were the reasons for why this type of abortion was more "gruesome" and "inhumane" than the D&E *in utero* dismemberment. The lines, however, had been drawn. Those who voted for the Act and the president who signed it into law believed they had found the "bright line" between abortion and infanticide and had struck the appropriate balance among the competing values involving the woman's health.

It remained for the courts to decide. The response was immediate. The day President Bush signed the Act, cases were brought almost simultaneously to the U.S. district courts in Northern California, Southern New York, and Nebraska. Citing well-known precedent, all three district courts found the Partial-Birth Abortion Ban Act of 2003 unconstitutional. There was continuing concern about whether the Act imposed undue constraints on the woman's choices, but most important was concern for the omission of any consideration given to exceptions for the woman's health. This was unacceptable.

When Attorney General Alberto Gonzales appealed these rulings to the relevant circuit courts, the outcome was the same. All three found the Act unconstitutional. In the Nebraska case, the circuit court noted, congressional claims notwithstanding, "If one thing is clear from the record in this case, it is that no consensus exists in the medical community." In this situation, "the Constitution requires legislatures to err on the side of protecting women's health by including a health exception." The conclusion followed, as night follows day: "Because the Act does not contain a health exception, it is unconstitutional."

By the end of January 2006, a total of six district and circuit court opinions, relying on the Supreme Court's findings in *Stenberg* and other supporting cases, now agreed in outcome. The Act signed into law by President Bush was unconstitutional. The attorney general appealed to the Supreme Court. The court agreed to hear the Nebraska case in February 2006 and combined it with the case from California in June. Although the parallels between the new federal law and the earlier Nebraska statute already declared unconstitutional by the Supreme Court were clear, there were important differences. The original *Stenberg decision* had been razor-thin— five–four. It had been aggressively argued, with strong dissents. The new federal Act had addressed concerns. Attorney General Gonzales was hopeful the outcome would be different. There were reasons for his hope.

It had been seven years since the Nebraska case had been decided. Two justices who had participated in that case were no longer on the court. Justice Alito had replaced Justice O'Connor, who had voted to strike down the Nebraska law. John Roberts, the attorney who had argued before the Supreme Court on behalf of the Summer of Mercy protestors, had replaced Chief Justice Rehnquist, who had found the earlier Nebraska law constitutional. With these two new justices siding with the majority, the Supreme Court, again voting five–four, found the constitutional shortcomings of the earlier Nebraska statue had been overcome. The Partial-Birth Abortion Ban Act of 2003 met Constitutional standards.[24]

Justice Kennedy, who had written a dissenting opinion when the Nebraska law was overturned, wrote for the majority. The concerns regarding overlap in D&X and D&E procedures, so evident in the Nebraska law, had been remedied. Intentional action was required. The protected boundaries of life had been specified. Depending on a head-first or breech delivery, the anatomical markers were clear. They were the baby's head or navel.

What about balancing the need to protect the mother's health? This was totally missing in the Partial-Birth Abortion Ban Act of 2003. Courts at all levels, including the Supreme Court, had previously underscored its importance numerous times. This go-around, contradictory medical testimony regarding the issue had been heard throughout the appeals process, as well as in final oral arguments before the Supreme Court. Unlike the circuit courts, where it was held that, in such uncertain circumstances, legislatures should "err on the side of protecting women's health," Justice Kennedy and colleagues voting with him were more willing to tolerate uncertainty. They wrote, "The Act is not invalid on its face where there is uncertainty over whether the barred procedure is ever necessary to preserve a woman's health." In such circumstances, remedies should be sought in an "as-applied challenge." Threats to the mother's health would have to be decided on a case-by-case basis. She and her doctor would have to ask for an exception to the law before proceeding with D&X procedures.

This was new. Writing in dissent, Justice Ruth Bader Ginsburg found this "piecemeal" approach "gravely mistaken" in that it jeopardized the woman's health and put the physician in an "untenable position." She also found portions of the all-male majority's vote to be a chauvinistic throwback to an earlier time. The court had heard in oral argument that doctors were sometimes reluctant to provide their patients with full information about the D&X procedures, desiring to shield them from the graphic details.

In a textbook example of paternalism, they wanted to protect her, even if her own values and assessment of the situation differed from theirs. Ironically, they grounded their concern in the mother's mental health. Justice Kennedy wrote,

> It is self-evident that a mother who comes to regret her choice to abort must struggle with grief more anguished and sorrow more profound when she learns, only after the event, what she once did not know: that she allowed a doctor to pierce the skull and vacuum the fast-developing brain of her unborn child, a child assuming the human form.

These procedures should be banned to protect the mother from her own, faulty, ill-informed judgment.

The single remaining woman on the court, joined by three of her male colleagues, found this reasoning inappropriate and condescending. It reflected, Justice Ginsburg noted, "ancient notions about women's place in the family and under the Constitution—ideas that have long since been discredited." Citing *Casey*, she reminded her brethren that they had previously found the "destiny of the woman must be shaped . . . on her own conception of her spiritual imperatives and her place in society." Further, Justice Ginsburg noted, the means "chosen by the State to further the interest in potential life must be calculated to inform the woman's free choice, not hinder it." The tension remained. This time, however, the razor-thin five–four majority fell on the side of banning, not the taking of life late in pregnancy, but a specified abortion procedure.

Adapting to a Strange and Strained Decision

The Partial-Birth Abortion Ban Act of 2003 was now the law of the land. Like the earlier decision in *Stenberg*, this was a strange and strained decision. It did not protect life. It simply affirmed the banning of a procedure based on the location of the fetus. It did not demand exceptions for the mother's health, though it did express concern for her mental anguish should she change her mind. The now-established legal boundary for protected life was whether the unborn child had been intentionally drawn out of the womb past its head or beyond its navel when its life was ended.

Mothers, their physicians, and supporting hospital abortion policies adapted. A few months later, the *Boston Globe* reported:[25]

> In response to the Supreme Court decision upholding the Partial-Birth Abortion Ban Act, many abortion providers in Boston and around the country have adopted a defensive tactic. To avoid any chance of partially delivering a live fetus, they are injecting fetuses with lethal drugs before procedures.

In some hospitals, the article continued, these alternatives had become policy:

> Three major Harvard-affiliated hospitals—Massachusetts General, Brigham and Women's, and Beth Israel Deaconess—have responded to the ban by making the injections the new standard operating procedure for abortions beginning at around 20 weeks' gestation . . . Boston Medical Center, too, has begun using injections for later surgical abortions . . . The decision came "after a lot of anguish about what to do."

The Partial-Birth Abortion Ban Act of 2003 established anatomical markers for the protected boundaries of life. It did not provide a quality-of-life rationale for why these markers were chosen. Still, if a child was protected once it emerged up to her navel or past his head, the protected status of an infant's life, fully born, would appear to be settled.

Not so. Following birth, questions swirled around the child's mental and physical capacities and projections of whether the just-born child would have a life worth living, protecting, and supporting.

Notes

1   *Jayne Bray, et al., Petitioners v. Alexandria Women's Health Clinic et al.*
2   *Gonzales, Attorney General v. Carhart et al.*, April 18, 2007.
3   The Partial-Birth Abortion Ban Act (Pub. L. 108–105, HR 760, S 3, 18 U.S. Code 1531).

4   Transcript of the Second Oral Argument in *Roe v. Wade*, October 11, 1972. Cited in Samuel W. Calhoun, "Ironic Misnomer: How the Term 'Partial-Birth Abortion' Reveals Why Attempts to Ban the Practice Have (so far) Been Largely Unsuccessful," (April, 2006). Washington & Lee Legal Studies Paper No. 2006–05. Available at SSRN: http://ssrn.com/abstract=899290. For an earlier discussion of these matters see: Stanley Atkinson, "Life, Birth and Live-Birth," *Law Quarterly Review* 20 (1904), 134.

5   Martin Haskell, "Dilation and Extraction for Late Second Trimester Abortion," presented at the National Abortion Federation Risk Management Seminar, September 13, 1992.

6   "2nd Trimester Abortion: An Interview with W. Martin Haskell, MD," *Cincinnati Medicine*, Fall (1993): 18.

7   "2nd Trimester Abortion," 18.

8   "2nd Trimester Abortion," 19.

9   www.prolifeaction.org/truth/objections.htm.

10 Testimony of Brenda Pratt Shafer, Subcommittee on the Constitution, U.S. House of Representatives, March 21, 1996.

11 See: Cynthia Gorney, "Gambling With Abortion: Why Both Sides Think They Have Everything to Lose," *Harper's Magazine*, November 2004, cover story.

12 http://mikeaustin.org/AAA/Partial%20Birth%20Abortion/PartialBirthAbortion.jpg.

13 Cited in Gorney, "Gambling With Abortion."

14 Cited in Gorney, "Gambling With Abortion."

15 House of Representatives: 288–139; Senate: 54–44.

16 Congressional Record, September 19, 1996.

17 House of Representatives: 295–136; Senate: 64–36.

18 *The Gallup Poll: Public Opinion 2002*, pp 206–7.

19 Roughly half of persons identifying with the Fundamentalist or Evangelical denominations reported praying several times a day, while roughly a third of self-declared "Mainline" and a fifth of "Liberal" Christians did the same.

20 530 U.S. 914 (2000).

21 Estimates varied, depending on how wording was interpreted.

22 In the Senate, the initial vote was 64–33–3. The House of Representatives passed its version without objection, but there were differences with the Senate. These were worked out, and, on October 2, 2003, a vote of 281–142–12 was recorded. The Senate then voted in support, 64–34–2.

23 "My Late Term Abortion," *Boston Globe*, January 25, 2004.

24 The votes in the two cases were: *Stenberg v. Carhart*: For the Majority: Breyer joined by Stevens, O'Connor, Souter, Ginsburg; Dissent: Kennedy joined by Rehnquist, Scalia, Thomas. *Gonzales v. Carhart*: For the Majority: Kennedy joined by Roberts, Scalia, Thomas, Alito; Dissent: Ginsburg, joined Stevens, Souter, Breyer.

25 Carey Goldberg, "Shots Assist in Aborting Fetuses—Lethal Injections Offer Legal Shield," *Boston Globe*, August 10, 2007.

CHAPTER 9

SHOULD THE BABY LIVE?

It was a long-established principle of law that infants born alive were considered persons and fully entitled to the protections of the law. But, as the twentieth century drew to a close, Representative Charles T. Canady, Chairman of the House Judiciary Subcommittee on the Constitution, was concerned. He saw "changes in the legal and cultural landscape" and what was increasingly referred to as an emerging "culture of death."[1] He aimed to clarify through proposed legislation, the Born-Alive Protection Act of 2000.

Introducing his legislation, Canady explained his concerns:

> The principle that born-alive infants are entitled to the protection of the law is being questioned at one of America's most prestigious universities. Princeton University bioethicist Peter Singer argues that parents should have the option to kill disabled or unhealthy newborn babies for a certain period after birth. According to Professor Singer, "a period of 28 days after birth might be allowed before an infant is accepted as having the same right to live as others." This is based on Professor Singer's view that the life of a newborn baby is "of no greater value than the life of a nonhuman animal at a similar level of rationality, self-consciousness, awareness, capacity to feel, etc." According to Professor Singer, "killing a disabled infant is not morally equivalent to killing a person. Very often it is not wrong at all."

Representative Canady went on to recount the implications of Singer's argument in the recent tragic treatment of an infant on the "outskirts of viability." The purpose of his bill, he told his congressional colleagues, was "to repudiate the pernicious ideas that result in tragedies such as this and to firmly establish that, for purposes of federal law, an infant who is completely expelled or extracted from her mother and who is alive is, indeed, a person under the law."

Representative Canady concluded his prepared statement with a specific proposal:

> Under the Act, an infant will be considered to have been born alive if she is completely extracted or expelled from her mother and breathes, has a beating heart, a pulsation of the umbilical cord, or definite movement of the voluntary muscles, regardless of whether the umbilical cord has been cut, and regardless of whether the baby was born as a result of natural or induced labor, caesarean section, or induced abortion.

As clear and specific as Canady's proposed legislation seemed to be, opposition remained. Final amendments were worked out, and President George W. Bush signed the all but unanimously passed Born Alive Infants Protection Act into law on August 5, 2002.

By the time the Act was signed into law, almost three decades had passed since the *Roe* and *Doe* decisions. An estimated 40 states had already passed related "born-alive" legislation. Over this period, the questions motivating this broad-based legal-reform movement had been posed, answered, and re-answered numerous times over. Why so much effort to resolve such a seemingly obvious question?

Lives Worth Living, Protecting, and Supporting

Concern was raised shortly after *Roe*, when James Watson, agreeing with his colleague Francis Crick, conjectured,

> If a child were not declared alive until three days after birth . . . the doctor could allow the child to die if the parents so chose and save a lot of misery and suffering. I believe this view is the only rational, compassionate attitude to have.[2]

Peter Singer and others were suggesting that the period when an infant had yet to attain the full protections of a person be extended to something approaching four weeks.[3]

A professor at American University, Jeffrey Reiman joined the fray and articulated his rationale in a book published in 1999.[4] "Killing children or adults is wrong," Reiman wrote, "because of properties *they* possess; killing infants [is wrong], because of an emotion that *we* naturally and rightly have toward infants." The implications of his rationale were elusive.

Reiman elaborated. It was a matter of empathy. We might love, identify with, and desire to protect infants, but infants "do not possess in their own right a property that makes it wrong to kill them." It followed that, while empathy and emotional attachments should be honored, "there will be permissible exceptions to the rule against killing [infants] that will not apply to the rule against killing adults or children." In particular, Reiman continued, "I think (as do many philosophers, doctors, and parents) that ending the lives of severely handicapped newborns will be acceptable." He left blurred the exact boundary separating less-protected infancy from fully protected children and adults. He was also unclear on the precise meaning of "handicapped newborns." Fully protected life depended on when and whether the infant possessed self-awareness and other attributes of "personhood" or "humanhood."[5]

No one, however, had more thoroughly, provocatively, and carefully explored the protective boundaries of early life and how some lives might be more worthy than others of living, protecting, and supporting than Peter Singer. Writing in 1985, Singer and his colleague, Helga Kuhse, introduced their book, *Should the Baby Live? The Problem of Handicapped Infants,*[6] with the bluntly provocative statement, "This book contains conclusions which some readers will find disturbing. We think that some infants with severe disabilities should be killed."

It was an intentionally jarring, directly stated claim. It had drawn a good deal of attention. It was grounded in the belief that the level of suffering must be taken into account and weighed in the balance against the duty to prolong and protect life. In some circumstances, the most humane course of action was to terminate an infant's life with care and compassion. Some lives, some moments and manifestations of life, were seen as more worthy of protection and support than others. We might want to deny this, we might think it morally wrong, there might be deeply troubling, ethical implications reminiscent of Nazi atrocities, but there was ample evidence for the ubiquitous presence of such actions based on these beliefs.

For Kuhse and Singer, such actions could be justified and should be defended. They built their argument by first reviewing the cases of two babies. Both had Down Syndrome. In both instances, the parents decided to let their child die. The first case occurred in 1980, in Derby, England; the second in Bloomington, Indiana, in 1982.

In Derby, the child had no complicating conditions. Shortly after the birth of her child, the mother was overheard by one of her sisters saying tearfully to her husband, "I don't want it, Duck." The doctor was informed and acceded to the parents' wishes. He wrote in the baby's records, "Parents do not wish baby to survive. Nursing care only." He also prescribed a pain killing drug to ease the child's suffering. It turned out this drug may have hastened death. Two days later, the infant was reported to be restless and struggling for breath. Early in the morning of the third day, he died in the arms of a nurse.

A troubled member of the hospital staff reported the doctor's actions to an advocacy organization, "Life." Members of the organization went to the police. The doctor was charged with murder. This charge was later reduced to attempted murder, as the baby had developed pneumonia, and it was unclear whether the baby had died from this or the doctor's action.

After a brief trial, the judge outlined several examples he felt might help the jury work through the legal and ethical issues defining the line between properly letting a patient die and unlawful murder. In reaching their decision, the jury's rationale remains unknown. They may have believed the doctor was not attempting to kill the child, but rather to alleviate suffering. They may have simply substituted their own moral judgment and negated the law in an exercise of jury nullification. Whatever the rationale, two hours after deliberations began, jurors returned with their verdict: "Not guilty."

In the Bloomington case, there was a complicating physical condition, frequently associated with Down Syndrome. For the baby to survive, a relatively simple operation with a high probability of success was necessary to remove a blockage in the infant's digestive tract. It would not affect the underlying mental handicap, but the child could be expected to lead an otherwise normal life.

The mother and father were in their early 30s. They had experience working with children with this condition. Both parents were of the opinion that such children "never had a minimally acceptable quality of life." They also had other children at home, whom they wanted and needed to support. After consulting with their physicians, they decided not to give permission for the operation.

The hospital doctors and administrators contacted a local judge, asking for a ruling. The judge sided with the parents. The baby was now three days old, and a decision was made not to appeal the judge's ruling. The local prosecutor, however, asked the judge to order intravenous feeding to keep the baby alive, at least temporarily. The judge refused. The prosecutor took his pleas for intervention to the State Supreme Court. Again, in support of parental autonomy, the answer was "No." Learning of the case, a number of families called the hospital and filed petitions with the court offering to adopt the baby. These requests were denied. The prosecutor, accompanied by a law professor from Indiana University, flew to Washington, DC, seeking emergency intervention from the U.S. Supreme Court. While en route to plead their case, the infant, now six days old, died.

Word spread immediately about the Bloomington case, producing an outcry among those who could not understand how the parents might let their child die and how physicians and the courts would stand idly by. One widely read newspaper columnist, published on both the east and west coasts, was a father of a child with Down Syndrome.

Writing a week after "Baby Doe" in Bloomington had died, George Will stated unequivocally how "common sense and common usage require use of the word 'homicide'." In addition to his consternation and condemnation of what had happened, Will wanted his readers to know of and learn from the childhood joys experienced by his son:

> Jonathan Will, 10, fourth-grader and Orioles fan (and the best Wiffle-ball hitter in southern Maryland), has Down's syndrome. He does not "suffer from" (as newspapers are wont to say) Down's syndrome. He suffers from nothing, except anxiety about the Orioles' lousy start.
>
> He is doing nicely, thank you. But he is bound to have quite enough problems dealing with society—receiving rights, let alone

empathy. He can do without people like Infant Doe's parents, and courts like Indiana's asserting by their actions the principle that people like him are less than fully human. On the evidence, Down's syndrome citizens have little to learn about being human from the people responsible for the death of Infant Doe.[7]

As compelling as his son's story was, not all parents agreed. Their children with Down Syndrome had not been so fortunate. One couple, living in Santa Barbara, California, replied. Unlike Will, they identified with the Bloomington parents. They too, "after much agonizing thought, prayer and discussion with family, friends, clergymen and other doctors," had made "the same painful decision." In their case, however, the hospital authorities did not cooperate. They knew how to successfully replace their son's missing esophagus and were going to proceed with or without the parents' consent. A court order was obtained, and the surgery was performed. The outcome was not good.

> Our baby has endured a great deal of pain, suffering and misery during his 18 months on Earth, due to the nature of his deformities, surgical procedures, and complications arising from them.
>
> He is not well today and is unable to eat orally. The doctors have told us there is a good probability that our son will suffer from lifelong problems ... It is indeed difficult to stand by and watch this occur.[8]

Regulations Emerge

George Will had helped craft the successful campaign of President Ronald Reagan. He remained close to the Reagan White House. A week after Will's column appeared in both the *Washington Post* and the *Los Angeles Times*, President Reagan issued memoranda to relevant federal agencies requesting that policies to prevent recurrences such as those in Bloomington be devised.[9]

The president's orders were grounded in a law passed in 1973 that forbade agencies receiving federal funds from withholding services ordinarily provided to handicapped citizens. In his communication with the attorney general, and perhaps recalling the scandals of Willowbrook,[10]

President Reagan noted, "Our nation's commitment to equal protection of the law will have little meaning if we deny such protection to those who have not been blessed with the same physical or mental gifts we too often take for granted."

It is important to recall how rapidly the rhetoric surrounding these matters was shifting. It was common through the 1950s to use the terms moron, imbecile, and idiot, or even monstrosities at birth, to characterize children not "blessed with the same physical or mental gifts we too often take for granted." In his influential but much criticized, *Morals and Medicine*, published in 1954, Episcopal clergyman Joseph Fletcher had reviewed the arguments of "those who favor involuntary euthanasia for monstrosities at birth," noting in a footnote, "It has always been a quite common practice of midwives and, in modern times, doctors, simply to fail to respirate monstrous babies at birth."[11]

Two years later, in 1956, less than a decade prior to the passage of the Civil Rights Act of 1964, a noted Cambridge University jurist, Glanville Williams, used similar terms. He had given a series of lectures at Columbia University. These were published in somewhat revised form in *The Sanctity of Life and the Criminal Law*. In a chapter titled "The protection of human life," Glanville noted, again in the dehumanizing parlance of the day, "There is, indeed, some kind of legal argument that a 'monster' is not protected under the existing law." Williams then went on to note, "Fortunately, the question whether a monster is human has small practical importance for the most extreme cases, because the acephalous, ectocardiac, etc., monster will usually die quickly after birth."[12]

By the 1980s, medical technology and greater sensitivity to civil discourse were changing both the probability of death and the rhetoric used. Medical technology had greatly enhanced the life chances of many of these infants and deepened our understanding of the underlying genesis of birth defects. Although the dehumanizing "monster" reference disappeared from legal and moral discourse, disagreements over the boundaries of protected life for otherwise imperiled infants remained.

The initial regulations following President Reagan's orders were hurriedly constructed. They were revised almost immediately to provide an oxymoronic "Interim final rule," which took effect March 22, 1983. They referred vaguely to "handicapped infants." They called for posters to be displayed in "a conspicuous place in each delivery ward." These posters were to carry the message that failure to feed and care for handicapped infants was a violation of federal law and that "Any person having knowledge that a handicapped infant is being discriminatorily denied food or customary medical care" should contact a "handicapped-infant hotline." A phone number in Washington, DC, was provided.

A good deal of confusion and suspicion followed. Critics began referring to the absurdity of Baby Doe Squads being dispatched from the nation's capital to hospital delivery wards all across the nation in response to anonymous phone calls. Within two weeks, suits were filed and injunctions sought by numerous professional associations, including the American Hospital Association and the American Academy of Pediatrics. The major complaints were focused: the federal government had no standing to intervene. The guidelines for treatment were too vague and had been drafted through inappropriate procedures. Physicians and parents should be trusted to make the right decisions.

Among the expressed concerns was poor specification of the many considerations faced by parents, doctors, and nurses, making decisions in time-constrained, emotion-laden circumstances. How viable was the newly born life? If saved, would the life be worth living? When were we prolonging death and the infant's suffering rather than protecting life? Should we simply let "vegetative" infants die? Indeed, with compassion and care, should we help the newly born child leave this life?

A pediatrician practicing in New Mexico reported,

> Because of the fear I had in being "reported," I recently spent one agonizing hour trying to resuscitate a newborn who had no larynx, and many other congenital anomalies. The sad part was that both the parents in the delivery room watched this most difficult ordeal. It was obvious to me that this was in no way a viable child but I felt compelled to carry on this way out of fear someone in the hospital would "turn me in." I am sure that you who sit in Washington are not faced with such difficult decisions at two o'clock a.m.[13]

A related and more general point of contention stemmed from the lack of recognition that not all handicaps were as minor as those faced by Jonathan Will or Baby Doe in Bloomington, Indiana. What about a "handicap" where the child was born with most of her brain missing? What about a condition known as intracranial hemorrhage, where the child might never breathe without a respirator and never have the capacity for cognition? What about a condition where a substantial portion of the digestive tract was missing, leaving an infant without the ability to digest food?

For many, including Jeffrey Reiman, Helga Kuhse, and Peter Singer, such handicaps raised questions about whether a life truly worth living, prolonging, and protecting was present. Medical treatment might be futile and serve no other end than prolonging the baby's suffering. Sometimes, we might simply want to let an infant die, even hasten its death, as peacefully and as comfortably as possible. The intention to let life go is profoundly different from the intention to destroy it. The boundaries of tolerable suffering, like the boundaries of protected life, would have to be more carefully drawn. Dilemmas infused with forced tragic choices between protecting life and alleviating suffering could not be avoided.

Nagging Uncertainties—Who Should Decide?

The courts agreed with those bringing the suit against the proposed Department of Health and Human Services (HHS) rules. As the Baby Doe Guidelines were being revised yet again, this time allowing specified exceptions and a period of comment,[14] a young baby girl, soon to be known as "Baby Jane Doe," was born on October 11, 1983, in Port Jefferson, Long Island, New York. She was the first child of a young couple, married about a year, born with numerous interrelated physical and mental defects, including spina bifida, kidney damage, microcephaly, a condition associated with incomplete brain development, and hydrocephaly, where fluid accumulates in the brain, sometimes causing brain damage.

Her physicians recommended operations to deal with the manifestations of spina bifida and to reduce the fluid in her skull. If performed, these operations might lengthen her life to a matter of weeks or months. Alternatively, she might live 20 years or more. There were risks and uncertainties all along the way. The child, in all likelihood and among other things, would be severely retarded, epileptic, paralyzed, and subject to infections.

This was the type of case Singer and Kuhse had in mind when arguing that suffering and the quality of life in these circumstances should be balanced against the duty to prolong and protect life. Baby Jane Doe's parents decided, after consulting with their clergy and attending physicians, to forego the operations and simply ensure that their baby girl was made comfortable and free from infection. Given the many uncertainties they faced, their physicians agreed.

The course of treatment would have been set, had it not been for a lawyer in Vermont, Lawrence Washburn, Jr., a dedicated pro-life activist and total stranger to the family. Given his convictions and commitments, he filed suit with a New York judge who had been the Right-to-Life party's candidate when he ran for the judgeship the previous year.[15] The judge appointed a guardian who stated at the subsequent hearing he thought the physicians and parents were wrong, arguing instead for immediate treatment. The judge agreed and so ordered.

The parents took the case to New York's Court of Appeals. With the appellate judges labeling Washburn's law suit "distressing and offensive," the court found that the parents had made "these decisions with love and thoughtfulness, and that strangers, however whimsical or well-intentioned, cannot subject them to this outrageous kind of proceeding."

As the case wound its way through the courts, publicity followed, and the parents agreed to an interview on *60 Minutes* with Ed Bradley. Bradley asked the infant's mother, "How do you feel when someone else who didn't know you, didn't know the child, had no connection with your family went to court to make a decision about your child's life?" With obvious emotion, she responded, "I think it is unbelievable. They don't have any right at all. They don't know our child. They don't love her. We are her parents. We are the only ones who can make this decision for her."

The father was of like mind:

It was very frightening to hear that a total stranger could force us into a state supreme court to answer for our decision making . . . It is very hard to understand his concern about our daughter's life when after all the court proceedings have ended, he would no longer be around, or heard from, or there to care for our daughter.

Washburn, who still had not met the parents or their struggling child, was unmoved. He responded in a subsequent interview that he remained convinced in the rightness of his actions, believing profoundly retarded children were, "'*l'enfants bon Dieu*,' the children of the good God, they are given to us because it is our call to heroism, to greatness, to have a child like this."[16] The case was taken to the U.S. Supreme Court, where judges declined, without comment, to review the New York Court of Appeals decision, and the parents' autonomy stood. Other accompanying issues, however, remained unresolved.

While Washburn was preparing his suit, and proceedings were progressing, an anonymous caller had used the U.S. HHS "hotline" to complain about the discriminatory treatment being given to Baby Jane Doe. In response, the case was referred to child protective services, where it was concluded there was no cause for intervention. Surgeon General C. Everett Koop, a pediatric surgeon closely aligned with the pro-life political movement, however, disagreed and wanted to examine the medical records.

Three weeks following Baby Jane Doe's birth, on November 6, Surgeon General Koop appeared on the national television show, *Face the Nation*, to discuss his involvement in the case and his decision to request related medical records. He had made similar requests for access in some 48 other cases. The focus was not on Baby Jane Doe but on the greater good. "We're not just fighting for this baby," he said. "We're fighting for the principle of this country that every life is individually and uniquely sacred." "Two different surgeons said different things," Koop noted. "One said, 'Operate. Operate now.' One said, 'Don't operate at all.' I think when you have that kind of a difference of opinion, there ought to be an independent review, there ought to be a third opinion."[17] The parents, doctors, and hospital felt they had reviewed the case appropriately and quite enough, and refused to provide the baby's medical records. A suit on behalf of HHS was filed to obtain them.

The U.S. Supreme Court agreed to review the case in *Bowen v. American Hospital Assn.*[18] The basic rationale for the Baby Doe Guidelines once again came under review. Some three years after Baby Jane Doe was born, in *Bowen*, the Court found:

> The [HHS] Secretary's own summaries of these cases establish beyond doubt that the respective hospitals did not withhold medical care on the basis of handicap . . . as a result, they provide no support for his claim that federal regulation is needed in order to forestall comparable cases in the future.

The opinion continued, "Concerned and loving parents had chosen one appropriate medical course over another." They had made an informed decision that was "in the best interests of the infant." The U.S. Supreme Court, as the New York Court of Appeals had done before them, affirmed parental autonomy to decide what was in the best interest of their handicapped child. Absent evidence of abuse, the government should stay out of these matters, and decisions should remain close to home.

When Doctors Say No

The cases that so bothered George Will, President Ronald Reagan, Lawrence Washburn, and C. Everett Koop had led to the Baby Doe Regulations. These regulations were initially grounded in civil rights-era legislation prohibiting discrimination against the handicapped. Subsequent revisions shifted justification of governmental oversight to evidence of child abuse and neglect. Whatever the justification, these regulations had evolved from cases where parents refused consent for treatment of their newly born infants. What if parents wanted treatment for their child, and their physicians refused?

This question was raised in *Bowen*. It was dismissed as too remote a possibility for serious consideration. Justices writing in the majority chided their dissenting colleagues for "speculating about nonexistent hypothetical cases in which a hospital might refuse to provide treatment requested by parents." If there was need for the Baby Doe Regulations, surveys of doctors showed and the Court concluded, it was "because parents refuse consent to treatment, and physicians acquiesce." The idea that doctors might refuse to treat infants with parental pleas to do so seemed far-fetched.

As medical technology continued to advance, and medical care became increasingly expensive, however, the remote possibility became increasingly real. On October 13, 1992, in Falls Church, Virginia, a baby girl was born lacking a major portion of her brain. While she was still in her mother's womb, anencephaly had been detected. The early indicators were severe enough that both the obstetrician and neonatologist counseled the mother to terminate her pregnancy.[19] They sensed the follow-on care would be quite expensive, and the baby's life would be profoundly limited and perhaps not worth living.

The mother disagreed, and her daughter was born. As predicted, the infant lacked a major portion of her brain, skull, and scalp. Her brain stem supported her autonomic functions and reflex actions, but without a cerebrum she was permanently unconscious. She was unable to see or hear, she lacked all cognitive abilities, and was unaware of, and otherwise unable to interact with, her environment. There was no known medical treatment that would improve her "vegetative" condition.

Anencephalic infants generally die within a few days after birth owing to breathing difficulties or other complications. When the baby's breathing became labored, mechanical ventilation was started, in part to allow the doctors time to explain more fully the baby's prospects to her mother (the father was only marginally involved). Within a few days, the physicians were urging that the artificial ventilation be discontinued. Because all known treatments would serve no therapeutic or palliative purpose, they recommended that the infant daughter, soon to be known to the outside world as Baby K, be provided nutrition, hydration, and warmth and allowed to die.

Again, the mother disagreed. She was firm in her belief "that all life is sacred and must be protected." This included her anencephalic daughter's life. She knew it looked hopeless. She believed God could work miracles. She wanted everything possible done, including the use of the ventilator. Given the profoundly limiting birth defects, the tending physicians remained firm in their belief that continuing their futile efforts was morally and professionally inappropriate.

The final iteration of the Baby Doe Regulations contained provisions for terminating treatment when, in the treating physicians' "reasonable medical judgment," any of three circumstances applied: the infant was chronically or irreversibly comatose; the treatment would merely prolong dying, and not be effective in ameliorating or correcting life-threatening conditions; the treatment itself would be inhumane. For one nurse caring for Baby K, it was clear. These conditions were present:

> I find it appalling to care for her each day. It is cruel and inhumane to keep her "alive." Animals are euthanized for far less problems and yet this is a human being who really has no voice and no rights other than her mother demanding she be kept alive.[20]

Other medical personnel agreed. They turned to the hospital's ethics committee for guidance.

Although the committee agreed with the physicians, the impasse with Baby K's mother continued. The hospital then sought to transfer the infant to another hospital. No other hospital would accept responsibility. Costs for hospital care were estimated to be about $1,400 per day. The mother had insurance, but nursing-home care would be less expensive. About a month after her birth, the baby's condition stabilized somewhat, and her mother agreed to have her daughter transferred to a nearby nursing home. The transfer agreement was reached only after an explicit agreement had been secured that, if an emergency with breathing or other functions reoccurred, the hospital would again admit her daughter.

In mid January 1993, the infant's breathing difficulties again became life threatening. She was returned to the hospital for a month of ventilatory support. Over the next few months, this back-and-forth transfer between nursing care and hospital occurred a total of three times. Following the second readmission, when the infant was now six months old, the hospital, joined by the guardian *ad litem* and the baby's father, sought, through legal action, to resolve the issue of whether the hospital was obligated to "provide emergency medical treatment to Baby K that it deems medically and ethically inappropriate."

The trial court found that they were. The appellate court agreed, noting that it was "beyond the limits of our judicial function to address the moral and ethical propriety of providing emergency stabilizing medical treatment to anencephalic infants."[21] The court's findings were not based on an assessment of Baby K's medical condition and treatment, which physicians found futile and ethically inappropriate, but on federal legislation—the Emergency Medical Treatment & Active Labor Act (EMTALA). This law, also known as the patient anti-dumping law, had been passed by Congress in 1986 to prevent Medicare-participating hospitals from refusing emergency treatment for patients simply because they could not afford it.

Baby K's breathing difficulties constituted an emergency. Parents had the right to request emergency medical treatment for their children. In this case, Baby K's parents disagreed with one another. In such circumstances, the court found priority should be given to the decision "in favor of life." The hospital was obligated to provide the requested treatment, regardless of the futility when it came to the baby's more serious underlying medical condition. Baby K lived to be two-and-a-half years old. Disagreements over whether her short, "vegetative" life had been worthy of heroic, expensive, and ultimately futile support measures would continue for many years.

Dealing With Futility

The physicians tending Baby K knew the ventilator would prolong her life. They also knew there was no known way to improve the profoundly limiting quality of her life. It was futile to try. The infant's mother disagreed. Her baby's life, even for a few moments, was worth fighting for. The ventilator provided those moments. It was not futile.

The meaning of futile treatment, when applied to particular life circumstances, can become as contentious as it is unclear. In one sense, however, there is absolute clarity. Unless there is a dramatic medical or genetic breakthrough, as of this writing, we will all eventually die, no matter how we might "rage against the dying of the light." There are no exceptions. In this sense, all medical treatment is futile. At the same time, until death occurs, nothing is futile. We can always fight for a final moment of life.

What then is the answer? Who should decide? There was a time when "doctor's orders" ruled the day. Trust was high, and relations with patients were direct and personal. The idea of questioning your doctor and relying instead on third-party review, including hospital ethics committees and litigation, was as remote as it was inappropriate. With increased emphasis on patient autonomy and specialized, sometimes highly technical and costly treatment, this changed.

Instead of close personal relations with their patients, in many ways doctors became "strangers at the bedside," health-care providers whose singular judgment, infused as it is with the uncertainties of rapidly evolving medical technology and treatments with uncertain outcomes, became routinely challenged and frequently reviewed. As David Rothman has noted, "The discretion that the profession once enjoyed has been increasingly circumscribed, with an almost bewildering number of parties and procedures participating in medical decision-making."[22]

Such was the case involving a young mother and her infant son, who died at the age of 19 months in Austin, Texas, on May 19, 2007. Emilio Gonzales was born with Leigh's Disease, a rare disorder causing the breakdown of his central nervous system and related motor skills.

Six months before his death, on December 28, 2006, he was admitted to the local Children's Hospital. By the time he was 17 months old, he was in an intensive care unit. He was not, as Baby K had been, vegetative. He was, however, losing his motor skills, he was deaf and blind, and his brain was shrinking. These conditions were getting worse day by day. As his condition worsened, he could still experience pain.

Efforts to reduce pain and discomfort meant he spent most of his time asleep from the effects of medication. He was kept alive with hydration, nutrition, and a respirator, the removal of which would result, his doctors estimated, in his death within minutes or hours. While his life could be prolonged, there was no known treatment for the degenerative effects of Leigh's Disease. In this sense, continued treatment was futile. Eventually, as his condition worsened, tending physicians wanted to remove Emilio from the respirator. It was inhumane, they felt, to do otherwise. Emilio's mother disagreed. She wanted to spend more time with her son. She did not want the timing of her son's death determined by physicians. God would decide.[23]

Eight years earlier, the state of Texas had passed an Advance Directives Act. This legislation, signed into law by then Governor George W. Bush, combined three existing laws, with revisions, into a single law. There were a number of provisions, including a new living will as well as definitions of terminal and irreversible illness, but the legislation became best known as the Texas Futile Care Law.[24] If a patient requested treatment the physician felt was futile, a seven-step process was outlined to resolve the dispute.[25] These steps were patterned after a report of the AMA, released that same year.[26]

Futility was not formally defined in the legislation. If consultation among the family and doctors resulted in disagreement, the dispute was to be taken to a hospital ethics consultation committee. The committee, with the invited participation of the family, was to decide. If disagreement remained, "the hospital, working with the family, must try to arrange transfer of the patient to another physician or institution willing to give the treatment requested by the family." Ten days were given for the transfer. At the end of this time, if no physician or hospital could be found, "the hospital and physician may unilaterally withhold or withdraw therapy that has been determined to be futile."

As a last resort, the dispute could be taken to court for an extension of the 10-day deadline. The extension was to be granted only if "the judge determines that there is a reasonable likelihood of finding a willing provider of the disputed treatment." If the family decided not to seek an extension, or the judge failed to grant one, "futile treatment may be unilaterally withdrawn by the treatment team with immunity from civil and criminal prosecution."

This was the situation Emilio Gonzales's mother and the hospital and health-care providers confronted. The consultation process had been completed. No agreement had been reached. The 10-day deadline had been passed. It had been extended once. A county judge had been persuaded to extend it again while a search continued, but a federal judge declined to intervene. Thirty-one facilities had been contacted with no success. For her part, Emilio's mother remained firm in her belief and wishes:

> I believe there is a hospital that is going to accept my son . . . I just want to spend time with my son . . . I want to let him die naturally without someone coming up and saying we're going to cut off on a certain day.[27]

Advocacy groups seeking stronger rights for the disabled developed petitions and wrote to the Texas governor, asking for a "stay of execution" of young Emilio. The Texas legislature, which convened every other year, was in session. A revised law was drafted. It provided more time to find alternative treatment. As the debate wore on, young Emilio's condition worsened, and he died while the legislature was in session, held by his mother in the last moments of his life. The revised legislation foundered in the 2007 legislative session. It was reintroduced in 2009. Once again, it failed to emerge from committee hearings.[28]

Futility involves both objective and subjective judgments. What is the time horizon sought—a year, a month, a day, a moment? What is the quality of life desired—restoration of function, an acceptable sense of self, a level of consciousness, the absence of pain or suffering? What are the chances that the desired outcome, whatever that might be, can be achieved? When numbers are used, is medical treatment futile if there is a very high probability (scientists like to talk about five 9s— 99.999 percent) that the procedure or treatment will not accomplish the ends sought? Even using the five-9s criterion, however, there is one chance in 100,000 that something might work. Why not try?

The improbable might become real. Miracles might happen. "Hope is what human beings summon up to seek a miracle against overwhelming odds. It is possible then to say in the same breath, 'I know this is futile, but I have hope.'"[29] Some argue hope should give way to realistic assessment. For others, nothing is futile even in the face of death. Two cases, one from New York, the other from California, are illustrative.

The criteria for declaring death had been revised in the late 1960s, and then refined and widely implemented through the Uniform Determination of Death Act in the early 1980s:

> An individual who has sustained either (1) irreversible cessation of circulatory and respiratory functions, or (2) irreversible cessation of all functions of the entire brain, including the brain stem, is dead.

These criteria were grounded in the Harvard Brain Death Committee's recommendations in the late 1960s, informed by common-law practices, refined through intervening events and discussions, and approved by the American Medical Association (AMA) and the American Bar Association in 1980 and 1981 respectively. The two criteria defining the boundary between life and death became widely accepted and put into law in all 50 states and the District of Columbia. The aim was to provide comprehensive scientific and legal bases for determining death in all situations. Seems straightforward enough. There was, however, a problem. The scientific and legal boundaries separating death from life may be definable and settled, but these same boundaries remain imbued with religious beliefs and personal emotions.

On November 4, 2008, a 12-year-old boy from Brooklyn, Motl Brody, who had been fighting brain cancer for several months, was declared brain dead by doctors at the Children's National Medical Center in Washington D.C. This was not a case of a persistent vegetative state, where the brain stem continues to function. This was more. There was no brain activity whatsoever. A ventilator and drugs were maintaining his respiratory functions and keeping Motl's heart beating. For his parents, supported by their Hasidic beliefs and support of their rabbi (Motl's father was also a rabbi), these were signs that life remained, and they wanted the ventilator and administration of drugs to continue—even in the face of no brain activity whatsoever. A family member reported with simplicity, "This has been a very traumatic time for both of his parents. We all want him to live his natural life and not have it terminated prematurely."

For attending physicians, this was not life support. Motl Brody was no longer living. Acting in ways that suggested life remained was "offensive to good medical ethics."[30] And so the debate was drawn. The case was taken to court, but never reached resolution, since 11 days after he was declared dead and during an agreed upon delay in court proceedings, on November 15, 2008, Motl Brody's heart stopped beating.

Some five years after Motl Brody's contested death, another case, this time involving a 13-year-old girl in California, came to the public's attention. Jahi McMath had been dealing with sleep apnea. On December 9, 2013, she was taken to the hospital in Oakland to undergo a commonly employed surgery to remove her tonsils, adenoids, and extra sinus tissue. Tragically, complications developed and there was a substantial loss of blood. Three days later, on December 12, doctors declared Jahi to be brain-dead. Again, as was the case with Motl Brody, a ventilator and drugs were maintaining Jahi's heartbeat and breathing. For her parents this signaled life. Her mother had a simple requirement, "I would probably need for my child's heart to stop to show me that she was dead. Her heart is still beating, so there's still life there."[31] Perhaps this reflected a lack of understanding that the ventilator and drugs were maintaining her daughter's beating heart and continued breathing, but not supporting "life." Perhaps in their grief, Jahi's parents were simply not yet able to accept the loss of their daughter. Whatever the case, for those providing care, maintaining a dead body with artificial means made no sense.

Jahi's conflicted, deeply disturbing case went to court, where it was decided, following negotiations, that the hospital could not be forced to continue the artificial support and perform additional procedures, such as a tracheostomy for the insertion of a feeding tube. Speaking to the parents, the judge noted with compassion, "This has been very, very hard on you. No one anywhere would wish this to happen to anyone." For family members, hope remained, the uncle reporting, "I don't know if we've accepted it yet. There's still time for a miracle. Christmas is tomorrow. It would be great if she woke up."[32]

On January 5, 2014 Jahi's body was released to the custody of her mother, who then took her daughter to an undisclosed location where reportedly a tracheostomy was performed and a feeding tube inserted. In late March 2014 Jahi's mother reported that her daughter was simply "still asleep."[33]

Dealing With Uncertainty

For the families of Motl Brody and Jahi McMath, as well as many others, futility is seasoned with belief, hope and emotion, in an uncertain mixture of religion, grief, science, and law. Making decisions with uncertain, differentially valued potential for life is never an easy task.[34] There are uncertainties, even with such clearly debilitating conditions as anencephaly, Leigh's Disease, spina bifida, hydrocephaly, microcephaly, and even no brain activity whatsoever. How extensively will mental capacities be diminished? How long is life likely to last? How much suffering will be endured? When should we abandon all hope and accept that life is no longer present?

There are also uncertainties of intentions embedded in such principles as the Doctrine of Double Effect, so widely discussed by philosophers and lawyers. Are drugs being administered to hasten death, to alleviate suffering, or both? Setting these questions aside, when there is a single-minded intention to let life go, even to hasten its end, this may reflect care, palliative healing, virtue, compassion, and justice. It may also reflect neglect and abuse, or perhaps, like Surgeon General Koop's intervention into the Baby Jane Doe case, a judgment that individual interests should be set aside for the greater good. The sanctity of *LIFE* should be protected, no matter the individual consequences, to prevent the emergence of a culture of death.

Finally, there are uncertainties of who should decide. In the case of newborns, the infant's wishes are not known. "It is nonsensical in general secular terms to speak of respecting the autonomy of fetuses, infants, or profoundly retarded adults, who have never been rational. There is no autonomy to affront."[35]

The same can be said with even greater emphasis for those declared brain-dead. In such circumstances, attention turns to others: mothers, fathers, relatives, doctors, nurses, surrogates, lawyers, government officials, and judges all have standing. They also frequently have competing assessments, preferences, interests, and intentions. Fully satisfying, consensus-filled boundaries of protected life and tension-free resolution of the embedded dilemmas, seasoned with uncertainty, remain elusive, perhaps unachievable.

These same uncertainties and competing interests were clearly manifest in the struggle to establish what came to be known as "the right to die."

Notes

1   See, for example, Wesley J. Smith, *Culture of Death: The Assault on Medical Ethics in America* (San Francisco, CA: Encounter Books, 2000).

2   "Children From the Laboratory," *American Medical Association Prism*, May (1973): 13.

3   Helga Kuhse and Peter Singer, *Should the Baby Live? The Problem of Handicapped Infants* (New York: Oxford University Press, 1985), 195.

4   Jeffrey H. Reiman, *Abortion and the Ways We Value Human Life* (New York: Rowman & Littlefield, 1999), 108.

5   See: Joseph Fletcher, *Morals and Medicine* (Princeton, NJ: Princeton University Press, 1954). Michael Tooley, "Abortion and Infanticide," *Philosophy & Public Affairs* 2 (1972): 37–65. Paul Ramsey, *Ethics at the Edges of Life* (New Haven, CT: Yale University Press, 1978). H. Tristram Engelhardt, Jr., *The Foundations of Bioethics*, 2nd ed. (New York: Oxford University Press, 1996), especially chap. 4.

6   Kuhse and Singer, *Should the Baby Live?*

7   George F. Will, "The Killing Will Not Stop," *The Washington Post*, April 22 (1982): A29.

8   Cited in Kuhse and Singer (1985), 16.

9   The genesis of President Reagan's several orders are somewhat unclear. See: Lawrence D. Brown, "Civil Rights and Regulatory Wrongs: The Reagan Administration and the Medical Treatment of Handicapped Infants," *Journal of Health Politics, Policy and Law* 11 (1986): 234.

10   David J. Rothman and Sheila M. Rothman, *The Willowbrook Wars* (New York: Harper & Row Publishers, 1984).

11   Joseph Fletcher, *Morals and Medicine* (Princeton, NJ: Princeton University Press, 1954), 207.

12   Glanville Williams, *The Sanctity of Life and the Criminal Law* (New York: Alfred A. Knopf, 1957), 20–4.

13   Cited in Kuhse and Singer, *Should the Baby Live?*, 43, gleaned from several illustrative statements of concern in materials submitted to the court by the American Academy of Pediatrics.

14   These exceptions were: (1) The infant is chronically and irreversibly comatose; (2) The provision of such treatment would merely prolong dying, not be effective in ameliorating or correcting all of the infant's life-threatening conditions, or otherwise be futile in terms of the survival of the infant; or (3) The provision of such treatment would be virtually futile in terms of the survival of the infant, and the treatment itself under such circumstances would be inhumane.

15 George J. Annas, "The Case of Baby Jane Doe: Child Abuse or Unlawful Federal Intervention?" *American Journal of Public Health* 74 (1984): 727–9.

16 Marcia Chambers, "Initiator of 'Baby Doe' Case Unshaken," *New York Times*, November 13 (1983).

17 See David Bird, "U.S. Role in 'Baby Doe' Case Defended by Surgeon General," *New York Times*, November 7 (1983); Ernest Van Den Haag and Lacey Washington "Baby Jane Doe," *National Review*, February 10, (1984): 36–8.

18 *Bowen v American Hosp. Ass'n*, 476 U.S. 610 (1986): 621, 632.

19 See Georg J. Annas, "Asking the Courts to Set the Standard of Emergency Care— The Case of Baby K.," *New England Journal of Medicine* 330 (1994): 1542–5.

20 Quoted in Ronald M. Perkin, "Stress and Distress in Pediatric Nurses: The Hidden Tragedy of Baby K.," 1996. Available online at: www.llu.edu/llu/bioethics/update 12_2.htm.

21 *In the Matter of Baby K*, 832 F. Supp. 1022 (E.D. Va. 1993). *In the Matter of Baby K*, 16 F.3d 590 (4th Cir. 1994).

22 David J. Rothman, *Strangers at the Bedside: A History of How Law and Bioethics Transformed Medical Decision Making* (New York: Aldine de Gruyter, 1991), 1.

23 This case received a good deal of local and national attention. See, "Dying Boy's Case Likely to Reverberate in Law, Religion," *Austin American Statesman*, April 15 (2007): A01; "Case Puts Texas Futile-Treatment Law Under a Microscope," *Washington Post*, April 11 (2007): A03; National Right to Life, "Emilio Gonzales Passes Away," May 22, 2007.

24 The Advance Directives Act (1999), Chapter 166 of the Texas Health & Safety Code, especially Section 166.046, Subsection (e).

25 Guidelines for resolving futility cases under the Texas Advance Directives Act, 1999.

26 "Medical Futility in End-Of-Life Care: Report of the Council on Ethical and Judicial Affairs," *Journal of the American Medical Association* 281 (1999): 937–41.

27 Quoted in: "Case Puts Texas Futile-Treatment Law Under a Microscope," *Washington Post*, April 11 (2007): A03.

28 House Bill 3325.

29 L.J. Schneiderman, N.S. Jecker, and A.R. Jonsen, "Medical Futility: Its Meaning and Ethical Implications," *Annals of Internal Medicine* 112 (1990): 949–54, 950.

30 www.washingtonpost.com/wp-dyn/content/article/2008/11/06/AR2008110603828.html

31 http://www.cnn.com/2013/12/28/health/life-support-ethics/index.html?hpt=hp_t1

32 David Debolt; Rick Hurd (December 24, 2013). "Jahi McMath: Judge denies petition to keep girl on ventilator past Dec. 30th," San Jose Mercury News. December 24, 2013.

33 www.latimes.com/local/lanow/la-me-ln-brain-dead-jahi-mcmath-mother-speaks-20140328-story.html#axzz2ybJmS8CF

34 For argument from potential in other bioethical settings, see: Peter Singer and Karen Dawson, "Technology and the Argument From Potential," *Philosophy and Public Affairs* 17 (1988): 87–104; Massimo Reichlin, "The Argument From Potential: A Reappraisal," *Bioethics* 11 (1997): 1–23.

35 H. Tristram Engelhardt, Jr., *The Foundations of Bioethics*, 2nd ed. (New York: Oxford University Press, 1996), 139.

PART III
THE BOUNDARIES OF TOLERABLE SUFFERING

Chapter 10

Limits to Tolerable Suffering

The "right to die" involves a now familiar dilemma. There is a duty to protect life. There is also a duty to give due reverence to the quality of life and the alleviation of suffering. These imperatives sometimes conflict. The dilemma produced has been around for a very long time. Advances in medicine have made it far more prevalent and urgent.

Writing in 1982, Eric Cassel, a physician concerned with the gap between medicine's technical objectivity and the subjective nature of suffering, prodded his colleagues, "Physicians' failure to understand the nature of suffering can result in medical intervention that (though technically adequate) not only fails to relieve suffering but becomes a source of suffering itself."[1] Many others were making the same point, including Dame Cicely Saunders, founder of the Hospice Movement, who was frequently quoted as saying, "We have to concern ourselves with the quality of life as well as its length."[2]

The Boundaries of Tolerable Suffering

The struggle to define and deal with suffering has been part of theological, philosophical, and public discourse for as long as stories have been told. Its meaning is interwoven in all major moral systems. Among Hindus, Karma offers a framework for the meaning of suffering, its causes, and remedies. The Four Noble Truths of Buddha's teachings deal with the meaning, causes, and end of suffering. God's testing of Job, with

Job's response, is an oft-told and frequently interpreted story from the Abrahamic faiths.

Science and medical technology have produced new questions and interpretations. Speaking at an International Conference on Euthanasia and the Future of Medicine in October 1988,[3] Surgeon General Koop was worried. He had been disappointed with the outcome of the Baby Doe cases, but his worries went far beyond. Pointing to a much-cited article written in the 1920s,[4] influential in shaping the tragedy of Nazi Germany, he saw a "euthanasian ethic" beginning to infuse the culture.[5] "We've had 'Baby Doe,'" he noted, "and, as sure as I'm standing here tonight, we're going to have 'Granny Doe,' too." The danger, the surgeon general asserted, resided in the rhetoric being used to frame the debate.

He saw a society replacing "its fundamental human values with a counter-framework outfitted with a new and fuzzy vocabulary that permits the healer to become killer." "We're snared," he continued, "in a marshland of new euphemisms and circumlocutions." These were fast becoming clichés, "a sure indication that the debate is deteriorating further from rationalization to imprecision." For Dr. Koop, the most worrisome phrases were "'quality of life,' 'withhold nutrition and fluids,' 'death with dignity,' 'assisted suicide,' 'heroic measures,' 'passive euthanasia,' 'surrogate,' 'extraordinary care,' and so on."[6]

He was particularly "confounded and angered" by the phrase "quality of life." He had no idea, he told his audience, "what anyone else's 'quality of life' was, is, or will be. No idea at all." Nor, in his opinion, did anyone else. For this experienced pediatric surgeon, the way to deal with these uncertainties was to relegate them to a distant corner and concentrate instead on the sanctity of all human life.

As compelling as Surgeon General Koop's argument might have been for many in his audience, there was room for disagreement. A decade before Dr. Koop expressed his worries about the uncertain edges of protected life, Paul Ramsey, whose published lectures had been so influential at the end of the "decade of conferences," had addressed these same questions. "All our days and years," Ramsey noted, "are of equal worth." There comes a time, however, when children should "not be stuck away . . . and have their dying prolonged through tubes." There comes a time when doctors ought to say, "We lost him several weeks ago; isn't it time to quit?"[7]

Even Dr. Koop, in his testimony in the recently completed judicial review of the Baby Doe Regulations, struggled with the competing demands to protect life and alleviate suffering. When pressed by the judge, Dr. Koop had acknowledged that giving due reverence to the qualities of life of a young infant born with serious mental and physical defects was widely and rightly practiced among physicians, including himself.[8] There were important qualities of life, infused with tragic suffering, that made efforts to prolong life futile, unwise, and inhumane. Some lives, some moments in life were more worthy of prolonging and protecting than others. As nebulous as they were, boundaries of protected life and the limits of tolerable suffering had to be drawn.

The claim that no one could truly judge the quality of life or the level of tolerable suffering experienced by another, coupled with the call for governmental regulations, presented Dr. Koop with a problem. If a patient suffered in a life unbearably filled with pain and wanted to let life go, why should these wishes not be honored? Why should the legal system intervene? If life had entered an irreversible cognitive state, void of higher brain functions, including awareness of surroundings, the ability to relate to others, and even the ability to experience suffering and judge the quality of life, why should efforts to prolong life be continued? Why should there not be a right to die, even if an individual simply wanted to avoid the anticipated suffering altogether?[9] If help was needed to end or avoid the suffering, why should physicians not provide it?

Troubling Cases in Troubled Times

Cassel, Saunders, and Koop were not working in a vacuum.[10] The 1930s had been troubled times, and stories of suffering and suicide permeated the news. Prominent individuals and professional organizations, most notably in Britain, were proposing the legalization of "mercy killing." In early November 1935, the year the Voluntary Euthanasia Society was founded in London, the first organization of its type, one such story ran in the *London Daily Mail*.

The physician, described as a kind-eyed, elderly country doctor, reported,

"Five times have I taken a life . . . The first case was a newborn child, clearly doomed to imbecility. With the squeeze of my finger and thumb, I had taken a life. In the second case, the child was born without a skullcap. The third case was that of a farmer suffering from an incurable and agonizing disease. He died clasping my hand, and murmuring, 'God bless you, doctor.' The fourth case was a man suffering from the same disease and unable to eat, drink or sleep. He was in agony beyond the torment of the damned. He also died with a smile on his face and with his hand in mine. The fifth case [had] the same disease. I had no hesitation in ending his life."

The doctor's actions were not legal. He did not care. When the story appeared a week later in the United States as a three-part summary in *Time Magazine*, readers learned that the doctor's conscience had "never stabbed him." He was ready to face "any tribunal in the land." He would act similarly, in similar circumstances, in the future.

This story followed closely a widely publicized murder conviction of Mrs. May Brownhill. "Mother May," as she was known, had been sentenced to hang. She had been tending her son, who "was an imbecile," for 30 years. She freely admitted, "I did put Dennis to sleep with 100 sleeping tablets, and before I left him I did turn on the gas." She was going to have an operation and "didn't want Dennis to be without care." It was a story that "stirred the well of British sentiment to its depths."[11] Two days after her conviction and sentence, Mother May was pardoned and reportedly driven home in a limousine.

These and similar cases formed the foundation for much debate in Britain, reviving sporadic reform efforts of the 1870s, with accompanying attempts to get a permissive euthanasia bill through Parliament.[12] Major proponents included prominent religious leaders, as well as members of the Society of Medical Officers of Health and the Royal College of Surgeons. In a speech delivered in the House of Lords, the royal physician, Lord Dawson, while not in favor of the proposed bill, spoke of euthanasia as a "mission of mercy," a matter best left to the conscience of individual physicians. "One should make the act of dying more gentle and more peaceful, even if it does involve curtailment of the length of life." "This may be taken," he continued, "as increasingly the custom, as something accepted."

"I would give as my deliberate opinion," he concluded, "that there is a quiet and cautious but irresistible move to look at life and suffering from the more humane attitude, and in face of disease which is undoubtedly incurable, and when the patient is carrying a great load of suffering, our first thoughts should be the assuagement of pain even if it does involve the shortening of life." Pointing to the wisdom of a "gentle growth of euthanasia," he urged his peers, "if we cannot cure, for heaven's sake let us do our best to lighten the pain." Lord Dawson was speaking from experience.

Some fifty years later, his personal papers were released. They revealed, for the first time, that, late in the evening on January 20, 1936, in just such a mission of mercy, he had hastened the death of King George V. He had injected the dying King with three-quarters of a gram of morphine and one gram of cocaine. He had done so, because, "It was evident that the last stage might endure for many hours, unknown to the patient but little comporting with the dignity and the serenity which he so richly merited and which demanded a brief final scene." Lord Dawson noted in his log, "The King's life is moving peacefully toward its close." Dr. Dawson had chosen late in the evening for his action of mercy to ensure the announcement would be carried "in the morning papers rather than the less appropriate evening journals." The King deserved to die with dignity. The headline the next morning read "A Peaceful Ending at Midnight"[13]

King George V was not alone. On September 23, 1939, Sigmund Freud died following his battle with cancer. He was 83 years old and had emigrated the previous year from Vienna to London, following Germany's take-over of Austria and several raids of his home by Gestapo agents. His former student, friend, and personal physician, Dr. Max Schur, had also emigrated. Schur would recall, in a book published a little over three decades later,[14] that Freud had only one wish left. It was best expressed in one of Goethe's most beautiful poems:

How tired am I of this struggle,
Why this senseless pain and joy?
Come, sweet peace,
Come, oh come into my breast.

The renowned founder of psychoanalysis had turned to Dr. Schur two days before his death: "My dear Schur, you certainly remember our first talk. You promised me then not to forsake me when my time comes. Now it is nothing but torture and makes no sense any more." Dr. Schur reassured his friend and patient that he did recall their earlier conversation:

> When he was again in agony, I gave him a hypodermic of two centigrams of morphine. He soon felt relief and fell into a peaceful sleep. I repeated this dose after about twelve hours. He lapsed into a coma and did not wake up again.

Efforts to craft permissive euthanasia legislation during the trying years of the Great Depression were ultimately unsuccessful. Nevertheless, most commentators suggest that, both in America and throughout Britain, Scandinavia, and Europe, the euthanasia movement was gaining momentum.[15] This was nowhere more evident than in Germany.

The German euthanasia initiative came to fruition in a decree issued by Adolf Hitler, sent to his personal physician and the director general of the Foundation for Welfare and Institutional Care. The decree was backdated to September 1, 1939 to correspond to the outbreak of war.

> Reich Leader Bouhler and Dr. Brandt are charged with the responsibility for expanding the authority of physicians, to be designated by name, to the end that patients considered incurable according to the best available human judgment of their state of health, can be granted a mercy death.[16]

The soul-searing consequences of this decree would all too soon become all too evident.

Although the phrase "granted a mercy death" implied carrying out a patient's request in the face of suffering, much like Dr. Schur had done for Sigmund Freud, the same month Hitler's decree was released, the practice of euthanasia in Germany would become something quite different. Instead of compassionate alleviation of suffering, its aim was to secure the public good. It was to rid society of the burden of those "unworthy of life." It was grounded in the 1933 German eugenics law, which in turn had been based on statutes stemming from the negative

Eugenics Movement advanced in the United States and legitimated in *Buck v. Bell* in 1927.

The German euthanasia program was clearly aimed at the excluded "other." It began with killing, first children and then adults, in Poland. The initial criteria were "serious hereditary diseases," specified in a slightly modified listing to those enumerated in Germany's 1933 eugenics law. This list soon came to include a wide range of persons seen more broadly as "useless eaters," those draining society of resources and contributing little, those, as Justice Holmes had put it in *Buck*, who "sap the strength of the State." Techniques of "mercy death" perfected in this euthanasia initiative were eventually used in a much broader genocidal holocaust.

Even though proponents of euthanasia based their arguments on patient autonomy, compassion, and the beneficence of a deeply held desire to alleviate suffering, those opposed would point to the Nazi experience as a dangerous precedent. For these opponents, death with dignity was in truth a thin edge of a wedge yielding unwanted and perhaps unanticipated outcomes. As Leon Kass put it, "It is easy to see the trains of abuses that are likely to follow the most innocent cases, especially because the innocent cases cannot be precisely and neatly defined so that they are distinguished from the rest."[17]

The Stages of Suffering

Religious traditions have long justified tolerance for suffering for the lessons learned. Following World War II, there was much discussion of this interpretive framework. Among the most poignant and influential was a small volume first published in German in 1946, and eventually translated in expanded form in 1959, titled, *Man's Search for Meaning*.[18]

Written by Viktor Frankl, this compelling commentary was a personal account of one man's encounters with the extreme boundaries of tolerable suffering in Germany's concentration camps. Frankl did not claim to be documenting "facts and events but . . . personal experiences, experiences which millions of prisoners have suffered time and again." If the boundaries of protected life were elusive, Frankl would show that the boundaries of tolerable suffering were even more so.

Although Frankl's experiences were extreme, they were not, he argued, restricted to concentration camps. His experiences were in many ways not unlike those encountered by patients faced with a terminal or debilitating disease, confronted with events over which they had little, if any, control. Frankl's account was influential in part because he so clearly and concisely addressed the connection between the meaning and quality of life and the significance of suffering. "If there is a meaning in life at all," he wrote, "then there must be a meaning in suffering. Suffering is an ineradicable part of life." For many, the importance of Frankl's message was that the meaning of suffering was ultimately personal: "No man can tell another . . . Each must find out for himself."[19]

As personal and private as suffering and the quality of life might be, Frankl noticed some general patterns. Prisoners in concentration camps seemed to adjust in stages. The first phase, Frankl recalled, was "shock." It was accompanied by confusion and denial, a "delusion of reprieve." "We clung to shreds of hope and believed to the last moment that it would not be so bad." "No one could yet grasp the fact that everything would be taken away." A newly arrived prisoner maintained, Frankl wrote, a "boundless longing for his home and his family." As reality set in, denial and the delusion of reprieve became more difficult, perhaps impossible, to sustain in the face of overwhelming evidence. A singular defining moment would sometimes bring to a close the first stage of shock, denial, confusion, and disgust.

For Frankl himself, this closure came when a fellow inmate scoffed at his concern over a manuscript he was writing. The manuscript contained, Frankl explained, his life's work. Could the inmate understand how important this was? "A grin spread slowly over his face, first piteous, then more amused, mocking, insulting, until he bellowed one word at me . . . a word that was ever present in the vocabulary of camp inmates: 'Shit!'" "At that moment," Frankl recalled, "I saw the plain truth and did what marked the culminating point of the first phase of my psychological reaction: I struck out my whole former life."

As inmates entered the second, perhaps more realistic, stage, separated from their former life and dealing with their surroundings, curiosity, rational assessment, even humor appeared as they found they could do things, endure things never thought possible. It was Dostoevsky who had noted that man was defined as a being who could get used to anything. To this, Frankl's fellow inmates replied, "Yes a man can get used to anything, but do not ask us how." This more realistic, in many ways isolating, assessment, however arrived at, generated depression and thoughts of suicide "born of the hopelessness of the situation." Paradoxically, for some this hopelessness also meant, "There was little point in committing suicide, since, for the average inmate life expectation, calculating objectively and counting all likely chances, was very poor."

Whether an inmate was suicidal or simply waiting for the high probability of death, the second phase was, Frankl concluded, "a phase of relative apathy, in which he [the inmate] achieved a kind of emotional death." Having encountered undeniable suffering, he "did not avert his eyes any more. By then his feelings were blunted, and he watched unmoved . . . Disgust, horror and pity are emotions that our spectator could not really feel . . . By means of this insensibility the prisoner soon surrounded himself with a very necessary protective shell."

Protected by a shell of insensibility, some, perhaps lucky, inmates coped by retreating "from their terrible surroundings to a life of inner riches and spiritual freedom." These inmates drew upon what Frankl called tragic optimism. This was of signal importance. By drawing on memories of a loved one, on the beauty of art, on a hope that somewhere, somehow, there was meaning, a purpose in life beyond what they were confronting, inmates were able to endure.

Those fortunate enough to come upon this moment and to find this inner wellspring experienced an extreme version of what Hans Selye would call "stress without distress."[20] With tragic optimism, they found value and meaning in the worst situation. They did not cater to the enormity of their suffering but instead drew strength from what was good in life, believing "it did not really matter what we expected from life, but rather what life expected from us." For Frankl, this inner strength and sense of purpose, whatever their source, determined the shifting boundaries of tolerable and intolerable suffering.

A decade after Frankl's account appeared in English, just as Paul Ramsey was closing out the decade of conferences with his *Patient as Person*, and the birth of bioethics was taking place, Elizabeth Kübler-Ross opened the door wider on our understanding of the stages of suffering. Her insights came from a series of conversations she had with terminally ill cancer patients.

As a teenager, Elizabeth had worked in Poland and Russia assisting persons recently released from German concentration camps. Later, as a trained psychiatrist, Dr. Kübler-Ross joined a group of physicians in the

United States conducting interviews with persons recently diagnosed with terminal cancer. She wanted to shed insight on what many tended to avoid—the experience of death and dying. She wanted patients to become teachers, "so that we may learn more about the final stages of life with all its anxieties, fears, and hopes."

She was telling their stories, she wrote, in the hope "that it will encourage others not to shy away from the 'hopelessly' sick . . . as they can help them much during their final hours." From these conversations and stories came *On Death and Dying*, an instant and influential bestseller, published in 1969. The five stages in Kübler-Ross's model continue to frame our understanding of what has come to be known as the grief process, more than 40 years after their publication.

Denial, anger, bargaining, depression, and acceptance closely parallel the stages leading to a tragic optimism outlined by Frankl. They have become something of a mantra. Subsequent researchers, and there have been many,[21] have criticized and suggested refinements, adding, dividing, or substituting stages. Some, including Kübler-Ross herself, question the inevitability of stages, noting that grief does not always occur in such regular fashion; that "stages" frequently occur simultaneously and not always in the same order. Criticisms and refinements notwithstanding, if ever there was a book that framed subsequent thinking on a topic, *On Death and Dying* was one.

Whatever the number, content, duration, intensity, or sequence of stages, there is widespread agreement that the experience of, and tolerance for, suffering shifts over time. There is also substantial evidence that cultural understandings and practices, networks of support and caring, an individual's sense of control over outcomes, and the ability to reconstruct meaning in the face of loss all influence the intensity and duration of suffering. These shifting cognitive–emotional, semi-regular stages add yet another element of uncertainty when defining the boundaries of tolerable suffering and the right to die. Namely, when should the decision be made?

These general principles and the vaguely specified boundaries of tolerable suffering are clarified through specific events. Such events provide examples of the hazy, uncertain boundaries of protected life and the reverence deservedly given to the importance of suffering. They clarify how the sometimes-contending principles of autonomy, justice, and beneficence are balanced. One such event was the tragic gas-line explosion on a rural East Texas road in the summer of 1973.

Please Let Me Die

Donald Cowart was severely burned when a leaking gas pipe exploded on a country road where he and his father were looking at some property. His father, Ray, died on the way to the hospital. Don survived, but was no longer the person he once was; no longer the person he had come to know and value; no longer a self-sufficient, independent athlete and jet pilot hoping to advance a career with commercial airlines. His appearance had been dramatically altered. He was without the use of his hands, legs, eyes, and some of his hearing. He needed assistance in every aspect of his life. He was enduring excruciating pain to save a life he no longer knew and no longer wanted. What Dax Cowart (he changed his name) wanted was the alleviation of his suffering.

Repeatedly, he pleaded, "Please let me die!" The problem was, his lawyer, doctors (most of them), and mother were not listening or did not agree. They wanted to save his life, even if he did not. Paternalism, defined as "nonacquiescence to a person's wishes, choices, or actions for that person's own benefit,"[22] was paramount. Dax's autonomy took second place to what his caretakers perceived as beneficence.

As Dax Cowart moved from Parkland Hospital in Dallas to the burn center at the University of Texas Medical Branch in Galveston, where his treatments and pleas for relief intensified, the Texas legal landscape was in transition.[23] In its 1973 legislative session, the Texas legislature passed a new penal code, greatly influenced by Herbert Wechsler's Model Penal Code project. When the legislative session was gaveled *sine die*, the new code's wide-ranging provisions contained sections outlawing both attempted and assisted suicide. Dax's accident occurred in July 1973. The new code took effect on January 1, 1974.

Many guidelines remained vague, and many questions unanswered. Dax Cowart's preferences, however, were crystal clear. They are documented in a 30-minute film, *Please Let Me Die*, produced while treatments were progressing and in a subsequent film *Dax's Case*, produced some 10 years later. Dax wanted his treatments stopped. What bothered him, in addition to the pain he was experiencing, were the bleak chances he foresaw for his life ahead. There was no way he wanted "to go on as a blind and a cripple." He did not wish to go through the pain of having his hands and fingers in traction and learning to walk again, especially when confronted with a life of helplessness. "It is a really sinking feeling . . . I like to do things for myself, my ways of doing things . . . now, I have to rely on someone else to feed me, all my private functions."

What really astounded Dax, was how,

> in a country like this where freedom has been stressed so much . . . a person can be made to stay under a doctor's care when he's objected to the painful treatment such as the "tankings" which are *very* painful against this person's wishes especially if he's demonstrated the ability to reason.

If he refused to undergo the tankings, which were like "alcohol was being poured over raw flesh," he was picked up out of bed and bodily placed on the stretcher and treated anyway. It was a painful process that continued "seven days a week, week after week, after week." Anticipating the right-to-die cases in the years ahead, Dax argued,

> Something should be done in the future so a person who did not want the care could be left alone and would not have to undergo the painful treatment. Like I am having to undergo this painful treatment regardless of my feelings.

Dax Cowart was twice found competent by psychiatrists. His pleadings were not the rantings of a deranged patient. How, then, could his pleas go unheeded? Competing interests among those involved seem to be the answer. When Donnie Cowart was first admitted to Parkland Hospital in Dallas, he was unable to sign consent forms for various procedures. His mother was asked to do so. As the treatments progressed, Dax and his mother would have repeated arguments about whether his treatment should continue. The doctors and his lawyer sided with his mother.

When asked about this, Ada Cowart replied, "As a mother it was hard for me to say that I could give up a child." Also, she knew the story of

Job: she believed God had a plan; there might be redemptive power in suffering.

> When Donnie wanted to discontinue treatment there were a number of things that kept going through my mind. I had prayed that he would never be killed instantly . . . I was hoping he would have time to realize his responsibility to God and come to the realization of what he should be doing . . . Had I believed it was God's will for him to want to die, I think I could have accepted that.

In addition, she realized her son was rational, but what if he changed his mind? If they stopped the treatments, it would be too late. She had lost a husband. She did not want to lose a son. She intended to do everything in her power to ensure that she did not.

For his part, her son had a good deal of empathy for his mother:

> I don't blame my mother for wanting to keep me alive. However, I feel that she should never have been placed in the difficult position of having to make such a decision. I feel that I as a patient should have been the only one to make that decision.

His doctors and lawyer also disagreed. They were driven by their sense of professional ethics and what, as professionals, they were called upon to do. These commitments transcended particular cases. Dax's lawyer, Rex Houston, was a long-time personal friend of the family. He was also representing Dax's mother. As a lawyer, he had fiduciary responsibilities. An important lawyerly concern was keeping Dax alive to maximize the monetary award from a pending lawsuit. Houston's explanation was straightforward:

> My reason for that was that Dax was a single man, 26 years of age. He had no dependents. He had no surviving children. He had no wife. He had no one dependent upon him. His lawsuit, were he dead, had no great value to it, because he had nobody surviving who was dependent upon him.

There was monetary value as long as Dax was alive. With a living plaintiff, the lawsuit, Houston continued,

> had tremendous value . . . Here you have a person who has lost both hands and both eyes . . . It [the law suit] has almost any value you can imagine . . . To me in taking care of the family and taking care of him, I had to have a living plaintiff at the time this went to trial.

An out-of-court settlement was soon reached, yielding a large sum.

Even with the lawsuit settled, there were other professional, paternalistic interests keeping Dax alive. Like lawyers, physicians are compelled by professional ethics. These standards, for some, transcend patient preferences and even the physician's own good intentions. "The deepest ethical principle restraining the physician's power," Leon Kass writes,[24] "is neither the autonomy and freedom of the patient nor the physician's own compassion or good intention. Rather it is the dignity and mysterious power of human life itself . . . the purity and holiness of the life and art to which the physician has sworn devotion. A person can choose to be a physician but cannot simply choose what physicianship means." If a patient's wishes are violated and suffering results to protect physicianship, so be it.

One of Dax's tending physicians seemed to reflect this paternalistic approach. In *Dax's Case*, he was troubled:

> I have a very difficult problem in terms of deciding not to treat a patient, because in my opinion when you do not treat a patient, you are in a sense killing that individual. I have the knowledge and the means of caring for this patient so that he does survive, and you are asking me not to do this . . . Why am I in medicine? . . . For me I cannot change my way of treating patients.[25]

With this grounding principle in place, however, Kass noted a way out. It was embedded in the Doctrine of Double Effect.

> Ceasing medical intervention, allowing nature to take its course, differs fundamentally from mercy killing . . . What is most

important *morally* is that the physician who ceases treatment does not intend the death of the patient. Even if death follows as a result of the physician's action or omission.

This was a distinction that drew the attention of another of Dax's tending physicians.

When he began practicing, the physician reported,

> I wanted to rehabilitate the world, and especially Don Cowart. That wasn't necessarily his priority. The difference now is that I am more comfortable with people choosing to not necessarily achieve the level of function that I think is possible for them, especially if it causes them acute discomfort or really may interfere with their quality of life.[26]

Dax understood clearly what was going on and how he had been put in such a subordinate position. "It's just a result of the doctors having the power. The doctors' interest has been to preserve life and also to benefit the patient on their own terms rather than the patient's. My case was an example of where the two are not the same." Reflecting more generally on the lessons that might be taken from what had happened to him, Dax was also clear in remedy:

> People who are terminally ill, today it is insane for anyone to require that person to undergo cancer chemotherapy or whatever if that is not that person's wishes . . . If we force people to undergo treatment, what we're doing is putting the individual at the mercy of whatever medical or scientific technology comes into being in the future. We may preserve . . . "life," but what is left of the patient may be only a shell. No quality of life left. No ability to function—even think. If you define life as just the fact that the individual is not decaying, it's not any life that anyone I know would have an interest in maintaining.[27]

Dax Cowart survived. His consternation and outrage, however, continued. Ten years later after *Please Let Me Die* was made, *Dax's Case* was produced. By this time, Dax was thriving as a lawyer. He remained adamant. "The view that the end result justifies whatever means necessary to achieve it is absurd," he asserted in the opening scene. "I suppose this would mean then that if the only way an individual's life could be saved would be with treatment that would be as equally painful as being boiled in hot oil or being skinned alive then we should go ahead and use that treatment. I totally disagree." He was alive and he was happy. He was also firm in his belief and quick to note, "My own life could have turned out much differently than it has. I could be stuffed away somewhere in a back room . . . Not going out and not living the happy life that I am now."

Dax's Case closed with Dax drinking, unaided, from a coffee cup and listening to the music he so enjoyed. Perhaps drawing on Frankl's tragic optimism, he had found a new self. He had obtained a law degree and gotten married. He acknowledged he was happy. He also remained firm in his claim. He should have been the one to determine whether the pain of his treatment passed the boundaries of tolerable suffering. His autonomy and his wishes should have been respected. Paternalistic beneficence, no matter its motivation or its results, was misplaced.

Dax Cowart's pleadings to stop treatment were never taken to court. The breadth of their impact, in this sense, was limited. The issues and competing interests that so troubled those involved—respect for the autonomy of patient wishes, the legal right to end treatment, the delegation of authority to others, the standing of professional responsibilities, the meaning of beneficence, the redemptive power of suffering, the unyielding protection of the sanctity of *LIFE*—would wind their way through moral debates and legal proceedings in the years ahead.

When Life Becomes Vegetative

It would remain for a case involving a young woman incapable of expressing any wish whatsoever to provide a legal cornerstone for the position Dax Cowart so adamantly sought—the right to determine his own destiny. In mid April 1975, a little over a year and a half after Dax's accident, a young woman in New Jersey, two weeks after she had turned 21, was out celebrating another friend's birthday. In the early hours of the morning, her mother received a phone call, "Mrs. Quinlan, this is the nurse from Newton Memorial Hospital. Your daughter was admitted to the intensive care unit. She is unconscious."[28] Apparently, Karen Ann had been dieting and, after ingesting a combination of Valium and alcohol, had become disoriented. She seemed, her friends would say, like she was drunk. They returned home, where Karen went to sleep and was later found not breathing. She was revived and taken to the hospital where she slipped into what had recently been labeled a "persistent vegetative state."[29]

One of the coiners of the phrase would later explain,[30] like other animals, humans have internal regulation mechanisms that control body temperature, breathing, blood pressure, heart rate, chewing, swallowing, sleeping, and waking. We also have, "a more highly developed brain, which is uniquely human, which controls our relation to the outside world, our capacity to talk, to see, to feel, to sing, to think." Karen Ann Quinlan had become a young woman with the capacity to maintain survival functions, but she no longer "had a functioning mind, capable of receiving or projecting information." Was this a life worthy of living, a life worth prolonging?

After much anguish, prayer, and consultation, her parents thought not. The doctors, considering their professional responsibilities and perhaps looking over their shoulders at potential civil lawsuits and criminal prosecutions, disagreed. Karen Ann Quinlan was not dead by any acceptable criteria. As doctors, they had the responsibility, professional, legal, and moral, to do what they could to maintain her life. This included continuing the use of a respirator to assist her breathing.

Several months later, Joseph and Julia Quinlan went to court to ask for authority to have their daughter removed from the respirator. The trial court denied their request. Joe and Julia appealed to the Supreme Court of New Jersey. Preparing their court arguments, lawyers for the Quinlans decided to seek advice.

By this time, the case had drawn national attention, including philosophers and theologians involved in the recently launched Hastings Center in New York and the Kennedy Institute of Ethics at Georgetown University in Washington, DC. For four days in early January, the lawyers met at the Kennedy Institute for "intensive dialogue with the priests, physicians, lawyers, and ethicists on the moral, constitutional, and religious issues" that would shape the heart of their pleadings. They then traveled to the Hastings Center for similar discussions with a prominent bioethicist, Robert Veatch. As the court date approached, their minds were, as their lawyer put it, "well honed for the task ahead."[31] Their case was presented on January 26, 1976. On March 31, 1976, two weeks short of the first full year following the vegetative-state diagnosis, the case was decided.

The time preparing for the appeal had been time well spent. The New Jersey court had listened carefully and was thorough in weighing competing values and interests. Most importantly, Karen was alive. There was no disagreement on this. There was also no disagreement that her life was of very limited quality. As the court summarized, "As nearly as may be determined, considering the guarded area of remote uncertainties characteristic of most medical science predictions, she can *never* be restored to cognitive or sapient life." There was no evidence of parental neglect. To the contrary, the court found, "The character and general suitability of Joseph Quinlan as guardian for his daughter, in ordinary circumstances, could not be doubted." There was "a high degree of familial love which pervaded the home of Joseph Quinlan and reached out fully to embrace Karen."

Ordinarily, religious convictions or dogma had no legal standing in a case like this. In this instance, however, the court felt they revealed important information about the father's concern for his daughter and his motives for wanting the respirator withdrawn. Joseph Quinlan's decision to ask for removal of the respirator had been reached after much thought, consultation, and prayer. The evidence clearly showed him "to be deeply religious, imbued with a morality so sensitive that months of tortured indecision preceded his belated conclusion . . . to seek the termination of life-supportive measures sustaining Karen." He had, the court noted, "sought solace in private prayer . . . first for the recovery of Karen and then, if that were not possible, for guidance with respect to the awesome decision confronting him."

Karen's father had also consulted with his parish priest and the Catholic chaplain at the hospital. He would not act contrary to the tennets of his faith. For this reason, the court admitted a statement of the New Jersey bishop, Lawrence B. Casey. By this time, advances in medical technology had led to a distinction between "ordinary" and "extraordinary" methods of treatment. The bishop, noting that extraordinary measures were being employed and citing Pope Pius XII, invoked the principle of double effect. Joseph Quinlan's request should "not be considered euthanasia in any way; that would never be licit. The interruption of attempts at resuscitation, even when it causes the arrest of circulation, is not more

The principle of double effect?

than an indirect cause of the cessation of life, and we must apply in this case the principle of double effect." As Karen's death was a known but indirect and unintended outcome, the proposed removal from the respiratory machine was acceptable. The request for discontinuance of treatment would be "according to the teachings of the Catholic Church, a morally correct decision."

With the facts of the case in hand, the character and motives of the parents assessed, and the justifying theological principle of double effect proposed, the New Jersey court turned to constitutional and legal issues. Of most concern was the recently established "right to privacy." In the cases leading up to and concluding with *Roe v. Wade* in 1973, this right had been drawn from the penumbras of the Constitution and was always to be balanced by compelling state interests. In the case of Karen Ann Quinlan, the court found, there were none.

In a unanimous opinion, the seven judges had "no hesitancy in deciding . . . that no external compelling interest of the State could compel Karen to endure the unendurable, only to vegetate a few measurable months with no realistic possibility of returning to any semblance of cognitive or sapient life." It was no different than a similar choice that might be made by "a competent patient terminally ill, riddled by cancer and suffering great pain; such a patient would not be resuscitated or put on a respirator . . . and *a fortiori* would not be kept *against his will* on a respirator."

The justices were aware that the state had an interest in "the preservation and sanctity of human life" and that a physician was sworn to "administer medical treatment according to his best judgment." In this case, however, "The respirator cannot cure or improve her condition but at best can only prolong her inevitable slow deterioration and death." Karen's life thusly preserved and thusly prolonged would not be worth living.

Although the court's conclusions were clear, unanimously grounded in the facts of the case and the relevant constitutional issues, the justices were also aware there were remaining problems. Of particular concern were the implications of rapidly evolving medical technology. What was ordinary? What was extraordinary? What implications did this ambiguity have for the clarity of professional, legal, and moral standards governing decisions physicians had to make? What was the resulting risk of malpractice litigation or criminal prosecution? In this arena, the court noted, there was a "paucity of pre-existing legislative and judicial guidance as to the rights and liabilities" of those involved.

The judges aimed to clarify. They stated and then restated their findings, specifying a decision process and shielding any participant from civil or criminal liability from charges of homicide, suicide, or assisted suicide should the decision be to take Karen Ann Quinlan off the respirator.

> We repeat for the sake of emphasis and clarity that upon the concurrence of the guardian and family of Karen, should the responsible attending physicians conclude that there is no reasonable possibility of Karen's ever emerging from her present comatose condition to a cognitive, sapient state and that the life-support apparatus now being administered to Karen should be discontinued, they shall consult with the hospital "Ethics Committee" or like body of the institution in which Karen is then hospitalized. If that consultative body agrees that there is no reasonable possibility of Karen's ever emerging from her present comatose condition to a cognitive, sapient state, the present life-support system may be withdrawn and said action shall be without any civil or criminal liability therefore, on the part of any participant, whether guardian, physician, hospital or others.
>
> By the above ruling we do not intend to be understood as implying that a proceeding for judicial declaratory relief is necessarily required for the implementation of comparable decisions in the field of medical practice.
>
> Modified and remanded.

After the decision, Julia Quinlan would remember returning home. She and Joe had very little to say. "It was a quiet evening. What do you say to one another when you know you are going to lose someone you love?" As weeks moved by, both Julia and Joe had noticed a deteriorating relationship with the doctors. They felt shunned in the hospital hallways. After one unpleasant meeting, the hospital even refused to comply and carry out the court's decision. Ultimately, however, on May 17, 1976, they began weaning Karen off the respirator.

It took five days. When the process was complete, on May 22, Julia recalled,

> Karen appeared tired but peaceful. She no longer had to struggle
> . . . I cannot put into words what a stressful week that was. We
> had no indication of how she would respond to the process.
> She could have died. We stayed at her bedside for a very long
> time. Finally, we had to say good night and pray that she would
> be there for us tomorrow. We had no idea how long she would
> survive.[32]

Their daughter would live for another nine years and twenty days. Around 5:30 in the evening of June 11, 1985, Joe and Julia, along with their friend and priest, Father Tom, were visiting in Karen's room and waiting for pizza. The pizza arrived, and Joe and Father Tom went to get it. Julia decided to stay.

> When I was alone with my daughter, I held her twisted hands
> in mine and prayed the Memorare.
>
> > Remember, O most Gracious Virgin Mary,
> > that never was it known that anyone who fled
> > to your protection, implored your help,
> > or sought your intercession was left unaided.
> > Inspired by this confidence, I fly to you,
> > O Virgin of Virgins, my mother.
> > To you I come; before you I stand,
> > sinful and sorrowful.
> > O Mother of the Word Incarnate,
> > despise not my petitions
> > but in your mercy, hear and answer me. Amen.

Julia sensed death was near. She called for Joe and Father Tom. "As we stood around her bed I continued to hold her hands, while Joe wiped her forehead. Suddenly, she was gone."[33]

The compelling faith, love, sadness, and profound parental connection, so vividly present in this final moment of life, hardly support an emergent culture of death, which so worried C. Everett Koop and those who dis-credited the importance of the quality of life and opposed decisions such as those Joe and Julia so lovingly made. Valuing life but letting life go can be profoundly life affirming.

Clearer distinctions needed to be made. They were soon forth-coming.

Notes

1   Eric J. Cassel, "The Nature of Suffering and the Goals of Medicine," *New England Journal of Medicine* 306 (1982): 639–45. This article was later expanded to a book-length discussion. *The Nature of Suffering and the Goals of Medicine* (New York: Oxford University Press, 1991).

2   David Clark, *Cicely Saunders: Founder of the Hospice Movement* (New York: Oxford University Press, 2005).

3   C. Everett Koop, "The Challenge of Definition," presented at the International Conference on Euthanasia and the Future of Medicine, Clark University, Worcester, Massachusetts, October 24, 1988.

4   In 1920, two distinguished German scholars, law professor Karl Binding and medical doctor Alfred Hoche, wrote a widely disseminated pamphlet, "The Permission to Destroy Life Unworthy of Life" (*Die Freigabe der Vernichtung lebensunwerten Lebens*). Leo Alexander, "Medical Science Under Dictatorship," *The New England Journal of Medicine*, July 14 (1949): 39–47.

5   Ezekiel J. Emanuel, "A Review of the Ethical and Legal Aspects of Terminating Medical Care," *American Journal of Medicine* 84 (1988): 291–301.

6   Presented at the International Conference on Euthanasia and the Future of Medicine, Clark University, Worcester, MA, October 24, 1988. Excerpted C. Everett Koop, *The Hastings Center Report* 19 (1989): 2–3.

7   Paul Ramsey, *Ethics at the Edges of Life* (New Haven, CT: Yale University Press, 1978): 191–2.

8   In the court cases challenging the HHS regulations, three debilitating conditions of newly born infants had been highlighted—babies born with a vastly diminished brain, with intracranial hemorrhage, or the absence of a substantial part of the digestive tract. In response to questioning by the judge regarding an infant born with essentially no intestine, Dr. Koop replied the regulations under review,

> never intended that such a child should be put on hyper-alimentation [i.e. artificially nourished] . . . we would consider customary care in that child the provision of a bed, of food by mouth, knowing that it was not going to be nutritious . . . nor do we intend to say that this child should be carried on intravenous fluids for the rest of its life.

Similarly, when asked about a child without a brain, he replied, "I suspect you meant an anencephalic child and we would not attempt to interfere with anyone dealing with that child. We think it should be given loving attention and would expect it to expire in a short time." See Kuhse and Singer, *Should the Baby Live?*, 25.

9   See: Jo Roman, "Choosing Suicide," in *Exit House: Choosing Suicide as an Alternative*, Ed. Richard Ellison, the Roman Tapes Company (New York: Seaview Books, 1980).

10 Some date modern interest to Samuel D. Williams' essay, "Euthanasia," published in 1870, in *Essays by Members of the Birmingham Speculative Club*. Williams' essay was reprinted and discussed widely, finding its way to the United States and forming the basis of much of the discussion surrounding the 1906 proposed legislation in Ohio, "An Act Concerning Administration of Drugs etc. to Mortally Injured and Diseased Persons," which was soundly defeated.

11 See *Time Magazine*, "Mother May's Holiday," March 11, "The Right to Kill," November 18, "The Right to Kill (Cont'd)," November 25, and "The Right to Kill (Cont'd)," December 2.

12 See the interlocking discussions of Glanville Williams, *The Sanctity of Life and the Criminal Law* (New York: Alfred A. Knopf, 1957), 329–50, and Yale Kamisar, "Some Non-Religious Views Against Proposed 'Mercy-Killing' Legislation," *Minnesota Law Review* 42 (1958): 696–1042.

13 Joseph Lelyveld, "1936 Secret Is Out: Doctor Sped George V's Death," *New York Times*, November 28 (1986).

14 Max Schur, *Freud: Living and Dying* (New York: International University Press, 1972), 528–9.

15 See, for example, Ian Dowbiggin, *A Merciful End: The Euthanasia Movement in Modern America* (New York: Oxford University Press, 2003), 32–62.

16 Robert Jay Lifton, *The Nazi Doctors: Medical Killing and the Psychology of Genocide* (New York: Basic Books, 1986), 63.

17 Leon R. Kass, "'I Will Give No Deadly Drug': Why Doctors Must Not Kill," in *The Case Against Assisted Suicide*, Eds. Kathleen Foley and Herbert Hendin (Baltimore: Johns Hopkins University Press, 2002), 26.

18 The original English title was, *From Death Camp to Existentialism*. Eventually, multiple millions of copies were sold. Some indication of the book's impact comes from a survey done by the Library of Congress Book of the Month Club, asking readers to name a "book that made a difference in your life." By this standard, *Man's Search for Meaning* was among the 10 most influential books in America.

19 Gordon W. Allport, in his preface to *Man's Search for Meaning*.

20 *The Stress of Life* (McGraw Hill, 1956); *Stress Without Distress* (Philadelphia, PA: J.B. Lippincott Co., 1974).

21 Margaret S. Stroebe et al., Eds., *Handbook of Bereavement Research: Consequences, Coping, and Care* (Washington, DC: American Psychological Association, 2001); Margaret S. Stroebe et al., Eds., *Handbook of Bereavement Research: Advances in Theory and Intervention* (Washington, DC: American Psychological Association, 2008).

22 James F. Childress and Courtney C. Campbell, "'Who Is a Doctor to Decide Whether a Person Lives or Dies?' Reflections on Dax's Case," in *Dax's Case: Essays in Medical Ethics and Human Meaning*, Ed. Lonnie D. Kliever (Dallas, TX: Southern Methodist University Press, 1989), 25. See, more generally, James F. Childress, *Who Should Decide* (New York: Oxford University Press, 1982).

23 See H. Tristam Engelhardt, Jr., Edmund L. Erde, and John Moskop, "Euthanasia in Texas: A Little Known Experiment," *Hospital Physician* 9 (1976): 30–1.

24 Leon R. Kass, "'I Will Give No Deadly Drug': Why Doctors Must Not Kill," in *The Case Against Assisted Suicide*, Eds. Kathleen Foley and Herbert Hendin (Baltimore, MD: Johns Hopkins University Press, 2002), 32, 36.
25 Interview in "Dax's Case."
26 Interview in "Dax's Case."
27 Quotes from "A Happy Life Afterward Doesn't Make Up for Torture," *Washington Post*, June 26 (1983): D3.
28 Julia Duane Quinlan, *My Joy, My Sorrow: Karen Ann's Mother Remembers* (Cincinnati, OH: St Anthony Messenger Press, 2005), 37.
29 Bryan Jennett and Fred Plum, "Persistent Vegetative State After Brain Damage," *The Lancet* April 1 (1972): 734–37.
30 *In Re Quinlan*, 70 N.J. 10, 355 A.2d 647 (1976).
31 Joseph and Julia Quinlan, with Phyllis Batelle, *Karen Ann: The Quinlans Tell Their Story* (Garden City, NY: Doubleday & Company, 1977), 252–3.
32 Quinlan, *My Joy, My Sorrow*, 53–4.
33 Quinlan, *My Joy, My Sorrow*, 105–6.

CHAPTER 11

ALLEVIATING SUFFERING AND PROTECTING LIFE

The case of Karen Ann Quinlan became a cornerstone for, indeed, all but synonymous with, the right-to-die movement over the decade and a half following the New Jersey Supreme Court's decision. While limited in jurisdiction, this decision's framing importance for the boundaries of protected life and patient autonomy was broadly felt and is hard to overestimate.

It specifically addressed the importance of the Harvard brain-death criteria and the humanizing importance of a "cognitive or sapient life." A person could be alive but not meaningfully human. Even under the dehumanizing circumstances of a persistent vegetative existence, however, the patient's life, autonomy, and right to privacy still deserved to be honored. Substituted judgment, when the immediate wishes of the patient were not evident, could be binding. The quality of life could be balanced against the state's unquestioned interests in protecting life. These were important points. Still, advances in science and medicine were making obsolete existing ethical and legal decision-making criteria, and further clarification was needed. It was soon forthcoming.

Following *Quinlan*, there were a burgeoning number of court cases aimed at clarifying these and many other related issues. They were heard across the nation. One involved a young woman, Nancy Cruzan, who, like Karen Ann Quinlan, was judged to be in a persistent vegetative state. She had been in a tragic car accident, and her parents wanted to stop medical treatment and let their daughter leave this life in peace. Their wishes were challenged, and a lengthy court battle ensued. Finally, in 1990, some 15 years after the New Jersey court's *Quinlan* decision, the U.S. Supreme Court heard its first right-to-die case—*Cruzan v. Director, MDH*.[1] The decade and a half between *Quinlan* and *Cruzan* marked a defining period in the right-to-die movement. Changes had been in the wind for some time.

Prolonged Death and the Public Good

In the years immediately following World War II, the "right to die," so clearly illustrated by Karen Ann Quinlan's parents' pleas, had not thoroughly entered the public's lexicon. "Euthanasia" was the more common term of choice. The distinction was important, and carefully crafted rhetoric emerged to frame the debate.

For some, as the literal translation implied, euthanasia allowed a dignified, merciful, and peaceful end to life. For others, euthanasia carried the connotation of Nazi atrocities. There were profound ambiguities when deciding when a life was no longer worth living and suffering no longer worth enduring. As Hitler's orders to Reich Leader Bouhler and Dr. Brandt evidenced, authority to "grant" a merciful termination of life could be abused.

There was clear evidence that physicians had for many years routinely allowed, even assisted, patients to die. These practices had evolved when little could be done to ease the suffering of a prolonged life. But this had changed. With effective drugs and life-prolonging technologies, doctors and patients had new tools and were presented with new, troubling, and frequently costly decisions. Guidance from the social, ethical, and legal climate lagged behind. In 1967, an experienced family doctor in Florida ran for office. He was elected, at the age of 60, as a state representative. He aimed to bring about legal acceptance of what he knew to be widespread medical practice, including his own.

Representative Walter Sackett was convinced by his own experiences that the legal vulnerability of physicians meant many patients were being kept tragically alive by a range of medical procedures, drugs, and technologies. His proposal to change this would soon be labeled the first piece of state legislation designed to secure "the right to die with dignity."

Dr. Sackett was clear in his intentions and beliefs that some moments in life were more worthy of protection and support than others.[2] He presented his proposal to his legislative colleagues:

> I come before you today with an unusual proposition, namely that of permitting the hopelessly ill patient to die with dignity and not keeping his life afloat when it has reached a meaningless state—meaningless to himself, his family, his community or his country.

When he first started practicing medicine, 30 years earlier, Sackett continued, "old folks with serious illnesses passed away with dignity." This was no longer true. "With the advent of the sulfa drugs, and later the antibiotics and with the great refinements of medicine, we have been able to keep these people alive."

To Dr. Sackett, prolonging these lives made very little sense. It had resulted in what he called, "the prolonged death syndrome." As he saw it, advancing medical technology presented doctors with an "awesome choice: to make the process of dying mercifully brief or to drag it out at a high cost in discomfort and—I must add even if it does sound crass—in dollars." These were difficult choices, infused with uncertainty. It was important, he emphasized, "to make the wishes of patients or of those close to them paramount in determining that choice."

During his first term, Representative Sackett had "impulsively entered" his constitutional amendment. Many, perhaps most, of his Florida legislative colleagues agreed with him, but, after about an hour of discussion, support weakened, and disagreement emerged, turning into "shocked" reaction and an "enthusiastic debate." The proposed amendment was defeated. Afterwards, Dr. Sackett recalled, several dozen of his legislative colleagues "came and knelt by my desk, or encountered me in the hallways, and urged me to return this bill in the next session." This he did. The second attempt also failed. Why?

Sackett had misjudged the opposition. He saw his proposal "applying to the old folks hopelessly ill, doomed to the life of a vegetable, and those severely retarded individuals in that same situation." Support came "from the old folks of the State of Florida who have seen their friends or loved ones go down the long trail of prolonged death, and they hardly relish an experience like this for themselves." Strong opposition, however, emerged when Sackett included the "severely retarded" among those whose lives were not worthy of protecting and prolonging.

Sackett had noted that severely retarded individuals were

> being condemned to live another 25 to 35 years . . . In this type of situation I am sure that it is more humane to let this person die a natural death rather than condemn him to an inhumane existence of another 25 years.

In addition, he continued, economic prudence dictated they pay attention to this matter. The State of Florida was then caring for some 1,500 individuals "who will never go beyond the diaper stage and whom some would have difficulty in recognizing as human beings." They "can live until an age of between 50 and 60." This meant the "care of these retarded can reach the sum of some 4–6 billion dollars." He had an example. One such patient was "a Negro boy 25 years of age staring up in the corner of the room, completely drawn up in a musculature contracture." For Representative Sackett, prudence, as well as recognition that some lives are not worth living or supporting, called for a remedy.

In Sackett's ill-chosen example, as well as the framing rhetoric he used, echoes of Germany's treatment of "useless eaters" were too obvious to miss. As the debates and successive submissions of his proposed legislation proceeded, Sackett had "been told to play down this aspect of the situation because everybody has a tremendous feeling for these [retarded] individuals." There was reluctance "to do anything that would interfere with their claim to existence."

Undaunted by two successive failures, and attentive to the criticism, Representative Sackett modified his euthanasia-for-the-greater-good argument and concentrated on individual rights to choose, introducing a revised bill in 1970. Again, his efforts failed. He had not, however, been totally without effect. His proposed legislation generated widespread national publicity, and he made appearances on syndicated daytime and nighttime talk shows, as well as the widely watched *60 Minutes*.[3] The public's attention to these matters was increasing.

By the mid 1970s, there had been much discussion of the competing points of view and a clearer articulation of arguments. The newly solidified right to privacy and autonomy of choice built a foundation for the right to die; the right to avoid what Sackett had called the prolonged death syndrome. "Living wills" were catching on and being widely distributed. Euthanasia as a means to ration health care in support of the public good, however, was quite another matter. Very little, if any, serious support could be found. As distinctions were drawn and the public became more informed, the chances of legislative success increased.

The Right-to-Die Movement Gains Momentum

By the early 1970s, "right-to-die" was accepted as the debate-framing phrase.[4] If euthanasia, with its troubling links to Hitler's Germany, was replaced by a right to choose to die with dignity, the sanctity of life might be questioned, and abuses might occur, but the decisions would remain in the hands of those most directly affected.

Among those convinced were members of the Euthanasia Society of America (ESA). In 1974, the year following *Roe*, the ESA, which had been founded in 1938, changed its name to become the Society for the Right to Die (SRD). For more than a decade, the ESA had been a small, elite, frequently splintered, and somewhat pariah operation. Intellectuals sparred in professional journals and book-length treatises,[5] but the appeal of their message remained narrow and for many off-putting. Tainted by the lingering connotations of "euthanasia," the ESA was even having trouble getting space for advertisements to spread their message and increase membership and revenue.[6] By reframing their message as a basic right, they aimed to join civil-rights forces and become part of "an awesomely large revolution," and perhaps "ride the crest of a 'great wave' of youthful protest sweeping the nation."[7]

There was reason for their optimism. It came in the form of a rapidly expanding demand for "living wills." The idea of the living will was proposed by Luis Kutner, a human-rights attorney practicing in Chicago and a cofounder in 1961 of Amnesty International, an organization growing out of the Universal Declaration of Human rights. In 1967, Kutner gave a talk at a gathering of the ESA. He was speaking from personal experience. Years earlier a friend had died a slow, painful death after a violent robbery. This prompted Kutner to suggest that individuals sign a document he referred to variously as a "declaration determining the termination of life," "body trust," "declaration of bodily autonomy," and "living will."

Whatever the label, the aim was to allow individuals to specify clearly their wishes for when life-sustaining medicine should be refused and systems shut off. "People do not want to accept the notion of death being final, and doctors, for differing reasons, have become obsessed with denying it," Kutner wrote. "But where there is the possibility of continuing a life without value, when heroic measures will keep someone alive without any hope of restoring that life, it is barbaric, cruel and costly to do so."[8]

Two years after his presentation to the ESA, and some seven years prior to when Karen Ann Quinlan's case was heard in New Jersey's courts, Kutner published his thoughts more formally in the *Indiana Law Journal*.[9] His ideas were beginning to draw attention. "Living will" became the phrase of choice. The living will seemed to provide a bridge between euthanasia and individual rights. Using Kutner's template, the Euthanasia Educational Fund (EEF), the educational arm of the ESA, drew up a living will and printed 5,000 copies. It began, "If the time comes when I can no longer take part in decisions for my own future, let this statement stand as the testament of my wishes." Within months, all 5,000 copies had been distributed.

Word spread, and demand grew. By the end of 1970, the EEF reported they had distributed some 60,000 copies. By the end of 1973, this had quadrupled to a reported quarter of a million. Living-will articles appeared in the public media and, perhaps most importantly for the expansion of ESA membership, in a widely popular advice column, "Dear Abby." On April 1, 1973, a letter from "Concerned" was published. The writer had heard "they are trying to pass a law making it legal to let people die just by discontinuing treatment." "The thought of this is frightening," Concerned continued. "WHO will decide who is old enough and sick enough?" Concerned's question would remain a central conundrum for years to come.

In reply, Abigail Van Buren, "Dear Abby," still using the increasingly contested term, "euthanasia," told Concerned, "'Euthanasia' literally means 'the good death,' and I am all for it." Dear Abby anchored her reasoning by quoting from the EEF's living will. In subsequent columns, readers were further informed and advised of how to secure a copy. They were also encouraged to support the cause by donating or at least sending a check to cover the costs of mailing. Many readers were convinced.

Records of the EEF reveal that the Dear Abby columns created a crisis of sorts. A decade earlier, paid membership numbered just over 300. Largely as a result of the Dear Abby columns, the staff suddenly found themselves "sorting thousands of letters, extracting the money and answering the most urgent." They were making deposits several times a day in a nearby bank. For the first time, because of the response to EEF's work, the ESA was on sound financial footing, with ballooning membership.

Clearly, an important nerve had been struck. What had been a small, elite, narrowly drawn organization grew from a few hundred members and a yearly budget on the order of $12,000 in the early 1960s to an organization with some 70,000 members and a budget of over $400,000 by the mid 1970s. By 1978, an estimated 3 million living wills had been distributed.[10] Abigail Van Buren had handed a gift to activists seeking the right to determine when life had lost meaning, when suffering became unbearable, and when life was otherwise not worth living.

Public Opinion and Legislative Action

Public opinion polls reflected this evolving moral landscape. In 1950, Gallup pollsters had asked respondents a question: "When a person has a disease that cannot be cured, do you think doctors should be allowed by law to end the patient's life by some painless means if the patient and his family request it?" Only five years had passed since World War II, and the full effects of the biological revolution were yet to come. Slightly over a third of the respondents, 36 percent, agreed with this brief depiction of what would later be called assisted suicide.

In July 1973, Gallup pollsters again asked the same question. By this time, supporters had become a majority, 53 percent. In 1977, the year following *Quinlan*, the National Opinion Research Center (NORC) released its poll, again asking the same question. The percentage in agreement had risen to 62 percent, leaving a little over a third in opposition. Over these two-and-a-half decades, the proportion of supporters to those opposed had reversed.[11] In the coming years, support would plateau at around 70 percent.

The NORC polls began asking the doctor-assisted, ending-of-life question the year following *Quinlan*. In Karen Ann's case, however, physicians were not administering "some painless means" to bring about death. They were withdrawing a respirator. Death was very likely in both cases, but there were important ethical and legal distinctions. Although the more passive right to die was less frequently part of opinion polling, public support for the withdrawal or refusal of treatment was, if anything, higher. In the late 1970s to the mid 1980s, support for the patient-requested withdrawal of treatment grew from 71 percent to 85 percent. In 1990, as Nancy Cruzan's case—detailed below—was being decided, a *Time/CNN* poll was conducted. Eighty-one percent of those surveyed agreed, if a patient was terminally ill and unconscious but had left instructions in a living will, the doctor should be allowed to withdraw life-sustaining treatment.[12]

As with abortion, support for an assisted right to die was not uniformly woven throughout the social fabric. Opposition followed lines of religious commitments and practices. The single strongest correlate, again mirroring attitudes toward abortion, was how frequently a person prayed. Why might this be the case?

Frequent prayer, in all likelihood, meant you believed in an active, concerned god, a god within reach, a god willing to intervene. A caring, all-knowing, and involved god could be trusted to do what was best in our lives, especially when it came to determining the moment of death. It took arrogant, inappropriate hubris to intervene in what God should control. A caring god had provided knowledge for life-prolonging technologies; they should be used. Although there were inconsistencies in this line of reasoning, and many antagonists would point them out, for believers we should use what God had given us and let His will be done.

Whatever the reasons, the NORC surveys revealed only one in eight (12 percent) of those who reported never praying stood in opposition to the active termination of life as reflected in the Gallup and NORC polls. By contrast, among those praying "several times a day," five out of ten (52 percent) were opposed. Those praying intermediate amounts varied accordingly.[13]

Leaving these variations aside and taking the polling data in the aggregate, the results were clear. They suggested a public receptive to change. As so often happens in receptive political climates, dramatic events can be like crystals dropped in super-saturated solutions. They precipitate action.[14] Joe and Julia Quinlan's widely publicized struggle to secure the removal of a respirator and their daughter's right to die was just such an event. Its influence would help precipitate legislative efforts in California in the early 1970s.

California Takes the Lead

Freshman Senator Barry Keene, author of the California legislation, drew motivation from personal experiences. He was a lawyer. Both his neighbor's wife and then his mother-in-law had been confronted with unwanted life-prolonging treatments. Keene had been called upon for legal assistance. He found little to work with. "The rights and duties of doctors and hospitals were unclear and the dying had no clear rights or way to refuse life-sustaining medical treatment."[15] In Keene's mother-in-law's case this was true even though she had signed a medical directive to limit treatment.

Similar to Walter Sackett's efforts in Florida, Keene's initial legislative efforts in 1974 were defeated. There was important opposition to his simple proposal that "every person has a right to die without prolongation of life by medical means." It came from three influential organizations—the AMA, the California Pro-Life Council (CPLC), an arm of the National Right to Life Committee, and the California Catholic Conference. The CPLC was most adamant, drawing the now familiar comparisons to Hitler and warning of the slippery slope leading to the extermination of undesirables.

Unlike Representative Sackett's efforts in Florida, however, Senator Keene hit upon a winning strategy. He aimed to avoid the economic or "common good" implications of euthanasia. His proposed legislation was narrowly crafted to concentrate on individual autonomy and the right to die. The new legislation provided that adult persons had the fundamental right to control decisions relating to their own medical care, including the decision to have life-sustaining procedures withheld or withdrawn.

He knew Catholic opposition had been softened by a declaration from Pope Pius XII a decade and a half earlier. The Pope had directly addressed the question of whether the doctor "[Has] a right, or is he bound, in all cases of deep unconsciousness, even in those that are considered to be completely hopeless . . . to use modern artificial respiration apparatus." The Pope's conclusion was:

> since these forms of treatment go beyond the ordinary means to which one is bound, it cannot be held that there is an obligation to use them, nor, consequently, that one is bound to give the doctor permission to use them.[16]

This was something Keene could work with. He sensed the AMA had not well understood the intent and specifics of his initial proposal. He would better explain. The California Medical Association (CMA) understood what he was attempting to accomplish and was quite receptive to legal clarification of how advancing technologies and new drugs might be restricted in use. They were actively advocating laws that would limit their personal legal liabilities. Such clarifications and protections could be crafted.

Keene was aware the polling data indicated he had support. He would work to neutralize the continued religious and ideological opposition of the CPLC by further strengthening public support by keeping the issue before the public. His public-relations efforts were assisted when Karen Ann Quinlan's case achieved maximum public exposure as final negotiations on the bill's wording were being worked out. Keene's colleagues in California's legislative bodies were now paying attention.

The eventual compromises yielded a bill more restrictive than Senator Keene hoped for, but the final vote was decisive. The California Assembly voted 43–22 and the Senate 22–14, in favor. When then Governor Edmund G. (Jerry) Brown, Jr. signed the California Natural Death Act (NDA) into law in 1976, it became the first piece of legislation that acknowledged, "modern medical technology has made possible artificial prolongation of human life beyond natural limits." It further established that, "adult persons have the fundamental right to control the decision relating to the rendering of their own medical care, including the decision to have life-sustaining procedures withheld or withdrawn in instances of a terminal condition."

Shortly after the NDA took effect, Senator Keene was asked to join a weekly staff conference of doctors at the University of California, San Francisco. The physicians wanted to understand better what this new legislation involved.[17] The physician introducing Senator Keene began with a review of the highly perplexing threads of the right-to-die Gordian knot:

> How long can we hold on to some hope for recovery? How can we justify continuing the anguish, and the false hope, for the family? How much of our resources, and manpower, can be appropriately diverted to this demoralizing exercise in futility, particularly when it is inevitably at the expense of our other patients?

Continuing his introduction, this physician breathed a sigh of relief. Help was on its way. The NDA, he concluded, "acknowledges public and legal involvement in a problem which, until now, the physician has had to shoulder alone and which many times has made him behave senselessly, inhumanely or, surreptitiously, illegally."

For his part, Senator Keene wanted the doctors to understand his role. He was a lawyer. He was concerned with constitutional rights and individual liberties. He believed that one of "the most intimate and potentially offensive acts is invasion of the human body itself without that decision having been made, or necessarily assented to, by the terminally ill person." Perhaps drawing from Representative Sackett's failed efforts in Florida, Senator Keene noted "opponents of the measure felt it was a foot-in-the-door leading to euthanasia." There were those who feared "soon we were going to be 'killing' other categories of people—the retarded and the elderly."

Senator Keen felt the NDA had gathered support and passed by large margins in part because it clearly addressed these fears. "It is not someone else deciding when a person ought to die." Rather, "The terminally ill patient in a prospective way, makes the decision." It was not a matter of "talking about a category of people and determining *whether* they ought to die, but *how* they ought to die. Those most affected by the prospect of dying ought to determine how their final days are to be spent."

With his neighbor's wife and his own mother-in-law's experiences fresh in his mind, and with Karen Ann Quinlan's case now well known, Senator Keene concluded:

> We felt there were people who in the event of terminal illness would not want to spend their final days tyrannized by machines when the only purpose (and this is the key language) of these machines is to postpone the moment of death artificially where no cure is possible and where death is, in any event imminent.

Although the California NDA marked an important turning point, it was in many ways limited. It was marred by a residue of concern over the slippery slope of "mercy killings" and weakened by the compromises of a negotiated settlement. In particular, it contained exclusions and special provisions for persons such as pregnant women and nursing-home patients. It only applied to situations where no cure was possible and where death was imminent. It was limited in application to those who were, or at one time had been, competent to make decisions. Still, it was an important benchmark. Many state statutes would follow. Seven related laws were enacted, mainly by neighboring states, the next year.

By 1990, the year the Supreme Court decided *Cruzan*, this number had grown to forty-two. Most of these subsequent statutes were less restrictive than California's pioneering effort. The path was partially cleared in 1982 when the AMA endorsed, for the first time, the position that it was ethical for physicians to withdraw life-support from hopelessly ill patients.

Working in tandem with the AMA, a presidential commission, initially convened in 1980 to develop a uniform definition of death, became troubled by cases such as Karen Ann Quinlan's and turned its attention to appropriate treatment of persons "who are dying but not dead." The commission's resulting set of recommendations, *Deciding to Forego Life-Sustaining Treatment*, was released in March 1983. Twenty state statutes were enacted in the next two years. Seven were passed in 1984, and thirteen followed in 1985.

These state statutes were joined by some 54 state court decisions, partially shaping and partially reflective of the newly passed laws. All were part of a continuing effort to clarify a range of remaining issues defining the boundaries of protected life, the significance of senseless suffering, and patient autonomy when it came to the right to die. This clarity was especially needed when the patients in question were not capable of expressing their wishes or understanding their conditions, treatment options, and potential suffering.

Alleviating Suffering and Protecting Life: Who Decides?

The *Quinlan* decision, living wills, and California's NDA all assumed persons were at one point capable of making rational decisions. But, who should decide if the capacity for rational decision-making was never present? What criteria should be used? In March 1976, shortly after *Quinlan* was decided, these issues, involving a severely retarded 67-year-old man, began winding their way through the courts of Massachusetts.

Joseph Saikewicz's IQ was assessed to be 10, with a mental age somewhere between two and three years. Since 1923, he had spent all of his life in state institutions. Although severely limited mentally, he was not "vegetative." As described by the court, he was "physically strong and well built, nutritionally nourished, and ambulatory." He had the ability, albeit minimal, to interact with those around him and to experience joy and discomfort. He did not, however, have the ability to communicate verbally. He communicated with grunts and gestures. He also had difficulty responding intelligibly to inquiries such as whether he was experiencing pain.

On April 19, 1976, Mr. Saikewicz was diagnosed as suffering from leukemia. If left untreated, the best prognosis was that he would live perhaps several weeks or months and would die with relatively little pain. Treated with then available chemotherapy, his life could most likely be extended for perhaps a year and possibly longer. The treatment would have many discomforting side effects, difficult to explain and hard to understand for the patient.

Although evidence was clear that most comprehending persons would choose to undergo this life-prolonging treatment, Joseph Saikewicz was not most comprehending persons. He was not capable of granting informed consent or refusing treatment with full understanding of the implications. It was very likely he would have to be restrained to allow the effective administration of the chemotherapy. What to do?

Family members were located, but they preferred not to become involved. A guardian was appointed. The guardian's recommendation was to forego treatment. Time was clearly a factor in that any delay meant the likely success of chemotherapy was diminished. Those who saw value in protecting and prolonging Joseph's life took the guardian's recommendation to court. Less than a month after the initial diagnosis, the judge agreed with the guardian. The judge's decision was immediately appealed to Massachusetts' highest court. On July 9, responding to the now urgent need, the court affirmed the trial judge's decision and promised a detailed decision in the months ahead. Before that decision was released, Joseph Saikewicz died on September 4, in relatively little pain, from the complicating condition of pneumonia.

Had he been mentally competent, in all likelihood, the life-prolonging chemotherapy would have proceeded. Was withholding treatment an act of compassion to minimize suffering or an instance where the life of a man with severely diminished mental capacity was deemed less worthy of protecting and prolonging than others? How was this any different from actions allowed by the constitutional amendment proposed by Representative Sackett, which the Florida legislators and many others had so firmly rejected?

The Massachusetts court was aware of these questions and meant to clarify. They did so in a detailed decision released in November 1977, some 14 months after Joseph died.[18] Their grounding assumption was clearly stated: "The chance of a longer life carries the same weight for Saikewicz as for any other person, the value of life under the law having no relation to intelligence or social position." The difference came, the court continued, from the patient's inability to understand what was happening and the absence of hope that would otherwise allow Joseph Saikewicz to understand treatment and tolerate suffering. The guardian had given voice to this "most troubling aspect" of the case in his trial testimony:

> If he is treated with toxic drugs he will be involuntarily immersed in a state of painful suffering, the reason for which he will never understand. Patients who request treatment know the risks involved and can appreciate the painful side effects when they arrive. They know the reason for the pain and their hope makes it tolerable.

The appropriate question was not what would most persons do, but,

> whether a majority of people would choose chemotherapy if they were told merely that something outside of their previous experience was going to be done to them, that this something would cause them pain and discomfort, that they would be removed to strange surroundings and possibly restrained for extended periods of time, and that the advantages of this course of action were measured by concepts of time and mortality beyond their ability to comprehend.

Persons such as Mr. Saikewicz, who were unable to "anticipate and prepare for the severe side effects of drugs," were left with only "confusion and disorientation." This meant, the court continued, that such a "naturally uncooperative patient would have to be physically restrained to allow the slow intravenous administration of drugs," compounding the "pain and fear," as well as possibly jeopardizing "the ability of his body to withstand the toxic effects of the drugs." Under these conditions, this elderly, mentally handicapped man "would experience fear without the understanding from which other patients draw strength."

At trial, the judge had weighed these confusing effects of chemotherapy against "the quality of life possible for him even if the treatment does bring about remission." This might be read as asserting Joseph's life, even if saved, would not be worth the effort. Advocates for the disabled saw it in just such a light. If this was the meaning taken, the Massachusetts court was quick to firmly reject it. "Rather than reading the judge's formulation in a manner that demeans the value of the life of one who is mentally retarded," the appeals court clarified, "the vague, and perhaps ill-chosen, term 'quality of life' should be understood as a reference to the continuing state of pain and disorientation precipitated by the chemotherapy treatment." Seen in this light, "the decision to withhold treatment from Saikewicz was based on a regard for his actual interests and preferences and the facts supported this decision."

A thin line was being drawn between intolerable suffering and the protective boundaries of life. In the years just ahead, many related cases would follow.[19] They were quick in developing. Hesitant, frequently waffling personal and professional decisions, along with conflicting court judgments, would emerge. The tolerable limits of suffering, the boundaries of protected life, the meaning of beneficence, justice, and individual autonomy, as well as the professional rights and responsibilities of care-givers would mix together and compete for primacy.

One such case, finally decided in 1981, involved a man in New Jersey who, like Joseph Saikewicz, was profoundly retarded and had spent all but the early years of his life in a state institution. He was suffering from terminal bladder cancer and needed blood transfusions from complicating conditions. This case yielded a decision in partial opposition to the Massachusetts' court's detailed findings for Joseph Saikewicz.

John Storar had just turned 50, with an estimated mental age of 18 months, when he was diagnosed with cancer of the bladder. He had lived in the Newark Development Center since he was 5. His widowed mother lived close by and visited him almost daily. When blood was found in her son's urine, after some hesitation, she consented to tests. When the tests came back indicating cancer, she agreed to a six-week regime of radiation treatment, beginning in August 1979.

This treatment sent John's cancer into remission, but it reappeared a few months later in March 1980. This time, attempts to cauterize blood vessels to stop the associated bleeding were unsuccessful, and his physicians concluded, "after using all medical and surgical means then available" the patient would die from the disease. By May, John Storar needed blood transfusions. His mother did not initially consent, but a day later withdrew her objection. For several weeks, transfusions were given.

The transfusions were clearly distressing to John, who was given sedatives to calm him down. After the transfusions, however, his energy picked up, and he was able to feed himself, shower, walk, run, and on occasion engage in mischievous activities "such as stealing cigarette butts and attempting to eat them." This continued for several weeks, until June 19, when his mother decided the good being done by the transfusions was outweighed by the problems produced for her son. She wanted them stopped.

The director of the center sought court authorization to continue the transfusions to save his patient's life. John's mother filed contending petitions. Pending a hearing, the court ordered that the transfusions could continue. At the subsequent hearing, it was noted that the cancer had spread to John's lungs and perhaps other organs. The loss of blood continued. With transfusions, John's life was likely to last perhaps three to six months. Without them he was likely to die within weeks. John did not comprehend the purpose of his treatment or possess the ability to make a reasoned choice.

Neither his mother, nor anyone else, was able to determine her son's wishes. She was also not sure whether stopping the transfusions would mean he would die sooner. What was clear was that John disliked the treatments and wanted to avoid them. His mother wanted her son to be comfortable and for his suffering to end. She wanted the treatments stopped. After hearing arguments, the court agreed. John's mother was the one best positioned to make the decision. The court denied the center's request to continue the transfusions.

This would have ended the story had this decision not been appealed and eventually heard in the Appellate Division of the Supreme Court of New York, where it was finally decided on December 15, 1981.[20] By this time, John Storar had died. Uncertainties and disagreements on how he should have been treated, however, remained. They had far-reaching implications. Reflecting these ambiguities and differences in opinion, the appellate judges were of split mind. The majority, however, like those involved with Joseph Saikewicz, felt there were larger issues, and they needed to provide guidance for future cases.

A few short months before events yielding the Baby Doe Regulations, this New York court, hearing the case of a 50-year-old man, wrote, "Mentally John Storar was an infant." This was "the only realistic way to assess his rights." Although parents had "a right to consent to medical treatment on behalf of an infant," they did not have the right to "deprive a child of lifesaving treatment, however well intentioned." Clearly, there were compelling state interests to protect the life of a child. Pointing to other cases in which parents had declined necessary life-saving treatment on the basis of religious beliefs (the transfusion of blood was a classic example), the court noted they had not been allowed to do so.

In John Storar's case, blood transfusions were likened unto food. Like nutrition and hydration, transfusions provided protection of life, no matter how short. "They would not cure the cancer, but they could eliminate the risk of death from another treatable cause." Weighing the consequent suffering John experienced in his prolonged life, the court found it was minor. It most certainly did not outweigh the state's duty to protect his life.

The need for "substituted judgment" for John Storar was clear. It was also clear that John's "best interests" should guide this judgment. On final appeal, the court decided its own substituted judgment was more compelling than that of John's mother. Unlike Karen Ann Quinlan, John Storar was not in a vegetative state. He was dying, but he had not lost all humanizing qualities. With transfusions, his life could continue, albeit for a short time, as it had before. These last moments of life, the court held, were worth protecting.

In a case like this, the court concluded, the protective boundaries of life should not be weakened or transgressed. They should be firmer than those drawn for Joseph Saikewicz. We should not, "allow an incompetent patient to bleed to death because someone, even someone as close as a parent or sibling, feels that this is best for one with an incurable disease." After John Storar had died, it was decided blood transfusions should have continued.

Those giving greatest weight to protecting life and the worthiness of severely mentally retarded persons praised the decision. Those looking to keep decisions about these uncertain matters in the hands of those most immediately impacted saw unwarranted governmental intrusion. As additional cases wound their way through various state courts over the next several years, the discrepancies in court findings began to narrow.

This was reflected in the case of Claire Conroy, an elderly woman living in a nursing home in New Jersey, suffering from multiple life-threatening illnesses. In 1985, the Supreme Court of New Jersey, again after Ms. Conroy had died, provided its written opinion.[21] By this time, patient autonomy was well established, and the legal and moral climate was better able to account for new medical technologies and procedures. There was widespread agreement in "terminal" cases, where patient wishes were known either through "living wills" or other explicitly determined sources, that patient autonomy was secure. This extended to "ordinary" and "extraordinary" life-/death-prolonging measures alike. "Life-sustaining treatment may be withheld or withdrawn from an incompetent patient," the New Jersey court held, "when it is clear that the particular patient would have refused the treatment under the circumstances." The standard was not what the "average person" would do, but "what the particular patient would have done if able to choose for himself."

Unfortunately, Claire's wishes were not well documented. She did not have a living will nor other formal documents. And, at the time, she was unable to express her wishes. Her closest relative was her nephew. Based on what he believed his aunt would have wanted, he decided that the various actions the physicians wanted to take, including the amputation of her leg and the removal of a feeding tube, should not be performed. The doctors in charge challenged his assessment.

Substituted judgment was again clearly called for. It was also clear that such judgment should be based on an assessment of the patient's best interests. If Claire's wishes had been known, the court wrote, they had "no doubt" she would have had the right to choose to refuse the recommended amputation of her leg and to have her nasogastric tube withdrawn. The "freedom from nonconsensual invasion of her bodily integrity" was well established and outweighed "any state interest in preserving life or in safeguarding the integrity of the medical profession."

Given the circumstances, who should decide? What criteria should be used? Here, there was less agreement. Lacking clear evidence of patient preferences, the New Jersey court, as other courts had before, seemed to wander through the hazy boundaries of tolerable suffering and a life worth protecting, supporting, and prolonging. "Pain, suffering, and possible enjoyment" of life could be considered. Treatment could be withheld or withdrawn if "the net burdens of the patient's life with the treatment" were "clearly and markedly" outweighed by "the benefits that the patient derives from life." What did this mean? When was a tipping point reached?

The "mere fact that a patient's functioning is limited or his prognosis dim," the court noted, in affirmation of the sanctity of life, "does not mean that he is not enjoying what remains of his life or that it is in his best interests to die." Other courts gave greater weight to the assessment of suffering, finding that the prolongation of life was not required "if there is no hope of return to a normal, integrated, functioning, cognitive existence." It was also true that a recent presidential commission had recommended that decisions could be made on the assessed best interests of the patient, taking into account "the relief of suffering, the preservation or restoration of functioning, and the quality as well as the extent of life sustained."

Absent the ability to communicate with the patient, the balance between tolerable suffering and protection of life was not easily determined. The relief of suffering, the assessment of a life worth living, and the sanctity of life more generally drawn remained in tension. The line between the duty to alleviate suffering and that to protect life was, indeed, quite thin. There was no clear-cut answer.

The Supreme Court Weighs In

Nevertheless, the state court decisions involving Karen Ann Quinlan, Joseph Saikewicz, John Storar, Claire Conroy, and a host of others provided important guidelines. They were, however, of limited jurisdiction.

Fifteen years after *Quinlan* and following the host of state court decisions, a related case finally wound its way on a seven-year journey to the U.S. Supreme Court. It involved a young woman, Nancy Cruzan, rendered "vegetative" from severe injuries she sustained in an automobile accident in Jasper County, Missouri, in early January 1983. Arguments before the U.S. Supreme Court were presented on December 6, 1989, and a decision was released six months later on June 25, 1990. *Cruzan v. Director, Missouri Department of Health*[22] would provide more broadly applicable findings regarding the rights and restrictions others had struggled so fervently to establish.

In 1983, Joe and Joyce Cruzan found themselves in circumstances equally tragic and perplexing to those experienced by the Quinlans. Nancy Cruzan, their 25-year-old daughter, had been severely injured in a car accident. Revisiting the site of the accident, her father would later recall:

> She was going east and she went off on this side of the road about 300 feet down from that mailbox. I imagine the car came to rest right along in here. It was upside down. It was on this side of the lane and Nancy was lying face down on the other side.
>
> I went down and talked to the trooper that worked the accident and then I also got a copy of the accident report from the state. It read, "Vital signs on arriving—blood pressure, 0 over 0. Pulse, 0. Respiration, 0." On the report it said, "Code blue. Clinical save." I asked them what a clinical save was and they said they have one maybe two or three times a year, and it's when someone

has gone into cardiopulmonary arrest, I think is the term they use, and that they're able to bring them back. And sometimes it works and sometimes it doesn't.[23]

Like Karen Ann, Nancy remained alive as determined by the Harvard brain-death criteria. Unlike Karen Ann, however, the treatment keeping Nancy alive was not deemed "extraordinary." It was nutrition and hydration provided through a tube. Some three years later, Nancy was diagnosed as being in a persistent vegetative state, and her parents requested that the hospital terminate treatment to let their daughter die in peace.

Joe later reflected on their decision:

> I signed the consent form to begin the artificial feeding of Nancy, to have the tube implanted. Looking back on it, I would like to have let her go that night because Nancy died—our Nancy died that night. We've got her body left, but she has no dignity whatsoever there and she was a very, very proud, independent person and you would see what was left there and you wondered why. Why? What's the purpose in this?[24]

Nancy's doctors, based on their understanding of a state law requiring "clear and convincing evidence" of the patient's wishes before withdrawing treatment, refused Joe and Joyce's request. The measures being used to sustain their daughter's life were not "extraordinary," and the physicians had professional and legal responsibilities to keep her alive.

The case went to trial. By this time, there was fairly widespread agreement that a person in Nancy's condition had a fundamental right to refuse "death-prolonging" procedures. But, what would Nancy want? There was no living will or other formal declaratory document. She had once expressed to a housemate and co-worker that she would not wish to continue her life if sick or injured unless she could live at least "halfway normally." Nancy's sister, Chris, also recalled a family conversation with the same conclusion. There was no doubt in their minds

> that, if we could call her up and ask, "Nancy, what do you want?", she would say, "Look, I realize it's hard on everyone else, but let me go. I've got other things to do, and I've got other places to go—so turn me loose."[25]

Joe was asked in trial, "Could you tell the court why you feel it is in Nancy's best interest that the feeding tube be discontinued." He responded, "Primarily it's because we believe it is what Nancy's wish would be." Chris was asked similar questions, as was Joyce. There were no specific detailed expressions of what Nancy would have wished, but, in emotional testimony as "her hands gripped the arms of the witness chair," Chris responded, "Nancy would want to live where she could live to the fullest. Where she lives to the fullest is within us. It is not within that body that's being maintained at Mt. Vernon."

On July 27, 1988, the trial court found, taken together, this was enough evidence. It directed that the "request of the Co-guardians to withdraw nutrition or hydration" be carried out. After reading the decision to his family, Joe's response was, "So, if that's winning, we won." Nancy's lawyer worried that the judge had not included a statement that Nancy was in a persistent vegetative state. Some others worried over the implications for vulnerable persons. "If somebody deems their quality of life is not sufficient, they could be starved to death." Very strong objections were expected from the staff where Nancy was being cared for.

The trial court's findings were immediately appealed to the state Supreme Court. In a split vote, the state appellate justices disagreed with the trial court. They found instead that the evidence of Nancy's wishes was not clear and convincing, as demanded by Missouri law. They reversed the trial-court decision. This reversal was, in turn, appealed to the U.S. Supreme Court. In December 1989, the U.S. Supreme Court agreed to hear its first right-to-die case. On June 25, 1990, some seven-and-a-half years after Nancy's accident, *Cruzan v. Director, Missouri Department of Health*[26] was decided. The five–four decision, along with the appeals process leading to it, was contentious. It mirrored the, by then, well-developed national right-to-die debate.

"This is the first case in which we have been squarely presented with the issue of whether the United States Constitution grants what is in common parlance referred to as a 'right to die,'" Chief Justice Rehnquist wrote. Developing the rationale of the court's majority, his detailed opinion read like a commentary on the years between the onset of Karen Ann Quinlan's vegetative state and Nancy's similar condition.

> Until about 15 years ago and the seminal decision in *In re Quinlan*, the number of right-to-refuse-treatment decisions was relatively

few ... More recently, however, with the advance of medical technology capable of sustaining life well past the point where natural forces would have brought certain death in earlier times, cases involving the right to refuse life-sustaining treatment have burgeoned.

More specifically, Rehnquist pointed to 54 reported decisions relevant to these issues between 1976 and 1988.[27]

By then, it was well established that competent individuals had the right to refuse medical treatment. Such decisions were private and protected by the Constitution. It was equally clear there was a compelling state interest in protecting the sanctity of life. In Nancy's case, there was the complicating condition that she was unable to express her wishes in the moment. This fell upon her parents, acting on her behalf, in what the courts now routinely called "substituted judgment." How did they know what their daughter would have preferred?

The Missouri statute required "clear and convincing evidence" of a patient's wishes when determining the acceptability of substituted judgment. The state appellate court found the available evidence did not meet this standard. Chief Justice Rehnquist and four of his U.S. Supreme Court colleagues found no reason to question this finding. The Cruzans had lost. As their lawyer, Bill Colby, would later write, the initial impact of the decision made him sick to his stomach.

He called Joe. Joe had already heard from a friend and, in a quivering voice, simply uttered, "Jesus" when he answered the phone. As their brief conversation came to a close, Joe began to cry. The decision was not what they had hoped for. It needed to be carefully read to determine what, if any, their next steps might be. Bill promised to get back to Joe as soon as he had time to consider the decision carefully.

At first, he was not optimistic. As he read he thought, "they should have simply pasted the words from the solicitor general's brief to the page, as it would have saved them some work." It turned out, however, there was a small but important opening. Chief Justice Rehnquist had written in the main opinion that there was a constitutional right for competent people to refuse medical treatment.

This was the first time the U.S. Supreme Court had reached this conclusion. Justice O'Connor, writing a concurring opinion, noted that artificial feeding qualified as medical treatment. This meant it could be withdrawn if the wishes of the patient were known. Then Bill Colby came upon eight words embedded in the legal language of the opinion— "discovery of new evidence regarding the patient's intent." If new evidence of Nancy's wishes was clear and convincing, the requests of Nancy Cruzan's parents should be honored.

Bill Colby knew from previous conversations there was additional evidence, not presented at trial. He called Joe and read Rehnquist's language to him. The wording was embedded in a longer paragraph, and Joe was unclear of the implications. "What's it mean?" he asked. "It means," Colby replied, "that the United States Supreme Court says we get a new trial."

Over the next few months, further evidence was gathered from family and friends regarding Nancy's previously expressed wishes. This new evidence was offered in a new trial. This time, it was deemed clear and convincing. The medical treatment keeping Nancy alive could be discontinued. There were no further appeals.

Joe and Joyce Cruzan were saddened, but relieved. Joe had made an early commitment to his daughter to "allow her to die with some dignity." Now it was time to do so. In a written statement, he pointed to the pride he took in the profound and lasting importance of Nancy's life. The reverence he held for both the sanctity of life and the power of suffering could not be missed. It had been a long and difficult journey.

> Today, 1,206 days later, we have that court order. She was our bright, flaming star who flew through the heavens of our lives. Though brilliant, her life was terribly short-lived, but she has left a flaming trail, a legacy that I do not think will shortly be forgotten. Because of Nancy, I suspect hundreds of thousands of people can rest free, knowing that when death beckons they can meet it face to face with dignity, free from the fear of unwanted medical treatment, unwanted and useless medical treatment. I think this is quite an accomplishment for a 25-year-old kid and I'm damned proud of her . . . Now we walk with her to the door of death so that she may at last pass through and be free.[28]

On December 15, 1990, the tube providing nutrition for Nancy Cruzan was removed. She died 11 days later.

The Gift of Death

During this final week and a half, protesters gathered outside the hospital. They were adamant in opposition. One regretted his inability to do anything: "If I could get up there . . . I would put the tube back in her myself. I had hoped to be able to try something like that, but we're not going to make it." Another voiced fear of the broader, dehumanizing implications. "'Vegetable' is going to be just like fetus was. That's the word they're going to use. It's not fully human and you can kill it. A vegetable isn't human." A third agreed, pointing to the emergent culture of death, "America has lost all sense of value for human life at all, you know, with abortion and now with this thing with Nancy."[29]

These protestors outside the Missouri hospital were not alone. They gave voice to a broad-based effort among those who saw an increased willingness to consider some lives less worthy of protection than others and a fading commitment to protect the inherent importance of *LIFE*. Standing in opposition were those such as Joe and Joyce Cruzan, who knew first hand and gave greater weight to the deeply tragic consequences of senselessly prolonging suffering and death.

In a tribute to his daughter at her burial on December 28, 1990, turning protestors' words back upon them, Joe wrote:

> Today, as the protestor's sign says, we gave Nancy the gift of death. An unconditional gift of love that sets her free from this twisted body that no longer serves her. A gift I know she will treasure above all others, the gift of freedom. So run free Nan, we will catch up later.[30]

Nancy Cruzan's grave marker has three dates:

Born: July 20, 1957
Departed: January 11, 1983
At Peace: December 26, 1990

It had taken a decade and a half to reach this point. California's NDA was passed less than a year after Karen Ann Quinlan's case was decided. It led the way for the passage of related legislation in 42 states. The *Cruzan* decision looked back on 54 related court cases decided in this interim.

Federal legislation, the Patient Self-Determination Act,[31] prompted by Nancy's family's struggles and introduced by Missouri's U.S. Senator John Danforth, became law.

Together they clarified the boundaries of protected life and tolerable suffering, as well as the right to choose to leave life peacefully. They dealt in specific detail with the general questions. The protection and support of life could, and frequently did, conflict with the alleviation of suffering. Prioritized choices were unavoidable. Justifications for a right to die were grounded in conclusions that some lives, some moments in life, are more worthy of protection, support, and prolonging than others.

From this defining *Quinlan*-to-*Cruzan* period, the core issue for the right-to-die movement became whether persons who now had the right to end their suffering or to leave life peacefully also had a right to assistance in doing so, even if they did not have an immediately terminal condition. On this, substantial social, legal, medical, and religious disagreement remained.

Notes

1 *Cruzan v. Director, MDH*, 497 U.S. 261 (1990).
2 Quotes that follow are taken from his later recollections: Walter Sackett, "Death With Dignity," *Southern Medical Journal* 64 (1971): 330–2. Walter Sackett, "I've Let Hundreds of Patients Die. Shouldn't You?," *Medical Economics* April 2 (1973): 92–7.
3 For a more complete account of Walter Sackett's endeavors, see: Henry R. Glick, *The Right to Die: Policy Innovation and its Consequences* (New York: Columbia University Press, 1992), 104–20.
4 Numerous detailed accounts have been provided of this period. See: Glick, *The Right to Die*. Peter G. Filene, *In the Arms of Others: A Cultural History of the Right-to-Die* (Chicago: Ivan R. Dee, 1998). Ian Dowbiggin, *A Merciful End: The Euthanasia Movement in Modern America* (New York: Oxford University Press, 2003).
5 See: Joseph Fletcher, *Morals and Medicine* (Princeton, NJ: Princeton University Press, 1954); Glanville Williams, *The Sanctity of Life and the Criminal Law* (New York: Alfred A. Knopf, 1957); and Yale Kamisar, "Some Non-Religious Views Against Proposed 'Mercy Killing' Legislation," *Minnesota Law Review* (1958): 969–1042.
6 Notably in *Harper's* and *Atlantic Monthly*. See Ian Dowbiggin, *A Merciful End: The Euthanasia Movement in Modern America* (New York: Oxford University Press, 2003), 107 and 205, fn 33.
7 Quotes from personal correspondence and annual presidential reports cited in Dowbiggin, *A Merciful End*, 119.
8 "The 'Living Will' Gains Acceptance," *New York Times*, September 20 (1984). "Luis Kutner, Lawyer who Fought for Human Rights, is Dead at 84," *New York Times* March 4 (1993); available online at: www.nytimes.com/1993/03/04/us/luis-kutner-lawyer-who-fought-for-human-rights-is-dead-at-84.html.

9   "Due Process of Euthanasia: The Living Will, a Proposal," *Indiana Law Journal* 44 (1969): 539–54.

10 Dowbiggin, *A Merciful End*, 121 and 211, fn 99.

11 See John Ostheimer, "The Polls: Changing Attitudes Toward Euthanasia," *Public Opinion Quarterly* 44 (1980): 123–8.

12 "Love and Let Die," *Time*, March 19, 1990. Harris Polls as reported in Glick, *The Right to Die*, 84.

13 Gallup Poll, "Public Historically Supports a Terminally Ill Patient's Right to Die," October 30, 2003. The General Social Surveys conducted by the National Opinion Research Center are available online at: http://sda.berkeley.edu/cgi-bin32/hsda?harcsda+gss06.

14 This pattern has long been noted and systematically developed in other arenas. See: Neil J. Smelser, *Theory of Collective Behavior* (New York: The Free Press, 1962).

15 Glick, *The Right to Die*, 94.

16 Pope Pius XII, "The Prolongation of Life," *The Pope Speaks* 4 (1958).

17 See transcript of this meeting held on January 19, 1977: "California's Natural Death Act—Medical Staff Conference, University of California, San Francisco," *Western Journal of Medicine* 128 (1978): 318–30.

18 *Superintendent of Belchertown State School et al. v. Joseph Saikewicz, Mass.*, 370 N.E.2d 417, 1977.

19 See: Ezekiel J. Manuel, "A Review of the Ethical and Legal Aspects of Terminating Medical Care," *The American Journal of Medicine* 84 (1998): 291–301.

20 *In re Storar* 52 N.Y.2d 363; 420 N.E.2d 64; 1981.

21 *In re Conroy*, 98 NJ 321. 486 A.2d 1209, 1261 (1985).

22 497 U.S. 261 (1990).

23 PBS Frontline, March 24, 1992.

24 PBS Frontline, March 24, 1992.

25 These and following quotes are taken from William H. Colby, *Long Goodbye: The Deaths of Nancy Cruzan* (Carlsbad, CA: Hay House, 2002), 41, 170, 178, 233, and 320.

26 *Cruzan v. Director, MDH*, 497 U.S. 261 (1990).

27 For specifics see: Manuel, "A Review of the Ethical and Legal Aspects of Terminating Medical Care," 291–301.

28 PBS *Frontline*, March 24, 1992.

29 PBS *Frontline*, March 24, 1992.

30 Cited in Colby, *Long Goodbye*, 391.

31 See Lawrence P. Ulrich, (1999) *The Patient Self-Determination Act: Meeting the Challenges in Patient Care* (Washington, DC: Georgetown University Press, 1999).

CHAPTER 12

GOD, DUTY, AND LIFE WORTH LIVING

The battle lines were drawn. On one side were persons concerned with keeping the uncertain, irrevocable decisions of assisted suicide in the hands of those most intimately involved. In circumstances of intense suffering and terminal illness, individuals should have the right to choose their moment of death. If they needed help, it should be provided. Although assisted suicide might be an anathema to medical ethics and religious or moral beliefs, there came a point when resistance to death and the prolongation of suffering made no sense. Assisted dying, not assisted suicide, should be the goal.

On the other side were those who feared a slippery slope of diminished respect for life. They saw assisted suicide as a diminution of the sanctity of life, with consequent weakening of life's protective boundaries. Practices of involuntary euthanasia, both subtle and overt, would soon follow. Suffering could and should be endured. God, not humans, should determine the moment of death. If needed, the machinery of law should be invoked to ensure that the timing of death was in God's hands.

Belief in an Efficacious, Caring God

As issues were framed and resources mobilized, the power of religious beliefs and practices was found everywhere. Agnostics and atheists were far more likely to support assisted suicide than believers. Among believers, there was wide variation among adherents to different faiths and denominations.

In the last chapter, we saw public opinion polls showing quite clearly that the frequency with which an individual prays is closely connected to attitudes toward the active termination of life through doctor-assisted suicide. A caring God would not push us beyond our abilities to endure. There was redemptive purpose in suffering. There were lessons to be learned. Only God should determine the time of death. If you did not believe in God, or your god was less involved or accessible through prayer, you were more likely to believe that tolerable levels of suffering should be determined by the individuals most intimately involved, and the protective boundaries of life were more appropriately subject to human intervention.[1]

These broad patterns were reflected as well in the religious beliefs of Dax Cowart's mother[2] as she struggled to resist her son's pleas to help him end his own life. Similarly, religious beliefs were a guiding influence on the mothers of Baby K[3] and Emilio Gonzales[4] as they fought to continue medical treatment. Each mother believed in a caring and concerned god; a god who watched over his children. These mothers were not alone.

When the National Opinion Research Center[5] asked respondents whether they believed "in a God who watches over me," some 60 percent indicated they "strongly agreed." This belief, not surprisingly, made a big difference in their prayer life. Just over seven out of ten (73 percent) of those believing strongly in an attentive god had an active prayer life—praying once or more a day. By comparison, only 5 percent of those not believing in a watchful god prayed on a daily basis.

Likewise, in seven separate national surveys between 1983 and 1991, NORC asked respondents, "How close do you feel to God most of the time?" Three out of ten respondents (31 percent) reported they felt "extremely close," an additional five out of ten (53 percent) felt "somewhat close." Only 6 percent reported they either did not believe in God or felt "not close at all." As one would expect, a close relationship with God was also linked to a life of frequent prayer. Some 85 percent of those persons feeling extremely close to God prayed once or several times a day. Among non-believers or those who did not feel close at all to God, the comparable figure was 3 percent. Attitudes toward assisted suicide varied accordingly.

Several related survey questions spoke to the respondent's daily spiritual experiences and how they dealt with difficult problems. To what extent, respondents were asked, did they "feel God's presence?" "desire to be closer to or in union with God?" Did they "find strength and comfort" in their religion? These same respondents were prompted by another set of questions asking how they dealt "with major problems in your life." Among the options were "I think about how my life is part of a larger spiritual force," "I work together with God as partners," "I look to God for strength, support, guidance." One prompt reversed the method of coping, asking whether the respondent tried "to make sense of the situation and decide what to do without relying on God."

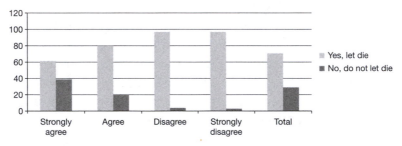

When a person has a disease that cannot be cured, do you think doctors should be allowed by law to end the patient's life by some painless means if the patient and his family request it? Please tell me whether you strongly agree, agree, disagree, or strongly disagree: I believe in a God who watches over me.

Figure 12.1 Support for Assisted Suicide in Relation to Belief that God Watches Over Respondent.

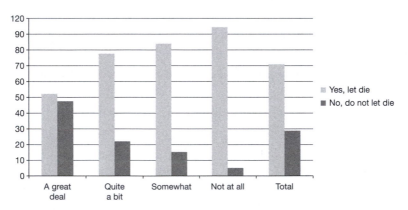

When a person has a disease that cannot be cured, do you think doctors should be allowed by law to end the patient's life by some painless means if the patient and his family request it?
Think about how you try to understand and deal with major problems in your life. To what extent is the following involved in the way you cope: I look to God for strength, support, guidance.

Figure 12.2 Support for Assisted Suicide in Relation to Tendency to Look to God for Support and Guidance.

If you believed in an active, concerned god, a god within reach, a god willing to work as a partner, to intervene in your life, you were, again not surprisingly, more likely to pray frequently. A caring, accessible god could be trusted to do what was best in your life. This trust held special importance when it came to determining who should control the moment of death. Opposition to, or support for, assisted suicide followed.[6]

Clearly, prayer and a sense of an active, caring, efficacious god are important influences on whether we support or oppose assisted suicide. If we feel close to God, if we pray, we are more likely to believe life belongs to God. If our belief in God is weak or non-existent, defining the protective boundaries of life and determining the tolerable boundaries of suffering are more likely to be guided by respect for the autonomy of the individual. Such patterned public opinion is important, but whether we assert the rights of individuals or the control of God, life and death decisions are firmly embedded in a system of costly medical care.

Resources sometimes do not match demand. Choices are forced. Health care is rationed. Who should have first call on medical resources? How much care is too much? Do we ever reach a point where there is not only a right but also a duty to die so that other lives might benefit?

Uncertainty, a Duty to Die, and Rationed Health Care

Sparring among competing advocates is easy to find. In 1958, a young, 27-year-old, soon to be well-known law professor, Yale Kamisar, then teaching at the Minnesota Law School, wrote of his "non-religious views" and concerns for gravely ill persons.[7] He took issue with liberalized euthanasia policies developed in a recently published and much-discussed book, *The Sanctity of Life and the Criminal Law*, written by a jurist from the University of Cambridge.[8]

Surely, Kamisar wrote, the "freedom to choose a merciful death" was an important right. But in circumstances of greatly diminished capacity, infused with suffering, and perhaps imminent death, there was a high probability of "confusion, distortion, or vacillation." Persons in the throes of dealing with suffering and the possible end of their life were not well positioned to make life-ending decisions.[9] It would be foolish to assume otherwise. A mountain of clinical research supported the idea that many, if not most, suicidal patients are depressed and ambivalent. As persons are doing something irrevocable in a state of uncertainty and shifting emotions, great care should be exercised.

Even assuming persons deciding to end their life were fixed in resolve and rational in thinking, Professor Kamisar foresaw problems. He wondered, was this really the kind of choice

> that we want to offer a gravely ill person? Will we not sweep up in the process some who are not really tired of life, but think others are tired of them; some who do not really want to die, but who feel they should not live on, because to do so . . . would be a selfish or a cowardly act?

"Will not some," Kamisar continued, "feel an obligation to have themselves 'eliminated' in order that funds allocated for their terminal care might be better used by their families or, financial worries aside, in order to relieve their families of the emotional strain involved?"[10]

As Leo Alexander had written a decade before Kamisar's cornerstone article, the "nonrehabilitable sick" could too easily become "unwanted ballast."[11] Resources, including health care funding and physicians' time and emotional energy, are limited. Priorities must be set. Setting these priorities, while unavoidable, involved dangers. Life for those near the end of life, those with resource-absorbing illnesses and debilitating conditions, could readily become life less worthy of protection. A less worthy life easily becomes a life too burdensome. Legalizing assisted suicide as a "therapeutic option" for those less worthy would lead to subtle and perhaps not-so-subtle shifts in the allocation of health-care resources and the quality of interaction between patient and physician.

Many shared Kamisar's fears of ethics gone awry. Years later, when the bioethics movement was well under way and when the slightly modified principles of the Belmont Report had become, for some, the Georgetown Mantra, these fears seemed to be confirmed in a speech given on March 27, 1984.

Three-term Colorado governor and health-care activist, Richard Lamm, was speaking to elderly constituents gathered on Senior Day in Denver. He was concerned over escalating costs of health care associated with the life-prolonging capabilities of new drugs, medical technologies, and procedures. It was time, Governor Lamm suggested, to consider setting limits. "We've got a duty to die and get out of the way with all of our machines and artificial hearts and everything else like that and let the other society, our kids, build a reasonable life."

The governor's words were picked up in the press. They created an immediate stir. Reports and editorials focused on the phrase "duty to die and get out of the way." Despite Governor Lamm's immediate protests of superficial mischaracterization of what he had said, this phrase repeatedly appeared for many years in subsequent academic discussions, press accounts, and congressional hearings.[12] Although the crassly stated duty-to-die message may not have been Governor Lamm's intended message, for many it was the message heard. Was this what patient autonomy had come to—a duty to die?

For Daniel Callahan, cofounder and director of the highly influential Hastings Center, Lamm's message, appropriately understood, deserved careful thought and even advocacy. Callahan had been worried about the same problem for many years. Shortly after Lamm's speech in Denver, Callahan decided it was time to present his own thoughts more systematically.

Setting Limits: Medical Goals in an Aging Society, published in 1987, was the result. Callahan began by asking a lengthy question; a question generated by the dilemmas inherent in increasingly costly medical advances.

> Is it possible that medicine's triumphant reconstruction of old age has also unwittingly created a demographic, economic and medical avalanche, one that could ultimately (and perhaps already) do great harm—a demographic avalanche by harmfully increasing the number and proportion of the elderly and also, in the process, distorting the ratio of old to young; an economic avalanche by radically increasing the burden of social and familial dependency; and a medical avalanche by lengthening life beyond a capacity to preserve its quality?

For Callahan, "the idea that the humane medical care and cure for the elderly sought in the 1960s and 1970s could turn out to be the occasion of a new social threat" was hard to accept. He was convinced, however, that it was true, regardless of how "appalling and distasteful the idea may be."[13]

The argument of this central figure in the bioethics movement was not simple. It was interlaced with many assumptions. It was also, however, grounded on clear evidence that limited resources were becoming increasingly strained. This trend was likely to continue into the foreseeable future. Like the early allocation of dialysis machines,[14] priorities would have to be set; life-protecting choices would have to be made to resolve the embedded dilemmas. Unlike access to dialysis, however, more machines or refined procedures were not the answer. We could not build our way out of this one. Any refinement would have to come through a new conception of what the waning years of life meant.

Callahan wanted to be clear. He was not arguing that lives of the elderly were less valuable, less worthy of protection than the young. Nor was he an advocate for "rational" suicide or euthanasia, then being proposed by organizations such as the Hemlock Society. His conclusion was exactly the opposite. "A sanctioning of mercy killing and assisted suicide for the elderly," he recognized, "would serve as a threatening symbol of devaluation of old age." Instead, he was simply recognizing that the length of life was finite, and that each generation should give way to the next. Letting life go, in recognition of life's importance, was profoundly different than destroying life.

Near the end of *Setting Limits*, Callahan wrote in italics for emphasis:

> *Cessation of life-extending treatment for the aged as a matter of social policy can be morally acceptable only within a context that accords meaning and significance to the lives of the individual aged and recognizes the positive virtues of the passing of the generations.*

Life was important and should be protected. It was also finite. At some point, given the high cost of medical treatments, we simply needed to step out of the way and let nature take its course. Such a shift in thinking would take time. It was not an idea to be accepted casually or immediately "without thought being given to its practical implications."[15] Even after his book-length development, however, many sympathizers were not exactly clear on what Callahan had in mind. Many more thought they understood exactly what he meant and strongly objected.

It did not take long for the critics to respond. Callahan had written, "As part of my approach to health care for the aged, they would cease being eligible for government-supported life extension beyond a certain age."[16] After his book was published, he appeared on the *McNeil/Lehrer News Hour*[17] to discuss what he had in mind. What would be the cut-off? When did the boundaries of life become less protected? Callahan thought it would be somewhere in the 80s. He understood that a sense of injustice might initially be generated, but "it seems to me in the nature of the case it [the injustice] would not be for a very long time."

A conference to address Callahan's ideas was held at the University of Illinois law school in October 1989.[18] Quoting this statement, one critic at the Illinois gathering warned, "Consider, then, the values that will flow from a societal decision that a compelling state interest in cutting costs justifies cutting off lives. That's not a slippery slope. That's an abyss."[19] No matter how you cut it, thinking of the elderly as Callahan suggested meant, after some specified age or age range, lives became less worthy of support and protection.

While he was not advocating the intentional killing of the elderly, Callahan's proposed policy, if adopted, contained not only fuzzy boundaries for protected life but also the fuzzy logic frequently found in the Doctrine of Double Effect. He did not intend to kill the elderly; they were going to die anyway. He simply wanted to restrict access to medical care near the end of life, so resources could be directed elsewhere. Protecting the lives of others, not ending the lives of the elderly, was the intent.

At about the same time critics were gathering at the University of Illinois law school, Leon Kass, a respected colleague frequently cited by Callahan, was also worrying over the unintended consequences of setting limits on who should be supported by health-care resources. It was not just a matter of economics. It would influence the nature of the doctor–patient relationship:

> Physicians get tired of treating patients who are hard to cure, who resist their best efforts, who are on their way down—"gorks," "gomers," and "vegetables" are only some of the less than affectionate names ... Won't it be tempting to think that death is the best treatment for the little old lady "dumped" again on the emergency room by the nearby nursing home?[20]

The implications of such thinking—for many, not-so-subtle dehuman-ization—were far too clear to miss. They were not restricted to the elderly who Richard Lamm and Daniel Callahan had in mind. The embedded, utilitarian, public-good rationale for rationing medical care was little different from the reasoning undergirding the policy to hasten the death of severely retarded patients proposed by first-term Florida legislator, Walter Sackett, some two decades earlier.[21] Advocates for the disabled were all too familiar with where this utilitarian logic, however refined, might lead.

Lives Less Worthy of Living?

Illustrative was a series of encounters between a young lawyer, Harriet McBryde Johnson, self-described as a disabled, liberal, atheistic Democrat, known widely as an opinionated, smart, fierce advocate for the disabled, and Peter Singer, both respected and reviled for his carefully constructed, thought-provoking and highly controversial "practical ethics."[22]

Harriet McBryde Johnson was among those who found Singer's writings disturbing. She had begun her legal practice in Charleston, South Carolina, around the time Governor Lamm had given his Denver speech and Singer and Helga Kuhse's *Should the Baby Live?* had been published. The young lawyer from Charleston knew that Singer had also written, in a frequently quoted section from his *Practical Ethics*, "The killing of a defective infant is not morally equivalent to the killing of a person; very often it is not morally wrong at all."[23] Her opposition to Singer's ideas was not grounded in a religious framework. Indeed, Singer's self-acknowledged efforts to "unsanctify life"[24] were consistent with McBryde Johnson's own atheism.

She had developed her own provocative, witty, and intelligent assess-ment of life as a disabled person. In her preface to *Too Late to Die Young*, she described herself as "thin, flesh mostly vanished, a jumble of bones in a floppy bag of skin." She spent her waking hours in a power chair, leaning forward to "rest my rib cage on my lap, plant my elbows on rolled towels beside my knees." Instead of grounding her opposition to Singer's practical ethics in God's purpose or to the redemptive power of suffering, she found his characterization of the disabled dehumanizing and offensive. The issue was personal.

McBryde Johnson's perspective had been shaped by her experiences and how she responded to persons who took pity on her, wished God's blessings for her, or expressed misplaced admiration. Writing with her own provocative candor, she noted,

> I used to try to explain that in fact I enjoy my life, that it's a great sensual pleasure to zoom by power chair on these delicious muggy streets, that I have no more reason to kill myself than most people. But it gets tedious. God didn't put me on this street to provide disability awareness training to everyone who happens by. In fact, no god put anyone anywhere for any reason, if you want to know.[25]

She and Singer had met when he gave a lecture at the College of Charleston. The lawyer from Charleston had challenged the philosopher from Princeton in the question-and-answer period that followed, and they had continued to correspond in the months following.

Not long after Singer's contested appointment to a prestigious position at the Center for Human Values,[26] Harriet was invited to debate Princeton's new professor. She subsequently published her account in a cover story for the *New York Times Magazine*[27] and later in *Too Late to Die Young*. Her account was laced with barbed wit. "He insists he doesn't want to kill me," she wrote. "He simply thinks it would have been better, all things considered, to have given my parents the option of killing the baby I once was, and to let other parents kill similar babies as they come along." If we acted in this manner we could "thereby avoid the suffering that comes with lives like mine and satisfy the reasonable preferences of parents for a different kind of child. It has nothing to do with me. I should not feel threatened."[28]

Harriet McBryde Johnson, and disability activists who agreed with her, aimed to protect the lives and rights of infants born with a range of birth defects, as well as the rights of adults who lived lives with various disabilities, variously acquired, and variously perceived. They had been moved to more aggressive action by what they saw as the pernicious implications of Singer's, Callahan's, and Lamm's utilitarian arguments.

They knew there were life-threatening consequences for those who might be perceived as a drain on public resources. Moreover, they were worried over a number of influences in popular culture consistent with the practical ethics discussed by philosophers, politicians, and bioethicists in the rather remote halls of academe. These worries included a play, *Whose Life Is it Anyway?* The play opened to rave reviews in London and New York in 1978 and 1979 and depicted a young sculptor paralyzed in a car accident and struggling with life-ending decisions. Further, the 1979 PBS airing of Jo Roman's *Choosing Suicide* and the publication of a companion book, *Exit House*, had brought the idea of "rational suicide" to the public's attention. Derek Humphry had founded the Hemlock Society that same year and went on to publish *Let Me Die Before I Wake* in 1981, a book outlining specific, nonviolent methods of suicide.

The intensity of the debate increased as the AIDS epidemic spread across the country and around the world throughout the 1980s. Eventually, Derek Humphry updated his earlier work in 1991, when he published the widely read, *Final Exit: The Practicalities of Self-Deliverance and Assisted Suicide for the Dying*.[29] This book, along with its parent organization, the Hemlock Society, would be praised and reviled in the early 1990s as laws legalizing assisted suicide began to take shape, and suicides modeled after the recommendations and depictions in *Exit House* became evident.

In addition to the concerns of disability activists, easy access to, and encouragement of, nonviolent rational suicide did not sit well with many otherwise sympathetic right-to-die advocates. A distinction was drawn between assisted suicide and assisted dying. Those seeking non-suicidal, compassionate, individually determined ways to deal with the end of life began to splinter off from those advocating ready access to methods advanced most importantly by the Hemlock Society.

Death With Dignity

A crystallizing event impacting these competing and frequently cross-cutting religious and secular movements came in 1983, when a young, disabled woman, suffering from severe cerebral palsy and quadriplegia, wanted assistance to die.[30] Elizabeth Bouvia did not have a terminal illness. Given the severity of her disabilities and recent life events, however, she had decided that her life was no longer worth living.

She knew of successes in the right-to-die movement and related court cases. She wanted the California hospital in which she was staying to provide pain-relieving medication to ease the pain while she starved herself to death. The hospital refused. Their responsibility was to keep her alive. They would not provide the medication, and they would force-feed her if necessary. With the help of an American Civil Liberties Union (ACLU) attorney, Elizabeth filed suit.

In many ways, Elizabeth Bouvia's suit was unique. Although Dax Cowart had pleaded for assistance to end his life, he did not take his pleas to court. Unlike Karen Ann Quinlan, Elizabeth was not in a vegetative state; she was clearly a "cognitive and sapient" being. Unlike Joseph Saikewicz, she had the ability to communicate in clear and rational terms and was not faced with an immediately terminal condition. Short of an unforeseen illness or accident, she was likely to live well into the foreseeable future. The question in her case was, how far we should go in assisting rational, non-terminally ill persons with disabilities to end their life, if they perceived their life to be filled with intolerable suffering?

Although there were similarities between Elizabeth's requests and those who refused blood transfusions or kidney dialysis, no one could find any case law where a non-terminally ill, competent individual had asked a hospital to let them stay in one of their beds and give them pain-relieving drugs while they starved themselves to death. In a memorandum outlining her argument, Elizabeth's lawyer, who had also trained to be a physician and was known to be a staunch right-to-die advocate closely associated with the Hemlock Society, pointed to the "pain, humiliation, and difficulty" Elizabeth's disabilities caused. Given her "incurable affliction" and "pitiful existence," her suffering had made life "intolerable."[31] She wanted to die. She should be given assistance to ease her pain while doing so.

Disability activists were caught in a bind. On the one hand, they were working hard to establish respect for the independence and autonomy of persons with disabilities, and their efforts would soon result in the Americans With Disabilities Act of 1990. Elizabeth was most certainly coping with a number of disabling conditions. She was acting in an autonomous and independent manner and needed assistance to exercise her rights. All these factors were consistent with the disabilities-rights agenda. Why should assistance not be provided? One major reason: the phrases and expressed wishes used by Elizabeth's lawyer were disturbing red flags. They depicted the disabled person as helpless and miserable, living a life less worthy of protection and support. They represented stereotypes Harriett McBryde Johnson and many others were fighting so hard to eliminate.

Elizabeth Bouvia's pleas for an assisted suicide drew strong opposition from the very persons she might otherwise have seen as allies. Two disability activists, Paul Longmore and Harlan Hahn, had recently launched the Program in Disability and Society at the University of Southern California. Elizabeth was staying in a hospital in Riverside California, some 60 miles away. Longmore and Hahn began to pay close attention as the case moved through the courts.

As someone who worked to establish respect for the autonomy and independent judgment of disabled persons, Longmore was concerned with how Elizabeth's life was being presented, not only by her lawyer, but in the media as well. It was an all-too-facile reflection of the prejudiced depictions the disabled all too frequently encountered in popular culture and media. Longmore used Woody Allen's comedy *Annie Hall* as an example. In one scene in the film, released in 1977, disabled people were lumped together with the terminally ill. The principle male character was found saying, "I feel that life is divided up into the horrible and the miserable . . . The horrible would be like, I don't know, the terminal cases, you know, and blind people, cripples. I don't know how they get through life." For Longmore, this comment, intended as comedic, represented a serious distortion—you might as well be dead as disabled.[32] The depiction of Elizabeth's experience, both directly and indirectly in popular media and the news, Longmore wrote, "epitomizes all of the devaluation and discrimination inflicted on disabled people by society."

What most worried Longmore and other like-minded activists was why Elizabeth found her life to be filled with intolerable suffering. Was it owing to her obvious and difficult disabilities, or to other recent events in her life that had clearly impacted her sense of loss and lack of support? Her marriage had recently failed. She had miscarried a child she wanted to have. She had lost her brother to death. For various reasons, she had moved several times. When in graduate school at San Diego State University, preparing to become a social worker, she was told her disabilities would preclude a successful career. Such life events, coupled with her disabilities, may have been the source of depression and a sense of hopelessness. It was well documented that both were among the strongest indicators of suicidal impulses.

Was Elizabeth simply in an early stage of unresolved loss and grief? Was she one of those persons, so worrisome to Yale Kamisar, who were "not really tired of life, but think others are tired of them?" If so, there was ample evidence that her perspective might change. Life was too important to let lack of support and transient emotions determine its end. A court hearing was held, and a decision was announced on December 16, 1983, the morning after closing arguments.[33] In support of her pleas, the judge found Elizabeth's requests were based on her physical disabilities and not on the transient emotions associated with troubling life events. She was judged to be rational and sincere in her requests. The judge also found, however, that her life expectancy was something on the order of 15–20 years. She was not only refusing medical treatment, Elizabeth Bovia was asking the hospital doctors and staff to help end her life prematurely as she starved herself to death.

This brought other considerations into play. Doctors, nurses, and hospital administrators were being asked to participate. They did not want to do so. Such actions put them at legal risk and ran directly counter to their professional ethics and commitment to protect and prolong life. Assisting their patient as she starved herself to death would have, the judge concluded, "a profound effect on the medical staff, nurses and administrators," as well as a "devastating effect on other patients within Riverside Hospital and other physically handicapped persons who are similarly situated in this nation."

Elizabeth's right to privacy and respect for her autonomy would have to be balanced against the impact terminating her life would have on other members of society, some of whom were directly involved. Balancing these competing values, the judge favored the greater public good. "Established ethics of the medical profession clearly outweigh and overcome her own rights to self-determination." Doctors and nurses on the hospital staff were protecting life, not experimenting with it, but right-to-die advocates were quick to note that the judge's public-good rationale to override patient preferences was not far afield from Nuremburg. Analogies drawn to Nazi practices cut both ways.

Tension emerging from the embedded dilemmas did not go away with the judge's ruling. Commentaries soon appeared, and, four months after the decision was issued, a prominent bioethicist published a critical assessment. He worried about where the public-good argument led. He wanted to remind the judge, the public, and his colleagues, "The right to bodily integrity and control of one's fate are superior to institutional considerations." He was sympathetic, but argued there was room for compromise. "If we simply accept her decision," he continued, "it is argued, we devalue all severely handicapped persons. But surely there is a middle ground between 'simply accepting' her decision, and violently force-feeding her."[34]

Others, arguing in support of the judge's ruling, found themselves turning the practical ethics embedded in Daniel Callahan's *Setting Limits* on its head. Prolonging life was the prime value. The public good demanded the continued use of medical resources, even when a person found their life not worth the struggle. Elizabeth Bouvia should be kept alive and not assisted in her efforts to die. The judge's decision was an affirmation of life. For these proponents, respect for individual autonomy was not the most important public-policy principle. "Considerations of autonomy," they argued, "must give way to the broader notion of the public good, which gives primacy to the respect for life."[35]

Elizabeth Bouvia did not give up. After changing hospitals and even moving to Mexico for a time, she returned to California. In 1986, her continuing requests found their way to the Court of Appeals in California.[36] Reflective of the power of competing values, the appellate court struggled, as the trial judge had before them, with where to place the hazy boundaries of protected life and intolerable suffering, and how to set priorities to resolve the associated dilemmas.

The priorities established and the boundaries drawn in 1986 by California's Court of Appeals, perhaps influenced by the growing number of right-to-die cases,[37] were quite different from those set by the trial judge in 1983. The trial judge had found compelling priorities in the public good and preserving life, even in the face of suffering and patient wishes to the contrary. The appellate court reversed these priorities, giving greater weight to the quality of life, the power of suffering, respect for the autonomy of the individual, and the right to make choices regarding one's life free from governmental interference.

In the eyes of the appellate judges, the trial judge had "mistakenly attached undue importance to the amount of time [15–20 years] possibly available to the petitioner." "Who shall say," the judges wondered, "what the minimum amount of available life must be? Does it matter if it be 15–20 years, 15–20 months, or 15–20 days, if such life has been physically destroyed and its quality, dignity and purpose gone? As in all matters lines must be drawn at some point, somewhere, but that decision must ultimately belong to the one whose life is in issue." This was not a medical decision to be made by Elizabeth's physicians. Nor was it to be resolved by lawyers or judges or hospital committees. Being a competent adult, it was Elizabeth's alone.

Force-feeding a patient against her will was troubling enough. If force-fed, Elizabeth would face a life of painful, difficult existence, made endurable only by the constant administration of morphine. She would have to be cleaned, turned, bedded, toileted by others for 15–20 years. "Her mind and spirit may be free to take great flights," the court continued, "but she herself is imprisoned and must lie physically helpless subject to the ignominy, embarrassment, humiliation and dehumanizing aspects created by her helplessness."

In Elizabeth Bouvia's view, such a dehumanized existence diminished her life "to the point of hopelessness, uselessness, unenjoyability and frustration." She was, "lying helplessly in bed, unable to care for herself." She considered her existence "meaningless," a life not worth living. The court found, in such circumstances, it was not

> the policy of this state that all and every life must be preserved against the will of the sufferer. It is incongruous, if not monstrous, for medical practitioners to assert their right to preserve a life that someone else must live, or, more accurately, endure, for 15 to 20 years.

Elizabeth Bouvia was entitled, the court concluded, "to the immediate removal of the nasogastric tube that has been involuntarily inserted into her body." The court further held, that the hospital "may not deny her relief from pain and suffering merely because she has chosen to exercise her fundamental right to protect what little privacy remains to her."

It was a troubling case, difficult to decide, and frequently, broadly, and aggressively argued. Implications of the decision reached far beyond Elizabeth Bouvia, and, in a concluding paragraph, a judge, writing his separate concurring opinion, expressed his hope that these implications would not be missed:

> Whatever choice Elizabeth Bouvia may ultimately make, I can only hope that her courage, persistence and example will cause

our society to deal realistically with the plight of those unfortunate individuals to whom death beckons as a welcome respite from suffering. If there is ever a time when we ought to be able to get the "government off our backs" it is when we face death—either by choice or otherwise.

The decision's strongly worded, sometimes emotional arguments, opinions, and conclusions would be met with equally strong and emotional criticism from those seeking to affirm the intrinsic importance of all life, even in the face of a severely disabling existence. Many disability activists, such as Paul Longmore, saw the court's reasoning as a victory for bigotry against the disabled.[38] Advocates for assisted suicide, Longmore wrote, engaged in "Orwellian newspeak." They

> assume a nonexistent autonomy. They offer an illusory self-determination . . . Their arguments for euthanasia, aid-in-dying, assisted suicide, and medical cost-containment simply rationalize the ultimate act of oppression. Their efforts are an assault on the rights and lives of people who are sick, old, or disabled.[39]

Elizabeth's attorney saw things differently. In his closing statement he noted simply,

> We do believe that this world will be a poorer place without that tortured but resilient and cheerful lady with so much potential, with so much to offer others. But Elizabeth Bouvia has no duty to make that offer nor does she have the obligation to endure what to her is unendurable.

Whether you agreed or disagreed, boundaries were drawn, priorities set, dilemmas resolved, and the decision issued. Elizabeth Bouvia was free to choose to die. The hospital was bound to comply and to provide relief from any pain or suffering that might result from her choice. Confirming the uncertainty and competing considerations these boundaries and dilemmas presented, Elizabeth Bouvia, once granted her right to decide, decided not to starve herself to death.

Notes

1   The connection between suicide and religion has long been noted. As a general rule, persons affiliated with religious faiths are, on average, less likely to commit suicide or support assisted suicide than are agnostics or atheists. Beyond this basic finding, however, the picture is clouded. Taken on average, Catholics are not as likely to support assisted suicide as are Jews or Unitarians. Persons identifying as "traditional," "moderate," or "liberal" Catholics differ among themselves, as do Protestants identifying as "evangelicals," "fundamentalists," "mainline," or "liberal."

Most attempts to clarify the links between religion and suicide point to the writings of French sociologist Emile Durkheim. Durkheim saw religion's influence on suicidal tendencies stemming from its ability to provide a sense of belonging through the integrative power of beliefs, rituals, and community. Life interwoven with the collective life of the church and community is life more immune to the threat of suicide. Religions vary in this regard. Some encourage individualism, theological and otherwise, and in this sense are more atomized. Atomized communities, Durkheim found, are communities more likely to have higher suicide rates. Subsequent studies have provided fresh insights into Durkheim's touchstone work. Emile Durkheim, *Suicide* (New York: Free Press, 1951). For literature review and related findings see: Amy M. Burdette, Terrence D. Hill, and Benjamin E. Moulton, "Religion and Attitudes Toward Physician-Assisted Suicide and Terminal Palliative Care," *Journal for the Scientific Study of Religion* 44 (2005): 79–93. See: Steven Stack, "Religion, Depression, and Suicide," in *Religion and Mental Health*, Ed. John F. Schumaker (New York: Oxford University Press, 1992), 87–97; Christopher G. Ellison, Geffrey A. Burr, and Patricia L. McCall, "Religious Homogeneity and Metropolitan Suicide Rates," *Social Forces* 76 (1997): 273–99.

2   Interview in *Dax's Case*. See also Lonnie D. Kliever, Ed., *Dax's Case: Essays in Medical Ethics and Human Meaning* (Dallas, TX: Southern Methodist University Press, 1989).

3   *In the Matter of Baby K*, 832 F. Supp. 1022 (E.D. Va. 1993). *In the Matter of Baby K*, 16 F.3d 590 (4th Cir. 1994).

4   "Dying Boy's Case Likely to Reverberate in Law, Religion," *Austin American Statesman* April 15 (2007).

5   The following data were gathered from the General Social Survey 1972–2006 Cumulative Data file, available online at: http://sda.berkeley.edu/cgi-bin32/hsda?harcsda+gss06.

6   Correlations among other GSS questions not reported in these tables reflect similar patterns. See also: J. Holden, "Demographics, Attitudes, and Afterlife Beliefs of Right-to-Life and Right-to-Die Organization Members," *The Journal of Social Psychology* 133 (1993): 521–7.

7   Yale Kamisar, "Some Non-Religious Views Against Proposed 'Mercy Killing' Legislation," *Minnesota Law Review* (1958) 969–1042.

8   Glanville Williams, *The Sanctity of Life and the Criminal Law* (New York: Alfred A. Knopf, 1957).

9   Kamisar saw, with less psychological and interpersonal precision, what Elizabeth Kübler-Ross, drawing from her conversations with the terminally ill, would give empirical substance to a decade later in *On Death and Dying*.

10 Kamisar, "Some Non-Religious Views", 990.

11 Leo Alexander, "Medical Science Under Dictatorship," *New England Journal of Medicine* (1949): 39–47.

12 See "Gov. Lamm Asserts Elderly, if Very Ill, Have 'Duty to Die'," *New York Times*. Available online at: http://query.nytimes.com/gst/fullpage.html?res=9E01E5D91E 39F93AA15750C0A962948260&sec=health&spon=&pagewanted=1.

13 Daniel Callahan, *Setting Limits: Medical Goals in an Aging Society*, 20–1.

14 Shana Alexander, "They Decide Who Lives, Who Dies: Medical Miracle and a Moral Burden of a Small Committee," *Life* November 9 (1962): 103–28.

15 Daniel Callahan, *Setting Limits*, 198.

16 Daniel Callahan, *Setting Limits*, 186.

17 *MacNeil/Lehrer News Hour*, Transcript no. 3399, March 30, 1989, LEXIS News Transcripts.

18 Robert L. Barry and Gerard V. Bradley, Eds., *Set No Limits: A Rebuttal to Daniel Callahan's Proposal to Limit Health Care for the Elderly* (Urbana, IL: University of Illinois Press, 1991).

19 Robert L. Barry and Gerard V. Bradley, Eds., *Set No Limits*, xvi.

20 Leon R. Kass, "Neither for Love nor Money: Why Doctors Must not Kill," *Public Interest* 94 (1989): 25–46.

21 Walter Sackett, "Death With Dignity," *Southern Medical Journal* 64 (1971): 330–2. Walter Sackett, "I've Let Hundreds of Patients Die. Shouldn't You?," *Medical Economics* April 2 (1973): 92–7.

22 Peter Singer, *Practical Ethics*, 2nd ed., (Cambridge: Cambridge University Press, 1993). Some of Singer's most relevant ideas were detailed in the book he wrote with Helga Kuhse, *Should the Baby Live? The Problem of Handicapped Infants*, published in 1985, the year after Governor Lamm spoke to his audience in Denver. As the reader may recall, the first sentence of *Should the Baby Live* contained a blunt warning:

> This book contains conclusions which some readers will find disturbing. We think that some infants with severe disabilities should be killed. This recommendation may cause particular offence to readers who were themselves born with disabilities, perhaps even the same disabilities we are discussing.

Singer and Kuhse were right—many readers did find their words disturbing.

23 Singer, *Practical Ethics*, 184.

24 Helga Kuhse, Ed., *Unsanctifying Human Life: Essays on Ethics*, Peter Singer (Oxford, UK: Blackwell Publishers, 2002).

25 *Too Late to Die Young*, 2.

26 "Princeton Appointment Creates an Uproar," *New York Times*, April 10 (1999).

27 "Unspeakable Conversations," *New York Times*, February 16 (2003).

28 *Too Late to Die Young*, 201.

29 For a detailed account of these events and this time period, see: Dowbiggin, *A Merciful End*, 136–62.

30 It should be recalled that this was the same year when the President Reagan Commission was issuing Baby Doe guidelines for the treatment of disabled infants.

31   Quoted in Adrienne Asch, "Disability, Bioethics and Human Rights," in *Handbook of Disabilities Studies*, Eds. Gary L. Albrecht, Katherine D. Seelman, and Michael Bury (New York: Sage Publications, 2001), 297–326, 311.

32   Paul K. Longmore "Elizabeth Bouvia, Assisted Suicide and Social Prejudice," *Issues in Law & Medicine* 3, 2 (1987): 146–7, 152.

33   *Bouvia v. Co. of Riverside*, No. 159780, Sup. Ct., Riverside Co., Cal., December 16, 1983, Tr. 1238–1250.

34   George J. Annas, "Law and the Life Sciences: When Suicide Prevention Becomes Brutality: The Case of Elizabeth Bouvia," *The Hastings Center Report* 14 (1984): 20–46.

35   Francis I. Kane, "Keeping Elizabeth Bouvia Alive for the Public Good," *The Hastings Center Report* 15 (1985): 5–8.

36   *Bouvia v. Superior Court (Glenchur)* (1986) 179 Cal.App.3d 1127, 225 Cal.Rptr. 297.

37   See: Ezekiel J. Manuel, "A Review of the Ethical and Legal Aspects of Terminating Medical Care," *The American Journal of Medicine* 84 (1988): 291–301.

38   "Urging the Handicapped to Die: Bouvia Decision is Victory for Bigotry, not Self-Determination," *Los Angeles Times*, April 25 (1986).

39   Longmore, "Elizabeth Bouvia," 168.

CHAPTER 13
ASSISTED DYING

The personal uncertainty that must have infused the troubling decisions Elizabeth Bouvia made also permeated the broader community. "As the 1980s dawned," one historian has noted, "a new chapter was opening in the history of the euthanasia movement in twentieth-century America. More Americans than ever believed in a right to die, but agreement about what the right to die actually meant was increasingly difficult to reach."[1] Right-to-die social movement organizations were redefining their missions, splintering, and reforming in uneasy coalitions. They were activating personal networks and recruiting members in attempts to mobilize resources to convince a seemingly supportive, but ultimately ambivalent, public. The evidence is easily found.

Social Movements Realign

The National Hospice Organization, founded in 1978, was refining and expanding opportunities for end-of-life palliative care. California's NDA was being replicated with increasingly permissive language across the country, and advanced directives and living wills were widely known and accepted. The Hemlock Society, founded in 1980, was growing rapidly, advancing the cause for what came to be known as rational suicide. More moderate and passive approaches, advocated by organizations such as the SRD and Concern for Dying (CFD), were frequently engaged in arguments among themselves over the strained moral standing of the

Doctrine of Double Effect and unintended but known consequences flowing from passive measures actively taken by physicians.

These strained arguments and outright disagreement among otherwise aligned advocates reduced focus and "severely compromised the chances of the [assisted-suicide] movement to win American public opinion precisely when attitudes seemed more receptive than ever."[2] Ineffectiveness at a moment of public receptiveness was nowhere more evident than in the early efforts of yet another new organization, Americans Against Human Suffering (AAHS), launched on July 18, 1986, just after California's Supreme Court rendered its decision in April supporting Elizabeth Bouvia's requests for assistance to help her die.

The AAHS aimed to organize a nationwide effort to secure physician aid-in-dying legislation. Robert Risley, an attorney, would spearhead this initiative. Like so many others, he was motivated by personal experiences, as his wife had died two years earlier after a difficult bout with cancer. The AAHS board of directors also included the cofounders of the Hemlock Society, Ann Wickett and Derek Humphry.[3] Organizers had followed closely the court battles of Elizabeth Bouvia, as well as two other recent cases in California,[4] and they saw a need to secure "the right to die for the terminally ill with the help of a physician." Their efforts began in California with a campaign to place the Humane and Dignified Death Initiative on the ballot in November 1988.[5]

Risley's immediate task was to secure some 450,000 signatures. He was optimistic. Depending on the exact wording, virtually all public opinion polls indicated somewhere between 60 and 70 percent support. In a state the size of California, with a two–one margin of support, 450,000 signatures should not be difficult. Or, so it seemed. There was well-funded and high-profile opposition coming from numerous disabilities activist groups, which were in loose coalition with the American and California Medical Associations and the Catholic Church. The Catholic Church's opposition translated into opposition among California's growing Latino population and organizations such as the League of United Latin American Citizens (LULAC). There may also have been more widespread but undetected ambivalence. It was one thing to support physician-assisted suicide in principle, when talking with a pollster. It was quite another to sign your name knowing there would be a vote on actual implementation.

Whatever the reasons, by 1988, the efforts of Robert Risley and the AAHS had foundered. They had produced approximately 130,000 signatures—less than one-third of those needed. Later, commentators would point to ill-focused leadership, lack of organization, funding difficulties, and well-organized opposition. They would also note, "The failure was almost certainly more than simply a product of bad organization. The extent to which it also involved deep-seated reservations about euthanasia cannot be known but must be suspected."[6] Citizens answering pollsters and signing petitions seemed to be struggling with the same competing values judges had worked so uneasily to resolve—the sanctity of life, the alleviation of suffering.

Although the initial California drive to get a proposed law on the ballot failed, others would join Risley's and the AAHS's efforts over the next several years. They concentrated in the states of Washington and Oregon and returned to California as the hub of efforts to secure aid-in-dying legislation moved solidly to the west coast.

A First-Hand Account Stimulates Debate

These continuing efforts were not, however, operating in a vacuum. The Supreme Court's *Cruzan* decision involving Missouri state law was just around the corner. Widely publicized events involving a physician assisting a woman from Oregon to die in the back of his Volkswagen van in Michigan would soon occupy the public media. Less-publicized actions taken quietly in New York would set the stage for further debate and another round of Supreme Court decisions.

More immediately, prompted in part by Risley's efforts in California, on January 8, 1988, the editors of the *Journal of the American Medical Association* (*JAMA*) decided to promote public debate on physician-aid-in-dying by publishing a brief first-hand account in *JAMA*'s "A Piece of My Mind" column.[7] It involved an unnamed young gynecology resident, rotating through a large, private hospital. He had been called in the middle of the night to assist a 20-year-old patient who was having trouble getting rest; she weighed 80 lb, and was suffering from ovarian cancer.

The young resident recalled that, as he walked into the room, a friend of the patient was holding her hand. The patient's "eyes were hollow," the resident reported.

She had not eaten or slept in two days. She had not responded to chemotherapy and was being given supportive care only. It was a gallows scene, a cruel mockery of her youth and unfulfilled potential. Her only words to me were, "Let's get this over with."

Leaving the room, the resident, who had just met the patient, recalled thinking, "The patient was tired and needed rest. I could not give her health, but I could give her rest."

He asked the nurse to draw 20 mg of morphine sulfate into a syringe: "enough to do the job." He took the syringe into the room "and told the two women [he] was going to give Debbie something that would let her rest and to say good-bye." Debbie laid her head on the pillow "with her eyes open, watching what was left of the world." Seconds after the injection, her "breathing slowed to a normal rate, her eyes closed, and her features softened as she seemed restful at last." As the friend stroked the hair of her dying friend, "With clocklike certainty, within four minutes the breathing rate slowed even more, then became irregular, then ceased." Debbie's friend "stood erect and seemed relieved." The resident's account closed with a simple "It's over, Debbie."

"It's Over Debbie" created an immediate stir. Over the next few weeks, *JAMA* received some 150 letters running four–one against the actions taken by the resident and three–one against the editors' decision to publish the piece. Three months later, in the April 8 volume of *JAMA*, 18 of these letters were printed, along with commentaries. The most scathing review came from four leaders of the bioethics movement. One of these critics would go on to publish a more detailed critique a year later.[8] It was a crystallizing event. The implications of "It's Over Debbie" sharpened the edges and clarified positions in the continuing debate.

For some, the conduct of the resident was "inexcusable." He hardly knew his patient. The publication of the resident's account was "incomprehensible." Active euthanasia was illegal in all 50 states. Debbie had not requested any assistance in dying. Why would *JAMA*'s editor knowingly publicize an account of a felony and shield the felon? Was this simply a (perhaps fictitious) trial balloon? "So-called active euthanasia practiced by physicians seems to be an idea whose time has come," one of the critics commented. "But, in my view, it is a bad idea whose time must not come

—not now, not ever."[9] "Is it morally responsible," others wrote to the editors, "to promulgate challenges to our most fundamental moral principles without editorial rebuke or comment, 'for the sake of discussion'? Decent folk do not deliberately stir discussion of outrageous practices, like slavery, incest, or killing those in our care . . . The very soul of medicine is on trial."[10]

For their part, *JAMA*'s editors acknowledged competing editorial ethical considerations, but remained firm in their position. "*JAMA* is the right place for issues in American medicine to be debated, and there is much debate." By publishing "It's Over Debbie," they hoped to demonstrate anew "that the ethics of euthanasia must be debated." Their hopes would not be disappointed.

If the very soul of medicine was on trial, it was not restricted to the pages of *JAMA* and other academic journals. Critics of *JAMA*'s decision to publish "It's Over Debbie" were worried. "These are perilous times for our profession," they noted:

> The Hemlock Society and others are in the courts and legislatures trying to legalize killing by physicians at patient request . . . Now is not the time for promoting neutral discussion . . . now is the time for the medical profession to rally in defense of its fundamental moral principles, to repudiate any and all acts of direct and intentional killing by physicians and their agents.[11]

The right-to-die cases accumulating in the courts were one thing. Perhaps persons such as Karen Ann Quinlan and Nancy Cruzan did have the right to have life-prolonging measures, even nutrition and hydration, stopped. This did not mean physicians should take measures, even upon patient request, and most certainly if no request was present, to end a life. This represented an unwarranted step toward a steep and dangerously slippery slope.

As the debate progressed, protagonists on both sides were startled by yet another galvanizing event. This time, it involved the widely publicized actions of a Michigan physician helping a woman from Oregon to die in his Volkswagen van. His actions took place three weeks before the Supreme Court announced its decision on Nancy Cruzan's pleadings.

A Suicide Machine and a Cookbook of Death

The account of Debbie's assisted death was dramatic, but its publication and impact were primarily among physicians reading their association's major journal. By contrast, the assisted suicide of Janet Adkins on June 4, 1990, permeated the media. Two weeks later, after many accounts had appeared, a *Newsweek* article reporting on these events[12] began with the sentence, "Sometimes, when ethical debates have run on interminably it takes a shocking incident to sear the old questions back into the public consciousness."

Janet Adkins, age 64, was a member of the Hemlock Society. She lived in Oregon. She had Alzheimer's. She had read a *Newsweek* article written several months earlier and had watched the popular *Donahue* talk show, both dealing with the activities of a Detroit pathologist, Jack Kevorkian, and his "Mercytron" suicide machine. With the support of her husband, she decided to investigate.

By all accounts Dr. Jack Kevorkian was an enigmatic figure. For some, he was an honest, direct provider of humane assistance. For others, he was a bombastic, offensive, and dangerous zealot. Over a period of months, Dr. Kevorkian talked, not only with Janet and her husband, but also with Janet's doctor. Eventually, Janet Adkins, along with her husband and a friend, flew to Michigan to seek Dr. Kevorkian's further advice and possible assistance. After several conversations, they decided to proceed.[13]

In a deluge of subsequent nationwide coverage, the public was told some version of the account *Newsweek* had summarized:

> While her husband waited at a nearby hotel, they [Janet Adkins and Dr. Kevorkian] drove to a suburban campsite in Kevorkian's rusty Volkswagen van. He inserted a needle in her arm and started saline flowing. She pressed a button on his death machine that first sent a sedative, then deadly potassium chloride racing to her heart.

With this action, "Janet Adkins reignited debate over the right to die with dignity, the ethics of assisting such deaths and the alarming rate of suicide among the elderly."

The list of accounts of Dr. Kevorkian's Mercytron continued to grow.[14] Even for many staunch advocates for physician-aided dying, the Michigan doctor had gone too far. Derek Humphry, quoted in many subsequent articles, noted that the jolting nature of Janet Adkins' death further under-scored the need for more rational, humane measures—most particularly, the measures he and the Hemlock Society advocated. Janet Adkins may have been a Hemlock Society member, but this was not what they had in mind. Traveling 2,000 miles from home to die in the back of a camper was not death with dignity. Discussion was needed, Humphry argued, to "clear the air on this gray area of what constitutes suicide and what constitutes homicide."

Michigan law-enforcement officials did not stand idly by. Four days after Janet Adkins died, a judge ordered that Dr. Kevorkian stop using his suicide device or otherwise helping people commit suicide until prosecutors decided whether to charge him with a crime. After a six-month investigation, on December 4, Dr. Kevorkian was arrested and charged with first-degree murder. The next week, after a two-day hearing, the judge, noting that Michigan had no specific law against assisting suicide, held that the prosecutors had failed to provide enough evidence to move forward with the charge of first-degree murder. Dr. Kevorkian was free to leave.

The saga of Dr. Kevorkian, however, was just beginning. He continued to assist patients to die. By 1993, he was appearing as Dr. Death on the cover of *Time*. A growing stream of feature stories appeared in newspapers across the country and international publications such as *The Economist*.[15] Even late-night talk shows were contributing their gallows humor. Among David Letterman's Top Ten promotional slogans for Kevorkian's suicide machine was, "Just try it once, that's all we ask." Estimates varied, but Dr. Kevorkian acknowledged he had aided a number close to 20 by the end of 1993.

Frequently, articles drew parallels between Dr. Kevorkian and Derek Humphry's activities with the Hemlock Society. This made Humphry uncomfortable. In *Final Exit*, he had revealed that, while the 1988 efforts in California were progressing, Dr. Kevorkian had approached the Hemlock Society with the idea to open a suicide clinic in Southern California. Writing of this conversation, Humphry recalled that Kevorkian, always the moral entrepreneur and advocate for confrontational politics, "argued that not only was this necessary for humanity but, if he was prosecuted for assisting suicides, as seemed likely, the resulting publicity would benefit the euthanasia cause."

Humphry saw such strategies as counterproductive. Kevorkian's idea was rejected. "Since the campaign in which the euthanasia movement was at that point engaged was to legitimize physician aid-in-dying for the terminally ill," Humphry noted, "any law-breaking would be bad publicity." Still, there was ambivalence. On the one hand, Humphry praised Kevorkian for "breaking the medical taboo on euthanasia," suggesting in June of 1993, "one could quibble about things with Dr. Kevorkian, but basically he's along the same lines as me."[16] Two months later, the connection was underscored. "It's a pincer movement. He's [Kevorkian] coming at it through the courts and we in the right-to-die movement are coming through the legislatures."[17] Humphry would later write, however, in less laudatory terms, that the Michigan pathologist's sudden appearance on the right-to-die scene "transformed the issue from polite debate and courteous informal assistance [Hemlock's way] to in-your-face, controversial death-on-request."[18]

In the minds of many, however, Dr. Kevorkian and the Hemlock Society were working hand-in-glove, fighting a common cause. Janet Adkins' involvement with both only accentuated this connection. Dr. Kevorkian and his suicide machine drew the loudest, most widespread criticism. But Derek Humphry and his arguments in *Final Exit* did not escape. This small "how-to" volume was characterized as "evil with a smile," in the normally reserved *HCR*.[19] If not evil, it was an "ill-advised cookbook of death," which failed to address, let alone resolve, the profound moral, ethical, and personal uncertainties surrounding the meaning of euthanasia and assisted suicide.[20]

For friend and foe alike, the how-to advice given by the Hemlock Society and the in-your-face tactics employed by Dr. Kevorkian began to frame the debate. Opponents used the extreme accounts of suicide vans and heightened fears of increased suicide rates to underscore what they saw as a dangerous slippery slope. Humphry and Kevorkian were seen "at once a spur for the death with dignity movement and a lightning rod for criticism of its potential excesses."[21] In July 1991, a year after Janet Adkins' death, a feature article in the *Wall Street Journal*, picked up in numerous newspapers across the country, pointed to the heated debate Humphry's book was stirring.[22] In August, the *New York Times*, noting a rare accomplishment for a book from a small, not-well-known publisher, reported *Final Exit* was topping its best-seller list.[23]

This small volume included specific dos and don'ts, a table of lethal dosages of various drugs, and what many considered its signature suggestion—"self-deliverance via the plastic bag." To ensure the recommended procedures were successful, *Final Exit* recommended that a plastic bag be placed over the head and secured with a rubber band. With this detailed advice in hand, *Final Exit* readers were provided a checklist for final review.

There was evidence that persons were not only reading, but also following, *Final Exit*'s quite specific, methodical advice. Although Humphry explicitly aimed at mature adults who were "suffering from a terminal illness and considering the option of rational suicide if and when suffering became unbearable," there were concerns. Many believed, by writing and promoting *Final Exit*, Humphry and the Hemlock Society were providing suicidal encouragement to troubled persons, including troubled adolescents and those simply discouraged or otherwise unable to deal with life. Strongly worded personal accounts, such as Wesley Smith's "The Whispers of Strangers," began appearing, charging Humphry and the Hemlock Society with complicity in deaths of their friends.[24] Many began to ask whether *Final Exit* was responsible for an asserted rise in the suicide rate among adolescents, the disabled, and the elderly.

In 1992, the *JAMA*, the *American Journal of Psychiatry* and the *NEJM* all published commentaries exploring this question.[25] In further pursuit, a systematic study of suicides in New York City was reported in the *NEJM* in November 1993.[26] Suicides involving "asphyxiation by plastic bag" did increase by over 300 percent (from 8 to 33) during the period investigated, but other methods were less frequently used. There seemed to be a substitution effect. Overall, the *NEJM* authors concluded, "It is therefore reassuring that despite the thousands of copies of the book in circulation in New York City, there was no increase in the overall rate of suicide."

Although these findings might have been reassuring, there were continuing concerns and widespread publicity surrounding Janet Adkins' death. Efforts succeeded in early February 1991 to get Kevorkian's death machine declared illegal. Undaunted, Dr. Kevorkian responded by devising a new instrument and procedure. Some eight months later, in October

1991, he assisted Sherry Miller, 43, and Marjorie Wantz, 58, both of whom wished to end their life peacefully.

Sherry Miller was not by any normal definition confronted with a terminal illness. Describing her 12 years of total dependence and debilitation, brought on by the complications of multiple sclerosis, she had testified for Dr. Kevorkian in the civil trial banning the initial version of his Mercytron. She shared with those in the courtroom how she had lost her will to live. She turned to Dr. Kevorkian for assistance. Again, widespread publicity and strong reactions, both for and against, followed Sherry Miller's and Marjorie Wantz's assisted suicides.

Their deaths came to light just days before the voters in Washington State went to the polls to vote on a death-with-dignity measure, Initiative 119. Washington Citizens for Death with Dignity had secured the necessary signatures. The physician-aid-in-dying measure was on the ballot. Public opinion polls continued to indicate something on the order of a two–one margin of support. As in the failed 1988 effort in California, however, the proposed law was opposed by a well-organized and substantially funded coalition of pro-life organizations. Again, ready access to assisted suicide, as defined in Initiative 119, was portrayed, not only as ill-advised, but also as possibly the initial step toward a policy wherein the lives of the elderly, disabled, and otherwise troubled and disadvantaged would be seen as somehow less worthy of support and protection than others.

Dr. Kevorkian's suicide machine(s) and the assisted suicides of Sherry Miller and Marjorie Wantz were used to illustrate potential dangers. Washington State's Initiative 119 was defeated—54 percent to 46 percent. A year later, on November 3, 1992, a similar proposal finally found its way to the California voters, again supported and opposed by the now familiar cast of activists and organizations. The California voters also rejected the proposal, by an identical margin to residents of Washington— 54 percent to 46 percent.

Back in Michigan, Dr. Jack Kevorkian continued to pursue his in-your-face strategy. He welcomed being arrested. When put in jail, he went on hunger strikes to gain added publicity. Jack Kevorkian was clearly a confrontational moral entrepreneur. He saw an injustice. Existing laws were flawed. He aimed to get them changed. Until they were changed, he would disobey them.

His disobedience was having an effect. Lower-court judges were divided on whether Michigan's law preventing assisted suicide met Constitutional standards as outlined in the *Roe* and *Cruzan* Supreme Court decisions.[27] In February of 1993, after several failed attempts, Michigan's law banning assisted suicide finally came into effect. Later that same year, on August 4, Dr. Kevorkian provided assistance to Thomas Hyde, age 30, suffering from amyotrophic lateral sclerosis (ALS)—"Lou Gehrig's disease." Following Hyde's death, charges were filed, and Dr. Kevorkian was arrested. When put in jail, as promised, he went on a hunger strike. While out on bond, he participated in several additional assisted suicides.

The trial involving Thomas Hyde's death was held in April of 1994. As written, Michigan's recently passed statute prohibiting assisted suicide applied to anyone who knew that another person planned to attempt suicide and knowingly provided the physical means or participated in a physical act by which the suicide was carried out. The law was aimed specifically at Dr. Kevorkian. Bowing to medical practice known to be widespread among physicians, however, it also contained an exception.

Exceptions to Michigan's law prohibiting assisted suicide should be granted, it was argued, "if the intent is to relieve pain and discomfort and not to cause death, even if the procedure may hasten or increase the risk of death." In his opening statement, Dr. Kevorkian's attorney underscored this provision as he spoke to the jury:

> Humanity and compassion are on trial. You will be deciding one of the great issues in the struggle for human rights . . . His intent is never to kill someone, but only to reduce suffering . . . You will decide how much suffering all of us must endure before we go into that good night—some of us, not so gently.[28]

The trial became a hazy examination of the Doctrine of Double Effect. Dr. Kevorkian's intention was not to kill but to alleviate suffering in a life that had become, or was rapidly becoming, not worth living. A prominent Detroit internist was called to testify. When pressed by the prosecutor he replied, "I think the procedure was a heroic effort on Dr. Kevorkian's part to control pain and suffering which was otherwise out of control." In his own testimony, Dr. Kevorkian noted, "I had a fairly good idea that he would die, but my expectation was that his suffering would end." He likened his own actions to a physician confronted with the unpleasant task of amputating a cancerous leg. It was not something the physician wanted to do. Like that physician, Dr. Kevorkian wanted to help his patient "end his suffering with the only means known and available to me."

A few days after this testimony was heard, a split jury acquitted Dr. Kevorkian of the charges on May 2, 1994. This would not be the last time Dr. Kevorkian would stand trial, but for now the jury was convinced. A member of the jury, a nurse's assistant, reported that Dr. Kevorkian's testimony had turned the case. "He convinced us that he was not a murderer, that he was really trying to help people out, and I can't see anything wrong with it." Another juror, a computer repairer, agreed, but with reservations: "I believe Dr. Kevorkian is doing the right thing, but he's not necessarily going about it in the right way. In the back of a van—I don't think that's the proper place for a medical procedure."[29]

Yale Kamisar, a legal scholar long involved in these matters, then teaching at the University of Michigan Law School, who knew Michigan's assisted-suicide law statute well, stated simply, "The jury was obviously badly confused." Exceptions contained in the law were aimed at the administration of pain medication, not inhalation of carbon monoxide. In Professor Kamisar's mind, the jury's decision effectively negated Michigan's law.[30]

Wise decision or confused negation, the jury's verdict was in. Dr. Kevorkian was free to continue his work. There would be other trials and other acquittals. By the end of 1996, Dr. Kevorkian had assisted nearly 45 suicides. In March 1999, after the list had grown to an approximated 130, Dr. Kevorkian was finally convicted of second-degree murder for his direct involvement in a videotaped death, eventually shown on the widely viewed *60 Minutes*. This time, he did not leave the final act to his patient. He had performed it himself. He was sentenced to prison.

Eight years later, in June 2007, the now 79-year-old doctor was released. A spokesman for the Archdiocese of Detroit issued a statement: "For 10 years, Jack Kevorkian's actions resembled those of a pathological serial killer. It will be truly regrettable if he's now treated as a celebrity parolee instead of the convicted murderer he is." In contrast, a group of sign-carrying supporters waited outside prison to greet the doctor on his day of release. A friend and colleague reported that the views of the doctor remained unchanged. He continued to believe, "this should be a matter that is handled as a fundamental human right that is between the patient, the doctor, his family and his God."[31]

A Calmer Voice

As Jack Kevorkian's suicide machines and Derek Humphry's *Final Exit* were gaining notoriety, a quiet, much calmer and cautious, though none-the-less insistent, voice joined the calls to open the door to legalized physician-assisted suicide. Dr. Timothy E. Quill aimed to bring wide-spread, hidden, but not-so-secret practices into the open. He did so by publishing "Death and Dignity: A Case of Individualized Decision Making." This article, published on March 7, 1991 in *NEJM*, was a brief, softly written personal account of how he had provided assistance to "Diane," a long-time patient and friend. Dr. Quill's initial advice to Diane drew in many ways on Derek Humphry and the Hemlock Society. His article was widely covered in the press and was credited by some as a primary reason *Final Exit* moved to the top of the *New York Times* best-seller list in the months immediately following.

Timothy Quill was well versed in palliative care and hospice operations. He knew first hand that suffering could be lessened, "but in no way eliminated or made benign," at least not within the current constraints of existing laws. He knew his efforts, along with those of the hospice staff, had helped Diane, but "bone pain, weakness, fatigue, and fevers" had begun to dominate her life. In the course of caring for his patient and friend, he had learned important lessons.

Diane had taught Dr. Quill that he could "take small risks for people that I really know and care about." The need to act indirectly, however, meant Diane ultimately had to die alone, with no one by her side in her final moments. For her family, friends, and physician, this was a painful thing to watch. This left Timothy Quill wondering.

> I wonder how many families and physicians secretly help patients over the edge into death in the face of such severe suffering. I wonder how many severely ill or dying patients secretly take their lives, dying alone in despair. I wonder whether the image of Diane's final aloneness will persist in the minds of her family,

or if they will remember more the intense, meaningful months they had together before she died. I wonder whether Diane struggled in that last hour, and whether the Hemlock Society's way of death by suicide is the most benign.

He wondered too whether the legal fiction of unintended consequences was in fact making things worse.

"If we do not acknowledge the inescapable multiplicity of intentions of most double-effect situations," he wrote two years later, "physicians may retreat from aggressive palliative treatment out of fear of crossing the allegedly bright line between allowing patients to die and causing their death." In his case, he had been accused by some of killing Diane. This implied "a desire to destroy a person's essence." Nothing could have been further from his intentions. For Dr. Quill, "the possibility of death may have helped to preserve her [life's] integrity." Diane had taken her life "only when her personhood was being irretrievably lost."[32]

Following his disclosure of the assistance he had given Diane, Dr. Quill "received a crash course in the politics of medical ethics." For his detractors, he was a killer. For supporters, he was a saint. In late July 1991, Dr. Timothy Quill was brought before a grand jury. Despite his admission of his obvious illegal involvement in Diane's death, after the assistant district attorney outlined the charges for three days, Dr. Quill, waiving immunity from prosecution, responded for some three hours. The grand jury failed to return an indictment. The state medical board also decided not to file disciplinary charges, reasoning the drug prescription for Diane did have a legitimate medical use. In a subsequent interview, Dr. Quill reported he was "tremendously relieved the ordeal is over." He remained clear, however, in his belief: "the debate needs to go on and be broadened."[33]

Dr. Quill entered the assisted-suicide fray with strong credentials. With fellow advocates, he began framing the right-to-aid-in-dying movement by working on a number of deeply informed, carefully argued publications, made more compelling by the personal experiences they contained.[34] In a book-length treatment, prompted by his experiences with Diane, Quill detailed how his position varied from cases such as those depicted in "It's Over Debbie." The young, tired physician responding to Debbie's late-night call had acted after a very brief encounter and with almost no background knowledge of his patient or her illness. If physicians were going to help their patients end their lives, they should do so with deep knowledge and extensive experience.

Dr. Quill was more upset, even frightened, by Dr. Kevorkian and the apparent ease with which the Michigan pathologist helped his patients die. Particularly disturbing was "his apparent lack of doubt, uncertainty, or careful analysis of his patients and their problems." In some cases, Dr. Kevorkian was helping non-terminally ill persons with their deaths. Was Dr. Kevorkian simply using receptive patients to advance his cause? Dr. Quill was similarly worried and unsettled by the "extreme over-simplification" contained in the self-deliverance advice offered in Derek Humphry's *Final Exit*. Humphry's widely available, seemingly cavalier advice, when combined with actions such as those being taken by Dr. Kevorkian, contained a deeper danger. Those who argued for caution in the face of a potential "slippery slope" had a point. Carefully crafted regulations were needed to avoid a slide into unintended and perhaps unforeseen practices.

Dr. Quill was convinced legal reform was needed to achieve a better balance between the alleviation of suffering and the protection of life. He wanted, however, to avoid the contentious, frequently demonizing mistakes of the abortion debate. "There must be," he argued, "some middle ground where we can maintain our reverence for life, while at the same time acknowledging the possibility of intolerable suffering." He recognized assisted suicide was an "extraordinary and irreversible treatment." Still, his experience had taught him there were essential elements of a humane yet safeguarded remedy:[35]

1. The patient must, of his own free will and at his own initiative, clearly and repeatedly request to die rather than continue suffering.
2. The patient's judgment must not be distorted.
3. The patient must have a condition that is incurable and associated with severe, unrelenting, intolerable suffering.
4. The physician must ensure that the patient's suffering and the request are not the result of inadequate comfort care.
5. Physician-assisted suicide should only be carried out in the context of a meaningful doctor–patient relationship.

6. Consultation with another experienced physician is required to ensure the voluntariness and rationality of the patient's request, the accuracy of the diagnosis and prognosis, and the full exploration of comfort-oriented alternatives.
7. Clear documentation to support each condition above is required.

These seven criteria were developed to provide a thoughtful, safeguarded approach, grounded in thorough knowledge of the patient as a person, with special emphasis on palliative care. They pointed to diagnostic and prognostic double-checks, as well as a set of specific clinical criteria physicians might use when working with those suffering and making life-ending decisions.

Dr. Quill and his colleagues knew there had been, was, and would be controversy.[36] It was controversy well worth engaging. With careful, thoughtful insistence, they became central figures in the legislative initiatives and court cases about to unfold.

A Foothold is Secured

Physician aid in dying received an unexpected boost from the Supreme Court in June 1992, just under a year following Dr. Quill's acquittal. *Planned Parenthood v. Casey* dealt with restrictions on abortion. It provided, however, a potential foundation for assisted suicide when justices wrote, "at the heart of liberty [is the] right to define one's own concept of existence, of meaning, of the universe, and of the mystery of human life." Such matters, the court noted, should not be "formed under the compulsion of the State."[37] For those paying attention, the implications for assisted suicide were clear. Armed with this broad-stroked inclusion of the right to define existence, meaning, and the mystery of life in the liberties protected by the Fourteenth Amendment, proponents of physician-assisted suicide, increasingly labeled death with dignity, fashioned what would become a successful effort in Oregon.

By framing the debate with detailed attention to criteria similar in principle to those outlined by Dr. Quill, Oregon activists aimed to protect life and acknowledge suffering with the reverence they both deserved. They took lessons from the failed campaigns in California and Washington State. Patients were more firmly in charge in the Oregon statute.

There were precisely defined, mandatory procedures to provide double-checked medical judgment and psychological assessment, with ample opportunity for patients to change their mind. With such provisions, it was argued, the much-discussed slippery slope could be avoided.

To be eligible under the new Oregon statute, a patient had to be an Oregon resident who was terminally ill—a prognosis that there were six months or fewer to live, confirmed by at least two physicians. There had to be repeated and fully informed requests to die—evidenced by at least two oral, and one written, requests for assistance. These requests had to be certified as voluntary, sincere, and not the result of "suffering from a psychiatric or psychological disorder or depression causing impaired judgment." The physician's prescription of drugs to be utilized could not be made until 15 days had passed from the initial request and 48 hours after the patient's final, written request. As a final safeguard, a request for assistance in dying could be rescinded at any time.

In their campaign, advocates for this Oregon voter initiative distanced themselves from the images of Dr. Kevorkian's methods. They also downplayed connections with Derek Humphry's plastic-bag advice, as well as his more recent and controversial advocacy of lethal injections.[38] The most difficult argument to counter was now quite familiar. It was based upon uncertain, perhaps unforeseen consequences. The "slippery slope" metaphor had been a warning sounded in virtually every assisted-suicide, quality-versus-sanctity-of-life debate following the revealed atrocities of World War II. If physician-assisted suicide were to be legalized, opponents argued, it would lead to widespread, unintended, unanticipated, dire outcomes. As the campaign in Oregon got under way, the recent release of a 1991 report from the Netherlands seemed to confirm these fears.[39]

The Remmelink Report, named after the head of the commission that released the report, documented that, despite long-standing, court-approved guidelines, assisted-suicide abuses were occurring in the Netherlands. During the period of study, Dutch physicians had reportedly ended the lives of 11,840 patients with overdoses of pain medication. In some 8,100 of these cases, the stated purpose was to end life, not to relieve pain. Most upsetting was evidence suggesting that, among these 8,100 patients, 61 percent (4,941) had been given the intentional overdose without the patient's consent.[40]

The meaning of these findings and the policy conclusions drawn would be disputed, but this was important evidence. It was countered in the Oregon campaign with pleas for empathy for the patient and appeals for balance among the options available. There were accounts of persons suffering, lingering in dehumanizing pain, with unheeded pleas for help. There were assurances that strong safeguards were built into the proposed statute to avoid the Netherlands' experience. Indeed, some otherwise supportive advocates worried these restrictions might be too onerous. As voting day approached, there were adamant advocates on both sides. There were dramatically different opinions across rural (opposed) and urban (supportive) districts across Oregon. The statewide vote was close— 51 percent to 49 percent (a difference of some 32,000 votes)—but, on November 8, 1994, the death-with-dignity forces had won a historic victory. Oregon voters had approved Measure 16, the Oregon Death With Dignity Law. It was the first such law in the United States.

Although a victory had been won, the fight was not over. Many religious leaders, disability activists, physicians, caregivers, and terminally ill patients standing in opposition did not give up. They filed suit in federal district court in November.[41] A temporary injunction was granted, and, eight months later, in August 1995, a federal district judge issued a permanent injunction against the Act's enforcement.[42] This decision was appealed and subsequently overturned on procedural grounds.[43] On October 27, 1997, the injunction was finally lifted, and physician-assisted suicide became an option for terminally ill patients in Oregon.

From coast to coast, 1994 marked an eventful year for energized assisted-suicide forces, both for and against. In New York, the Task Force on Life and the Law had been in existence for a decade. Reversing its long-standing affirmation of individual autonomy, it issued a unanimous recommendation in May of 1994, just months before the historic vote in Oregon, to retain barriers to physician-assisted suicide and active euthanasia. The task-force members were attentive to the alleviation of suffering. They encouraged more systematic use of palliative care. They even suggested that quiet, surreptitious agreements between patient and doctor would take care of the remaining cases. Like many others, however, they were worried about threats to the sanctity of life if even small and well-protected steps were taken. Legalizing assisted suicide and euthanasia would, "pose profound risks to many individuals who are ill and vulnerable." The "potential dangers of this dramatic change in public policy would outweigh any benefit that might be achieved."[44]

Is There a Right to Assisted Suicide?

Throughout the 1990s, court cases were filed to challenge the constitutionality of existing laws prohibiting physician-assisted suicide. The litigated issues coalesced around whether assistance in this most assuredly private decision was not only acceptable, but also a constitutionally protected right. In 1994, a case from Washington State began winding its way to the Supreme Court.

Since 1854, even before Washington had become a state, it had been a crime to assist suicide. In 1994, Washington law read simply that a person was guilty of assisting suicide "when he knowingly causes or aids another person to attempt suicide." Violations could result in imprisonment for a maximum of five years and a fine of up to $10,000. A month after the initial passage of the Oregon death-with-dignity law, four Washington physicians and their attorneys, asserting the rights of three terminally ill, competent patients who wished to "hasten their deaths with help from their physicians," went to court to challenge this prohibition.[45]

After hearing the case, the federal district judge, Barbara Rothstein, promptly issued her opinion, ruling against the state's law. In so doing, Judge Rothstein became the first judge to hold that assisted suicide was a right guaranteed by the U.S. Constitution. The underlying constitutional issue was

> whether the State of Washington can resolve the profound spiritual and moral questions surrounding the end of life in so conclusive a fashion as to deny categorically any option for a terminally ill, mentally competent person to commit physician-assisted suicide.

Pointing to the *Casey* decision, Judge Rothstein found the answer was, No. The suffering of a terminally ill person could not "be deemed any less intimate or personal, or any less deserving of protection from unwarranted governmental interference, than that of a pregnant woman." The conclusion followed: "A competent, terminally ill adult has a constitutionally guaranteed right under the Fourteenth Amendment to commit physician-assisted suicide."[46]

By this time, two of the three patients had died. On appeal, a three-judge Ninth Circuit Court panel disagreed with Judge Rothstein's finding and voted two–one to reverse. The two circuit court justices noted in support of their reversal: "In the two hundred and five years of our existence no constitutional right to aid in killing oneself has ever been asserted and upheld by a court of final jurisdiction." There was no such right to assisted suicide guaranteed by the Constitution. Washington's statute should stand.[47] This was in March, 1995. By this time, the third patient had died. Still, the issue remained unresolved. "Because of the extraordinary importance of this case," the Ninth Circuit Court justices decided to hear the case *en banc*.[48]

As they introduced their decision, they noted, this was "the first right-to-die case that this court or any other federal court of appeals has ever decided." It compelled them to "address questions to which there are no easy or simple answers, at law or otherwise." It required them to "confront the most basic of human concerns—the mortality of self and loved ones—and to balance the interest in preserving human life against the desire to die peacefully and with dignity."

In echoes reminiscent of *Roe v. Wade*, the Ninth Circuit Court justices knew there was controversy. "People of good will can and do passionately disagree about the proper result, perhaps even more intensely than they part ways over the constitutionality of restricting a woman's right to have an abortion." As the *Roe* court before them had done, the justices aimed to remain above the political fray, to "determine whether and how the United States Constitution applies to the controversy before us, a controversy that may touch more people more profoundly than any other issue the courts will face in the foreseeable future."

There were two competing values—the alleviation of suffering and the protection of life. Who should decide? Assuming an individual was terminally ill and competent, was there "a constitutionally-protected liberty interest in hastening what might otherwise be a protracted, undignified, and extremely painful death"? Assuming this protected-liberty interest existed, did the State of Washington have a competing and compelling interest to ban "a form of medical assistance that is frequently requested by terminally ill people who wish to die"?

Reversing their colleagues' two–one vote of a year earlier, on March 6, 1996, the U.S. Ninth Circuit Court of Appeals, in an eight–three decision governing seven western states (California, Oregon, Washington, Arizona, Nevada, Idaho, and Montana), sided with the alleviation of suffering over the state's interest in protecting life. The decision should be kept close to home. The majority opinion announced there was indeed a "constitutionally-protected liberty interest in determining the time and manner of one's own death, an interest that must be weighed against the state's legitimate and countervailing interests, especially those that relate to the preservation of human life." There were no compelling state interests strong enough to override individual autonomy in these matters. "Insofar as the Washington Statute prohibits physicians from prescribing life-ending medication for use by terminally ill, competent adults who wish to hasten their own deaths, it violates the Due Process Clause of the Fourteenth Amendment." The Washington statute was in violation of the U.S. Constitution.

There were few, if any, bright-line distinctions. As Supreme Court justices had done in *Roe v. Wade*, the Ninth Circuit Court justices searched frequently imprecise constitutional penumbras to anchor their arguments. They reasserted the importance of privacy and individual autonomy. They drew analogies with right-to-die findings in the 1980s. They found moral and legal equivalence when comparing the removal of medical equipment, stopping hydration and nutrition, and prescribing or administering drugs to terminate life. They continued to struggle with the hazy distinctions of intent to alleviate suffering or to hasten death.

While the justices knew they were breaking new legal ground, they sensed solid footing. "While the cases we have adverted to lend general support to our conclusion," the justices concluded, "we believe that two relatively recent decisions of the Court, *Planned Parenthood v. Casey*, and *Cruzan v. Director, Missouri Dept. of Health*, are fully persuasive, and leave little doubt as to the proper result." A little over a year later, these Ninth Circuit Court justices sitting on the west coast would find whether their colleagues on the Supreme Court in Washington, DC, agreed with their analogies, linkages, boundaries, and balancing of competing values and interests.

Clearly, court decisions resolving challenges to the Washington State statute were swaying back and forth in pendulum-like fashion, reflecting the enduring and deeply embedded dilemmas and shadowed boundaries of constitutional provisions and personal intent and interests. The same pattern would be found in a case being decided at about the same time in New York.

As in the Washington case, the New York case involved doctors arguing on behalf of themselves and their patients, then in the final stages of terminal illnesses—a 76-year-old retired physical education instructor dying of thyroid cancer, a 48-year-old publishing executive suffering from AIDS, and a 28-year-old former fashion editor also under treatment for AIDS. Each patient wanted to end their life "in a certain and humane manner."[49] Their physicians wanted to assist them.[50] Such assistance was against the law in New York. Drawing parallels to the removal of life-support systems, recently approved by the Supreme Court in Nancy Cruzan's case and asking for equitable treatment, the patients and their doctors wanted New York's law declared unconstitutional.

Dr. Timothy Quill and two of his colleagues filed the New York case in July, 1994,[51] two months after the New York Task Force on Life and the Law had issued its report opposing such practices. The district court judge was not persuaded. By his assessment, "the type of physician assisted suicide at issue in this case does not involve a fundamental liberty interest." A long tradition of practice and law supported the judge's conclusion. Nor was it a matter of equitable treatment. There were important differences when comparing what was being proposed and the removal of life-support measures from patients such as Nancy Cruzan.

In the judge's opinion, it was not "unreasonable or irrational" for the state to recognize a difference between allowing nature to take its course and intentionally using an artificial death-producing device:

> The State has obvious legitimate interests in preserving life, and in protecting vulnerable persons. The State has the further right to determine how these crucial interests are to be treated when the issue is posed as to whether a physician can assist a patient in committing suicide.

Dr. Quill and his colleagues had failed to convince him.

The decision was appealed. Arguments were heard, and, seven months later, on April 2, 1996, three justices for the Second Circuit Court of

Appeals (covering Connecticut, New York, and Vermont) issued their opinion.[52] Unlike the district court judge, they found moral and legal equivalence between disconnecting life support and prescribing life-ending drugs. Physicians did not fulfill the role of "killer" by prescribing drugs to hasten death, any more than they did by disconnecting life-support systems. "In point of fact," the circuit court decision continued, "[terminally ill patients] themselves are entitled to hasten death by requesting such withdrawal and should be free to do so by requesting appropriate medication to terminate life during the final stages of terminal illness."

We may not know the precise boundaries of tolerable suffering, the circuit court justices argued, there might not be a bright line signaling when prolonging life becomes prolonging death, but we should treat equally situated individuals equitably. "It seems clear," the justices concluded, "that New York does not treat similarly circumstanced persons alike: those in the final stages of terminal illness who are on life-support systems are allowed to hasten their deaths by directing the removal of such systems; but those who are similarly situated, except for the previous attachment of life-sustaining equipment, are not allowed to hasten death by self-administering prescribed drugs." There was no compelling state interest to justify this inequitable treatment. New York's law prohibiting physician-assisted suicide was unconstitutional.

This decision was announced a month after the Ninth Circuit Court decision involving the Washington law. By April 1996, two federal courts of appeals, with jurisdiction over ten states on the east and west coasts, had found prohibitions against assisted suicide unconstitutional. Applauded by many and deeply disturbing to others, both circuit court decisions were appealed to the U.S. Supreme Court. They were argued on January 8, 1997.

In the Washington case, the argument was based upon an assertion of a fundamental liberty of terminally ill persons to determine the time and manner of their death. In the New York case, Dr. Timothy Quill and his colleagues, along with the patients under their care, sought equity. Persons kept alive by medical technology, including the provision of hydration and nutrition, had the right to refuse treatment and thereby end their life. Persons suffering from terminal illness but living without medical assistance should have the same right to end their suffering and leave this life.

Unanimous Ambivalence

The U.S. Supreme Court issued separate decisions, *Washington v. Glucksberg* and *Vacco v. Quill*,[53] on June 26, 1997. With "ambivalent unanimity,"[54] both decisions reviewed the now well-discussed and frequently competing interests embedded in the hazy boundaries of tolerable suffering and protected life.

By this time, the moral as well as legal standing of individual autonomy to refuse medical treatment was secure. Just as clear was a compelling state interest to protect life. The now more mature bioethics movement had dealt repeatedly and in depth with the Doctrine of Double Effect. The boundaries of tolerable suffering and the point where protecting a life became prolonging a death, infused with pain and suffering, remained hazy. Judging from public opinion polls, as well as more narrowly drawn surveys of physicians and hospital staff, most felt that persons immediately impacted—patients and their physicians—should determine where these boundaries lie. Laws permitting physician-assisted suicide, with the exception of Oregon, had, however, repeatedly fallen short of passage.[55] The Supreme Court justices had a rich, frequently contradictory foundation on which to build.

They had plenty of help. The list of "friend of the court" briefs, providing what proponents of one position or another hoped was compelling information and advice, was long and read like a "Who's who" of the legal and ethical debates of the past two decades. They came from attorney general offices across the country, from religious and social-movement organizations both for and against, from persons more personally involved, and from ethicists, philosophers, and lawyers outlining their persuasive reasons to decide one way or another.

After considering these briefs and hearing arguments, the frequently divided Supreme Court came to a unanimous decision, elaborated with five separate concurring opinions, laced with ambivalent references to troubling and unresolved issues and suggestions that other cases might appropriately be brought to the court in the future. With multiple voices, the justices unanimously found that access to assisted suicide was not a fundamental liberty interest. The state had ample compelling interests to restrict its availability. Nor was access to assisted suicide a matter of equity. There were legitimate distinctions to be drawn between letting a patient die and providing the drugs to hasten death.

History and contemporary practices told them so. Chief Justice Rehnquist, writing for the court, noted that assisted suicide had been punished or otherwise disapproved for over 700 years. More recently, this prohibition had been reaffirmed in votes throughout the country—with the one exception of Oregon. Most recently, even as their opinions were being researched and written, Congress had passed by a wide margin, and President Clinton had signed, the Assisted Suicide Funding Restriction Act of 1997.[56] When signing the Act, President Clinton had noted, "While I have deep sympathy for those who suffer greatly from incurable illness, I believe that to endorse assisted suicide would set us on a disturbing and perhaps dangerous path." Once taken, the path too easily led to policy and practice where protective boundaries of, and respect for, life were weakened.

With reference to the permissive assisted-suicide laws in the Netherlands, along with the cases of Elizabeth Bouvia, Nancy Cruzan, and Jack Kevorkian, as well as others, the Supreme Court justices saw many reasons for governmental regulation. It was justified when

> preventing the serious public health problem of suicide, especially among the young, the elderly, and those suffering from untreated pain or from depression or other mental disorders; protecting the medical profession's integrity and ethics and maintaining physicians' role as their patients' healers; protecting the poor, the elderly, disabled persons, the terminally ill, and persons in other vulnerable groups from indifference, prejudice, and psychological and financial pressure to end their lives; and avoiding a possible slide towards voluntary and perhaps even involuntary euthanasia.

For these reasons, the Supreme Court justices disagreed with their circuit court colleagues. The findings of the Second and Ninth Circuit Courts were overturned. States could pass laws prohibiting assisted suicide. They also had the latitude to pass laws permitting the same. In his closing comments reviewing the case from Washington, Chief Justice Rehnquist acknowledged the unresolved state of affairs: "Throughout the Nation, Americans are engaged in an earnest and profound debate about the morality, legality, and practicality of physician assisted suicide. Our holding permits this debate to continue, as it should in a democratic society."

The boundaries and dilemmas of assisted suicide were matters voters in each of the states would have to decide.

Voters Decide (Again) and Are Challenged (Again)

Voters had done so in 1994 when approving Oregon's Death With Dignity Act. Legal maneuverings had delayed implementation until October 27, 1997, when an injunction against the voter-approved measure was finally lifted. A week later, on November 4, Oregon voters, in a turnout judged to be the largest in three decades,[57] voted, this time overwhelmingly, to rebuff ongoing efforts to repeal their state's law allowing physician-assisted suicide.

Oregon voters had twice voted to allow physician-assisted suicide under tightly controlled circumstances. Still, unlike Justice Rehnquist and his Supreme Court colleagues, there were those who felt these deeply important matters transcended the "will of the people." This time, continuing opposition came in the form of a letter from the director of the Drug Enforcement Agency (DEA), Thomas Constantine. It was written in response to a request he had received in July, a month following the Supreme Court's companion decisions, from two U.S. congressmen, Representative Henry Hyde and Senator Orin Hatch. Constantine's response was dated November 5, 1997—one day after Oregon voters had expressed their preferences for the second time.[58]

The congressmen were both closely associated with what had come to be known as the pro-life side of the debate. They were concerned. They were encouraged by many influential constituents, including a representative of the National Conference of Catholic Bishops. As congressmen, they had important oversight authority over the DEA. They knew that physicians could prescribe controlled substances only for a "legitimate medical purpose." Writing to Director Constantine, they wanted an agency opinion on whether "delivering, distributing, dispensing, prescribing, filling a prescription, or administering a controlled substance with the deliberate intent of assisting in a suicide [such as permitted by the Oregon statute] would violate the Controlled Substance(s) Act." Referring to the recently passed Assisted Suicide Funding Restriction Act, Hyde and Hatch noted there would be "serious concern [in Congress] were any federal agency to construe the intentional prescribing of legal drugs for suicide as a legitimate medical practice."

The DEA depended on Congress for funding. Director Constantine knew an only vaguely veiled threat when he saw it. He asked his staff to carefully review the matter. Some four months later, the day after the Oregon voters affirmed their state's law permitting the practices of concern, the staff finished their assessment, and Director Constantine sent his reply. He and his staff were persuaded "that delivering, dispensing or prescribing a controlled substance with the intent of assisting a suicide would not be under any current definition a 'legitimate medical purpose'." Such activities would be, in their opinion, a violation of the Controlled Substance Act. This was the answer Representative Hyde and Senator Hatch had hoped for.

The congressmen then approached Attorney General Janet Reno to seek appropriate enforcement. Here, they hit a brick wall. Attorney General Reno, in her June 5, 1998, reply, did not agree with Director Constantine and his staff. She found no reason to conclude that the intent of the Controlled Substance Act was "to displace the states as the primary regulators of the medical profession." Even more importantly, with reference to Chief Justice Rehnquist's closing comment in *Washington v. Glucksberg*, she found no evidence that the DEA was assigned "the novel role of resolving the 'earnest and profound debate about the morality, legality, and practicality of physician-assisted suicide'." "Such a mission," Reno continued, "falls well beyond the purpose of the CSA." The pendulum swing of opinions continued.

The attorney general's response may have been anticipated. The same day Reno's letter was dated, Representative Hyde introduced legislation that would more clearly allow the DEA to discourage the prescription of life-ending drugs. A companion bill was filed in the Senate. A month later, hearings were held.

In his remarks on July 14, Representative Hyde drew upon now quite familiar images to make his case. "Today," he wanted his colleagues to know, "we are forced to squarely face the reality of what has been called a culture of death." The slippery slope he had warned about,

> back in 1973, when the Supreme Court sanctified abortion . . . now appears before us as a precipitous cliff, where the elderly, the infirm, the sick, the disabled are lined up at the top and invited to do the right thing and relieve their loved ones of their

burdensome existence by plunging off this cliff under the care of a physician who will assist them in their suicidal journey.

The slippery slope metaphor was appropriate, Hyde continued,

> when one considers exterminating life in a womb has become a constitutional right; partial birth abortion . . . is as we speak legal . . . We now move from this tragedy to assisted suicide . . . Who is to say the slippery slope won't become steeper and the un-wanted, the despised, the useless eaters will soon join the unborn as candidates in this journey to oblivion.

Speaking in opposition, Oregon's governor, himself a licensed physician, saw this opposition not as a guard against a slippery slope but as an inappropriate challenge to the will of the Oregon voters. It was also "an unprecedented expansion of federal power over the practice of medicine." A representative of the AMA agreed. The AMA was a powerful organization, long opposed to physician-assisted suicide. This time, however, it weighed in against the proposed federal legislation. There was professional concern over the thin line of intent. Drugs prescribed to alleviate pain could readily be used to end a life. The AMA feared that the "real world" consequences of the legislation being proposed by Representative Hyde and his colleagues would have a chilling effect on the prescription of pain-relieving medication and thereby discourage appropriate palliative care.

In the end, the proposed federal legislation failed. With tenacity befitting a committed believer, however, Representative Hyde immediately introduced yet another legislative proposal to ban the use of drugs required to carry out the provisions of Oregon's law. This, too, failed. By this time, the political significance of these life-and-death matters in the U.S. Congress was fading, as legislative attention turned to efforts to impeach President Clinton.

A year later, George W. Bush was elected president. He came to office with the narrowest of margins, but strong support from pro-life forces. He appointed John Ashcroft, closely associated with President Bush's evangelical right-to-life supporters, as attorney general. In his home state of Missouri, Governor Ashcroft and his Department of Health had been thoroughly involved in the Nancy Cruzan case. Attorney General Ashcroft was well versed in the issues at hand. He took a different view of federal oversight of the medical profession and physician-assisted suicide laws than had his predecessor, Janet Reno.

On November 9, 2001, Ashcroft sent a memorandum to the administrator of the DEA, with specific reference to his disagreement with Janet Reno's assessment. For the new attorney general, Director Constantine's original assessment had been correct. Assisting suicide was not a "legitimate medical purpose." Prescribing, dispensing, or administering controlled substances to assist suicide violated the Controlled Substance Act. Given this assessment, Ashcroft directed the DEA, effective with the publication of his memorandum and "notwithstanding anything to the contrary" in the attorney general's letter to Director Constantine, to enforce and apply the law based on his new assessment. This directive was a not unexpected. Still, it was a stunning reversal.

Not many persons, however, were paying attention. The nation's and the world's attention had turned elsewhere. A month earlier, on September 11, terrorists had forced planes to fly into the World Trade Center, the Pentagon, and a field in Pennsylvania. More than 3,000 persons had been killed. The nation was under attack. Concern for physician-assisted suicide laws in Oregon were a minor distraction at best.[59]

In March 2005, however, another high-profile right-to-die case, in Florida, drew substantial national attention.[60] Following prolonged, contentious, and highly politicized events involving the state legislature and courts, as well as the U.S. Congress, Terri Schaivo's feeding tube was removed, and she died amid protests and the now frequent assertions that we were moving rapidly toward a culture of death.

Two years later, on the west coast, passage of laws that would provide easier access to assisted dying once again gained attention. This time, two-term governor, Booth Gardner (1985–1993), was at the forefront. Governor Gardner was suffering from Parkinson's Disease. He wanted to die and he wanted to do it with dignity. He, along with a coalition of state and national activists, aimed to change Washington's law, which they saw as standing in the way. "Under no circumstances," Governor Gardner reasoned, "should my fate be put in the hands of a pinhead politician who can't pass ninth-grade biology."[61] In what he saw as his last campaign and the biggest fight of his career, the governor saw his logic as impeccable. "[It is] my life, my death, my control."[62]

The arguments had been heard and reheard numerous times. This time they were persuasive. On November 4, 2008, the voters in Washington went to the polls and, by a wide margin (59 percent to 41 percent), Washington became the second state to pass a death with dignity law. A year later, on December 31, 2009, the state Supreme Court in Montana ruled there was nothing in Montana court rulings or state statutes indicating physician aid in dying was against public policy.[63] The man for whom the case had been filed, Robert Baxter, had died the previous December, "so skinny he couldn't sit because his skin hurt."[64] The debate over these perhaps ultimately irresolvable issues continues.

Notes

1   Ian Dowbiggin *A Merciful End: The Euthanasia Movement in Modern America* (New York: Oxford University Press, 2003), 135. More generally, see chap. 5.
2   Dowbiggin, *A Merciful End*, 135.
3   Humphry and Wickett were married and had co-authored *Jean's Way and the Right to Die*, an account of Humphry's first wife's assisted suicide. Wickett's and Humphry's troubled relationship and its disruptive impact on the Hemlock Society would become a source of public discussion in the years ahead.
4   *Barber v. Superior Court*. California Court of Appeal, Second District, 1983. 147 Cal.App.3d 1006, 195 Cal.Rptr. 484. *Bartling v. Superior Court* (1984) [209 Cal.Rptr. 220].
5   See, Robert L. Risley, *A Humane and Dignified Death: A New Law Permitting Physician Aid-in-Dying* (Americans Against Human Suffering, 1987).
6   Allan Parachini, "The California Humane and Dignified Death Initiative," *The Hastings Center Report* 19 (1989): 10–13.
7   "It's Over, Debbie," *Journal of the American Medical Association* 259 (1988): 272.
8   W. Gaylin et al., "Doctors Must Not Kill," *Journal of the American Medical Association* 259 (1988): 2139–40; K.L. Vaux, "Debbie's Dying: Mercy Killing and the Good Death," *Journal of the American Medical Association* 259 (1988): 2140–1; G.D. Lundberg, "'It's Over, Debbie' and the Euthanasia Debate," *Journal of the American Medical Association* 259 (1988): 2142–3. Leon Kass, "Neither for Love Nor Money: Why Doctors Must Not Kill," *Public Interest* 94 (1989): 25–46.
9   Kass, "Neither for Love Nor Money," 26.
10 Gaylin et al., "Doctors Must Not Kill."
11 Gaylin et al., "Doctors Must Not Kill."
12 "The Doctor's Suicide Van," June 18, 1990.
13 For an account of these early dealings, see Neal Nicol and Harry Wylie, *Between Dying and the Dead* (Madison, WI: The University of Wisconsin Press, 2006): 147–50.

14   See for example: http://topics.nytimes.com/top/reference/timestopics/people/k/jack_ kevorkian/index.html?offset=15&s=oldest.

15   "Death's Dissident," *Economist*, November 13 (1993): 34.

16   "Founder Defends Euthanasia Action," *The Lima News*, October, 16 (1993): B1. Paul Verschuur, "Euthanasia Advocates Say Death Machine Raises Few New Issues," Associated Press wire service, June 7, 1990.

17   Quoted in: "Dr. Death's Trial Intrigues Legal Experts," *The Beacon Journal*, August 19 (1993): A6.

18   Derek Humphry and Mary Clement, *Freedom to Die: People Politics and the Right-to-die Movement* (New York: St. Martin's Griffin, 2000), 132.

19   Leon Kass, "Suicide Made Easy, the Evil of 'Rational' Humaneness," *Hastings Center Review* (1991): 19–24.

20   See Sherwin Nuland, *How We Die: Reflections on Life's Final Chapter* (New York: Random House, 1993), 156–7.

21   Daniel Hillyard and John Dombrink, *Dying Right: The Death With Dignity Movement* (New York: Routledge, 2001), 245.

22   M. Cox, "Suicide Manual for Terminally Ill Stirs Heated Debate," *Wall Street Journal*, July 12 (1991): B1, B8.

23   L.K. Altman, "How-to Book on Suicide is Atop Best-Seller List," *New York Times*, August 9 (1991): A10.

24   Wesley J. Smith, "The Whispers of Strangers," *Newsweek*, June 28 (1993). *Forced Exit: The Slippery Slope from Assisted Suicide to Legalized Murder*. This 1997 publication would be followed by *Culture of Death: The Assault on Medical Ethics in America*.

25   Phillip B. Chappel, Robert A. King, Michael Enson, "Final Exit and the Risk of Suicide," *Journal of the American Medical Association* 267 (1992): 3027. M.H. Sacks and I. Kemperman, "Final Exit as a Manual for Suicide in Depressed Patients," *American Journal of Psychiatry* 149 (1992): 842–843. M.R. Lavin, G. Martin, and A. Roy, "Rational Suicide and Psychiatric Disorders," *New England Journal of Medicine* 326 (1992): 890.

26   "Increase in Suicide by Asphyxiation in New York City After the Publication of Final Exit," *The New England Journal of Medicine* 329, November 11 (1993): 1508–10.

27   See: "Dr. Kevorkian's Legal Victory," *New York Times* December 16 (1993).

28   Geoffrey Fieger, in his opening statement in the 1994 trial of Jack Kevorkian. Cited in Neal Nicol and Harry Wylie, *Between Dying and the Dead* (Madison, WI: The University of Wisconsin Press, 2006), 189.

29   Quotes taken from, "Kevorkian Takes Stand in Own Defense," *New York Times*, April 28 (1994).

30   David Margolick, "Jury Acquits Dr. Kevorkian of Illegally Aiding a Suicide," *New York Times*, May 3 (1994).

31   Kathy Barks Hoffman, "Kevorkian Leaves Prison After 8 Years," The Associated Press, June 1 (2007).

32   "The Ambiguity of Clinical Intentions," *The New England Journal of Medicine* 329 (1993): 1039–40.

33   Lawrence K. Altman, "Jury Declines to Indict a Doctor who Said He Aided in a Suicide," *New York Times* July 27 (1991).

34 Timothy E. Quill, *Death and Dignity: Making Choices and Taking Charge* (New York: W.W. Norton & Company, 1993). See also: Franklin G. Miller, Timothy E. Quill, Howard Brody et al., "Regulating Physician-Assisted Death," *The New England Journal of Medicine* 331 (1994): 119–23; Timothy E. Quill, Christine K. Cassel, and Diane E. Meier, "Care of the Hopelessly Ill: Proposed Clinical Criteria for Physician Assisted Suicide," *New England Journal of Medicine* 327 (1992): 1380–1. Timothy Quill, "The Rule of Double Effect—A Critique of its Role in End-of-Life Decision Making," *The New England Journal of Medicine* 337 (1997): 1768–71. Timothy Quill, *Caring for Patients at the End of Life* (New York: Oxford University Press, 2001); and Timothy E. Quill and Margaret P. Battin, Eds., *Physician-Assisted Dying: The Case for Palliative Care & Patient Choice* (Baltimore, MD: Johns Hopkins Press, 2004).

35 *Death and Dignity: Making Choices and Taking Charge* (New York: W.W. Norton & Company, 1993): 161–5.

36 See, for example: Daniel Callahan, letter, *New England Journal of Medicine* 331 (1994): 1656. Daniel Callahan and Margot White, "The Legalization of Physician-Assisted Suicide: Creating a Regulatory Potemkin Village," *University of Richmond Law Review* 30 (1996): 1–83.

37 *Planned Parenthood v. Casey*, 505 U.S. 833 (1992) at 851.

38 See editorial written shortly after the Oregon initiative passed: Derek Humphry, William K. Kaula, and Geoffrey N. Fieger, "To the Editor," *New York Times* Dec. 3 (1994): 14.

39 *Medical Decisions About the End of Life*, I. Report of the Committee to Study the Medical Practice Concerning Euthanasia. II. The Study for the Committee on Medical Practice Concerning Euthanasia (2 vols.), The Hague, September 19, 1991.

40 See page 72 of the Remmelink Report.

41 *Lee v. Oregon*, 869 F. Supp. 1491 (D.Or. 1994).

42 *Lee v. Oregon*, 891 F. Supp. 1429 (D.Or. 1995).

43 *Lee v. Oregon*, 107 F.3d 1382 (9th Cir. 1997).

44 *When Death is Sought: Assisted Suicide and Euthanasia in the Medical Context*: www.health.state.ny.us/nysdoh/provider/death.htm 120. See also: John D. Arras, "On the Slippery Slope in the Empire State: The New York State Task Force on Physician-Assisted Death," *American Philosophical Association Newsletters* 95 (1996): 80–3.

45 As summarized in the circuit court's decision: Jane Roe was a 69-year-old retired pediatrician who had suffered since 1988 from cancer, now metastasized throughout her skeleton. She had been completely bedridden since June of 1993 and experienced constant pain, which became especially sharp and severe when she moved. The only medical treatment available to her at the time did not fully alleviate her pain. In addition, she suffered from swollen legs, bedsores, poor appetite, nausea and vomiting, impaired vision, incontinence of bowel, and general weakness.

     John Doe was a 44-year-old artist dying of AIDS. Since his diagnosis in 1991, he had experienced two bouts of pneumonia, chronic, severe skin and sinus infections, grand mal seizures, and extreme fatigue. He had lost 70 percent of his vision, which would eventually result in blindness and loss of his ability to paint.

     James Poe was a 69-year-old retired sales representative who suffered from emphysema, which caused him a constant sensation of suffocating. He was connected to an oxygen tank at all times and took morphine regularly to calm the panic reaction associated with his feeling of suffocation. Mr. Poe also suffered from heart failure related to his pulmonary disease, which obstructed the flow of blood to his extremities and caused severe leg pain. There were no known cures for his pulmonary and cardiac conditions, and he was in the terminal phase of his illness.

46 *Compassion In Dying v. State of Washington*, 850 F.Supp. 1454, 1456 n.2 (W.D. Wash. 1994).

47 *Compassion In Dying v. State of Washington*, 49 F.3d 586 (9th Cir. 1995).

48 *Compassion in Dying v. Washington*, 79 F. 3d 790, 798 (1996).

49 The pleading of Jane Doe, suffering from thyroid cancer, is illustrative:

> I have a large cancerous tumor which is wrapped around the right carotid artery in my neck and is collapsing my esophagus and invading my voice box. The tumor has significantly reduced my ability to swallow and prevents me from eating anything but very thin liquids in extremely small amounts. The cancer has metastasized to my plural [sic] cavity and it is painful to yawn or cough . . . In early July 1994 I had the [feeding] tube implanted and have suffered serious problems as a result . . . I take a variety of medications to manage the pain . . . It is not possible for me to reduce my pain to an acceptable level of comfort and to retain an alert state . . . At this time, it is clear to me, based on the advice of my doctors, that I am in the terminal phase of this disease . . . At the point at which I can no longer endure the pain and suffering associated with my cancer, I want to have drugs available for the purpose of hastening my death in a humane and certain manner. I want to be able to discuss freely with my treating physician my intention of hastening my death through the consumption of drugs prescribed for that purpose.

50 In a document filed with the court, Dr. Quill stated:

> The removal of a life support system that directly results in the patient's death requires the direct involvement by the doctor, as well as other medical personnel. When such patients are mentally competent, they are consciously choosing death as preferable to life under the circumstances that they are forced to live. Their doctors do a careful clinical assessment, including a full exploration of the patient's prognosis, mental competence to make such decisions, and the treatment alternatives to stopping treatment. It is legally and ethically permitted for physicians to actively assist patients to die who are dependent on life-sustaining treatments . . . Unfortunately, some dying patients who are in agony that can no longer be relieved, yet are not dependent on life-sustaining treatment, have no such options under current legal restrictions. It seems unfair, discriminatory, and inhumane to deprive some dying patients of such vital choices because of arbitrary elements of their condition which determine whether they are on life-sustaining treatment that can be stopped.

51 *Quill v. Koppell*, 870 F. Supp. 78 (S.D.N.Y. 1994).

52 *Quill v. Vacco*, 80 F.3d 716.

53   21 U.S. 702 (1997) and 521 U.S. 793 (1997).

54   See: Sonia Suter, "Ambivalent Unanimity: An Analysis of the Supreme Court's Holding," in *Law at the End of Life: The Supreme Court and Assisted Suicide*, Ed. Carl E. Schneider (Ann Arbor, MI: The University of Michigan Press, 2000).

55   See *Washington v. Glucksberg*, n. 15 for listing of failed legislative proposals between 1994 and 1997. For more up-to-date listing, see Appendix A in Neil M. Gorsuch, *The Future of Assisted Suicide and Euthanasia* (Princeton, NJ: Princeton University Press, 2006). Washington State's 2008 Death With Dignity Law was a decade away.

56   Neither federal funds nor federal facilities could be used to provide "assisted suicide, euthanasia, or mercy killing." The Congressional vote had not been close. In the Senate, it was 99–0. In the House of Representatives, it was 398–16.

57   Timothy Egan, "The 1997 Elections: Right to Die," *New York Times*, November 6 (1997): A22.

58   These documents and related materials have been brought together in a very useful volume: Susan M. Behuniak and Arthur G. Svenson, Eds., *Physician-Assisted Suicide: The Anatomy of a Constitutional Law Issue* (New York: Rowman & Littlefield Publishers, 2003).

59   As attention turned elsewhere, Ashcroft's directive was appealed and eventually overturned by the U.S. Supreme Court on January 17, 2006. Oregon's law was finally fully implemented. Assessments were published. In many cases, the yearly assessments showed, the prescribed drugs were never used. See: www.oregon.gov/DHS/ph/pas/ar-index.shtml.

60   Arthur L. Caplan, James J. McCartney, and Dominic A. Sisti, Eds., *The Case of Terri Schiavo: Ethics at the End of Life* (Amherst, NY: Prometheus Books, 2006).

61   Claudia Rowe, "Ex-Governor Seeking Death With Dignity—Booth Gardner Devotes His Final Days Fighting to Legalize Physician-Assisted Suicide," *Seattle Post Intelligencer* May 18 (2007). Available online at: www.seattlepi.com/local/316298_gardner18.html.

62   Daniel Bergner, "Death in the Family," *New York Times*, December 2 (2007).

63   *Baxter v. Montana*.

64   See http://abcnews.go.com/Health/MensHealth/story?id=8466212.

Part IV
Taking Life and Inflicting Suffering

Chapter 14

Removing the Protective Boundaries of Life

Allowing, even assisting, a terminally ill person to die is one thing. Taking life from one person to prevent or discourage the misdeeds of others is quite another. This is an often-heard deterrence justification for capital punishment. Likewise, executing the offender is seen as a retributive and perhaps restitutive means to redress suffering and bring closure to the grief inflicted by brutal acts. These justifications, grounded in the protection of life and the alleviation of suffering, are often coupled with a thoroughgoing dehumanization of the offender, who, transformed into a subhuman beast, deserves death.[1]

Transforming a fully protected citizen into a convicted, dehumanized felon whose life can be taken is an uncertain business. It has been so for a very long time. Many actions have called for the taking of life: disobeying parents, disregarding the Sabbath, blasphemy, sodomy, adultery, abortion, robbery, rape, and murder have all been included at one time or another. Communities have also differed on how they remove the protective boundaries of life. Sometimes, trials are prolonged and detailed. Sometimes they are abbreviated, better characterized as "Lynch law." One thing is constant. Those already close to the edges of protected life are those most vulnerable to the punishment of death. This finding has been widely noted and repeatedly illustrated across time, place, and life circumstances.[2] It is nowhere more evident than when lynchings soiled the landscape in the United States.[3]

Lynching and the Margins of Life

By all accounts, the post-Civil War years were marked by social turmoil. Power and influence were being renegotiated. Governments were being re-established. Property was being redistributed and rights redefined. The resulting communal instability was amplified by the serious economic depressions of the 1870s and 1890s. These decades were characterized by a heightened sense of Us and Them, with an important accompanying sense in which belonging begets separation. Along the exclusionary boundaries of a fissured community life, empathy faded; ostracism and animosity built; demonization, anger, and lethal violence became more likely; and a paradox of community in which the ties that bind us together become the ties that keep us apart was manifest.

A 1905 study of this period[4] was introduced by telling readers,

> As will be made clear in the following pages, lynch-law has been resorted to in the United States in times of popular excitement and social disruption; it has been inflicted upon Negroes, Indians, Italians, Mexicans; it has been inflicted upon disreputable characters.[5]

The same year this study was published, an editorial appeared in the *Times Clarion*, a Longview, Texas, community newspaper.

Longview is located in an area of East Texas where slaveholding had been dominant, an area wherein the slaveholding South met the rough-and-tumble West. Lynchings were justified as a way to preserve lives and a way of life deemed more worthy. "Almost every day," the *Times Clarion* editorial began, "some Negro brute assaults a white woman in this state, and often one to a half-dozen murders are committed in an effort to hide the crime ... If rape and murder by brutish Negroes are to become common, the Negro must expect extermination."[6] This Longview editorial did not stand alone. Similar articles and editorials, especially throughout the former Confederacy, joined in chorus in constant refrain that was exclusionary, dehumanizing, and fearful.

Although this palpably exclusionary mindset was widespread, it did not proceed without resistance. As editors across the country were publishing opinion pieces and graphic articles such as the one in Longview, a group of 29 influential activists gathered in July 1905, on the Canadian side of Niagara Falls. Their aim was to counter the inflammatory conversation taking place across the nation and to seek a more inclusive society.

William Edward Burghardt (W.E.B) DuBois, who had been educated at both Fisk and Harvard universities, was among their leaders. The location of their first gathering was selected carefully and was purposively symbolic. DuBois and his colleagues knew the caste-like society was threatening the lives of those they aimed to support. Like Niagara Falls, they would create a mighty current for change. They aimed to weaken the exclusionary sense of Us and Them and thereby strengthen the protective boundaries of life. At their second meeting, they outlined their objectives:

> We shall not be satisfied with less than our full manhood rights ... We claim for ourselves every right that belongs to a free-American—political, civil, and social—and until we get these rights, we shall never cease to protest and assail the ears of America with the story of its shameful deeds toward us.[7]

Three-and-a-half years later, in early February 1909, some of those associated with this *Niagara Movement* founded the National Association for the Advancement of Colored People (NAACP). This organization would become a powerful, guiding force in a movement to eliminate exclusionary policies, laws, and practices. A half a century later, associated efforts would form the cornerstone for the abolition of capital punishment. In the early days of 1909, however, the NAACP's eventual influence was on the distant, hoped-for, but not-clearly-foreseen, horizon. The immediate concern was with lynchings.

Lynchings, more than anything else, illustrated the dehumanizing, suffering-inducing, life-threatening consequences of an exclusionary society. A year after the NAACP was founded, to help frame more clearly the issues defining the inclusive society, the NAACP began publishing *The Crisis: A Record of the Darker Races*. Topics were wide ranging, but special place was reserved for lynching. Anti-lynching efforts soon became part of an aggressive campaign aimed at mobilizing resources to oppose this egregious affront to a common humanity.[8]

These efforts yielded some fruit. Working closely with the NAACP, a Missouri Republican congressman, Leonidas Carstorphen Dyer, who represented a district including parts of St. Louis with a high concentration of black citizens, introduced a piece of anti-lynching legislation into the U.S. Congress in mid April, 1918.[9] Shortly thereafter, the Senate Majority Whip, Senator Charles Curtis from Kansas, who traced his roots to the Kaw and Osage people, introduced related legislation to launch an investigation into lynching. Although these legislative efforts would ultimately flounder, the battle lines were drawn. Three months after Dyer's bill was introduced, in late July, President Woodrow Wilson responded to the mounting pressure from members of the NAACP and called upon "the governors of all the states, the law officers of every community and, above all, the men and women of every community" to end the "disgraceful evil" of lynching.[10]

At the time, the nation was at war. Those most susceptible to lynching were being trained and deployed to take life and protect a way of life that was putting their own lives at risk. There was a deep irony afoot. It did not go unnoticed. The Armistice ending World War I was signed on November 11, 1918. Six months later, W.E.B. DuBois, on behalf of war-weary black veterans, published "Returning Soldiers" in the May 1919 issue of *The Crisis*. He wrote with force:

> This is the country to which we Soldiers of Democracy return. This is the fatherland for which we fought! . . . It was right for us to fight . . . Under similar circumstances, we would fight again. But by the God of Heaven, we are cowards and jackasses if now that the war is over, we do not marshal every ounce of our brain and brawn to fight sterner, longer, more unbending battle against forces in our land.
>
> > We return.
> > We return from fighting.
> > We return fighting.
> > Make way for Democracy! We saved it in
> > France, and by the Great Jehovah, we will
> > Save it in the United States of America, or
> > Know the reason why.

DuBois wanted to be clear. He was not going to stand idly by while others justified grotesque, dehumanizing lynchings.

There were some reasons for optimism. Although lynchings threatened significant numbers of the black population, opportunities were expanding for many others. There was a Renaissance of sorts taking place. The Great Migration of black citizens moving north, usually said to have started sometime around 1915, was under way. Precise numbers are hard to come by, but no account puts the total below hundreds of thousands in the first few years. Harlem became a cultural Mecca. Chicago, South Chicago in particular, became known as the Black capital of the nation. By 1919, persons, both black and white, had begun referring to an awakening of the New Negro.

To some, this awakening brought hope. Optimism was reflected in the words of a Negro spiritual, "O, Rise, Shine for Thy Light is a' Coming."[11] While some progress was evident, a now well-focused anti-lynching campaign remained at the vortex of the swirling and frequently contradictory social transformation. The same year DuBois published "Returning Soldiers," others in the NAACP published a comprehensive study of lynching. Their report, *Thirty Years of Lynching in the United States (1889–1918)* was released in April 1919. The stated purpose of the report was simple. It aimed to present, without embellishment, a factually accurate picture. The authors wanted, "to give concreteness and to make vivid the facts of lynching." With direct reference to President Wilson's admonition to the nation, the report went on to note: "Despite President Wilson's earnest appeal, made under such extraordinary circumstances, lynchings continued during the remaining period of the war . . . Sixty-three Negroes, five of them women, and four white men fell victims to mob ruthlessness during 1918."[12] This largely statistical report was compiled from a number of sources. Although the data were incomplete and in all likelihood underestimated the true incidence of lynchings, the patterns were clear.

Lynchings were still very much in evidence, but, by 1918, the data suggested some reason for hope. There had been a sustained two-and-a-half decade decline in lynchings, from a high of 226 in 1892 to 67 in 1918. The decrease was most noticeable in the frontier west. The more settled regions of New England and Mid Atlantic states had always had far fewer lynchings, though even here they had decreased. Lynchings

remained most tenacious in states infused with the exclusionary, dehumanizing legacy of slavery. There were signs, however, that things were
changing. They provided a ray of hope that would quickly dim.[13]

Despite the noted decline in lynchings, immediately following the
release of *Thirty Years of Lynching*, and DuBois's article depicting the intentions of returning soldiers, there was a dramatic upswing in lynchings and
a rash of mob violence in what came to be known as the Red Summer
of 1919. A May 10 race riot in Charleston, South Carolina, marked the
beginning of this five-month period of violence.[14] Throughout the summer, there were riots and lynchings all across the country, north and south,
east and west. Violent events in rural Phillips County Arkansas in late
September and early October marked the final burst. Years later, Walter
White, centrally involved in investigating these incidents for the NAACP,
would write in his autobiography, "The blood lust which World War One
was too short to satiate made the year 1919 one of almost unmitigated
horror and tension."[15]

The final burst of violence in the neighboring rural communities in
Arkansas clearly demonstrated how the line between lynching and more
elaborate legal procedures of state-sanctioned execution could be razor
thin. The violence and subsequent trials in these isolated rural Arkansas
communities would become a crystallizing event on the road to reform.

Crystallizing Events on the Road to Reform

Seemingly small and isolated events can have an impact far beyond their
immediate circumstances. Such events frame issues with clarity and
influence the evolution of moral thinking. One such event occurred in
late September 1919, when a group of black farmers gathered in a small
church in rural Phillips County.

The legacies of slavery along the Mississippi River in Arkansas were
alive and well, but they were being challenged. Disputes in the nearby
communities of Hoop Spur, Helena, and Elaine were festering over the
price paid for cotton and the wages given to cotton pickers.[16] Periodic
violence broke out. Citizens, both black and white, kept guns nearby
for protection. Although whites constituted a large majority (close to
75 percent) in the state, in rural Arkansas they were in the distinct minority
—some 80 percent of the roughly 35,000 Phillips County residents
were black. Plantation owners in these rural areas retained their traditional

power through intimidation and legal privilege. Local black citizens, to secure their rights and increase their collective bargaining power, had hired lawyers to help found the Progressive Farmers and Household Union of America. These organizing activities were seen as a threatening affront to a way of life among the greatly outnumbered local whites.

Following the founding of the Union, organizing sharecroppers contacted a well-respected white lawyer, Ulysses Simpson Bratton, along with his sons and associates. The Brattons agreed to pursue the claims of some 68 black farmers. They were known for pursuing the interests of tenant farmers with commitment and skill. The elder Bratton's name, Ulysses Simpson, was a constant reminder of his political sympathies and the general and president for whom he was named. The Brattons also had a record of winning. As a central figure in these events would eventually note, hiring Bratton

> caused the landlords to take the new organization seriously because they knew Bratton would pull the cover from the unsavory system and, possibly, send some of them to federal prison for violation of the Thirteenth Amendment against slavery and the laws against peonage.[17]

It was with this background that, on the night of September 30, 1919, local black farmers gathered in a small church in Hoop Spur to further discuss their plans. The church was packed. Guns were carried for protection, and guards were posted outside the church. Rumors spread among whites that the meeting was part of a sharecroppers' plot to launch an insurrection. Worried this might be true, three white citizens drove by the church and parked to observe.

There are various versions of what followed and who fired the first shot,[18] but, from one account, those attending the gathering were "thrown into panic as fusillade after fusillade of bullets poured into the crowded church, killing a number of women and men and wounding others." Shots from those guarding the meeting killed one of the whites riding in the car and wounded another. It was as if "the match had been applied to the powder keg."[19]

Word quickly spread of a "Negro insurrection." An estimated 600–1,000 whites from neighboring communities in Arkansas and from across the river in nearby Mississippi and Tennessee gathered for a "nigger hunt."[20] As the Supreme Court would later note in less racially loaded terms, "The report of the killing [outside the church] caused great excitement, and was followed by the hunting down and shooting of many Negroes."[21]

An eyewitness account came from a World War I veteran, who was among those being hunted:

> It was a Good many Negros down their killed and the white Peoples called for the troops from Little Rock and they went down their and killed Negros like they wont nothen But dogs and did not make no arrest and unarmed a lots of Negroes and left the white with their armes and the Negro with nothen But their Hands and face to stand all the punishment the white wished to Give them.[22]

The initial shootings had occurred on Tuesday evening. The next day, the governor requested federal troops to control the situation. In a later account, a reporter known to be an ardent supporter of the whites wrote with conflicted consternation. Even he was offended by the actions being taken:

> The thing that "stumps" us, however, is by what authority did a coterie of Federal soldiers, aided and abetted by a collection of low-lived creatures who call themselves WHITE MEN, march down among the ramshackle homes of good old innocent, hard-working Darkeys, and then and there unlimber their guns . . . finally snuffing out their lives before passing on to the next house, where the same cruel scene was enacted.[23]

The exact number of black men, women and children killed was never firmly established, but eventual estimates settled on a total in excess of 200, with a high estimate of 856.[24] In addition, over 1,000 black men, women, and children were arrested and put in a stockade.

The governor convened a committee of seven prominent white citizens to investigate. They began their work on Saturday, October 4. Two days later, on Monday, October 6, they issued their report. It affirmed what a local newspaper, *The Arkansas Gazette*, had asserted the previous day in a headline reading: "Negroes Plan to Kill All Whites." This basic story was picked up in papers across the country, with the *New York Times* reporting "Negroes Seized in Arkansas Riots Confess to Widespread Plot; Planned Massacre of Whites Today."[25] In this manner, the violence erupting from the rural church gathering was framed as a situation in which outnumbered local whites were being threatened and attacked in an insurrection. The widespread lethal violence that followed was justified as an attempt to protect life.

The U.S. Supreme Court would later summarize the committee's findings. The church gathering in Hoop Spur had been part of "a deliberately planned insurrection of the Negroes against the whites, directed by an organization known as the 'Progressive Farmers and Household Union of America' established for the purpose of banding Negroes together for the killing of white people."[26] The committee's conclusion and the accounts in the media had been immediately challenged by federal agents and eventually proved false beyond any doubt.[27] In the immediacy of the moment, however, these stories stirred emotions, precipitated action, and justified the killings of black citizens.

Following the violence, something in excess of 120 black citizens were indicted on a range of charges. In an atmosphere of violent intimidation, witnesses and defendants were tortured to confess and give testimony supportive of the prosecution.[28] One of the white participants in the interrogations would later reveal:

> I saw a great many Negroes whipped . . . to compel them to give evidence against themselves and others . . . They were not only whipped but formaldehyde was put to their noses and they were stripped naked and put into an electric chair . . . I not only personally saw a great many Negroes whipped with a leather strap that would cut blood at every lick, but I whipped probably two dozen of them myself.[29]

Trials were held, and court decisions were rendered. The trials were perfunctory, defendants having little or no contact with their lawyers and scant, if any, testimony or evidence presented in their defense.

The first trial was held on November 3, a month after the violence had broken out. Once the defendants were arraigned, the trial took just under an hour and a half. Reportedly, about fifteen seconds after the prosecution rested, the defense attorney cleared his throat and said in a loud voice: "The defense has no witnesses, Your Honor."[30] The jury, all white, took eight minutes to reach a guilty verdict.

It took only seven minutes in the shorter second trial, held immediately following the first. The remaining trials were held in rapid-fire succession. With each successive trial, time for testimony and jury deliberation decreased, with the last verdict taking the jury only two minutes, making it perhaps "some sort of national record for the fastest verdict ever in a capital case."[31] By the end of two weeks, twelve blacks had been sentenced to death, and some seventy others had been sentenced to prison terms ranging from one to twenty-one years. No whites were tried for the widespread killing that had followed the initial incident.

This was not what the framers of the Fourteenth Amendment to the Constitution and the Habeas Corpus Act of 1867 had in mind shortly after the Civil War, when they aimed to protect former slaves from continuing enslavement and crafted the words "nor shall any State deprive any person of life, liberty, or property, without due process of law; nor deny to any person within its jurisdiction the equal protection of the laws." The problem was, intermittent Supreme Court decisions in the five decades between 1867 and 1919 had left confusion over how this Amendment and Act should be applied when there was a conflict between state and federal jurisdictions.[32]

Although the door of equal protections for those otherwise on the margins of life had been cracked open in 1907 by the only criminal case ever heard by the U.S. Supreme Court,[33] never before, no matter how egregious the violation, had a state criminal verdict been set aside by the U.S. Supreme Court. These were matters for local communities and the states to decide. Local officials seemed to be on firm legal footing.

If the sentences of organizing sharecroppers, now convicted of murder, were to be challenged, the appeals would have to be carefully crafted. Although a "lynching" had not occurred, the difference between a lynching and these trials was razor thin. At stake was whether the perfunctory trials, backed by evidence gathered through torture, intimidating threats, and no formal defense, were a legitimate forum for removing the protective boundaries of life.

A small group of lawyers in Arkansas decided to appeal the verdicts. They approached the national office of the NAACP for support. It was fitting that the son of a former slave, Scipio Africanus Jones, born in 1863, stood most prominent among them. As a young man, Jones had managed to secure a basic education and bachelor's degree and then moved into legal practice through an apprenticeship at a Little Rock law firm in the late 1880s. Judge Jones, as he was known locally, though he was not a judge, would carry the major responsibility for crafting the appeals. Over the years, Jones had developed a successful practice. By 1919, he had argued before the Arkansas Supreme Court some 17 times, winning 8. Judge Jones was well versed in how the Fourteenth Amendment and the wider ranging Habeas Corpus Act might be used effectively to strengthen the protections that should have surrounded the lives of his clients.

For reasons not altogether clear, the NAACP was not immediately responsive to Judge Jones' request for help.[34] Eventually, however, a visit from Ulysses Bratton, who had traveled north to vouch for Jones, secured some action. After this visit, the NAACP began mobilizing resources and cooperating. The cases of six defendants, who had been sentenced to death, included two brothers, Ed and Frank Hicks, as well as fellow organizers of the farmers union, J.C. Knox, Ed Coleman, Paul Hall, and Frank Moore. It took legal skill, diplomatic tenacity, and three-and-a-half years, but in the end these cases found their way to the U.S. Supreme Court in *Moore et al. v. Dempsey*.[35] The NAACP would eventually refer to this appeal as the "most important case of its kind in the history of America." "Out of the ashes of the Elaine [County] massacre," one later commentator wrote, "came a legal victory that set the country on a new course."[36]

Justice Oliver Wendell Holmes wrote the decision for the six–two majority of the court (one seat on the court was vacant), released in mid February, 1923, some three-and-a-half years after the Phillips County violence had exploded.[37] Summarizing the court's findings, Justice Holmes was clear and to the point: "A trial for murder in a state court in which the accused are hurried to conviction under mob domination without regard for their rights is without due process of law and absolutely void." With this language, *Moore et al. v. Dempsey* marked a turning point for how free citizens could be transformed into convicted felons. Local citizens and state courts of appeal were not free to run rough shod over the protective boundaries of life, no matter if the life in question was a life deemed less worthy and seen as a threat to a way of life.

The violent events and accompanying trials in these neighboring rural Arkansas communities on the banks of the Mississippi River dramatically illustrated how the infliction of suffering and the taking of life to protect lives deemed more worthy could be justified by a dehumanizing, fear-ridden, fissured sense of Us and Them. In its *Moore* decision, the Supreme Court planted the seeds for reinforcing the protective boundaries of life in a more inclusive fashion. Once planted, these seeds would take five decades to reach fruition.[38]

Evolving Protections for Those on the Margins

Between 1891 and 1893, there had been a reported average of some 189 lynchings per year, or on average about one every other day.[39] Thirty years later, between 1920 and 1922, the three-year average was 61. Starting with 1923, the year of the *Moore* decision, the yearly numbers fell over the following three years to 33, 16, and 17. There was a slight increase in 1926, but the overall downward trend continued, until the early 1930s, when the effects of the Great Depression were being felt. In 1933–1935, reported lynchings were 26, 15, and 20 per year. Thereafter, the decline continued, and, by 1939–1941, reported lynchings had decreased to three, five, and four per year.

What appears to have happened is that, as lynchings fell off, more formal trials and state-sanctioned executions rose. A substitution of sorts was taking place.[40] Once again, the impact of singular events was evident and dramatically illustrated by the response to the gruesome burnings and hangings of nine black citizens, accused of a range of crimes in a small Texas community about 70 miles east of Waco in May 1922.[41] A local citizen, J.W. Thomas, deeply disturbed by these events, ran for the state senate with the single-minded intent of passing a law that would remove hangings from the frequently frenzied emotional environment in local communities. Local hangings were to be replaced by electrocutions in the state's main prison.

With the passage of Thomas's legislation, Texas joined a growing number of states forbidding local hangings and choosing electrocution as a more humane method of execution.[42] Shortly after midnight of February 8, 1924, in Huntsville, Texas, the first application of the new law resulted in what one newspaper called a "harvest of death."[43] Starting at 12:09 a.m., four executions were carried out within an hour and a half. A fifth man, after a last-minute temporary stay of execution, was electrocuted and pronounced dead shortly after 2:00 a.m. All five were black convicts. All had been convicted of murder.

Safeguards for defendants had been somewhat strengthened following the Supreme Court's *Moore* decision. Further protections were provided by state statutes, such as the one in Texas, which removed legal hangings from the heightened emotion of local communities. For those on the margins of life, however, protective boundaries were still all too readily breached. Many of these offenses involved crimes grounded in what came to be called a peculiar kind of chivalry. One such event occurred in 1930 in Sherman Texas, located 65 miles north of Dallas. It involved a black man, recently arrived to the community as a farm laborer, later said to be "ignorant and feeble-minded." He was charged with the rape of his employer's wife, a white woman. It had been a little over six years since the Texas electrocution statute had yielded the initial "harvest of death." On May 9, as the alleged victim arrived on a stretcher just prior to the scheduled trial, an enraged crowd set fire to the courthouse.

The only person left inside was the defendant. He was locked up on the second floor. His body was later removed and, according to one account, as the police directed traffic, the corpse was dragged "to a cotton-wood tree in the Negro business section. There it was burned; afterward the crowd looted and destroyed most of the black-owned property in town."[44]

The repulsive nature of this event, combined with concern over a recent upsurge in lynchings in the early 1930s, precipitated further reform efforts on two fronts. On one, a group of concerned writers and academics, centered primarily at the University of North Carolina, began compiling reports and publishing articles, pamphlets, and books on lynchings and related subjects. The objective was to better understand and inform the public of the nature of racial violence. Among this group were legal scholars, including James Chadbourn, who wrote *Lynching and the Law*, published in 1933. A companion book, *The Tragedy of Lynching*, written by a social scientist, Arthur Raper, was published that the same year. Both works would frame much of the academic discussion in the decades ahead. Although these scholars, along with their colleagues at Tuskegee, Atlanta, and Fisk universities, were thorough and persistent, they were exclusively males.

Jesse Daniel Ames was one of the women left on the sidelines by the lawyers and academics producing reports and writing books in North Carolina. She was intensely interested and invested in the issues at hand. She had grown up in East Texas, just south of Dallas and east of Waco, in the small community of Palestine. She had long been concerned by the negative consequences of a "peculiar chivalry" she saw all around her that placed white women on a pedestal, separated from full participation in community affairs, and seen in need of protection. Ames saw this ill-conceived chivalry as the cornerstone used to justify lynchings involving the charge of rape of a white woman by a black man.[45]

Ames was well connected through a series of religious and social networks with women throughout the south. Some six months following the burning of the Sherman courthouse, just north of the region of Texas in which she had grown up, she became convinced that something had to be done. Excluded from the work of the male scholars in North Carolina, Ames decided that women could and should organize reform efforts of their own. "The men were out making studies," she once remarked, "and so the women had to get busy and do what they could to stop lynchings!"[46]

Ames invited 26 women from six southeastern states to join her in Atlanta on November 1, 1930, some six months after the Sherman incident. Together, they founded the Association of Southern Women for the Prevention of Lynching (ASWPL). Over the ensuing decade, they mobilized church communities and local action groups by giving speeches and distributing pamphlets. Their aim was to eliminate the unjust practices they saw as the illegitimate taking of life.

Their message was focused. "Public opinion has accepted too easily," Ames stated in an interview given some eight months after ASWPL was established, "the claim of lynchers and mobsters that they were acting *solely in the defense of womanhood*." "Women dare no longer to permit the claim to pass unchallenged nor allow themselves to be the cloak behind which those bent upon personal revenge and savagery commit acts of violence and lawlessness."[47] Galvanized by the egregious inhumanity of lynchings, emerging from a misplaced and peculiar chivalry, the ASWPL would not suspend their campaign until 1942, when lynchings had all but disappeared from the nation's landscape.

Another Crystallizing Event

These early efforts of the male intellectuals and female activists were further energized by yet another charge of rape in 1931. The ensuing trials would eventually provide further momentum to a broader civil rights movement then taking shape. The incident occurred on a freight train traveling from Chattanooga, Tennessee, through Alabama on its way to Memphis, only four months after the founding of the ASWPL. Like the trial of Frank Moore and his fellow sharecroppers, this trial would further crystallize thinking and motivate national concerns over how easily the lives of those on the margins of life could be taken.

On a sunny afternoon, March 25, 1931, some two-dozen hoboing young men, mostly teenagers, both black and white, caught a ride on a freight train. They were looking for work as the Great Depression began moving through its darkest days. There were also two young white women, 17 and 21 years of age, riding in one of the cars. The women were returning home to Huntsville, Alabama, after a failed search for work in Tennessee.

As the train wound its way through northern Alabama, there was some scuffling, and words were exchanged between two of the young travelers, one black, one white. Something to the effect: "Nigger bastard . . . you better get off. All you black bastards better get off." To which the challenging reply was, "Okay, you just try to put us off."[48] A fight broke out, and the young black men won out.

With one exception, the whites were forced from, or voluntarily left, the train. Word of the fight went ahead, and, when the train made a scheduled stop in Paint Rock, some 19 miles west of the county seat in Scottsboro, the remaining hoboing travelers were told to get off the train. A short time later, one of the young women riding the train approached the sheriff and accused the nine black men of gang-raping her and her companion after the whites had left the train.

The incident became a story often told and well documented.[49] The accused were arrested and taken back to the county jail in Scottsboro. A black man's rape of a white woman was seen as a particularly egregious offense. The fact that nine blacks were charged escalated the emotion to a fever pitch. Word spread throughout the surrounding communities, and, by that evening, one of the accused remembered a threatening crowd of several hundred, "howling like dogs . . . throwing rocks and threatening to burn us out."[50] The militia was called to restore order.

On Monday, April 6, not quite two weeks after the incident and six days after the defendants had been indicted, the trials of the nine defendants began. Three days later, all nine of the "Scottsboro Boys" had been found guilty of rape. Eight death sentences were scheduled for July 10, three months later. The ninth defendant, 13 years old, was found guilty, but the jury could not decide whether to sentence him to death or life in prison.

The trials, held two weeks after the arrests, took a total of three days to convict nine defendants and sentence eight of them to death. These abbreviated proceedings soon drew long-lasting attention. The national offices of the NAACP and the International Labor Defense (ILD) arm of the Communist Party of the United States became involved. The ILD eventually took charge of the legal matters. Appeals were developed. The Alabama Supreme Court rejected these on March 24, 1932, almost a year to the day after the initial incident. On further appeal, however, the U.S. Supreme Court agreed to hold a hearing seven months later, on October 10, 1932. On November 7, *Powell v. Alabama*, a seven–two decision consolidating the nine cases,[51] was released.

Justice George Sutherland, writing for the court, reviewed the facts:

> [On] April 6, six days after indictment the trials began. When the first case was called, the court inquired whether the parties were ready for trial. The state's attorney replied that he was ready to proceed. No one answered for the defendants or appeared to represent or defend them.

After a bit of discussion in the courtroom, an attorney indicated he was willing to represent the defendants, and the trial proceeded with a defense attorney identified. This meant, Justice Sutherland's opinion continued,

"Until the very morning of the trial, no lawyer had been named or definitely designated to represent the defendants."

As a result,

> During perhaps the most critical period of the proceedings, from the time of their arraignment until the beginning of their trial, when consultation, thoroughgoing investigation and preparation were vitally important, the defendants did not have the aid of counsel in any real sense.

Clearly, the accused did not have effective representation. They were not prepared to defend themselves and were at serious disadvantage.

Justice Sutherland continued,

> The defendants, young, ignorant, illiterate, surrounded by hostile sentiment, hauled back and forth under guard of soldiers, charged with an atrocious crime regarded with especial horror in the community where they were to be tried, were thus put in peril of their lives within a few moments after counsel for the first time charged with any degree of responsibility began to represent them.

For seven of the Supreme Court justices, the evidence was clear, and the outcome unacceptable.

The state could not negate the protective boundaries of life in such a cavalier manner. When it did, there was precious little difference between a trial and a lynch mob. "A defendant, charged with a serious crime, must not be stripped of his right to have sufficient time to advise with counsel and prepare his defense," Sutherland wrote. "To do that is not to proceed promptly in the calm spirit of regulated justice, but to go forward with the haste of the mob."

As clear and compelling as the evidence might have been, the seven concurring justices realized they were breaking new legal ground. They were fully convinced, however, the ground needed to be broken. As their written decision drew to a close, the conflicting jurisdictional issues between federal and state rights were put squarely on the table, as they had been with the Arkansas violence resolved in *Moore* a decade earlier. Although the Supreme Court had never before categorically determined the question before them, they would do so on this occasion. "We think the failure of the trial court to give [the defendants] reasonable time and opportunity to secure counsel was a clear denial of due process." There were, "certain immutable principles of justice which ... no member of the Union may disregard." The right to counsel in a capital case, when the protective boundaries of life were removed and death was inflicted, was one of those immutable principles.

Following the *Powell* decision, the cases of the nine young men who had been riding a train looking for work in depression-ridden Alabama, only to be charged with raping two women, would be retried, re-retried, and then retried again. In the process, other reinforcements for the protective boundaries of life would emerge.[52] What began in 1931 with the nine young men's arrest and conviction finally ended in 1976, when then governor of Alabama, George Wallace, pardoned the last of the Scottsboro Boys remaining in jail, noting that the conviction of all nine had been a tragic mistake. It had taken four-and-a-half decades to right this wrong.

The two Supreme Court decisions, *Moore v. Dempsey* and *Powell v. Alabama*, became important reinforcements for the protective boundaries of life. No matter how ignorant, illiterate, or otherwise marginal persons might be, no matter how hostile the community's sentiment or atrocious the crime, life could not be taken without due attention to the protective boundaries of life surrounding those charged. These decisions went straight to the heart of a deep sense of injustice stemming from an exclusionary and dehumanizing society. They drew strength from, and further reinforced, a broader civil rights movement aimed at securing related protections for those on the margins of life. Resistance to this newly anchored inclusiveness, however, remained.

Stark Inhumanity Energizes a Movement

The fragility of life's protective boundaries was dramatically evident in the trials of Frank Moore and his fellow sharecroppers. The same was true for the newly arrived farm hand in Sherman, Texas, and the young Scottsboro Boys riding the train in Alabama. The clear injustices embedded in these events had crystallized issues of injustice and galvanized action. There were other, similarly clarifying, events. One involved a teenage boy brutally murdered for an alleged insult to a white woman.

Emmett Till (Bo to his family and friends) was 14 in the summer of 1955 when his mother's uncle, Moses Wright (Papa Mose), came to Chicago in August for a funeral of a family member. Mamie Till (Emmett's mother) had migrated north from Mississippi with her parents in 1924 when she was only two. Her family moved to a small community just outside Chicago. Contact with Mississippi family members who decided to stay in Mississippi, however, remained strong.

They were delighted to see Papa Mose. He could tell great stories. He loved to entertain the family with tales of the simple pleasures of fishing and long summer nights in the Mississippi Delta. For the young boys listening, including Emmett, the Delta became the land of adventure. "For a free-spirited boy who lived to be outdoors," Mamie Till would later write, "there was so much possibility, so much adventure in the Mississippi his great-uncle described."[53]

When Emmett found out two of his cousins were going south a few weeks later to visit Papa Mose, he began working on his mother and grandmother to let him join the fun. At first, both refused. Emmett persisted. Eventually, like "two hens coming to fuss over this one little chick," his mother and grandmother drove to Papa Mose's daughter's house, where Papa Mose was staying. To the amusement of those present, both mother and grandmother came seeking promises of care and reassurances of safety. With the sought after promises and reassurances given, Emmett's mother consented to let Emmett take the trip.

First, however, she would have to give him the talk. "It was the talk every black parent had with every child sent down South back then," Emmett's worried mother would later recall. "We went through the drill." Chicago and Mississippi were very different places. Emmett should not start up conversations with white people. He should always put a polite handle on his answers, "Yes, ma'am," "No ma'am," "Yes, sir," "No sir." If a white woman was approaching him on the street, he should not look her in the eye. He should step off the sidewalk and lower his head. He should make every effort to humble himself.

For a free-spirited young teenager, who knew only of life in Chicago, this all seemed quite incredible. "Oh mama," he said. "It can't be that bad." Perhaps knowing that, only months earlier, on separate occasions, two black men, who were attempting to vote, had been shot and killed in full view of others not far from where her son was going to visit, Bo's mama replied, "Bo, it is worse than that." As the talk continued, Mamie took pains to reemphasize various points. Emmett listened and finally said, "Mama, I know how to act. You taught me how to act."

On Saturday morning, August 20, 1955, Papa Mose, Emmett, and one of his cousins, Wheeler, boarded *The City of New Orleans* and headed south. Another cousin, Curtis, would join them later. They would not be able to use the diner on the train, so Emmett's mother fried some chicken and included cake, treats, and a drink in a shoebox as she and her son left for the train station. She would recall later that it was a bit like sending Emmett to summer camp. A few days after he left, missing her son, Mamie decided to call to see how he was doing and if he wanted to come home early.

Instead, Bo asked if she could send him some more money. "More money?" His mother wondered. He had left home with plenty as far as she was concerned. Well, he had been buying sweets for some of his new friends. He could use a bit more. Bo also asked if she would make sure his motorbike got fixed before he got home. On August 27, Mamie received a short letter from her traveling son. He closed with the sentence "I am going to see Uncle Crosby Saturday. Everybody here is fine and having a good time. Tell Aunt Alma hello. (out of money), Your son, Bobo." Bo's mother had her answer. Her son was doing fine and having a grand time, "too good a time to even think about returning sooner."

Early the next morning, Sunday, August 28, her phone rang. It was Willie Mae, Papa Mose's daughter. Her son, Curtis, had called. "I don't know how to tell you. Bo . . ."

"Bo, what?" Mamie remembered asking as she sat up with a jerk. "Willie Mae, what about Bo?"

"Some men came and got him last night."

That's all Willie Mae knew. Some men had come to Papa Mose's house very early, around 2:30 a.m., Sunday morning, and taken Bo. Bo's now deeply troubled mother needed more information. After several attempts, they couldn't reach Papa Mose. They finally called another uncle and learned the other boys were OK. The uncle and Papa Mose were going to the sheriff to report the incident.

The next day, Monday, two men, Roy Bryant, owner of the small grocery store in Money, and his half-brother, J.W. Milam, who managed local cotton pickers, were arrested. They admitted to forcibly taking Bo from Papa Mose's house, but said they had let him go. Why had they done this? Bo had insulted Roy's wife. It had happened the previous Wednesday.

Emmett and his cousin Wheeler had arrived in Mississippi on Sunday, August 21. They had been given various chores around the house and helped pick cotton during the day with adults and other teenagers. On Wednesday, after working in the fields, Emmett, along with seven others, six boys and a girl, went to Bryant's Grocery and Meat Market to relax and buy some candy that evening.

Accounts of what came next vary, but all agree Emmett eventually went into the store to buy some bubble gum and, prodded by his friends, apparently forgot some of the details his mother had outlined in "the talk." After buying the bubble gum, he spoke directly to Carolyn Bryant, Roy's 21-year-old wife, and placed the money in her hand instead of on the counter where local custom dictated. There were also reports that, a short time later, he whistled at Carolyn when she came out of the store. Offense was taken. The peculiar chivalry that had for so long bothered Jessie Daniel Ames was about to be enraged.

Mrs. Bryant was taking care of the store that day, with Juanita Milam, J.W.'s wife, as Roy was away in Texas delivering some shrimp. At first, the two women decided not to tell their husbands, but the story started circulating, so, when Roy returned from Texas on Friday, Carolyn recounted what had happened. It took Roy until Saturday night to finish up some work. He then called J.W. and, early Sunday morning, August 28, the two brothers headed for Papa Mose's house in their pickup.

What followed was cruelly gruesome, well documented, and admitted to.[54] Bo was taken from Papa Mose's home, driven to numerous locations, beaten, mutilated, shot through the head, and thrown into a nearby river with a large cotton-gin fan tied around his neck with barbed wire. Three days later, on August 31, Emmett Till's decomposed body was discovered and sent back to Chicago, where his mother could bury her son. After an abbreviated trial, Roy Bryant and J.W. Milam were acquitted less than a month after the killing.

Papers throughout the country began carrying various accounts of Bo's murder and the trial that followed. His mother insisted on an open-casket funeral, so the world could see what had happened to her son. Two weeks after the funeral, *Jet Magazine*, on September 15, 1955, carried graphic images of Emmett's mutilated body. Subsequent coverage was widespread, sometimes in serialized stories. Following the trial, *Look Magazine* paid $4,000 to Roy Bryant and J.W. Milam for their account of what had really happened. The story ran on January 24, 1956.[55]

Both men admitted kidnapping, torturing, and killing Emmett Till. The writer of the article had covered the trial for *Look*. He introduced this sometimes-rambling account with a note:

> In the long history of man's inhumanity to man, racial conflict has produced some of the most horrible examples of brutality. The recent slaying of Emmett Till in Mississippi is a case in point. The editors of *Look* are convinced that they are presenting here, for the first time, the real story of that killing—the story no jury heard and no newspaper reader saw.

J.W. Milam was satisfied with *Look's* portrayal. Reportedly smiling as he talked to a newsman after the article appeared, "I'll say one thing for the article, it was written from a Mississippi viewpoint. I've gotten a lot of letters from people commending me for what *Look* did."[56]

The published graphic photos, made possible by Emmett's mother's decision to let the world see what had happened to her son, coupled with widespread media coverage of the killing, the subsequent perfunctory trial and acquittal in the face of clear guilt, and the callous response of those responsible, struck a deep chord of revulsion. Life should be protected. It had not been. Suffering should be alleviated. It had been inflicted.

A clearer example of the exclusionary, dehumanizing consequences of deeming some lives less worthy of support and protection could hardly be found. Such events were accumulating, and Emmett Till's death, in jarring detail, clarified issues and deepened a sense of injustice. It provided one of several immediate sparks that would ignite a soon-to-be powerful civil rights movement.

Reform Efforts Coalesce

On a Thursday evening, December 1, 1955, a few months after Emmett Till's brutal murder had been widely discussed, the still struggling, but now reenergized Civil Rights Movement gained further momentum in

Montgomery, Alabama, when a volunteer secretary for the Montgomery chapter of the NAACP boarded a bus to go home after a day of work at a local department store. Rosa Parks was tired. She was asked to get up to release her seat for a white rider. She refused.

Rosa had long experienced the humiliating irritations of being asked to move to the back of the bus. She was involved in growing efforts to protest such treatment. Her husband had been working for some time in the legal battles to free the Scottsboro Boys, putting his own life in danger.[57] Riding the bus after work, Rosa later would recall how she thought back on the times when her grandfather would keep his gun within easy reach for protection. She thought also of Emmett Till, the teenage boy from Chicago who had been visiting his relatives in Money, Mississippi. Writing of her experiences, Rosa Parks would state,

> People always say that I didn't give up my seat because I was tired, but that isn't true. I was not tired physically, or no more tired than I usually was at the end of a working day . . . No, the only tired I was, was tired of giving in.[58]

The soft-spoken, steel-willed Rosa Parks would soon become a household name. She was not alone. Also in Montgomery at the time was a young, soon to be 27-year-old, largely unknown minister, Martin Luther King, Jr. He would be elected as president of the Montgomery Improvement Association, and a year later would help establish the Southern Christian Leadership Conference. He would soon rise to international prominence and deep historical importance.

The breadth and depth of the social movement set in motion would reach far beyond the tragedy of lynchings and the injustices of capital-punishment trials. Concern over a broadly held exclusionary mindset, however, would remain at the root of the movement. Among many, both black and white, there was growing fatigue with the dehumanizing policies and treatment that greeted marginalized persons in many ways, every day.

Any exclusionary system of laws that allowed, even encouraged, such callous disregard for life and suffering was no law at all. The broad-based movement for change increased in intensity, sometimes with violence of its own. Among the many reforms pursued were those aimed at arbitrary and capricious procedures of capital-punishment trials, wherein sham procedures allowed clearly guilty persons to go free, offering little or no protection for those deemed less worthy. Laws allowing, even encouraging, these outcomes lacked legitimacy. They needed to be changed. A powerful campaign to do so was launched.

Notes

1   Examples abound: Justice Brennan's oft-quoted comment in *Furman v. Georgia*: "The calculated killing of a human being by the State involves, by its very nature, a denial of the executed person's humanity." See: Robert M. Cover, "Violence and the Word," *The Yale Law Journal* 95 (1986); Charles L. Black, Jr., *Festschrift*, 1601–29. Albert Bandura, "Moral Disengagement in the Perpetration of Inhumanities," *Personality and Social Psychology Review* 3 (1999): 193–209. Dov Cohen and Richard E. Nisbett, "Self-Protection and the Culture of Honor: Explaining Southern Violence," *Personality and Social Psychology Bulletin* 20 (1994): 551–67.

2   See, in particular, Donald Black, (1976) *The Behavior of Law* (New York: Academic Press, 1976).

3   NAACP, *Thirty Years of Lynching in the United States (1889–1918)* (NAACP, 1919). Arthur F. Raper, *The Tragedy of Lynching* (Chapel Hill, NC: University of North Carolina Press, 1933). Ralph Ginzburg, *100 Years of Lynchings* (Baltimore: Black Classic Press, 1962). Stewart E. Tolnay and E.M. Beck, *A Festival of Death* (Urbana, IL: University of Illnois Press, 1995). W. Fitzhugh, Ed., *Under Sentence of Death: Lynching in the South* (Chapel Hill, NC: North Carolina Press, 1997).

4   James Elbert Cutler, *Lynch-Law: An Investigation into the History of Lynching in the United States* (1905, reprint, Montclair, NJ: Patterson Smith, 1969).

5   Cutler, *Lynch-Law*, 2–3.

6   The Longview, Texas, *Times Clarion*, quoted in James W. Marquart, Sheldon Ekland-Olson, and Jonathan R. Sorensen, *The Rope, the Chair, and the Needle* (Austin, TX: University of Texas Press, 1994), 7.

7   Cited in Mary White Ovington, *The Walls Came Tumbling Down* (New York: Schocken Books, 1947), 100.

8   See Robert L. Zangrando, (1980) *The NAACP Crusade Against Lynching 1909–1950* (Philadelphia: Temple University Press, 1980).

9   *Congressional Record*, 65 Congress, 2 Session, LVI (April 19, 1918), 5362.

10 Cited in NAACP, *Thirty Years of Lynching*, 5.

11 These words were used to dedicate an edited book of articles on the topic, published in 1925. Alain Locke, Ed., *The New Negro: An Interpretation* (New York: Albert & Charles Boni, 1925).

12 NAACP, *Thirty Years of Lynching*, 5.

13 NAACP, *Thirty Years of Lynching*, 8, 11, and 28.

14 See for example: "For Action on Race Riot Peril," *New York Times*, October 5 (1919).

15 *A Man Called White* (1948; reprint, Viking Press and University of Georgia Press, 1995), 44.

16 First-hand reports of the events in Phillips County come from newspaper accounts, the trial record, the writings of Walter White, who traveled to Arkansas to investigate, and a subsequent Supreme Court decision released in February, 1923. For contemporary summaries, see, "The Real Causes of Two Race Riots," *The Crisis* 19 (1919): 56–62. *Moore v. Dempsey*, 261 U.S. 86 (1923). Ida B. Wells-Barnett, *The Arkansas Race Riot* (Chicago: 1920). For later, well-documented histories see: Richard Cortner, *A Mob Intent on Death: The NAACP and the Arkansas Riot Cases* (Middletown, CT: Weskean University Press, 1988); Grif Stockley, *Blood in Their Eyes: The Elaine Race Massacres of 1919* (Fayetteville, AR: The University of Arkansas Press, 2001); and Robert Whitaker, *On the Laps of Gods: The Red Summer of 1919 and the Struggle for Justice That Remade a Nation* (New York: Crown Publishing Group, Random House, 2008).

17 Walter F. White, *A Man Called White*, 48.

18 See, Grif Stockley, *Blood in Their Eyes: The Elaine Race Massacres of 1919* (Fayetteville, AR: The University of Arkansas Press, 2001), chap. 3.

19 *A Man Called White*, 48.

20 See chronology of events in Grif Stockley, *Blood in Their Eyes: The Elaine Race Massacres of 1919* (Fayetteville, AR: The University of Arkansas Press, 2001).

21 *Moore v. Dempsey*, 261 U.S. 86 (1923), 87.

22 Quoted in Robert Whitaker, *On the Laps of Gods: The Red Summer of 1919 and the Struggle for Justice That Remade a Nation* (New York: Crown Publishing Group, Random House).

23 Quoted in Whitaker, *On the Laps of Gods*, 118.

24 Stockley, *Blood in Their Eyes*, xiv.

25 *New York Times*, October 6 (1919).

26 *Moore et al. v. Dempsey*, 261 U.S. 86 (1923), 88.

27 See: Cortner, *A Mob Intent on Death*; Whitaker, *On the Laps of Gods*.

28 See Walter F. White, "' Massacring Whites' in Arkansas," *The Nation*, 109 (1919): 715–16.

29 Cited in Stockley, *Blood in Their Eyes*, 197. For further detailed accounts of the measures used, see Whitaker, *On the Laps of Gods*, chap. 9.

30 Whitaker, *On the Laps of Gods*, 175.

31 Whitaker, *On the Laps of Gods*, 176.

32 *Slaughter-House Cases*, 83 U.S. 36 (1873), *United States v. Cruikshank*, 92 U.S. 542 (1875), *Hodges v. United States*, 203 U.S. 1 (1906), and *Frank v. Magnum*, 237 U.S. 309 (1915).

33 *U.S. v. Shipp*, 214 U.S. 386 (1909) See Mark Curriden, "A Supreme Case of Contempt: A Tragic Legal Saga Paved the Way for Civil Rights Protections and Federal Habeas Actions," *ABA Journal*, June (2009); available online at: www.abajournal.com/magazine/a_supreme_case_of_contempt/.

34 For an interesting account of this at times contentious connection between the NAACP and the Arkansas lawyers, see Whitaker, *On the Laps of Gods*, chap. 10; Stockley, *Blood in Their Eyes*, chap. 6.

35 *Moore et al. v. Dempsey*, 261 U.S. 86 (1923).

36 Whitaker, *On the Laps of Gods*, 312.

37   In the years just ahead, Holmes would write in more exclusionary language in *Buck v. Bell*.

38   *Furman v. Georgia*, 408 U.S. 238 (1972).

39   These and the statistics that follow come from the records kept by the Tuskegee Institute.

40   See: http://users.bestweb.net/~rg/lynching_century.htm and www.ojp.usdoj.gov/bjs/glance/exe.htm.

41   See: James W. Marquart, Sheldon Ekland-Olson, and Jonathan R. Sorensen, *The Rope, the Chair, and the Needle* (Austin, TX: University of Texas Press, 1994).

42   The electric chair had been first adopted in New York in 1890. By 1920, 15 states had established an electric chair to carry out executions. In 1924, Florida and Georgia passed similar laws to Texas.

43   "Midnight Appeal Causes Pause in Harvest of Death," *Austin American Statesman*, February 8 (1924): 1.

44   Jacquelyn Dowd Hall, *Revolt Against Chivalry: Jessie Daniel Ames and the Women's Campaign Against Lynching* (New York: Columbia University Press, 1974), 130.

45   Hall, *Revolt Against Chivalry*.

46   Quoted in Hall, *Revolt Against Chivalry*, 162.

47   Quoted in Hall, *Revolt Against Chivalry*, 194.

48   David Aretha, *The Civil Rights Movement: The Trial of the Scottsboro Boys* (Greensboro, NC: Morgan Reynolds Publishing, 2008), 11–12.

49   See, *Powell v. Alabama*, 287 U.S. 45 (1932); Dan Carter, (1979) *A Tragedy of the American South* (Baton Rouge, LA: Louisiana State University Press, 1979). James R. Acker, *Scottsboro and its Legacy* (Westport, CT: Praeger Publishers 2008); Aretha, *The Civil Rights Movement*.

50   Aretha, *The Civil Rights Movement*, 17.

51   *Powell v. Alabama*, 287 U.S. 45 (1932).

52   Important among these decisions was *Norris v. Alabama*, 294 U.S. 587 (1935), argued on February 15 and 18, 1935, and decided April 1, 1935. It held that the systematic exclusion of Negroes from juries was a violation of equal-protection provisions in the Constitution.

53   This and quotes that follow, unless otherwise specified, come from Mamie Till-Mobley and Christopher Benson, *Death of Innocence: The Story of the Hate Crime That Changed America* (New York: Ballentine Books, 2003), chaps. 11 and 12.

54   Stephen J. Whitfield, *A Death in the Delta: The Story of Emmett Till* (Baltimore: Johns Hopkins Press, 1988); Till-Mobley and Benson, *Death of Innocence*. For a summary, see: www.pbs.org/wgbh/amex/till/timeline/timeline2.html.

55   Two days after the *Look* article appeared, *The California Eagle* began a five-part story that would run from January 26 through February 23. See also, *Life Magazine* photos: www.life.com/image/52757602/in-gallery/23001/civil-rights-emmett-tills-murder.

56   Quoted in Amos Dixon, "The Truth, the Whole Truth," *The California Eagle*, January 26 (1956).

57   Rosa Parks with Jim Haskins, *Rosa Parks: My Story* (New York: Puffin Books, 1992), 60–71.

58   Rosa Parks with Jim Haskins, *Rosa Parks*, 116.

CHAPTER 15

A CAMPAIGN TO STOP
THE EXECUTIONS

The profound injustices so readily evident in the lynchings of the early twentieth century, the perfunctory trials and convictions of the Scottsboro Boys, and the unpunished torture and murder of young Emmett Till did not go unnoticed. These and similar events formed a motivating backdrop for questioning the legitimacy of capital punishment and for launching a campaign for its abolition.

A Sense of Injustice and Questioned Legitimacy

The attorney most frequently identified as the architect of the campaign to challenge and eventually abolish capital punishment was Tony Amsterdam. He would later recall,

> I think that in the minds of everyone [involved in the NAACP's Legal Defense Fund (LDF) efforts to abolish capital punishment] the Scottsboro Boys trial stood as a constant background symbol of "Judge Lynch"—the constant danger of perversion of the criminal justice system into an instrument of oppression and subordination of African Americans.

Amsterdam continued:

> Lou Pollak was an adviser to LDF in a lot of its projects; his father, Walter, had been one of the Scottsboro Boys' lawyers;

Lou's presence was something of a reminder of those cases. It was because the Scottsboro Boys cases had demonstrated the need to go to the defense of African Americans charged with capital crimes against whites that LDF was still sending lawyers into that breach in the early 60s; that tradition led us into the cases that, in turn, turned into the campaign against the death penalty.[1]

As the initial sequence of trials for the Scottsboro Boys drew to a close in 1937, the Carnegie Corporation decided to commission a study of what many saw as a deeply flawed moral–legal system in the United States, and in particular what had come to be called the Negro problem. A prominent Swedish economist, Gunnar Myrdal, was chosen to lead the effort. He began his work in 1938, combing through statistics and government reports and interviewing schoolteachers, clergy, academics, journalists, and others across the United States. Six years later, he published *An American Dilemma: The Negro Problem and Modern Democracy*.

Myrdal's findings and message were by this time familiar. Five years before the project began, in 1933, James Weldon Johnson, a prominent leader of the NAACP, had published his autobiography, *Along This Way*. Included in the events that had shaped his thinking was the time he had been asked to investigate a particularly gruesome burning of a black man in Memphis, Tennessee. There had been no trial. A large crowd, estimated to be 5,000 men, women, and children, had watched. As they dispersed, some were heard complaining, "They burned him too fast." Reflecting on this experience, Johnson recalled,

> I tried to balance the sufferings of the miserable victim against the moral degradation of Memphis, and the truth flashed over me that in large measure the race question involves the saving of black America's body and white America's soul.[2]

Myrdal's conclusions would echo Johnson's assessment time and time again. *An American Dilemma* was a thorough, wide-ranging and voluminous report.[3] It became one of the most influential pieces of social-science research of the twentieth century, and the Carnegie Corporation would eventually consider its grant to Myrdal among the most important it had ever given. Indeed, in the decade after World War II, those seeking a more inclusive society in the United States built on Myrdal's work to construct a case headed for the Supreme Court, *Brown v. Board of Education*, in which the long-standing, separate-but-equal doctrine justifying exclusionary practices and an unyielding sense of Us and Them would be overturned.

The injustices of an exclusionary society, so carefully documented by Myrdal, and underscored in *Brown*, were pervasive. Mountains of evidence, found in virtually every corner of life, demonstrated that the lives of those standing on one side of the racial and ethnic divide were considered less worthy of support and protection than those standing on the other. When it came to the administration of criminal justice, Myrdal wrote:

> The Negroes . . . are hurt in their trust that the law is impartial, that the court and the police are their protection, and, indeed, that they belong to an orderly society which has set up this machinery for common security and welfare. They will not feel confidence in, and loyalty toward, a legal order which is entirely out of their control and which they sense to be inequitable and merely part of the system of caste suppression. Solidarity then develops easily in the Negro group, a solidarity against the law and the police.[4]

Just as supply responds to demand, legitimacy rises and falls with a sense of injustice. A sense of injustice and the consequent withdrawal of legitimacy have powerful implications.[5] Law's legitimacy provides a reservoir of trust in, and support for, a community's institutions, especially important during times of crises and uncertainty. When absent, instability follows. In these circumstances, social movements designed to bring about change are likely to emerge.

As the Civil Rights Movement moved through its most unsettling days, charges of injustice and the withdrawal of legitimacy were readily evident. Of particular concern were the injustices found in the coercive power of the state.[6] Following the bus boycott in Montgomery, Alabama, protests escalated. They were met with force. Coercive actions accompanied by a sense of injustice become an illegitimate exercise of naked power.[7] Many would shout loud and long that the use of force against civil-rights protesters was just such an exercise. Among those protesting was a young activist minister. In April 1963, Martin Luther King, Jr., not yet 35 years old, found himself in jail for disobeying the dehumanizing, exclusionary policies and laws he saw all around.

Writing from his Birmingham jail cell, addressing most directly his fellow clergymen, the now widely recognized leader of increasingly frequent civil-rights protests and demonstrations turned to Saint Augustine for support:

> One may ask, "How can you advocate breaking some laws and obeying others?" The answer is found in the fact that there are two types of laws: There are *just* and there are *unjust* laws. I would agree with Saint Augustine that "Any unjust law is no law at all."

Protest followed protest, as the growing sense of injustice and illegitimacy gained momentum. Only weeks after King's widely distributed letter was written, fire hoses and police dogs were turned loose on Birmingham protesters. Images of these actions further awakened a national sense of injustice, galvanizing the withdrawal of legitimacy among a broad array of citizens committed to achieving a more inclusive society.

In June 1963, the month following the Birmingham protest, Medgar Evars, who had attempted to desegregate the University of Mississippi Law School in 1954, a 37-year-old man (he would have turned 38 in July) who at the time was the field secretary for the NAACP, was shot in the back as he got out of his car in his home driveway in Jackson, Mississippi. It would not be until some 30 years later, in February 1994, that a conviction of this assailant was secured.

Shortly before he was shot, Medgar Evars had been investigating the death of Emmett Till. Traveling with him one night in the backwoods of Mississippi was the author, James Baldwin. Two years earlier, in 1961, Baldwin had published *Nobody Knows My Name*, which included his reflections on growing up in Harlem. They echoed Myrdal's conclusions, the claims of Martin Luther King, Jr., and the experiences of Medgar Evars. Baldwin told of how, in his experience, Harlem policemen were like occupying soldiers "in a bitterly hostile country; which is precisely what, and where he is, and is the reason he walks in twos and threes."[8]

Baldwin would soon also write about the night he spent with his friend Medgar Evars, talking with local residents in rural Mississippi. He saw parallels to his experiences in Harlem. It was like traveling in an occupied country.

> Many people talked to Medgar that night, in dark cabins, with their lights out, in whispers; and we had been followed for many miles out of Jackson, Mississippi, not by a lunatic with a gun, but by state troopers. I will never forget that night, as I will never forget Medgar—who took me to the plane the next day. We promised to see each other soon.[9]

After his friend was shot, James Baldwin decided to complete a play he had been working on for some time. *Blues for Mister Charlie* was based on the murder of Emmett Till. Once completed, Baldwin wrote in the preface of the impact of Medgar's death:

> Something entered into me which I cannot describe, but it was then that I resolved that nothing under heaven would prevent me from getting this play done. We are walking in terrible darkness here, and this is one man's attempt to bear witness to the reality and the power of light.

Blues for Mister Charlie was dedicated to the memory of Medgar Evars, his widow and children, and to the memory of "the dead children of Birmingham."

Two-and-a-half months after Medgar Evars was shot, light for the terrible darkness also came from another source. On August 28, 1963, Martin Luther King inspired the country with his "I Have a Dream" speech on the steps of the Lincoln Memorial. "Now is the time," King told the crowd of some 200,000, "to rise from the dark and desolate valley of segregation to the sunlit path of racial justice. Now is the time to lift our nation from the quick sands of racial injustice to the solid rock of brotherhood. Now is the time to make justice a reality for all of God's children."

There was common ground on which God's children walked. The state's policies, laws, and actions, taking life and inflicting suffering, negated this common humanity. While urging nonviolent, patient, and tenacious commitment, King also wanted no one to miss the "fierce urgency of now." "There will be neither rest nor tranquility in America until the Negro is granted his citizenship rights. The whirlwinds of revolt will continue to shake the foundations of our nation until the bright day of justice emerges."

When should their efforts cease? King answered,

> We can never be satisfied as long as the Negro is the victim of the unspeakable horrors of police brutality. We can never be satisfied, as long as our bodies, heavy with the fatigue of travel, cannot gain lodging in the motels of the highways and the hotels of the cities . . . No, no, we are not satisfied, and we will not be satisfied until justice rolls down like waters and righteousness like a mighty stream.

It was a powerful speech. It moved a nation. It also provoked anger and fear. Two weeks later, again in Birmingham, four young girls, the children to whom James Baldwin dedicated his play seven months later, died when a bomb exploded while they were attending Sunday school on September 15, 1963. Two months later, President Kennedy was assassinated. Over the coming years, additional riots broke out, protests continued, and others were murdered.

Even in the face of this climate of reciprocated violence, however, the Civil Rights Movement became a powerful force for nonviolent change. Ten months after the bombing of the Birmingham church, on July 2, President Johnson signed the Civil Rights Act of 1964 into law. It struck directly at the heart of the dehumanizing, exclusionary policies, practices, and laws then so apparent. It marked important progress toward a more inclusive society. There remained, however, the glaring and dehumanizing legacy of lynchings, still evidenced in a disturbing pattern of state-sanctioned executions of black men for the rape and even attempted rape of white women.

Remaining Legacy of a Misguided Chivalry

In the midst of the deeply troubling, yet hope-inspiring events of 1963, a small group of lawyers and social scientists, organized by the NAACP and the LDF, began to plot a course to eliminate capital punishment from the life of the nation. Efforts were based on a deep sense of well-documented injustice. The LDF lawyers were convinced that, "By 1963," as a member of the legal team would later recall, "capital punishment in the United States was in good measure arbitrarily applied, infrequently employed, and of questionable utility."[10] For the director-counsel of the NAACP LDF, this assessment had been long building. "One of the first cases I became involved in (end of 1949, beginning 1950 and onwards)," Jack Greenberg recalled, "was known as 'Groveland,'[11] named after a community in which an alleged crime occurred. Four young blacks were charged with rape of a white woman. One was killed while hunted by police, one killed by the sheriff en route to trial, one sentenced to life imprisonment, one sentenced to death but after a lengthy effort his sentence was commuted."

"Another early case," Greenberg continued, "was that of a black man executed for rape of which I'm confident he was innocent. He happened to have been circumcised shortly before the alleged crime. It would have been physically impossible (or nearly so) for him to have committed the crime. 90 percent plus of those executed for rape were blacks accused of having raped whites. I vowed that if I could I would end that some day."[12]

In 1963, that day had come. The injustice Jack Greenberg and his colleagues saw was widely shared, but LDF resources were limited. They had to focus. What Jessie Daniel Ames and the women she mobilized had labeled a peculiar chivalry is what particularly disturbed them. It had long justified the taking of life in cases involving a black defendant and the rape of a white woman. This is where they would start.

Statistics coming from the Department of Justice clearly suggested a problem. Although the dramatic patterns were most evident in the south, they were found throughout the nation. Over the years, there had been 455 executions for rape. Of these, 405 (90 percent) had involved black defendants. These data would later be expanded and refined, confirming the dramatic differential in executions for rape and an even sharper discriminatory pattern for attempted rape. Of the 98 persons executed in the United States for crimes involving an attempted rape, but no murder, all but three were black defendants.[13]

Although capital cases involving rape, with particular attention paid to black defendants charged with raping a white woman, were the first priority for LDF lawyers, as their work progressed they soon broadened their strategy. They decided to defend murderers as well as rapists, whites as well as blacks, all across the country. As a lead attorney for this now broad-based effort would later put it, "We said, 'What the hell! Are we going to let these guys die?' It was like somebody was bleeding in the gutter when you've got a tourniquet." At that point, "We were in the execution-stopping business."[14]

The now-expanded aim became to create a crisis of litigation, "one that was discussed, attracted attention and, in a more immediate way than in the past, affected the work lives of the judges and prison officials who administered it."[15] "We were living in the demands of our times," Michael Meltsner would recall, "which meant capital cases with racial issues of other pressing constitutional claims dumped on our desks. We were probably all abolitionists before then, if you took a survey, but none that I know of had become an abolitionist activist, until after the legal cases were brought . . . We had to do this because we could. That may sum it up best."[16]

Over the course of the next nine years, starting in 1963, a small band of litigating reformers would expand into a nationwide network representing over 300 death-row inmates. Their objective was simple—a national moratorium on all executions.

A Campaign is Launched

There was reason to believe success was within reach. Executions in the United States had been declining for years. The five-year average for the highest point, 1935–39, had been 178. By 1945–49, this yearly average was 128. By 1955–59, it was down to 61. In 1963, when the LDF lawyers launched their initial efforts, the number had fallen to 21. Two years later, as the network of litigating lawyers broadened and reform efforts gained steam, the number of executions was seven. There would be one execution in 1966 and two in 1967, the last one in June. In 1968 there were none.[17]

Capital punishment laws, however, remained on the books. The moratorium on executions did not mean an end to death sentences. Trials were held, convictions secured, and persons continued to arrive on death rows across the country. In the early 1960s, the number of inmates on the nation's death rows passed 500. By 1968, the first year when executions fell to zero, the reported daily average of death row inmates was 517. By 1971, the year prior to a landmark Supreme Court decision that would change the legal landscape, this daily average had risen to 642, with a year-end total of just under 700.[18]

These were the numbers LDF lawyers and a growing number of colleagues across the country considered as they pursued remedies for perceived injustices. Jack Greenberg had graduated from Columbia Law School some 15 years prior to the launching of the campaign in 1963. As a young lawyer, he had been intimately involved in the preparation of the *Brown v. Board of Education* case, and had succeeded Thurgood Marshall as chief counsel for the NAACP when President Kennedy appointed Marshall to the Second Circuit Court of Appeals in 1961.

In October of 1963, Greenberg received "what could only be called an invitation to start attacking capital punishment."[19] It came from Justice Arthur Goldberg, who disagreed with his Supreme Court colleagues' refusal to review a case involving the conviction of a black man sentenced to death in Alabama for rape.[20] Justice Goldberg thought the case should be reviewed because it involved "a convicted rapist who [had] neither taken nor endangered human life."

Was the taking of human life in such circumstances, Goldberg wondered, "consistent with the constitutional proscription against punishments which by their excessive severity are greatly disproportioned to the offenses charged"? Couching his thinking in constitutional terms, Golberg asked, were such practices consistent with "evolving standards of decency that mark the progress of our maturing society?" Could legitimate aims of punishment be achieved "as effectively by punishing rape less severely than by death?" If so, did a death sentence in such cases constitute "unnecessary cruelty?" Pointing to punishments once accepted but now abhorrent, Goldberg noted that opinions change over time. Given evolving standards of decency, the time had come, Goldberg argued with support from two other justices, to call into question the constitutional acceptability of removing the protective boundaries of life for crimes where life was not taken.

Jack Greenberg did not miss the import of Justice Goldberg's concerns. Here was a justice of the Supreme Court outlining a road map for a possible attack on capital punishment. Writing years later, Greenberg recalled, "[Goldberg's] opinion signaled that the time to launch the effort had arrived. Shortly afterward, I announced to the board that we would launch a full-scale attack on capital punishment for rape. By mid-decade, we had seventeen cases."[21]

Greenberg asked a young attorney, Anthony Amsterdam, to join the effort. Amsterdam was a 1960 graduate of the University of Pennsylvania Law School, where he had been editor-in-chief of the *Pennsylvania Law Review*. Because Greenberg and Amsterdam knew that systematic data collection and analysis would be needed if they were to succeed, they sought expertise of another kind. A social-science colleague at the University of Pennsylvania, Marvin Wolfgang, seemed to be the perfect person to join their efforts. In 1958, still in his early 30s, Wolfgang had published, to wide acclaim, *Patterns in Criminal Homicide*. He recognized the importance of carefully collected and analyzed data. He was well versed in the issues of capital punishment, having just published an article on differential death sentencing patterns the previous year.[22] In addition, he was sympathetic to the LDF's reform efforts.

Together, Greenberg, Amsterdam, and Wolfgang became a formidable team to lead the charge. They were joined by a contingent of lawyers that eventually grew into an informally organized, nationwide network. The first task was to systematically collect data on executions for rape in the former Confederacy. For this, they needed help. In the spring of 1965, they approached the Law Students Civil Rights Research Council (LSCRRC) for assistance. This multiracial group of law students had been founded two years earlier with the explicit purpose of supporting the Civil Rights Movement.[23] In June, Marvin Wolfgang and his colleagues brought a group of LSCRRC students who were interested in summer internships to the University of Pennsylvania in Philadelphia for orientation and training.

During the summer, some 28 interns were trained to collect information, covering the previous three decades, on rape cases in 12 southern states.[24] They were given a 28-page data-collection form, with explicit instructions on how to record information from court records, newspaper accounts, lawyers' files, and interviews with actual participants. The list of factors was long. The aim was to ferret out explanations other than blatant discrimination that might account for the widely recognized disproportionate execution of black defendants.[25]

Each student received a geographic assignment, along with a list of friendly local contacts, should they need assistance. As the training drew to an end, one student remarked, "I feel as if we're parachuting behind enemy lines."[26] The seven-year journey leading to the landmark case, *Furman v. Georgia*,[27] had begun. Over the summer, the rape-case data were collected. In the fall, Professor Wolfgang enlisted a group of graduate students to begin the analysis. Transferring the data to punch cards for computer analysis would take time. Death penalties continued to be imposed. Fortunately for the now focused reformers, the Supreme Court, building on the *Moore* and *Powell* decisions, had expanded the bases for appeals. The time between conviction and execution had been rising in recent years.[28] What had been days and then weeks had become months and frequently years. Still, the time pressures were real. Getting the data in shape for analysis was a time-consuming, labor-intensive task. Priorities were set by the appeals being pursued.

An early case came from Arkansas. It involved a black man in his early 20s, William L. ("Willie Lee") Maxwell. Maxwell had been convicted in Hot Springs, Arkansas, for the 1961 rape of a 35-year-old white woman. The case had moved forward through several appeals, including an unsuccessful trip to the U.S. Supreme Court in 1965, just as the LSCRRC students began collecting data.[29] Maxwell was scheduled to die on September 2, 1966. In early August of that year, LDF lawyers convinced a judge to review the data they had collected. Perhaps overwhelmed by the sheer volume of the information, there was no objection from the other side.[30]

The appellate hearing began on August 22. Marvin Wolfgang had been working with his colleagues, rehearsing how to best present the sometimes complex and frequently mind-numbing statistics. When called upon to testify, he reported that, after statistically adjusting for a multitude of contending explanations, the data were compelling. The discriminatory punishment of blacks in Arkansas for the crime of rape was clear. It was very unlikely that these findings were due to random chance. Put in lay terms, if race was not systematically related to receiving a death sentence for rape in Arkansas, the results observed would have occurred by chance in only two or fewer similar time frames since the birth of Christ.[31]

The judge was listening, though not altogether sympathetic. He was impressed by, and accepted, Wolfgang's findings, but still he had questions.

The alternative explanations Wolfgang had considered were numerous, but not exhaustive. Racial discrimination was a subtle process. Statistical patterns did not define actions taken in this particular case. Besides, the judge concluded, in a statement that must have made Marvin Wolfgang cringe, "Statistics are elusive things at best, and it is a truism that almost anything can be proven by them."[32] On Friday, August 26, 1966, the judge dismissed the petition and declined to stay Maxwell's execution. It would proceed as planned the following week.

Tony Amsterdam and his colleagues persisted and petitioned the Eighth Circuit Court. They hit a brick wall. There would be no rehearing. Maxwell's execution would not be postponed while further appeals were pursued. Time was now running very short, as the execution was scheduled for Friday. Three LDF attorneys flew to Washington, DC, to file a request for a stay of execution with the U.S. Supreme Court. Here, the outcome was positive. Just days before William L. Maxwell was to be executed, the Eighth Circuit was told by the Supreme Court that issues raised by LDF attorneys regarding sentencing guidelines for juries, the structure of the trial, and the exclusion of jurors who expressed reservations about the imposition of capital punishment were important. A stay of execution should be granted while these issues were resolved.

LDF lawyers knew of many similar cases across the country. With the decision from the nation's highest court in hand, they now had the criteria on which their appeals could proceed. They acted quickly. The aim was to secure a stay on all executions in the country. Driven by both tactical and moral concerns, Amsterdam worked with a newly hired graduate of Harvard Law School, Jack Himmelstein, to create what came to be known as the "Last Aid Kit." As Amsterdam would later put it,

> We needed form documents to (1) ship out to lawyers all across the U.S. who were handling cases which were approaching an execution date and (2) enable us to move into new cases quickly ourselves if there were no other lawyers capable of handling the case.[33]

Following the flurry of activity surrounding Willie Lee Maxwell's case, it took until June 11, 1968, almost two years, to secure a decision from the Eighth Circuit. Judge Harry Blackmun wrote the opinion. He was writing in tumultuous years. Civil-rights demonstrations were in full swing. The 1967 Six-Day War in Israel had concluded almost exactly a year prior. Opposition to the war in Viet Nam was mounting. The Reverend Martin Luther King, Jr. had been fatally shot just two months earlier on April 4, 1968, and Senator Robert Kennedy had been assassinated on June 5, the previous Wednesday. LDF lawyers might be fighting to abolish capital punishment, but on many other fronts, calls for law and order and tough action on crime were being increasingly heard.

Judge Blackmun first concentrated on the most prominent assertion of injustice—that death sentences for rape were racially biased. Having received a mathematics degree as an undergraduate, Blackmun was perhaps comfortable with statistical arguments. Although impressed with Wolfgang's data, he rejected the associated legal claims. Statistics dealt with averages and patterns of behavior. They did not go directly to the question of whether this particular defendant had been discriminated against.

It should be noted, Blackmun wrote,

> whatever suspicion [statistical evidence] may arouse with respect to Southern interracial rape trials as a group over a long period of time, and whatever it may disclose with respect to other localities, we feel that the statistical argument does nothing to destroy the integrity of Maxwell's trial.

"Improper state practice of the past," Blackmun continued, "does not automatically invalidate a procedure of the present." Moreover, he wrote, "We are not yet ready to condemn and upset the result reached in every case of a Negro rape defendant in the State of Arkansas on the basis of broad theories of social and statistical injustice."[34]

Blackmun closed his written opinion, however, with an unusual personal note, not signed by his Eighth Circuit colleagues. Removing the protective boundaries of life so an individual could be executed was for him "excruciating." He was "not personally convinced of the rightness of capital punishment." He questioned the collective-good justifications for capital punishment as an effective deterrent. Capital punishment was, however, "a policy matter ordinarily to be resolved by the legislature or through executive clemency and not by the judiciary."[35] This would not be the last time Blackmun and Amsterdam would engage one another on when, by whom, and through what procedures life's protective boundaries should be removed. Nor would it be the last time Judge Harry Blackmun would be bothered by his own decisions.

Judge Blackmun's personally excruciating 1968 decision was appealed to the Supreme Court. It was decided on June 1, 1970.[36] By this time, President Nixon had appointed Blackmun, after two initial nominations had failed, to the U.S. Supreme Court. Justice Blackmun did not participate in the appeal of the case he had decided, but would take his seat on the court the following week.[37]

By this time, the sense of injustice was intense. Whatever the justification for the taking of life, whatever the constraints on judicial action, whatever the structure of the trial, or the selection of jurors, there was very little doubt that capital-punishment trials for rape were yielding highly discriminatory results.[38] For many, it was this deep sense of injustice that drove them forward. How could the taking of life by the state, so blatantly infused with inequitable application, be seen as anything but an illegitimate exercise of naked power?

Tony Amsterdam presented his final argument for William Maxwell to the Supreme Court on May 4, 1970. Many were waiting for the Court's answer. Since the call for a review of William L. Maxwell's case in 1966, several states had declared moratoria on executions, awaiting the Supreme Court's decision. Capital-punishment trials and convictions, however, continued. As a result, over 500 condemned persons waited on death row. Some 67 petitions for hearing were pending before the Supreme Court as Amsterdam began his presentation.

If blatantly discriminatory outcomes would not move the court, Amsterdam began, perhaps arguments based on flawed procedures would. There were three problems. They related to standards used by jurors, the structure of the trial, and the manner in which jurors were selected. In the first instance, it seemed self-evident that, when removing the protective boundaries of life, juries should be given appropriate guidelines. There were none. Jurors were brought in off the street. They had unbridled, unreviewable discretion over whether or not to condemn a man to death. Without standards, Amsterdam argued, there was no rule of law. The taking of life was like the rolling of dice. The outcome depended on the whims and biases of the moment. Emmett Till and the Scottsboro Boys were not-so-distant reminders of what this meant.

In the second instance, Amsterdam argued, justifying the removal of life's protective boundaries should be done on the basis of the act committed. This was the purpose of court proceedings designed to establish guilt. That much was agreed. Given the profoundly important implications of taking life, however, decisions to execute an individual should be reached only after securing full information about the circumstances surrounding the offense, as well as the defendant's background and character. The singular structure of capital-punishment trials in the vast majority of states precluded this. If the defendant's character and background were introduced during the guilt-or-innocence phase of the trial, it would likely be seen as an admission of guilt. Some separate procedure should be established, Amsterdam argued, that did not "whipsaw [a] capital defendant between his privilege against self incrimination and his right to provide the jury with adequate information to make an informed sentencing choice."[39]

Finally, there was the matter of jury selection. In states all across the nation, potential jurors expressing any reservations about imposing capital punishment had been routinely removed from the jury pool. This meant that jurors empaneled were biased in favor of a sentence of death. In 1968, two years prior to the hearing in which Amsterdam was now speaking, the Supreme Court had released a decision declaring this winnowing of jurors unconstitutional.[40] Amsterdam reminded the court of their *Witherspoon v. Illinois* decision and noted such exclusion of jurors was widespread and had occurred in the trial of William Maxwell.

After listening for almost two-and-a-half hours to arguments on both sides and considering the voluminous amount of supporting material, the Supreme Court justices, in a six–one opinion,[41] agreed at least in part with Amsterdam and sent the case back to the trial court for reconsideration. Reiterating its earlier *Witherspoon* decision, the court held,

> A sentence of death cannot be carried out if the jury that imposed or recommended it was chosen by excluding [potential jurors] simply because they voiced general objections to the death penalty or expressed conscientious or religious scruples against its infliction.[42]

courts opinion

The court was silent on Amsterdam's remaining two issues.

Efforts Intensify

It was a narrowly drawn decision, focused only on the manner in which jurors were selected. If juror selection procedures were adjusted, death sentences could be imposed, and executions continue. The lack of death sentencing guidelines and the structure of the trial, which precluded a full examination of the defendant's character and background, remained. Still, William L. Maxwell would receive another trial, as reformers moved ever so slightly toward the goal.

Six months later, on Tuesday, December 22, 1970, there was another positive development. Arkansas Governor Winthrop Rockefeller, in many ways sympathetic with the abolitionist arguments, hosted a group of LDF lawyers, prison officials, and personal aids in Hot Springs to discuss the wisdom of commuting death sentences in Arkansas. Turning to Amsterdam, who had been speaking as the meeting drew to a close, the governor was admiring and appreciative: "Thank you very much," he said. "I had made up my mind, but what you were saying was so interesting that I did not want to interrupt you . . . I have decided to commute them all."[43] A week later, on December 29, 1970, Governor Rockefeller, urging other governors to follow his lead, formally announced the commutation of 15 Arkansas death sentences to life in prison. William L. Maxwell was among them.

For those seeking the abolition of capital punishment, it was a moment to celebrate. The moment was, however, only a moment. A little over four months later, another Supreme Court decision was released on May 3, 1971. It involved two cases, *McGautha v. California* and *Crampton v. Ohio*.[44] These cases raised once again the questions of whether guidelines were needed when juries sentenced a defendant to death, and whether the capital-punishment trial should be split into guilt-or-innocence and punishment phases—questions left unresolved in the court's *Maxwell* decision.

In a six–three opinion, the court decided in the first instance that juries could operate without guidelines. Although guidelines for removing the protective boundaries of life might be helpful, they were not mandatory. As the court put it,

> In light of history, experience, and the present limitations of human knowledge, we find it quite impossible to say that

committing to the untrammeled discretion of the jury the power to pronounce life or death in capital cases is offensive to anything in the Constitution.

Constitutional standards likewise were not violated by trial procedures combining consideration of guilt and punishment, even if defendants were, as Amsterdam had put it, whipsawed between self-incrimination and the right to provide adequate information for an informed sentencing choice.

Following these latter two decisions, Jack Greenberg sensed, "The capital punishment effort looked hopeless."[45] The court had specifically rejected the two remaining mainstays of the LDF's strategy. Although there were over 100 cases on death rows across the country that had been favorably impacted by the court's holding on the biased selection of jurors, this was an issue easily remedied. Once addressed, executions would continue.

Those seeking to abolish capital punishment were now down to a last-ditch effort. Their strategy needed to be adjusted and clarified. A meeting, originally scheduled for nine months later in February, was now to be held just two weeks hence at Columbia University Law School. Interested colleagues from around the country were invited.[46]

The Core Question for a Last-Ditch Effort

The major focus of the LDF strategy had been to attack the legitimacy of procedures used to redefine a free citizen into a person whose life could be taken, but that was all they were—procedures. What about the core question? Was the taking of life for a crime committed ever appropriate, no matter the procedures? The Supreme Court had never directly ruled on this question. Looking forward, however, for those who were working to abolish capital punishment, the prognosis was not good.

There were signs all around that the taking of life for acts committed could be justified under the Constitution. Justice Hugo Black, writing a separate concurring opinion in the Ohio and California cases just decided, went out of his way to say so. It was inconceivable, Black noted, that the framers of the Constitution would consider executions unacceptable. For almost a century, convicted felons had been deemed civilly dead.

Executions for crimes committed had been imposed since the birth of the nation, and long before. On what rationale was capital punishment unconstitutional? He could think of none.

For others, however, it was not so clear. In his dissenting opinion in 1963, Justice Arthur Goldberg had argued just the opposite. Moral systems evolved. They had done so for as long as anyone could tell. Many punishments, once acceptable, were no longer allowed. Jack Greenberg had seen Goldberg's dissent as an invitation to launch the LDF's anti-death penalty crusade. Tony Amsterdam would later note, with a poetic touch, "The Goldberg dissent was an important item on the legal horizon that bounded the playing field on which we made our decisions and plans. It was one peak in a mountain chain whose tops were visible over the horizon."[47]

As the Supreme Court was deliberating their decision in *Maxwell*, now former Justice Goldberg had further elaborated his argument for abolition when he and his former law clerk, Alan Dershowitz, published, "Declaring the death penalty unconstitutional."[48] "We are in the midst of a great national debate over capital punishment," Goldberg and Dershowitz began. "The debate is being carried on in the legislative, executive and judicial chambers of our state and national governments." At issue was whether the nation should take, as Camus had called it, the "great civilizing step" of abolishing the death penalty.

The hoped-for civilizing step, however, would have to be taken as the country was passing through an uncivil time. In recent years, violent crime had risen dramatically. Public opinion polls indicated that the perceived need to control violent behavior was widespread and on the rise. In the mid 1950s, the yearly homicide rate per 100,000 population hovered between 4.0 and 4.2. In the mid 1960s, the rates were closer to 5.0. By the first three years of the 1970s, they were 7.9, 8.6, and 9.0. They had more than doubled over a 20-year period.[49]

Particularly gruesome events had captured the nation's attention. In households across the country, Richard Speck and Charles Manson had become, as brutal murderers, much-discussed demons.[50] Something needed to be done. Even within the LDF, objections to defending such demons were heating up. On one occasion, they boiled over when two secretaries refused to type legal briefs defending a man convicted of brutally raping and fatally stabbing two women, one 60 years old and the other a mother of two, who at the time was five months pregnant with her third child.[51] Why would we not put such demons to death?

Charges were increasingly heard that the courts were part of the problem. They were soft on crime. They had tied the hands of the police. Tougher responses to crime were called for. Public opinion polls indicated increased support for capital punishment. To make matters worse, the nation was engaged in an unpopular war that precipitated violence of a different sort on home soil. Destructive urban riots linked to civil discontent were occurring. The phrase associated with urban rioters, "burn baby burn," had entered the nation's vocabulary.

President Nixon had won the 1968 presidential election with a strong law-and-order, get-tough-on-crime platform. In California and New York, between 1968 and 1970, laws were being considered and passed in support of capital punishment for narcotics peddlers as well as those who killed police officers, firemen, and persons aiding these public servants. Violent offenders were portrayed as a "threatening evil."[52] Life needed to be protected. To protect life, crime and criminals needed to be dealt with, and dealt with harshly. For many, taking life to preserve and protect life seemed quite reasonable.

Still, hesitation remained. Immediately following the clarification of procedural matters in the California and Ohio cases, the governors in those states, along with the governor of Maryland, halted executions, awaiting resolution of the core questions: Was it ever legitimate to take life for acts committed? If the answer was yes, what were the limits?

LDF lawyers felt an increased urgency. As bleak as the prospects were for those who found capital punishment an affront to human dignity, this yet-to-be-resolved core issue provided a small glimmer of hope. They had intended to hold a planning conference in February 1972. It would now take place on May 15 and 16, 1971, some eight months earlier than originally planned. Tony Amsterdam would provide the keynote address. Among the materials distributed to those attending was a revised Last Aid Kit, first put together in 1968. It included advice and updated forms taking into account recent legal developments, along with a listing of related law review articles and a bibliography of relevant books.[53] These materials were useful. Those gathered at Columbia Law School did not wait long to put them to use.

A month later, on June 28, the Supreme Court agreed to review the remaining core question: "Does the imposition and carrying out of the death penalty . . . constitute cruel and unusual punishment, in violation of the Eighth and Fourteenth Amendments?" This was the moment LDF lawyers had been working toward.

After a short delay due to the need to replace Justices Hugo Black and John Harlan—both abruptly resigned from the court for health reasons —arguments were heard. Four cases were being reviewed. One was from California, two from Georgia, and one from Texas. The California State Supreme Court was hearing the California case simultaneously. It involved a particularly gruesome set of facts and a defendant twice convicted of rape and murder. Given the heinous offense involved and the background of the defendant, if the California case were combined with the other three cases, the argument before the U.S. Supreme Court would be diffi-cult. The LDF attorneys were relieved when, even in the face of the extreme nature of the offenses and offender, the California State Supreme Court accepted Amsterdam's argument that capital punishment was degrading, dehumanizing, incompatible with the dignity of man, unneces-sary to any legitimate goal, and therefore in violation of the state's constitution.[54]

This California decision was released a month after oral arguments in the four Supreme Court cases were heard. The California case was separated from the other three, where the charges were much less severe. One was for a murder in Georgia, resulting when a burglar tripped while fleeing after being discovered by the owner of the home. The gun he was carrying went off and killed a member of the household, apparently by accident. The other two cases involved death sentences for rape, one from Georgia and one from Texas. Were these crimes, absent the taking of life, worthy of execution? The stage was thus set for yet another Supreme Court decision. This time, the boundaries of protected life, along with the moral dilemmas associated with their removal, would be explored in great detail.

Arbitrary and Capricious Procedures

It was hard to argue that the Constitution forbade executions, but there was room to note that things change. Clearly, executions had been allowed for a wide range of offenses, but so had whippings, brandings, and the

cutting off of ears. There had been times when boiling in oil and disem-
boweling were also seen as effective deterrents or acceptable retribution, both justifications for inflicting suffering and death. They were no
longer acceptable. Instead, they were repulsive offenses to the dignity of
all humanity, no matter the crime, no matter the impact on future offenses.
Clearly, moral systems evolved over time. The question was: Had the
U.S. evolved to a point where killing individuals for crimes committed
was no longer acceptable?

No clearly defined standards for justifying the infliction of suffering
and death were available. Should persons be executed for stealing live-
stock, for selling drugs, for robbery, for rape, for murder? Were there
circumstances that made these crimes more or less deserving of death?
What standards should be used? Standards depended on subjective
judgments. These clearly varied over time, place, and life circumstance.
Tony Amsterdam, arguing his case before the Supreme Court on January
17, 1972, underscored this well-documented point and drew parallels with
the dramatic decline in executions over the past several decades. Although
not determinative, this trend was as clear as it was important. It suggested
that moral standards had shifted toward the total abolition of capital
punishment.

Even if moral standards justifying capital punishment remained in
place, Amsterdam continued, there was another important matter: there
was ample evidence that the existing procedures for removing the
protective boundaries of life for convicted felons were not even-handed.
An updated version of the Wolfgang study documenting the inequality
of punishment was reintroduced. Capital punishment had been, and continued to be, unpredictably and unevenly applied. Those most vulnerable
were those already on the margins of life. There was a strong racial bias
in the imposition of death sentences, especially in cases involving rape.
Although the Constitution might not prohibit the death penalty per se,
it most certainly did not tolerate such inequality. For reasons of both
equity and evolving moral standards, capital punishment should be
abolished.

This basic rationale was repeated and rebutted several times over, as
the Supreme Court justices listened to oral arguments for four hours.
As the arguments drew to a close, optimism among opponents of capital
punishment was hard to find. Among LDF lawyers, "It was not overstating

the matter to say that a victory for abolition would rank among the greatest surprises in American legal history."[55] Five-and-a-half months later, that surprise came. The Court released *Furman v. Georgia* on June 29, 1972.[56] It was a contentious, five–four decision. There was little agreement, even among justices who reached the same conclusion. The majority concluded that capital punishment was not categorically unconstitutional, but, as then practiced, it was deemed constitutionally unacceptable.

A landmark decision had been reached. Chief Justice Burger announced simply, "The Court holds that the imposition and carrying out of the death penalty in these cases constitutes cruel and unusual punishment in violation of the Eighth and Fourteenth Amendments." Those paying attention knew the phrase "in these cases" was important. Taking life for crimes committed had not been deemed totally unacceptable, but in these cases it was. The same was true for some 120 other cases then pending before the Court.

In total, there were 631 men and 2 women on death row at the time. All were affected in one way or another. New sentences were to be determined by the state courts. Although the taking of life was not totally eliminated, the impact of *Furman* was far reaching. Among those working for reform, "Fantasy had become reality. Against every expectation, by the slimmest of margins, the future of the death penalty in America had been irrevocably altered."[57]

Justice Brennan was totally unwilling to accept the exclusionary, dehumanizing implications of taking life for crimes committed. Writing what would become one of the most frequently quoted sentences from the *Furman* decision, he stated simply, "The calculated killing of a human being by the State involves, by its very nature, a denial of the executed person's humanity." For Justice Brennan, such dehumanization did not protect life. It degraded life. It offended the very core of a civil society. Capital punishment was unacceptable, no matter the crime.

Justice Marshall arrived at the same conclusion, though along a somewhat different path. Moral standards had evolved, and capital punishment had become abhorrent to the public. Executing persons served no useful purpose not otherwise achieved through less-severe punishments. It followed that capital punishment, no matter the crime, was cruel and unusual. The remaining seven justices disagreed.

For varying reasons, three of the seven found that the death penalty, although not totally unacceptable in theory, as practiced yielded arbitrary and capricious, and therefore unconstitutional, results. The problem resided in the procedures used to justify the termination of life. The absence of sentencing guidelines for juries, which the court had so recently deemed acceptable, meant that the death penalty was "wantonly" and "freakishly" applied. Receiving a death sentence was like being struck by lightning. Standards were now seen as necessary.

In another analogy, death-penalty procedures were likened, not to lightning strikes, but to a biased lottery. There were well-documented and pervasive findings that death sentences were disproportionately visited upon "the poor, the Negro, and the members of unpopular groups." It was not clear, however, when or under what conditions a sentence of death would be imposed. Such unpredictable inequity was unacceptable. If life was to be taken by the state, clear guidelines to ensure equality of treatment were needed.

Among justices voting against capital punishment as then practiced, there was also the belief that capital punishment was not serving any public good. Killing one person so that others would not kill might be asserted as a justification for taking life, but evidence for such an impact was tissue-thin at best. Numerous studies, with one or two highly criticized exceptions, had shown that a general deterrent effect from capital punishment was nowhere to be found. Any slight evidence for a deterrent effect that might show up from time to time had been rebutted. There was even evidence in a handful of studies that murder rates rose immediately following a highly publicized execution. Taking life was not saving life in any detectable way, at least not in any way that could not more readily be accomplished through lesser punishments.

Retribution was another asserted public good. It affirmed the importance of protecting life. The counter-assertion was that taking life was just as likely to "lower our respect for life and brutalize our values." If lives were not being saved, if taking life brutalized as much as it affirmed life, there was "no substantial reason to believe that the punishment of death, as currently administered, is necessary for the protection of society."[58] Life should be protected. It should not be taken if other, equally effective means for achieving the desired end were available.

And so the patchwork rationales of five Supreme Court justices voting against capital punishment were pieced together. As a whole, they read more like a mosaic than a coherent argument. The four remaining justices disagreed. Like those in the majority, they did so on varying grounds. They wrote together and separately to outline their reasoning.

Most consistently, they focused on who should decide. This was a matter for the legislature, not the court. Indeed, had it not been for this assessment, Justice Blackmun, repeating his previously voiced personal reluctance, would have voted with the majority. In his brief separate opinion he wrote,

> I yield to no one in the depth of my distaste, antipathy, and, indeed abhorrence for the death penalty . . . It is antagonistic to any sense of "reverence for life." Were I a legislator, I would vote against the death penalty.

Blackmun remained convinced, however, as he had been when he issued his *Maxwell* decision, that such matters were reserved for legislative action. He would later change his mind.

By the slimmest of margins and for kaleidoscopic reasons, in 1972 capital punishment, as then administered, was declared arbitrary and capricious and therefore null and void. If states could come up with remedies for the various procedural problems when removing the protective boundaries of life, capital punishment once again could be justified. States were not long in responding.

Justifications for Taking Life Are Clarified

Furman was released in the midst of a wave of law-and-order sentiment.[59] Thirty-seven states would soon pass post-*Furman* capital-punishment statutes. Given the turmoil and rising crime rates of the late 1960s, many agreed with a lawyer defending North Carolina's revised capital-punishment law. When compared with abolishing capital punishment, "[Stripping] the state of its ultimate punishment to stem the tide of robberies and murders would more likely offend society."[60]

Every state with a capital-punishment statute prior to *Furman* passed new death-penalty statutes. The new laws were responsive to the procedural and substantive concerns a deeply divided Supreme Court had raised. They differed in specifics, but, taken as a whole, the new laws narrowed the number of capital crimes (arson, burglary, and robbery were eliminated). All but a few states restructured trials to consider guilt and punishment separately. They specified listings of mitigating and aggravating circumstances to guide jury deliberations. A handful of statutes eliminated judge and jury discretion altogether by declaring capital punishment mandatory for specified offenses.

Using these statutes, trials were held, and convictions were secured. By the end of 1975, only three short years after *Furman* had emptied death rows across the nation, 400 new inmates were awaiting execution. Attorneys working with the LDF were representing some 100 of these.[61]

On January 22, 1976, the Supreme Court agreed to review five death sentences emerging from the revised statutes. These were representative of the new laws that had been passed. All five came from southern states— Florida, Georgia, Louisiana, North Carolina, and Texas.[62] In 1977 and then in 1978, two additional cases, one from Georgia and one from Ohio, would be decided.[63] Together, these seven cases mapped the new roads along which death sentencing could travel. There would be additional refinements, but, by the end of 1978, the major routes for justifying the taking of life for acts committed were once again in place.

Under the new statutes, life could only be taken after "judicious and careful review" of the facts and circumstances of the case. An important improvement, the court noted, was that the majority of revised laws now included a bifurcated proceeding wherein guilt and sentencing were decided separately. Tony Amsterdam's concerns were being addressed. Likewise, the new laws specified a variety of sentencing guidelines for jurors and judges, including the consideration of mitigating and aggravating circumstances.

In upholding the new Florida statute, the court noted with approval that the law required focus on both the crime's circumstances and the defendant's character by weighing eight aggravating factors against seven mitigating factors. In principle and in various forms, such balancing allowed juries and judges to more rationally reach conclusions as to the severity of the crime and the nature of the defendant. In principle at least, this balancing was also more likely to yield equitable sentencing across similar cases.

Some statutes sought to eliminate biased outcomes altogether by calling for a mandatory sentence of death, no matter the character or background of the person or circumstances of the crime. These were not acceptable. Fundamental respect for humanity demanded that each case be carefully considered on its own merits.[64] Without weighing the specific circumstances of the case and the character and background of the persons involved, removing life's protective boundaries, even from persons found guilty of taking life, could not proceed. In the years to come, it would be repeatedly noted that, by so holding, the court put capital-punishment procedures in a bind. Individualized justice demanded discretion. Discretion was the door through which biased outcomes passed.

Respect for humanity also demanded that the death penalty not be "grossly disproportionate" to the crime committed. Reviewing a rape case from Georgia, the court held that, because the rape of an adult woman "did not involve the taking of another human life . . . the death penalty [was] excessive in its severity and revocability."[65] Standards of decency had evolved to the point where such punishments were no longer allowed. A threshold for the severity of acts needed for taking the defendant's life had been set.

As Tony Amsterdam noted while arguing before the court in the 1976 case from Texas, taken as a whole, the revised statutes were designed to provide, "the road to death with avenues of discretionary mercy shooting off from the beginning of the process to the end."[66] With the court's various affirmations and rejections written and released, the revised path for removing the protective boundaries of life and imposing death was somewhat clearer. Bifurcated trials, separating the finding of guilt from the assessment of punishment, were a good idea but not required. Guidelines for judges and juries, aimed at balancing mitigating and aggravating circumstances of the defendant's character and the nature of the offense, were mandatory. Mandatory sentences or sentences grossly disproportionate to the crime committed were not permissible.

While some fog had been lifted, a good deal remained. What constituted a sentence being "grossly disproportionate" to the crime? What were the important dimensions of a defendant's background and character? A pattern of past violent behavior was relevant, but did age matter? If so, what was the appropriate threshold? Related to chronological age, did mental retardation mitigate the crime? If so, what level of retardation was required? Was it possible to prohibit mandatory sentences and demand consideration of a defendant's character and the circumstances of the crime, without introducing personal bias and associated inequalities?

As lawyers and appellate justices grappled with the still vaguely defined boundaries of tolerable suffering and protected life, as they set priorities to resolve the dilemmas produced when taking life to protect life, frustration and mixed messages frequently emerged. As with other issues involving life and death decisions, the uncertain complexity of conflicting imperatives led key players to change their minds.

Notes

1 Personal correspondence, November 21, 2009.
2 James Weldon Johnson, *Along This Way* (New York: Penguin Books, 1933), 317–18.
3 It drew instant, not totally anticipated or welcomed, attention. Shortly after it was published, German doctors and governmental officials went on trial in Nuremberg. As the trials progressed, defense lawyers took note of Myrdal's work and pointed time and time again to the parallels between charges facing their clients and the now well-documented injustices in the United States.
4 *An American Dilemma: The Negro Problem and Modern Democracy* (New York: Harper & Bros., 1944), 2: 525
5 M.S. Weatherford, "Measuring Political Legitimacy," *American Political Science Review* 86 (1992): 149–66. Tom R. Tyler, "Psychological Perspectives on Legitimacy and Legitimation," *Annual Review Psychology* 57 (2006): 375–400. John T. Jost and Brenda Major, Eds., *The Psychology of Legitimacy* (New York: Cambridge University Press, 2001).
6 Oliver Wendell Holmes, who played such a prominent role in both the *Moore v. Dempsey* and *Buck v. Bell* decisions, once bluntly wrote, "All Law Means is that I Will Kill You if Necessary to Make You Conform to My Requirements." Quoted in Alschuler, *Law Without Values*, 26.
7 Max Weber, *On Law in Economy and Society*, Ed. M. Rheinstein (Cambridge, MA: Harvard University Press, 1954): 322–48. Jack P. Gibbs, "Sanctions," *Social Problems* 14 (1966): 147–59.
8 James Baldwin, *Nobody Knows My Name* (New York: Dial Press, 1961), 65–7.
9 James Baldwin, preface to *Blues for Mister Charlie* (New York: Dell Publishing Co., 1965).
10 Michael Meltsner, *Cruel and Unusual: The Supreme Court and Capital Punishment* (New York: Random House, 1973): 72–3.
11 For a detailed account of this case, see: Eric W. Rise, *The Martinsville Seven: Race, Rape, and Capital Punishment* (Charlottesville: University of Virginia Press, 1998).
12 Personal correspondence, November 21, 2009.
13 Of the remaining three, two were other minorities, and one was "white." See: www.deathpenaltyinfo.org/executions-us-1608-2002-espy-file.

14   Anthony Amsterdam, quoted in Nadya Labi, "The Man Against the Machine," *New York University Law School Magazine* (2007): 11–19.

15   Michael Meltsner, *Cruel and Unusual*, 106–7.

16   Michael Meltsner, personal correspondence, November 21, 2009.

17   See: www.ojp.usdoj.gov/bjs/glance/tables/exetab.htm.

18   See: www.deathpenaltyinfo.org/death-row-inmates-state-and-size-death-row-year# year.

19   Jack Greenberg, *Crusaders in the Courts: Legal Battles of the Civil Rights Movement* (New York: Twelve Tables Press, 2004), 474.

20   *Rudolph v. Alabama*, 375 U.S. 889 (1963).

21   Greenberg, *Crusaders in the Courts*, 474.

22   Marvin E. Wolfgang, Arlene Kelly, and Hans C. Nolde, "Comparison of the Executed and the Commuted Among Admissions to Death Row," *Journal of Criminal Law, Criminology, and Police Science* 53 (1962): 301–11.

23   See: http://diglib.princeton.edu/ead/getEad?id=ark:/88435/hd76s005t.

24   These included Alabama, Arkansas, Florida, Georgia, Louisiana, Mississippi, North Carolina, South Carolina, Tennessee, Texas, and Virginia. Maryland was also initially included, but time limitations eventually precluded its inclusion. See: Marvin E. Wolfgang and Marc Riedel, "Race, Judicial Discretion, and the Death Penalty," *Annals of the American Academy of Political and Social Science: Blacks and the Law* 407 (1973): 119–33.

25   These lengthy forms included information on the background and social and marital status of the victim and offender, any prior relationship between the victim and offender, the circumstances of the offense, the place of the offense, the degree of violence involved. Where other crimes such as burglary or robbery involved? Were drugs used? What was the nature of the intercourse? Were other defendants or victims involved? What issues, such as insanity or consent, were raised at trial?

26   Michael Meltsner, *Cruel and Unusual*, 87.

27   *Furman v. Georgia*, 408 U.S. 238 (1972).

28   See for example: James W. Marquart, Sheldon Ekland-Olson, and Jonathan R. Sorensen, *The Rope, the Chair, and the Needle* (Austin, TX: University of Texas Press, 1994), 64 and 95.

29   *Maxwell v. Stephens, cert. denied*, 382 U.S. 944 (1965).

30   Michael Metsner would later write, "Lawyers often fight hard for such tactical advantages, knowing that their adversary may be too overwhelmed by bulky documents, or simply too lazy to dispute the facts." Meltsner, *Cruel and Unusual*, 97.

31   Meltsner, *Cruel and Unusual*, 100.

32   Cited by Meltsner, *Cruel and Unusual*, 101.

33   Personal correspondence, September 7, 2009.

34   *William L. Maxwell, Appellant, v. O.E. Bishop, Superintendent, Arkansas State Penitentiary*, United States Court of Appeals Eighth Circuit—398 F.2d 138. As he continued outlining the court's decision, Judge Blackmun took note of two recent Supreme Court decisions, released just months before in April: *United States v. Jackson*, 390 U.S. 570 (1968); and June: *Witherspoon v. Illinois*, 391 U.S. 510 (1968). They had already begun to reshape the capital-punishment landscape. Nevertheless, he was not persuaded and rejected the appeal.

35 *William L. Maxwell, Appellant, v. O.E. Bishop, Superintendent, Arkansas State Penitentiary*, United States Court of Appeals Eighth Circuit—398 F.2d 138.

36 *Maxwell v. Bishop*, 398 U.S. 262 (1970).

37 Given what he wrote in his Eighth Circuit *Maxwell* decision, it is interesting as a side note that, in 1973, Justice Blackmun authored another opinion, *Roe v. Wade*, a decision many saw as overstepping the boundaries of judicial intervention that had so constrained him in the case of Willie Lee Maxwell.

38 Later analysis of Wolfgang's data collected in the summer of 1965 would only strengthen this conclusion. See: Wolfang and Riedel, "Race, Judicial Discretion, and the Death Penalty," 119–33.

39 Oral argument, May 4, 1970, *Maxwell v. Bishop*, 398 U.S. 262 (1970).

40 *Witherspoon v. Illinois*, 391 U.S. 510 (1968).

41 Thurgood Marshall did not participate, and Harry Blackmun, who had written the opinion of the Eighth Circuit being appealed, would take his seat on the court the next week.

42 Citing *Witherspoon v. Illinois*, 391 U.S. 510 (1968)

43 Meltsner, *Cruel and Unusual*, 235–6.

44 *McGautha v. California*, 402 U.S. 183 (1971). *Crampton v. Ohio*, 402 U.S. 183, 210–211 (1971).

45 Jack Greenberg, *Crusaders in the Courts*, 483.

46 See Meltsner, *Cruel and Unusual*, 246.

47 Anthony Amsterdam, personal correspondence, September 7, 2009.

48 Arthur J. Goldberg and Alan M. Dershowitz, "Declaring the Death Penalty Unconstitutional," *Harvard Law Review* 83 (1970): 1773–819.

49 See: www.ojp.usdoj.gov/bjs/homicide/tables/totalstab.htm

50 See: www.time.com/time/2007/crimes/9.html.

51 Greenberg, *Crusaders in the Courts*, 484.

52 Theodore Caplow and Jonathan Simon, "Understanding Prison Policy and Population Trends," in *Prisons*, Eds. M. Tonry and J. Petersilia, vol. 26 of *Crime and Justice: A Review of Research*, Ed. M. Tonry (Chicago: University of Chicago Press, 1999).

53 I would like to add here a special note of thanks to Tony Amsterdam and Michael D'Amelio for their kindness in digging up and providing these documents, which by 2009 were beginning to gather a good deal of dust.

54 *People v. Anderson*, 100 Cal Rpt. 152 (Cal. 1972).

55 Meltsner, *Cruel and Unusual*, 287.

56 *Furman v. Georgia*, 408 U.S. 238 (1972).

57 Meltsner, *Cruel and Unusual*, 289.

58 Justice Brennan, concurring opinion in *Furman v. Georgia*, 408 U.S. 238 (1972).

59 In 1966, when the moratorium on executions was in place, support for capital punishment for murder was at its lowest point. Polls, for the first time, indicated that less than a majority of the population supported the taking of life from those who had taken life. By the early 1970s, however, support had risen and began hovering closer to 70 percent.

60 Sidney S. Eagles, arguing before the Supreme Court in *Woodson v. North Carolina*, 428 U.S. 280 (1976), March 31, 1976.

61   Greenberg, *Crusaders in the Courts*, 487.
62   *Gregg v. Georgia*, 428 U.S. 153 (1976), *Proffitt v. Florida*, 428 U.S. 242 (1976), *Jurek v. Texas*, 428 U.S. 262 (1976), *Roberts v. Louisiana*, 428 U.S. 325 (1976), and *Woodson v. North Carolina*, 428 U.S. 280 (1976).
63   *Coker v. Georgia*, 433 U.S. 584 (1977) and *Lockett v. Ohio*, 438 U.S. 586 (1978).
64   *Woodson v. North Carolina*, 428 U.S. 280 (1976).
65   *Coker v. Georgia*, 433 U.S. 584 (1977).
66   Oral argument in *Jurek v. Texas*, 428 U.S. 262 (1976), March 30, 1976.

CHAPTER 16

THE PENDULUM SWINGS, THE DEBATE CONTINUES

The first post-*Furman* execution occurred on January 17, 1977.[1] It had been almost a decade since the last execution had taken place in June of 1967. There were no executions in 1978, and a total of five over the next four years, between 1979 and 1982. In 1983 and 1984, several details of the post-*Furman* statutes were clarified.[2] In 1983, there were five executions. Then, in 1984, there were 21. The post-*Furman* era of executions had begun.

Yearly fluctuations characterized the second half of the 1980s, with a high of 25 (1987) and a low of 11 (1988). In the 1990s, executions turned sharply upward, more than quadrupling from 23 to 98 between 1990 and 1999. It had been almost 50 years since the yearly total had reached this level. Public support for capital punishment was firmly in place, hovering at 80 percent, or so it seemed.

The Pendulum Swings

By 1994, however, this upward trend was drawing the attention of a now thoroughly disenchanted Justice Harry Blackmun. In February of that year, Blackmun wrote,

> From this day forward, I no longer shall tinker with the machinery of death. For more than 20 years I have endeavored—indeed, I have struggled—along with a majority of this Court, to develop

procedural and substantive rules that would lend more than the mere appearance of fairness to the death penalty endeavor. Rather than continue to coddle the Court's delusion that the desired level of fairness has been achieved and the need for regulation eviscerated, I feel morally and intellectually obligated simply to concede that the death penalty experiment has failed.[3]

Justice Blackmun had specific reasons for his disenchantment, which had been building for several years. There was continuing evidence of inequitable punishment.[4] Referring to a 1987 case from Georgia,[5] Justice Blackmun chided his colleagues on the court who had turned their backs on "staggering evidence" that racial prejudice continued to infect Georgia's capital sentencing scheme.[6] Since that decision, broad-ranging evidence had continued to mount,[7] and Blackmun had come to question whether the problem was resolvable. Was there truth in the suggestion, he wondered, "that discrimination and arbitrariness could not be purged from the administration of capital punishment without sacrificing the equally essential component of fairness—individualized sentencing?"[8] Blackmun's growing concerns over inequitable outcomes had been further prodded in 1990, when the U.S. General Accounting Office issued a wide-ranging report.[9] This report reviewed and summarized an avalanche of research done over the post-*Furman* years. There had been some improvement, but the evidence continued to reveal serious patterns of race-based inequities. There was little room for doubt, Justice Blackmun, among many others, was convinced.

Inequitable sentencing was only part of the story. In the same year, the staggering evidence of continuing racial bias had been presented, and in Blackmun's mind ignored, the *Stanford Law Review* published a detailed examination of some 350 cases involving convictions of individuals, later found to be innocent. The conclusions were again unequivocal. If the evidence failed "to convince the reader of the fallibility of human judgment," the authors wrote, "then nothing will."[10] Five years later, in 1992, the study was updated.[11] The conclusions remained the same.

Science, Technology, and Innocence

While these and similar studies were being conducted, forensic science was advancing, most importantly through the Human Genome Project, launched in 1990. As so often happens, these scientific advances had a dramatic impact on the evolving moral assessment. The emerging techniques of DNA "fingerprinting" or "profiling" were increasingly used over the ensuing years. The forensic significance of these techniques was quickly recognized, and, in 1992, two lawyers who had been litigating cases based on the new technologies founded the Innocence Project.[12] The next year, 1993, Kirk Bloodsworth, who had been sentenced to death in 1984, left Maryland's prison as the first man exonerated on the basis of DNA evidence.[13]

Bloodsworth had been sentenced to death and held in prison nine years for a crime he did not commit. In 1995, two additional DNA-related exonerations were uncovered in Illinois. More would follow.[14] These cases clearly demonstrated that innocent persons had been convicted and sentenced to death. They raised the specter of a seriously flawed system, as DNA evidence, as important and compelling as it was, could be gathered and used in only a small fraction of cases. What about other mistakes being made; mistakes that were not discovered through the use of genetic profiling?

The same year Kirk Bloodsworth left prison, and a year prior to Justice Blackmun's decision to no longer tinker with the machinery of death, the majority on the Supreme Court refused a request for a stay of execution of Leonel Herrara. Eight years after Herrara's trial, evidence had come to light suggesting his innocence. It was not based on DNA, but on new testimony of persons associated with the crime. On appeal, the Supreme Court concluded Herrera's case had not passed the "extraordinarily high" threshold for mandating further review of evidence presented at trial. If the court granted this request, six justices concluded, a flood of cases would surely follow, and the system would fall of its own weight.

With barely restrained anger, Justice Blackmun wrote,

Of one thing I am certain, just as an execution without adequate safeguards is unacceptable, so too is an execution when the condemned prisoner can prove that he is innocent. The execution of a person who can show that he is innocent comes perilously close to simple murder.[15]

The court's decision refusing review was released on January 25, 1993. Three-and-a-half months later, on May 12, Leonel Herrera, an immigrant to South Texas, was executed. He had been on death row for almost eleven-and-a-half years. His last words were,

> I am innocent, innocent, innocent. Make no mistake about this; I owe society nothing. Continue the struggle for human rights, helping those who are innocent, especially Mr. Graham. I am an innocent man, and something very wrong is taking place tonight. May God bless you all. I am ready.[16]

Gary Graham, the man for whom Leonel Herrera urged continuing efforts, was executed some seven years later.[17]

For Justice Blackmun, the proper course to take in the face of a deeply flawed system, inequitably executing individuals and refusing to respond to possible innocence, was clear. Contradictory demands were being placed on those assigned the task of removing the protective boundaries of life and sentencing individuals to death. Sentencing needed to be individualized, but individualized sentencing was the route through which bias entered the decision-making process. Focusing on the contradictory demands of two earlier decisions,[18] the remedy was not, Blackmun wrote,

> to ignore one or the other, nor to pretend that the dilemma does not exist, but to admit the futility of the effort to harmonize them. This means accepting the fact that the death penalty cannot be administered in accord with our Constitution.[19]

Progress had been made, but important and perhaps irremediable problems remained.[20] For Blackmun, the time had come to call a halt to an inherently flawed system for removing life's protective boundaries.

A Messy and Meaningless System

Justice Blackmun's change of mind was not shared among the majority of his colleagues on the Supreme Court, but Justice Lewis Powell was of like mind. After leaving the court, Powell too had changed his mind about the capital-punishment system he had helped build. Like Blackmun,

Powell had voted to uphold executions. Speaking with his biographer in 1991, some four years after his retirement from the court, Powell was asked whether he would change his vote in any case. He replied, "I would vote the other way in any capital case . . . I have come to think that capital punishment should be abolished." The convoluted procedures that had emerged in the post-*Furman* years had led Justice Powell to believe that the seemingly endless litigation in capital cases brought "discredit on the whole legal system."[21]

Justice Blackmun's expressed disenchantment in 1994, coupled with Justice Powell's equally negative assessment, was reflected in a broader arena. The pioneering Innocence Project, begun in 1992, was soon joined by some 80 similar efforts anchored in a number of law schools, journalism programs, and public-defender offices across the nation. Together, they formed the core of what came to be called the "Innocence Network."[22] Numerous articles began appearing in both academic journals and the popular press. Issues were explored in detail when, in 1995, two law professors, writing in the *Harvard Law Review*, published a lengthy account of how the court had created a body of law "at once so messy and so meaningless."[23]

The number of exonerations of those wrongfully convicted continued to mount. On November 13–15, 1998, a National Conference on Wrongful Convictions and the Death Penalty was held at Northwestern University School of Law, just outside Chicago. It had been motivated by recent findings of innocence, most immediately in Illinois. It brought together 28 persons from around the country; all had been sentenced to death for crimes they had not committed. Some 1,200 academics, lawyers, and activists involved in the now growing Innocence Network joined the occasion. From this conference, the Center on Wrongful Convictions at Northwestern University's Law School was launched.[24]

As the strength of Northwestern's operation, along with the growing Innocence Network, mounted, concern deepened. In February and April of 2000, Senator Patrick Leahy and Representatives Bill Delahunt and Ray LaHood (with 81 cosponsors) introduced versions of an Innocence Protection Act in both houses of Congress. Six months later, on June 12, 2000, three colleagues, working at Columbia University Law School and New York University's Sociology Department, released: *A Broken System: Error Rates in Capital Cases, 1973–1995*.[25]

The executive summary of this lengthy report was clear and direct. Justice Blackmun's and Justice Powell's concerns were well founded. Serious, documented, reversible errors had been found in 68 percent of the 4,578 cases since capital punishment had been reinstated. Introducing their findings, the authors of *A Broken System* began, "There is a growing bipartisan consensus that flaws in America's death-penalty system have reached crisis proportions." Many feared, they continued, that a substantial number of persons on death row did not belong there. As the first statistical study ever undertaken of modern American capital appeals, the research suggested that both claims were correct. "Our 23 years' worth of results," the authors concluded, "reveal a death penalty system collapsing under the weight of its own mistakes."

A year after *A Broken System* was released, on July 3, 2001, Justice Sandra Day O'Connor, who, like Powell and Blackmun, had upheld capital punishment on numerous occasions, gave a widely reported speech to the Minnesota Women Lawyers Association. "If statistics are any indication," she reported, "the system may well be allowing some innocent defendants to be executed." On April 8, 2002, Ray Krone became the 100th former death-row inmate freed because of innocence in the post-*Furman* years—the twelfth on the basis of DNA evidence. He had spent 10 years in Arizona's prison system for a crime he had not committed. In the coming years, the number continued to mount.[26]

Around this same time, an unexpected trend began to emerge. The number of yearly executions began to decline. Executions had quadrupled from 23 in 1990 to a total of 98 in 1999. In the year 2000, there were 85 executions. By 2005, the total was 60. By the end of the decade, they had dropped to roughly half what they were in 2000.[27] Statistics published by the Bureau of Justice reflected a parallel decline in the number of death sentences imposed. In the mid-to-late 1990s, they were hovering around 300. By 2010, they were closer to 100. This reduction in death sentences signaled a further decline in executions in the years ahead.

The reasons for this unexpected decline remain unclear, but in all likelihood there was a confluence of influences. Importantly, there had been a noticeable decline in violent-crime rates. The homicide rate had peaked in the 1980s, and by the 1990s it was in decline. In 1991, there were 9.8 homicides per 100,000 persons. In 1995, there were 8.2. By 2000, this rate had fallen to 5.5.[28] By 2005, the total violent crime rate had reached the lowest level ever recorded by the Bureau of Justice. This trend would continue through the remainder of the decade.[29] Violent crime as metaphor for a threatening evil[30] was weakening.

A Watershed Decision

More immediately influential on the decline in executions, however, was the heightened concern for innocence. Building on the growing chorus for reform, on January 31, 2000, less than two weeks prior to the introduction of the Innocence Protection Act in Congress, Illinois Governor George Ryan declared a moratorium on executions in his state. The specter of possibly killing innocent persons had become too great, and Governor Ryan's actions, occurring as they did in a receptive climate, crystallized thought and precipitated dramatic action for reform across the country.

The Conference on Wrongful Convictions, held at Northwestern University a little over a year earlier, had drawn the governor's attention. Four cases of wrongful convictions in Illinois were spotlighted. There was further evidence that, while 12 persons had been executed in Illinois since *Furman*, another 13 of those sentenced to death had been found innocent. The *Chicago Tribune* had recently published a series of articles on a range of death-penalty issues. The week prior to Govenor Ryan's announcement, underscoring the findings reported in *A Broken System*, one headline read, "Half of State's Death-Penalty Cases Reversed."[31] The story began with the "amazing figure" that, among death-penalty cases in Illinois, exactly half (130) had been reversed for a new trial or sentencing hearing. Like Justices Blackmun and Powell, Governor Ryan was convinced that the system of capital punishment was flawed beyond repair.

During the Illinois moratorium, the governor established a commission to investigate what appeared to be the state's flawed system of justice. On January 11, 2003, after the commission had reported its findings, the governor spoke to an overflow crowd at the Center on Wrongful Convictions. Preaching to the choir, he told his audience,

> Our capital [punishment] system is haunted by the demon of error, error in determining guilt and error in determining who among the guilty deserves to die. What effect was race having? What effect was poverty having? Because of all these reasons, today I am commuting the sentences of all Death Row inmates.[32]

Ryan granted outright pardons to four men. The death sentences of some 170 (estimates varied slightly) convicted offenders were commuted to life in prison without parole. Echoing Justice Blackmun, Governor Ryan reviewed his decision while talking with inmates on death row. "Because the Illinois death penalty system is arbitrary and capricious—and therefore immoral," he told them, "I no longer shall tinker with the machinery of death."

Not everyone, however, viewed the governor's decision as a mark of progress. Whereas anti-capital-punishment activists across the country, along with those awaiting execution on Illinois's death row, may have seen Governor Ryan's actions as a positive watershed moment, family members of the victims, such as the mother whose daughter had been killed in a fire started by one of the convicted men, did not. Instead, she saw it as a mockery. The man responsible for her daughter's death had been duly convicted and sentenced to death. With the stroke of a pen, the governor now said he could live. This still grieving mother simply did not understand: "How could he do that?"[33]

As the first decade in the twenty-first century unfolded, those opposing capital punishment had successfully shifted the framing argument away from an emphasis on inequity and toward the question of innocence. A sense of urgency was growing. Effects from the efforts of those who would abolish or drastically revise the death-penalty system began to be felt. Almost five years after Governor Ryan first announced his moratorium in Illinois, a revised version of the Innocence Protection Act was passed and signed into law by President George W. Bush, on October 30, 2004.[34]

Given the documented conviction of innocent persons and the high probability of further mistakes, the willingness to remove the protective boundaries of life from those convicted of even very severe offenses was on the wane. "A social cascade, starting with legal clinics and innocence projects," the authors of a 2008 study reported, "has snowballed into a national phenomenon that may spell the end of the death penalty in America."[35]

Whether this prognosis proves correct is yet to be seen. By 2006, public support, although still strong (hovering around 65–70 percent), seemed to be dropping from the highs noted in the mid 1990s (around 80 percent). Support fell dramatically (to an estimated 47 percent) when evidence of a flawed system of justice was introduced, and preferences for capital punishment were compared with preferences for sentencing to life without the possibility of parole.[36] Images of a flawed system seemed to be producing a deepening sense of injustice. If society could be protected without the taking of life, an increasing number began to think that it should be.

In the post-*Furman* era, 37 states had enacted capital punishment statutes, leaving 13 without such laws. In December 2007, 25 years after its new death-penalty statute had been enacted in 1982, New Jersey became the first state post-*Furman* to abolish capital punishment and replace it with life in prison without the possibility of parole.[37] In 2009, repeal bills were pending in 11 states. New Mexico's passed in March, and, when announcing his signing, Governor Bill Richardson, a former supporter of capital punishment, pointed to the dehumanizing impact a flawed system was having. "The potential for . . . execution of an innocent person," Governor Richardson announced, "stands as anathema to our very sensibilities as human beings."[38] Two years later in March 2011, Illinois joined the growing repeal efforts when it became the sixteenth state to prohibit capital punishment. Governor Pat Quinn noted simply, "We cannot have a death penalty system in our state that kills innocent people."[39]

Although dominating the public debate, innocence was not the only issue. There was a growing conviction that the protective boundaries of life were being removed from those less culpable for their actions.

Mental Retardation and Age

On June 26, 1989, the Supreme Court had released its five–four decision in a case from Texas involving Johnny Paul Penry.[40] There was no expressed belief that Penry was innocent. Before the victim died, she had described her assailant, and Penry fitted the description. Penry had twice confessed to the brutal rape, beating, and stabbing, which had taken place in Livingston, Texas, in October of 1979. One problem: although Johnny Penry was 22 years old chronologically, his mental age was that of a six-and-a-half-year-old, with the social maturity of a 9- or 10-year-old. His IQ was assessed to be in the seriously retarded range, set somewhere close to 55.

At issue on appeal to the Supreme Court was whether the Constitution categorically prohibited Penry's execution because he was mentally retarded. In a set of divergent opinions, reflecting the hazy boundaries and dilemmas involved, the justices had expressed both support for, and opposition to, this assertion. In the end, Justice Sandra Day O'Connor, writing for the five–four majority, found no "sufficient objective evidence today of a national consensus against executing mentally retarded capital murderers." The majority of justices were aware that public opinion might someday turn against executing the mentally retarded, but, they noted, the "petitioner has cited only one state statute that explicitly bans that practice, and has offered no evidence of the general behavior of juries in this regard." O'Connor's written decision expressed skepticism, "Opinion surveys indicating strong public opposition to such executions do not establish a societal consensus, absent some legislative reflection of the sentiment expressed therein."

This was June, 1989.[41] Some 13 years later, on June 20, 2002, half a year before Governor Ryan commuted the sentences of death-sentenced inmates in Illinois, the court, in a six–three decision involving a case from Virginia, *Atkins v. Virginia*, found that "much has changed since *Penry's* conclusion."[42] This time, the conviction being appealed involved a robbery and murder committed by two men in 1996. One, Daryl Atkins, was judged to be mentally retarded, with an IQ in the range of 59 and a mental age of a 9-to-12-year-old. There was some question of his innocence of the actual killing, as he said one thing, and his co-defendant said another. During the 13 years since the *Penry* decision, 18 of the 37 states with post-*Furman* death-penalty statutes had passed laws limiting execution of the mentally retarded. The court now noted:

> Given that anticrime legislation is far more popular than legislation protecting violent criminals, the large number of States prohibiting the execution of mentally retarded persons (and the complete absence of legislation reinstating such executions) provides powerful evidence that today society views mentally retarded offenders as categorically less culpable than the average criminal.

For the majority of the court, arguments for retribution and deterrence, when applied to the mentally retarded, were also not persuasive. When it came to retribution, the court noted, "The severity of the appropriate punishment necessarily depends on the offender's culpability." Because of reduced culpability of those lacking substantial mental capacity, death could not be justified. The same could be said about deterrence. By this time, the vast majority of studies and the considered judgment of professionals directly involved in law enforcement suggested there was very little, if any, deterrent effect gained by capital punishment. Among the mentally retarded, the court found, the already lacking deterrent influence of threatened death would be even further reduced. "The same cognitive and behavioral impairments that make the mentally retarded defendants less morally culpable," Justice Stevens wrote for the majority, "also make it less likely that they can process the information of the possibility of execution as a punishment and, as a result, control their conduct based upon that information." Finally, the court found executing the mentally retarded offender heightened the chances of taking life from those factually innocent of committing the act. "They [the retarded] will unwittingly confess to crimes they did not commit." They have a lessened ability to "give their counsel meaningful assistance." Their general demeanor "may create an unwarranted impression of lack of remorse for their crimes."

For reasons of evolving standards of decency, reduced justification based on deterrence and retribution, and for heightened probabilities of killing the innocent, executing mentally retarded offenders was now deemed to violate the Constitution's prohibition against cruel and unusual punishments. Taking life under these circumstances would no longer be permitted.

Writing in harsh dissent, Justice Antonin Scalia, joined by two of his colleagues, suggested that the majority's attempt to "fabricate" evidence for a shifting moral consensus was feeble at best. As for culpability, there was a long, well-established legal tradition, Justice Scalia noted, that, "only the *severely* or *profoundly* mentally retarded, commonly known as 'idiots,' enjoyed any special status under the law ... Mentally retarded offenders with less severe impairments—those who were not 'idiots'—suffered criminal prosecution and punishment, including capital punishment." Conflating mental retardation with mental illness and insanity, Scalia and his dissenting colleagues pointed in support to the hazy boundaries of a defendant's mental state, noting, "This newest invention promises to be more effective than any of the others in turning the process of capital trial into a game."

Justice Scalia's views were well known. Years earlier, in the same session as Johnny Paul Penry's case was decided, he had elaborated his views.[43] Two cases, one from Kentucky and one from Missouri, had been consolidated. Both involved very brutal murders. Instead of mental retardation, the issue before the court was chronological age. One case involved the murder a 20-year-old woman, Barbel Poore. She had been raped, sodomized, and then shot pointblank in the face and the back of the head in the course of a robbery in Jefferson County, Kentucky. The robbery had netted 300 cartons of cigarettes, two gallons of fuel, and a small amount of cash. The offender, Kevin Stanford, was eight months shy of his eighteenth birthday at the time of the offense, which had taken place some eight years earlier on January 7, 1981.

Belying the deterrent effect of capital punishment, and perhaps suggesting the threat of execution had actually encouraged Kevin Stanford, a correctional officer had testified of a conversation he had had with Stanford. The accused had an explanation for his behavior.

> I had to shoot her, [she] lived next door to me and she would recognize me . . . I guess we could have tied her up or something or beat [her up] . . . and tell her if she tells, we would kill her . . . Then after he said that, he started laughing.

Kentucky law allowed Kevin Stanford to be tried as an adult. He had been sentenced to death.

The second case was from Missouri, where the law permitted individuals between the ages of 14 and 17 to be tried as adults. The crime involved an offender, Heath Wilkins, approximately 16½ years old when the crime occurred on July 27, 1985. Wilkins and an accomplice had planned to rob a store in Avondale, Missouri. Again, there was some indication that a looming death sentence yielded little deterrent effect and perhaps encouraged their actions. Before the robbery, Wilkins and his accomplice intended to kill whoever was behind the counter because "a dead person can't talk." The victim, Nancy Allen, was a 26-year-old mother of two. She had been repeatedly stabbed in the heart and neck and left to die after Wilkins and his accomplice left with liquor, cigarettes, rolling papers, and approximately $450 in cash and checks.

Reviewing these two cases in 1989, Justice Scalia and four of his colleagues on the court found nothing in the Constitution that would prohibit executing individuals such as Heath Wilkins and Kevin Stanford. They had done things, no matter their age, that negated their right to live. Writing for the majority of his colleagues, Justice Scalia concluded,

> We discern neither a historical nor a modern societal consensus forbidding the imposition of capital punishment on any person who murders at 16 or 17 years of age. Accordingly, we conclude that such punishment does not offend the Eighth Amendment's prohibition against cruel and unusual punishment.

This was in 1989.

Whereas evolving standards of decency that mark the progress of a maturing society did not categorically prohibit the execution of persons who were 16 or 17 years of age in 1989, 16 years later, in yet another a five–four decision, announced on March 1, 2005, the majority of the court said they did.[44] The case involved two offenders. At the age of 17, still a junior in high school, Christopher Simmons and a 15-year-old accomplice set out at 2:00 a.m. with the intention of robbing and killing Shirley Crook, who had been involved in a car accident with Simmons. They entered Mrs. Crook's home and awakened her. They bound her and drove her to a nearby park. There, they further secured her hands with electrical wire, wrapped her face in duct tape, and threw her off a bridge, where she drowned in the water below. Simmons had told his accomplice they could get away with it because they were minors. The day after the murder, Simmons was heard bragging about how he had killed the victim "because the bitch seen my face." There was no question. He had committed the crimes charged—robbery, kidnapping, and murder.

The convictions were appealed. The Supreme Court was asked to reverse its 1989 decision. The request was based on an extension of the same reasoning used to prohibit the execution of the mentally retarded. Was there evidence that standards of decency had evolved to the point where executing convicted offenders under a certain age was no longer acceptable? Did the court believe that, owing to reduced culpability, the death penalty was a disproportionate punishment for juveniles?

In 1989, when the cases involving Kevin Stanford and Heath Wilkins had been decided, 25 states prohibited the death penalty for juveniles. In the intervening years, five additional states had abandoned the practice. No state had lowered the minimum age for capital punishment. Even in those states permitting the execution of individuals who were juveniles at the time of the offense, the practice was rarely carried out. Even in Kentucky (over the outrage of the victim's family), the governor had commuted Kevin Stanford's sentence to life.

In 2005, for the majority of the court, this was enough evidence. Moral standards had changed. As they had found in the case of mental retardation, the court now found "the susceptibility of juveniles to immature and irresponsible behavior" meant their wrongful conduct was "not as morally reprehensible as that of an adult." Juveniles also had "a greater claim than adults to be forgiven for failing to escape negative influences." Finally, given their still malleable identity, it was "less supportable to conclude that even a heinous crime committed by a juvenile is evidence of an irretrievably depraved character." Justices voting with the majority recognized that drawing a line at 18 years was subject "to the objection always raised against categorical rules." Still, a line had to be drawn.

For five justices, reaching their decision in 2005, this reasoning and evidence were sufficient. The court's 1989 decision was no longer binding. "Today our society views juveniles as categorically less culpable than the average criminal . . . the death penalty may not be imposed on offenders who were under 18 when they committed the crime."[45]

Justice Kennedy had announced the court's decision. Justice Scalia again gave strong voice to those who stood in opposition. Chief Justice Rehnquist and Justice Thomas joined him. These three found little reason to grant mercy. The crime was as calculated as it was chilling. The offenders knew precisely what they were doing. They should be held accountable.

Justice Scalia found it implausible that evolving moral standards for capital punishment had evolved so dramatically in so short a time and that "a national consensus that could not be perceived in our people's laws barely 15 years ago now solidly exists." This was a horrendous crime; it easily crossed the threshold of acts deserving of death. The three dissenting justices took offense and viewed with disdain that the court would proclaim itself "sole arbiter of our nation's moral standards." This was better left to legislators and juries.

Scalia disagreed also with the majority's assessment of culpability. Had not the American Psychological Association (APA) asserted, on the basis of "a rich body of research" just the opposite in a case occurring only a few years earlier. In this case, Scalia noted, the decision was to secure an abortion without parental consent.[46] Had not the APA noted that, by age 14–15, the ability to make moral judgments was well in place? Had they not stated that juveniles had developed "abilities similar to adults in reasoning about moral dilemmas, understanding social rules and laws and reasoning about interpersonal relationships and interpersonal problems?" Which took greater maturity, Justice Scalia wondered, "deciding whether to have an abortion or deciding what the 17-year-old defendant in this case had to decide, whether to throw a live and conscious woman to her death over a bridge?"[47] Such contradictory conclusions by the APA were scientifically disturbing. When used by the court to justify their decisions, they were a travesty.

Uncertain Boundaries, Innocent Lives, Scarce Drugs, and Botched Executions

In *Atkins v. Virginia*, Justice Scalia and two of his colleagues had scornfully noted the vague nature of the boundaries defining mental retardation and how allowing such persons who were convicted of horrible crimes to escape execution turned the criminal justice system into a cynical, easily manipulated game. The majority of the court, however, disagreed, finding instead that the execution of individuals with substantial intellectual disabilities was an anathema to a civilized society and prohibited by the Eighth and Fourteenth Amendments to the Constitution. With execution prohibited on the basis of reduced intellectual abilities, the question became where to draw the line. In a brief sentence glossing over the embedded vagaries, the majority in *Atkins* simply stated, "[W]e leave to the states the task of developing appropriate procedures to enforce these substantive constitutional restrictions."

In response to *Atkins*, States established, clarified, and adjusted their statutes. One of the most precise was found in Florida. In Florida the point of substantial intellectual disability at or below which execution was unconstitutional was set at the score of 70 on the Wechsler IQ test.

There were also provisions for less crisp clinical considerations of significant limitations in adaptive skills such as communication, self-care, and self-direction, but if your score was above 70 you could be sentenced to death. No further questions asked. In 2014 a case involving a Florida man, Freddie Lee Hall, was brought before the U.S. Supreme Court for review.

Oral arguments were presented in *Hall v. Florida*, starting at 10:05 in the morning of the third of March. It had been a long road. Mr. Hall had been on death row since 1978 (almost 36 years) for the murder of a 21-year-old woman who was pregnant at the time, as well as a related murder of a deputy sheriff shortly thereafter. The Florida Supreme Court had thrown out Hall's conviction in 1989, but he was reconvicted with a new death sentence in 1991. Twenty-three years after this second conviction, the arguments of lawyers before the Supreme Court and the questions posed by the listening Justices as the hearing began would make an excellent case study for an introductory statistics class.

Speaking on behalf of Freddie Lee Hall was Seth P. Waxman. After a brief introduction, Mr. Waxman began by focusing on the standard error of measurement (SEM).

Mr. Waxman: Because of the standard error of measurement that's inherent in IQ tests, it is universally accepted that persons with obtained scores of 71 to 75 can and often do have mental retardation . . .

Justice Sotomayor: Mr. Waxman, a line has to be drawn somewhere. And, we did say in *Atkins* that we would leave it up to the States to determine the standards for this issue . . . How would you announce the rule?

Mr. Waxman: . . . The rule that we advocate is—and the only real question presented in this case is just this: If a State conditions the opportunity to demonstrate mental retardation on obtained IQ test scores, it cannot ignore the measurement error that is inherent in these scores . . .

The point attorney Waxman was making was that there was uncertainty, scores on IQ tests (indeed, all tests) varied. Not only did they vary from one individual to another, if the same individual took the test multiple times, scores would have a central tendency, but would also vary. What was the "true" score? The Florida statute did not allow for consideration of this variation. It did not allow for the consideration of SEM.

The presence of SEM had consequences. In Florida, if a defendant's score was 72 he would be eligible for the death sentence, no further questions asked, even though his "true" score (i.e. the central tendency taking into account variation across tests) was 69. Florida's statute ignored this important point. About a half an hour later, after much discussion of the importance of SEM and related implications, Mr. Waxman closed in summary:

> Well, in our view, the Eighth Amendment requires that if a State chooses to use IQ test scores as a proxy for intellectual functioning rather than a full inquiry into intellectual functioning, it cannot refuse to employ the standard error of measurement that is inherent in the test.

The attorney for the State of Florida, Allen Winsor, now took his turn. He began by noting that while the statute might not take into account SEM, Freddie Lee Hall's scores, 71, 72, 73, 74, and 80 indicated he was eligible for the death sentence. Justice Scalia interrupted. Wait a minute. Was he arguing that each set of scores would have to be considered by the Supreme Court? Noting the implications for the Court of considering cases one at a time, based on unique sets of scores, bothered Justice Scalia, "I mean, I'm not very happy having to go through this and all future cases where you have somebody who has 69, 73, 74, 75, and 81. I mean, don't you have some more general principle, other than the particular scores in this case are good enough?" Attorney Winsor responded with a brief comment that the standards should be left to the States.

This time, Justice Kennedy broke in wondering why Florida was declining to follow standards set by those who designed, administered, and interpreted the tests. It was not looking good for Florida. It got worse when Justice Ginsburg noted issues of equity, that Florida's law allowed differential treatment of defendants with scores above or below 70. In the latter case the State could consider additional factors making the defendant eligible for death, but if the score was above 70 such considerations were not allowed. Why? Now it was time for Mr. Winsor to worry about the capacity of the justice system. He replied, "What is so terrible about doing it [looking at additional factors] is you would end up increasing the proportion of people, the number of people who would be eligible for a mental retardation hearing."

As his argument drew to a close, Allen Winsor, perhaps in some frustration, noted that nobody disputes "that the true IQ is something that is incapable of being measured . . . but the IQ test is what the community has . . . which is why we believe it's particularly important to focus on because it's the most objective test that we have." The boundaries justifying the taking of life were being drawn with a blunt instrument, clouded by SEM, resulting in much ambiguity. For proponents it was the best we could do. For opponents it confirmed the presence of a meaningless and messy system.

Some three months later, on May 27, 2014 a 5–4 decision was released. Writing for the majority of the Court, Justice Kennedy noted:

> Florida law defines intellectual disability to require an IQ test score of 70 or less. If, from test scores, a prisoner is deemed to have an IQ above 70, all further exploration of intellectual disability is foreclosed. This rigid rule, the Court now holds, creates an unacceptable risk that persons with intellectual disability will be executed, and thus is unconstitutional.

Florida would have to find another way to determine a legitimized boundary justifying the execution of those with intellectual disabilities. If test scores were to be used, there would need to be recognition that IQ test scores should be read not as a single fixed number but as a range. The SEM would have to be taken into consideration. In further deference to professional standards, the Court also noted with approval those statutes that evenhandedly took into account life factors whatever the test scores. For instance, in Mr. Hall's case there was evidence that his upbringing appeared to make his deficits in adaptive functioning (communication, self-care, and self-direction) more severe. As a child he had been mistreated, constantly beaten because he was slow and his mother would strap him to his bed at night "with a rope thrown over a rafter. In the morning, she would awaken Hall by hoisting him up and whipping him with a belt, rope, or cord." The case was reversed and remanded, which meant it was sent back to Florida to address the issues noted. Freddie Lee Hall's 36-year stay on death row would be extended.

Determining the boundaries of substantially impaired mental abilities was only one source of lingering uncertainty. As we moved well into the second decade of the twenty-first century, there was a more deeply troubling issue. The evidence was clear. We were sentencing innocent persons to death. More than any single factor, this now well-established fact was driving broad-based reconsideration of the wisdom of continuing the practice of capital punishment.[48] Gallup polls reported that public support (still at 60 percent) was at its lowest point since 1972. States across the nation were witnessing reform and abolition legislation[49] In 2013, Maryland continued a six-year trend of States repealing the death penalty. Executions had dropped by almost two-thirds, from a post-*Furman* high of 98 in 1999 to 39 in 2013. Signaling continuing future decline, nationwide there was a 75 percent reduction in new death sentences from the peak years in the mid-1990s. Even in Texas, widely regaled and reviled as the leading death penalty state, the number of new death sentences was 9, compared to 48 in 1999.[50]

While concern for convicting innocent persons was undoubtedly the strongest reason for these shifts, the downward trend in executions received increased energy from an unexpected source: scarce drugs, botched executions, and pressure on corporations.[51] It is unconstitutional to execute persons while inflicting cruel and unusual suffering. While the switch to lethal doses of drugs[52] was widely supported as a more humane means of killing persons, compared to shooting, hanging, electrocution, and gas chambers, questions were being raised. In 2008 a case from Kentucky came before the Supreme Court.[53] The Court found that the use of drugs was constitutional, but special care needed to be taken with the appropriate dose of the initial anesthetic. It was, Chief Justice Roberts wrote:

> Uncontested that, failing a proper dose of sodium thiopental that would render the prisoner unconscious, there is substantial, unconstitutionally unacceptable risk of suffocation from the administration of pancuronium bromide and pain from the injection of potassium chloride.

A related problem arose three years later when, in 2011, the only company with governmental approval to make the anesthetic announced it was suspending production. Other sources were sought and found. Some States adjusted by opting for a single-drug protocol, similar to how animals were "put to sleep." Death penalty opponents began filing requests to identify producers of drugs used for execution and organize protests against them. States responded by refusing to reveal sources, which in turn precipitated open-record requests.[54]

As new drug protocols developed, mistakes were made. In 2014 botched executions in Ohio, Oklahoma, and Arizona received nationwide publicity. In April, the man being executed in Oklahoma reportedly spent 40 minutes gasping for air, fading in and out of consciousness and finally dying of a massive heart attack. In May of that year, a U.S. District Judge in Ohio ordered a moratorium following the execution of an inmate, which resulted in choking and a clenched body for some 26 minutes after the drugs were administered. As drugs became scarce, protocols questioned, and botched executions noted, politicians considered bringing back long-abandoned alternatives like the gas chamber or firing squads. In May 2014 Tennessee reauthorized the use of the electric chair.

For many opponents these events only underscored the continuation of a terribly flawed system. Still, it continued. This quandary was noted by Justice Stevens, who wrote in *Baze v. Rees* that although experience demonstrated that imposing capital punishment constituted a pointless and needless extinction of life, with only negligible social or public returns, the current issues swirling around lethal injections did not justify a reversal of previous Supreme Court decisions upholding the constitutionality of capital punishment. In other words, the debate seeking justification for the taking of life and the boundaries of acceptable suffering would continue. As this book goes to press, we continue to pursue the issues of equity in the execution of individuals. The lack of evidence suggesting that we protect life by taking life remains troubling. The ambiguous thresholds and flawed procedures for removing the protective boundaries of life remain clouded by uncertainty. Convicting innocent persons looms large. The related questions of who should live, who should die, and who should decide are being answered for some in the best way we can. For others we are perpetuating an unacceptably messy and meaningless system.

Notes

1 See Norman Mailer's *Executioner's Song* (Boston, MA: Little, Brown and Company, 1979).

2 See: *Godfrey v. Georgia*, 446 U.S. 420 (1980); *Beck v. Alabama*, 447 U.S. 625 (1980); *Adams v. Texas*, 448 U.S. 38 (1980); *Hopper v. Evans*, 456 U.S. 605 (1982); *Enmund v. Florida*, 458 U.S. 782 (1982); and *Pulley v. Harris*, 465 U.S. 37 (1984).

3 Blackmun was dissenting from the court's decision not to review a case from Texas. *Callins v. Collins*, 510 U.S. 1141 (1994).

4 See, for example, Edwin Brochard, *Convicting the Innocent: Sixty-Five Actual Errors of Criminal Justice* (New Haven, CT: Yale University Press, 1932). Hugo A. Bedau, "Murder, Errors of Justice, and Capital Punishment," in *The Death Penalty in America: An Anthology*, Ed. Hugo A. Bedau (Garden City, NY: Anchor Books/Doubleday, 1964): 434–52.

5 *McCleskey v. Kemp*, 481 U.S. 279 (1987)

6 David C. Baldus, Charles Pulaski, and George Woodworth, "Comparative Review of Death Sentences: An Empirical Study of the Georgia Experience," *The Journal of Criminal Law and Criminology* 74 (1983): 661–753.

7 For example, Samuel R. Gross and Robert Mauro, *Death and Discrimination: Racial Disparities in Capital Sentencing* (Lebanon, NH: University Press of New England, 1989). Raymond Paternoster, *Capital Punishment in America* (Lanham, MD: Lexington Books, 1991).

8 *Callins v. Collins*, 510 U.S. 1141 (1994).

9 *Death Penalty Sentencing: Research Indicates Patterns of Racial Disparities* (Washington, DC, 1990), 3.

10 Hugo Adam Bedau and Michael L. Radelet, "Miscarriages of Justice in Potentially Capital Cases," *Stanford Law Review* 40 (1987): 24.

11 Michael L. Radelet, Hugo A. Bedau, and Constance Putnam, *In Spite of Innocence* (Boston, MA: Northeastern University Press, 1992).

12 See: www.innocenceproject.org/about/.

13 Tim Junkin, *Bloodsworth* (Chapel Hill, NC: Algonquin Books, 2004).

14 See: www.deathpenaltyinfo.org/innocence-list-those-freed-death-row.

15 *Herrera v. Collins*, 506 U.S. 390 (1993).

16 See: www.tdcj.state.tx.us/stat/herreraleonellast.htm.

17 Gary Graham was executed June 22, 2000. See: www.txexecutions.org/reports/222.asp and *Jet*, July 10 (2000): http://findarticles.com/p/articles/mi_m1355/is_5_98/ai_63537150/. Most final statements are brief. Gary Graham prepared a lengthy review of his case and those who had helped him. See: www.tdcj.state.tx.us/stat/grahamgarylast.htm.

18 *Furman v. Georgia*, 408 U.S. 238 (1972) and *Lockett v. Ohio*, 438 U.S. 586 (I978).

19 *Callins v. Collins*, 510 U.S. 1141 (1994).

20 By this time, there was a growing mountain of research. See, for example, David C. Baldus, George G. Woodworth, and Charles A Pulaski, (1990) *Equal Justice and the Death Penalty* (Boston, MA: Northeastern University Press, 1990), especially chap. 12; Marquart, Ekland-Olson, and Sorensen, *The Rope, the Chair, and the Needle*, 158–62, fn 8. See also: www.deathpenaltyinfo.org/.

21 John C. Jefferies, Jr., *Justice Lewis F. Powell, Jr.: A Biography* (New York: Charles Scribner's Sons, 1994): 451–2.

22 See: www.innocencenetwork.org/.

23 Carol S. Steiker and Jordan M. Steiker, "Sober Second Thoughts: Reflections on Two Decades of Constitutional Regulation of Capital Punishment," *Harvard Law Review* 109 (1995): 355–438.

24 See: www.law.northwestern.edu/wrongfulconvictions/aboutus/.

25 James S. Liebman, Jeffrey Fagan, and Valerie West.

26 See: www.deathpenaltyinfo.org/anthony-graves-becomes-12th-death-row-inmate-exoneated-texas.

27 See: www.deathpenaltyinfo.org/execution-2010.

28 See: www.ojp.usdoj.gov/bjs/homicide/tables/totalstab.htm.

29 *Washington Post* Editorial, January 2 (2010); available online at: www.washington post.com/wp-dyn/content/article/2010/01/01/AR2010010101829.html.

30 Caplow and Simon, "Understanding Prison Policy and Population Trends."

31 Ken Armstrong and Christi Parsons, "Half of State's Death-Penalty Cases Reversed," *Chicago Tribune*, January 22 (2000): 1.

32 See: www.northwestern.edu/observer/issues/2003-01-23/deathpenalty.html. This speech was widely reported. See, for example, Reynolds Holding, "Historic Death Row Reprieve Illinois: Gov. Ryan Spares 167, Ignites National Debate," *San Francisco Chronicle*, Sunday, January 12 (2003). "Guarding Death's Door," *Time*, January 14 (2003); see: http://dir.salon.com/story/news/feature/2003/01/14/ryan/index.html.

33 BBC, "Activists Hail Death Penalty 'Watershed,'" Sunday, 12 January, 2003; see: http://news.bbc.co.uk/2/hi/americas/2650021.stm.

34 The Justice for All Act of 2004 (HR 5107; Public Law No. 108–405).

35 Frank R. Baumgartner, Suzanna L. DeBoef, and Amber E. Boydstun, *The Decline of the Death Penalty and the Discovery of Innocence* (New York: Cambridge University Press, 2008).

36 National Opinion Research Center: General Social Surveys, 1972–2006 (Cumulative file). Gallup News Service, June 1, 2006.

37 Jeremy Peters, "Death Penalty Repealed in New Jersey," *New York Times*, December 17, 2007.

38 Richardson's announcement was quoted widely. See: www.huffingtonpost.com/2009/03/18/new-mexico-bans-death-pen_n_176666.html.

39 See: www.nytimes.com/2011/03/10/us/10illinois.html and: www.correctionsreporter.com/2011/03/11/quinn-repeals-illinois-death-penalty/.

40 *Penry v. Lynaugh*, 492 U.S. 302 (1989).

41 In 2008, Johnny Paul Penry's death sentence was commuted to life.

42 *Atkins v. Virginia*, 536 U.S. 304 (2002).

43 *Stanford v. Kentucky*, 492 U.S. 361 (1989).

44 *Roper v. Simmons*, 543 U.S. 551 (2005).

45 All immediate quotes come from Justice Kennedy's announcement of the decision, March 1, 2005.

46 *Hodgson v. Minnesota*, 497 U.S. 417 (1990).

47 Quotes from Justice Scalia's verbal announcement of Justice Thomas's, Chief Justice Rehnquist's, and his dissent.

48 www.pewstates.org/projects/stateline/headlines/state-of-the-death-penalty-as-2013-ends-85899527826.

49 www.deathpenaltyinfo.org/recent-legislative-activity?did=236&scid=40.

50 http://deathpenaltyinfo.org/documents/YearEnd2013.pdf.

51 www.propublica.org/article/a-prolonged-stay-the-reasons-behind-the-slow-pace-of-executions.

52 A three-drug protocol was in general use: Sodium thiopental was used to render the prisoner unconscious to avoid the pain of the second and third drugs used. This was followed by pancuronium bromide which paralyzes the diaphragm and lungs and finally potassium chloride which causes death by cardiac arrest.

53 *Baze v. Rees*, 128 S.C. 1520.

54 See for example, "AG Shifts Stance on Drug Supplier: Execution Drug Source Should Remain Secret, Abbott's Office Says." Austin American Statesman, May 30, 2014 .

CHAPTER 17
LESSONS LEARNED

We come to the end. The journey has been long, and the landscape varied. Throughout, we have been guided by two deeply important moral imperatives: life is sacred (intrinsically important) and should be protected, and suffering, once detected, should be alleviated. A single question has been asked: how do communities go about justifying the violation of these imperatives while holding firm to their importance? The short answer is this: boundaries are drawn, priorities are set, and dilemmas are resolved. In the process, a sense of differential social worth is established, as moral imperatives involving the protection of life and alleviation of suffering remain operable but not applicable. What general lessons can be drawn from the journey we have taken?

Lesson One: The Power of Assessed Social Worth

Most evident is that the protective boundaries of life and the associated sense of social worth are structured and rearranged through exclusionary logic and the power of empathy. Persons become parasites, fetuses become nonpersons, lives become vegetative, convicted felons become demons. In each case, the protections are removed or maintained by socially defined and historically variable definitions of worth. Along these lines, moral systems evolve.

Lesson Two: Change Comes Along a Jagged and Contentious Path

We have seen that moral evolution rarely progresses along a straight path. Instead, it winds along a jagged and often contentious route, as science and technology introduce new and unanticipated possibilities, and crystallizing events clarify issues and motivate reform. With unexpected scientific and technological breakthroughs, along with unanticipated emerging events, new questions arise. Current moral and legal systems are simply not up to the task. We have seen many examples of the ensuing cultural lag. Newly refined kidney machines, respirators, and organ transplant procedures brought hope to people previously facing certain death. On what basis should limited life-prolonging resources be distributed: first-come, first-served; random assignment; ability to pay; or assessment of social worth? New medical treatments have provided the ability to prolong the lives of young infants. Should these treatments be used, even if they mean the child's short life will be filled with suffering and resource-draining medical care? Medical technology now allows a life to be maintained, even when the person in question has lost all cognitive and emotional capacity. In other situations, these technologies can be used to keep someone alive, only to face a life filled with suffering. Is life in a vegetative state, or a life filled with suffering, a life worth prolonging and protecting?

Likewise, moral shifts have occurred when crystallizing events clarified the implications of one action or another. Again, supporting evidence is abundant. *Buck v. Bell,* the thalidomide scare, the *Quinlan* case, the radiation, Willowbrook, and Tuskegee experiments, the trials of the Scottsboro Boys, and the torture and killing of Emmett Till all clarified issues and precipitated otherwise elusive reforms. The Civil Rights Movement proceeded with increased force, a set of bioethical principles aimed at enhancing and clarifying the moral significance of individual autonomy, justice, and beneficence were put in place.

Lesson Three: The Importance of Analogies, Metaphors, Images, and Stories

This much is clear: existing moral principles, judicial decisions, and legislated statutes are frequently do not keep pace with the implications of new scientific findings and technologies. To address this cultural lag, metaphors are built, analogies are drawn, empathy-generating images are fashioned, and stories are told. Again, evidence for the power of analogies, metaphors, images, and stories is readily found. Supreme Court justices find analogies in the penumbras of constitutional language. Theologians, as well as religious zealots, look to the similarly shadowed niches of sacred scriptures. Pro-choice stories are told to emphasize existing injustice. Pro-life films and graphic posters, designed to generate empathy, are carried to underscore the human qualities of a fetus. Partial-birth abortion becomes a phrase of political art. From such rhetoric, analogies, metaphors, images, and stories, the protective boundaries of life and tolerable suffering are drawn and redrawn. In the process, the legitimacy of existing understandings and practices is reassessed. Given the fundamental nature of the moral dilemmas in question, tension remains.

Lesson Four: Who Decides?

From this tension, competing social movements are spawned. They are organized to address the contending demands of moral imperatives, to rectify perceived injustices, and to question the power and authority of laws judged to be illegitimate. We have seen, time and time again, social movements succeed or fail according to their ability to mobilize resources, coalesce networks, and frame issues. The dynamics of such purpose-driven reform efforts is evidenced in the Eugenics Movement of the late nineteenth and early twentieth centuries. It is manifest in abortion protests, clinic blockades, and violence. It is found in contending efforts debating the right to die, as well as in contradictory court decisions that followed. It is no less evident in efforts in the shifting reform movements aimed at limiting and refining capital-punishment practices.

Lesson Five: Dilemmas Lead to Cyclical Change

From evidence gathered in these widely varying arenas, a general proposition emerges: dilemmas, especially ones involving competing and deeply important moral principles, produce cyclical social change. In the early twentieth century, loosely linked networks of individuals and organizations, building on the findings and theorizing of Charles Darwin and others, coalesced, mobilized resources, and framed issues to produce a Supreme Court decision that legitimized the mandatory sterilization of those judged to be feeble-minded, less worthy of support and protection. The attendant logic of exclusion, aimed at enhancing and protecting life of the greater whole, formed a cornerstone for eliminating persons judged to be parasites—useless eaters as they were called. In Hitler's Germany, legal boundaries were drawn, and empathy-diluting rhetoric was devised to further divide society. Suffering and death were inflicted on Them to support and protect lives among Us. It was not until the soul-searing consequences of the Final Solution became evident that a civil rights movement, aimed at achieving a more inclusive sense of social worth, was fully energized. As barbaric as it was, Germany was not alone. Testimony during the Nuremburg trials pointed to exclusionary injustices of a fissured social structure in the United States, and the legitimacy of existing law and practice was brought into question. Unjust laws were no laws at all.

In the aftermath of the Nuremburg Trials, a rethinking and restructuring of social worth began to take place. There emerged renewed interest in human rights, rights transcending the civil rights defined within legal jurisdictions. Occurring at the same time was a scientific and technological revolution, which also impacted how we defined, protected, and prolonged life. One thing became clear. Without a careful, more inclusive restructuring of our sense of social worth, we stood in danger of becoming scientific giants but ethical infants.

The glaring presence of cultural lag was undeniable, and a movement to advance the importance of applied ethical thinking was launched. What did it mean to be a person? What were the limits of individual autonomy? Where should the boundaries of tolerable suffering be drawn? When did life worthy of protection and support begin? What role should social worth play in the allocation of scarce, newly devised medical treatments?

The major testing grounds for the emerging moral adjustments were abortion, neonatal care, and assisted dying, with capital punishment entering the discourse from time to time. The political arena separated into camps: pro-life and pro-choice. Those claiming the pro-life position accused their opponents of devaluing life and promoting a culture of death. The pro-choice movement countered by saying that none of its proponents was anti-life or in favor of a culture of death, dismissing such claims as nonsense. Rather, the pro-choice mindset gave reverence to the autonomy of individuals, the quality of life, and the elimination or reduction of suffering.

As the debates unfolded, it became clear that the embedded definitions of personhood and boundaries and dilemmas of life and death decisions were not limited to abortion. Medical technology had become proficient at keeping patients alive in what was labeled a persistent or permanent vegetative state. Like a vegetable, some life was totally absent emotion and cognition. Was such a life worth prolonging? Who should decide? Medical technology was also capable of keeping persons alive in the face of suffering and a personal sense that life had lost its meaning. What were the boundaries of tolerable suffering? When should the alleviation of suffering and the loss of meaning take precedence over prolonging and protecting life? Were we really prolonging death rather than life? Who should decide?

Driven by these dilemma-defined issues, the political arena separated into camps. Those claiming the pro-life position accused their opponents of devaluing life and promoting a culture of death. No one, it was countered, was anti-life and in favor of a culture of death—that was nonsense. Rather, it was a matter of giving credence to suffering. Highly contentious life and death decisions, shrouded as they were in uncertainty and ambiguity, should be kept firmly in the hands of those most immediately involved. The law, by its very nature, was ham-handed, unable to balance the qualities of life against an equally compelling demand for individual autonomy and the alleviation of suffering.

Besides, many noted with more than a little irony, it was often the case that those claiming the pro-life position were frequently in favor of imposing death. How could this be? Was life no longer worthy of protecting when bad deeds were done? What was the threshold of offense? Clearly, this had shifted over time. Those in the anti-capital-punishment camp chided those in favor of imposing death sentences by referring to scripture, where death was called for when children disobeyed their parents, when persons blasphemed God, when contractors performed shoddy work, when farmers did not control their animals, when consenting same-sex adults engaged in sexual behavior.

With more immediacy, it was noted that persons, mainly minorities, had been put to death for robbery, rape, and even attempted rape. Compelling evidence of continuing injustices, rooted in a peculiar chivalry and the legacies of slavery, brought the legitimacy of current practices into question. Reform efforts were weak and only partially successful until DNA profiling provided undeniable evidence that innocent persons were being sentenced to death. The image of a messy and meaningless system evolved. A pattern of escalating executions began to drop off.

In counterargument, proponents of the death penalty replied, "Where has the concern for the alleviation of suffering gone?" What about the victims? Should we not be concerned with their suffering? Although a death sentence might not deter others, it would most certainly stop this offender from killing again. It would bring closure and relief to those surviving the victim. Life should be taken to protect life and to heal the harm inflicted.

Lesson Six: Tension Remains

When the desire to identify the protective boundaries of life competes with the desire to alleviate suffering, unavoidable dilemmas, infused with uncertainty, emerge. Such dilemmas, by definition, are not resolvable without residual tension. In an important sense, both sides are right. If so, tension will always remain. Perhaps this is the final lesson learned.

INDEX

Page numbers followed by 'f' refer to figures and followed by 'n' refer to notes.